BUT NOW THEY ARE ANGELS

REFLECTIONS ON MY LIFE IN SERVICE TO PUBLIC HEALTH

EUGENE J. GANGAROSA, MD, MS, FACP

WITH THE COLLABORATION OF

RAYMOND E. GANGAROSA, MD, MPH, MSEE AND

RACHEL M. BURKE, MPH, PhD

WITH AN APPENDIX: THE EMERGING ROLE OF PUBLIC HEALTH IN CIVILIZATIONAL EVOLUTION: HEALING THE SCHISM BETWEEN SCIENCE AND RELIGION

BY RAYMOND E. GANGAROSA, MD, MPH, MSEE

WITH THE COLLABORATION OF

DIANE DOUGHERTY, MAE, MSE, EDS

Printed in the United States of America

First Printing, 2016

ISBN 978-1-48357-466-0

Eugene J. Gangarosa gratefully acknowledges the Rochester Museum
and Science Center for provision of and permissions for the
photographs of the Children's Hospital.

Raymond E. Gangarosa gratefully acknowledges the publishers and
authors of the epitaphs selected for the Appendix.

To Rose—for her courageous and steadfast support even in the worst of times

To my mother, Carmella Gangarosa—the only breadwinner in the worst days of the Great Depression, who stood firm in her decision to stay in the USA rather than return to Italy

To my brother Sam E. Ganis—whose academic achievements set professional standards that shaped my career

Table of Contents

BUT NOW THEY ARE ANGELS

A FOREWORD BY WILLIAM FOEGE, MD, MPH

There are some important triads in medicine and public health. One concerns the traditional pathways of medical graduates to clinical medicine, teaching or research. Most medical graduates choose one; some are able to do two. But it is a rare person who does all three and does them well. Gene Gangarosa has excelled at all three. However, this book reveals that he went far beyond the usual combination. Gene integrated all these skills while being involved in military service, global health programs, international travel, teaching in the Middle East, developing public health academic programs, and doing history-changing research.

Many are familiar with oral rehydration, which both despite and in virtue of its simplicity has profound power in saving the lives of millions of children and adults suffering from diarrhea. A myriad of organisms can be responsible for diarrhea; the extreme is represented by cholera, which can wring out the fluids in a patient and cause death within hours of the onset of symptoms. Oral rehydration in such cases is truly lifesaving. Up until relatively modern times, medical students were taught that the intestinal lining had sloughed, as one would see with a burn, and the proper treatment was to withhold fluids. Few know that it was Gene's ingenious research that showed that the intestinal lining is structurally intact, but for some reason is not absorbing fluid and electrolytes.

This was not simple research. Imagine being sick and dehydrated, feeling absolutely miserable, and then being asked to swallow an object, a stainless steel capsule the size of a large multivitamin tablet, secured to a long, flexible, hollow, plastic tube. This object would travel through the stomach into the small intestine. Once the capsule was in place, a vacuum created with a syringe would suck in a small portion of the intestinal wall and thus activate a small spring-loaded knife that would secure a biopsy. Gene would then retrieve the capsule by reversing its journey upwards through the stomach and esophagus and out of the patient's mouth. How do you talk people into doing that? Gene's biopsies of the intestinal lining at the time of illness contradicted the accepted theory, as they proved that the intestinal epithelium in the case of cholera is entirely intact and functional. This enabled other researchers to pursue other theories and treatment approaches, eventually leading to the finding that glucose was necessary to enable the intestine to absorb electrolytes. This was the critical discovery that led to the invention of oral fluid therapy, a treatment for all diarrheal illnesses that has saved millions. Gene combined research, clinical medicine, and teaching to make the case for his findings and advance the science to save lives.

Another triad exists in public health, in the belief that public health education seeks three outcomes: the development of a basic philosophy, the acquisition of skills, and the gathering of knowledge. Philosophy is eternal, skills are for a lifetime, but knowledge is ephemeral. And yet attaining knowledge is where much time is spent in schools of public health. The development of philosophy is heavily dependent on mentors. Gene describes a rich tapestry of mentors who influenced his life over many decades. He begins with the mentors he will never meet, those who wrote about hunting microbes, establishing an interest that never left him. He also describes the people who took an interest in him in school, in graduate programs and in employment in the military, at the Centers for Disease Control and Prevention, the American University in Beirut, Emory University, in Pakistan and elsewhere.

Gene, in developing public health academic programs, gave attention to the development of skills and the transfer of knowledge, but he paid back his mentors by becoming a mentor himself—a mentor to medical students, public health students, coworkers, and contacts by the dozens.

The book will thrill students with an interest in global health—they will discover that you cannot draw up a life plan as a student. You simply have no way to know which scientific techniques and findings that will present opportunities. You have no idea of the political and social changes to be confronted, and you have no knowledge of the mentors you will meet who will inspire you with new ideas for you to explore. But, just as Gene was able to discover mentors at every turn of his career, so can the student of today see Gene as a mentor by reading his book.

This book describes life in the raw, not an idealized summary of the best things that ever happened to the author. Gene met challenges in every endeavor, often in people who could not be trusted, had their own objectives to pursue, or simply didn't share the vision of a more perfect world.

Students will find other surprises. It has been observed that medical students assume they will be financially rewarded, while public health students will never expect high salaries. Imagine the surprise in store for public health students who read this book and discover they can spend a lifetime in public health and still be millionaires. It is the old story of consistent savings, compound interest, and the patience of decades. Gene shows how he and his wife, Rose, became millionaires, which allowed them to provide generously to charities and their special interest of improving water supplies and sanitation throughout the world. In time they even endowed two chairs to promote this field at the Rollins School of Public Health at Emory University.

This is a story of a first-generation American, benefiting from a country that rewards merit. He then went on to enrich the world, medicine, and the future through a life well lived.

Dr. William Foege is an Emeritus Presidential Distinguished Professor of International Health, Emory University as well as a Gates Fellow, and has held numerous other distinguished positions in public health.

GENE GANGAROSA: CLASSMATE, SCHOLAR, DEAN

A FOREWORD BY D.A. HENDERSON, MD, MPH

Sixty-one years ago, two classmates of the University of Rochester School of Medicine received doctoral hoods signifying that they were officially Doctors of Medicine. Neither Gene nor I anticipated that we might spend the rest of our lives dedicated to the practice, research, teaching, and administration of public health. Public health, as a profession, was little known to us at that time. So far as I can recall we had just two lectures in medical school that were identified as "public health": "Syphilis" and "The Construction and Maintenance of Pit Privies." Neither provided any special motivation to embark upon public health careers. The critical factor that changed our lives stemmed from the requirement that we serve at least two years in the uniformed service. Gene spent some five years in the Army and I, 22 years in the public health service. Each of us served to introduce to the fields of public health and medicine a range of remarkable approaches and diverse opportunities for treatment and prevention in public health. Gene explored new areas in the understanding and treatment of enteric organisms, while I spent fully 11 years endeavoring to eradicate smallpox.

Many years later, we both became deans of schools of public health. I can say from personal experience that serving as a dean offers experiences and adventures that are unique in their ability to present insoluble problems and an incalculable breadth of opportunities. I had the opportunity to speak with Gene and Rose in Beirut as he struggled to bring to life a school of public health in the midst of one of the most serious eras of the Middle-East conflict. Although there was a dire need for public health throughout the entire area, as well as potential faculty in the university, there was barely the semblance of a critical mass.

5

Despite problems including resistance on the part of the administration, Gene brought to life a respected school of public health drawing students from a number of countries. Funding for this endeavor derived primarily from tuition, in addition to sparse voluntary donations. My discussions during a visit with Gene and his ever-patient wife, Rose, served to bolster my own courage as I was learning to become the Dean of the Johns Hopkins School of Hygiene and Public Health.

There was a second chapter, however, as Gene took up residence in Atlanta and began a slow and difficult trek to create a school of public health at Emory University. Again, I had opportunities to meet and talk with Gene about schools of public health and, in particular, why the needs in faculty, research, practice, and resources necessarily were so unique unto themselves and had to develop an ethos distinct from the traditional environment of a school of medicine. This was of a particular value to me as it heightened my own appreciation of the unique qualities of schools of public health and why so many different aspects of management, structure, and creativity were important in order for both schools to appreciate their potential.

I would be remiss if I failed to offer a special salute to Rose Gangarosa, who weathered all manner of difficulties and storms with cheerful equanimity. Throughout their lives, both Rose and Gene have been especially honored for their hospitality, while Gene has been noted as an exceptional teacher and internationally renowned scientist.

The story of Gene and Rose is intriguing and unique, replete with every imaginable challenge as they succeeded in bringing to life not one but two schools of public health. Their lives together have been nothing short of remarkable.

Dr. D.A. Henderson is a University Distinguished Service Professor and Dean Emeritus at the Johns Hopkins Bloomberg School of Public Health, and has held many other distinguished positions in public health.

PREFACE

In my long career in public health, I've experienced and learned much, gaining not only knowledge, but hopefully wisdom as well. It is my goal with this book to impart some of that to the reader.

Specifically, this book may be of interest to the following audiences:

All students I have taught and will continue to teach surveillance methods to control food and waterborne diseases—I recount my own experiences in developing these systems and my perspective on their importance.

All who have read the textbook I use for my courses, Steven Johnson's *Ghost Map*—I complement his perspective with my own experiences over decades of dealing with cholera and other water borne diseases.

All who are concerned about childhood deaths still common in places lacking safe water and sanitation—I give my own perspective as to why four of my siblings died in similar environmentally soiled settings.

All who aspire to exciting careers in public health—I describe my experiences as an epidemic detective at the Centers for Disease Control and Prevention followed by two challenging academic careers.

Any want-to-be millionaires—I share my story of the magic of compounding dividends from quality stocks, which enabled a pathway from depression-era food stamps to gratifying philanthropy.

– Gene Gangarosa, June, 2016

ACKNOWLEDGEMENTS

I gratefully acknowledge the editing assistance of an earlier draft of this book provided by Dr. John J. Farmer, III, Associate Dean Kathryn Graves, Dr. D.A. Henderson, and Dr. William H. Foege.

I also thank Ms. Mona Katul, executive officer at FHS, and Ms. Amal Kassis, student services officer at FHS, for the assistance they provided us in writing this story.

BUT NOW THEY ARE ANGELS

REFLECTIONS ON MY LIFE IN SERVICE TO PUBLIC HEALTH

INTRODUCTION

Georg Wilhelm Friedrich Hegel, influential German philosopher. Peter Ilyich Tchaikovsky, Russian composer. James Polk, 11th President of the United States. Charles X, exiled King of France. Nicolas Carnot, engineer and the "father of thermodynamics." William Gamble, Union general in the American Civil War.

These people were among the tens of millions who died of cholera in the nineteenth century. Cholera was the most fearsome infectious disease then, at a time when infections were already the most common cause of death.

Intestinal infections often occur in epidemics—defined as an increase in the incidence of illnesses. This happens because of changes in the underlying conditions that facilitate transmission. In my teaching, I use Stephen Johnson's book *The Ghost Map* to demonstrate foundational concepts of public health, including how intestinal infections are transmitted. In the Broad Street outbreak of cholera described in this book, Johnson uses a metaphor, "a monstrous cancer," to explain the conditions from which cholera emerged: the accumulation of human and animal waste in homes of people who had no plumbing, no toilets, and had to deposit their wastes in basement cesspool. These people were immersed in shit! This is the way cholera is transmitted, as well as other intestinal pathogens.

Cholera takes the pattern of epidemics to another level. Cholera is absent for long periods—typically years or even decades—and then strikes large geographic regions in massively widespread outbreaks, or pandemics. There have been eight cholera pandemics. Five of these occurred in the nineteenth century, and one overlapped the nineteenth and twentieth centuries. The last two are going on concurrently at this writing, with the seventh pandemic occurring since the late 1950s through the present and the eighth pandemic, involving different strains of the bacterium, from early 1990s to the present.

The pandemic nature of cholera is one important feature that long contributed to the terror of this disease. Before 1816, cholera had been restricted to the Bengal region of India and what is now Bangladesh, so it appeared in the West very late in historical times. It didn't reach Western Europe and America until the second pandemic, 1829 – 1851, when it caused the deaths of many hundreds of thousands of people. The third pandemic, 1852 – 1860, killed over one million in Russia and many hundreds of thousands in Western Europe, the rest of Asia, and the Americas. All the other pandemics except the last have exacted similar or greater tolls.

The most dreadful aspect of cholera was the rapidity with which it could kill a previously healthy person. Acute symptoms of cholera start 6 to 48 hours after the ingestion of an infectious dose of organisms, typically from water or food contaminated with the feces of infected individuals. Often, a person would leave for work in the early morning feeling fine. After the infection takes hold, a vicious cycle ensues in the untreated. Copious diarrhea initiates the process, quickly leading to metabolic acidosis[1], which induces severe nausea, and then in turn, profuse vomiting. Each step in the cycle greatly exacerbates fluid and electrolyte imbalances. In just 24 hours, fluid losses can amount to as much as 20 liters, sometimes corresponding to

---

[1] Metabolic acidosis is the buildup of hydrogen ions in blood and tissues, typically determined as a decrease in blood pH below 7.35. In diarrheal diseases, this condition of acidic buildup results from loss of bicarbonate ions in stool.

over one-fourth of total body weight. After such enormous losses, the victim would likely be reduced to a skeletal appearance. The fluid losses and electrolyte imbalances often cause agonizing muscle cramps. Before the next day, and sometimes within hours, the infected person, if untreated, can die because of insufficient blood volume, metabolic acidosis, and acute renal failure. In perhaps the most tragic aspect of a historically all-too-common scenario, a family might see their loved one leave for work as usual and never return—only hearing later of the person's rapid death and terrible fate.

Characteristically, a frightfully high percentage of those with untreated cholera—including virtually all of those who progress to hypovolemic shock[2]—die within hours or days of contracting the disease. In 1831, the French physiologist François Magendie called it "a disease worse than death, which begins where other diseases end, with death." In 1854, cholera killed 5.5% of the population of Chicago. From 1858 to 1860, an estimated 100,000 to 200,000 people died of cholera in Tokyo alone.

In the early stages of historical outbreaks, cholera had a particularly devastating economic impact because it predominantly affected adult males, who were typically the family breadwinners.[3] In the nineteenth century, most infectious diseases commonly struck infants and young children in large numbers, so their deaths were accepted with stoical resignation.

---

[2] This refers to a state of shock induced when the body loses copious amounts of water and the electrolytes critical to life, causing a low blood volume.

[3] Indeed, a similar pattern of laboring males being the earliest cholera victims played out even in the early stages of later cholera outbreaks, even into the mid-1990s. This is due to their differential exposure to various sources of contaminated water as they move throughout the community, as opposed to women who stay at home and thus are only exposed to a single source of water.

By contrast, cholera did not generally affect infants, who often drank breast milk, sparing them from exposure to contaminated water. However, the workers in the family drank water both at home and at various worksites, thereby increasing their chances of contracting cholera. In a period when most of the poor depended critically on the earnings of the male head of the household, the sudden death of the main provider of income was an appalling prospect that threatened financial ruin for everyone in the family.

Another common scenario, which often occurred later in pandemics, was exposure of households to contaminated water. In this setting, entire families often became ill and died at the same time. Needless to say, this had an alarming impact on the community.

Another terrifying aspect of the disease was its mysterious character and unknown cause. During the first two pandemics virtually nothing was understood scientifically about the transmission source and disease mechanism of cholera. Some people attributed the outbreaks to the wrath of God; others blamed uncleanliness of immigrants, the poor, and/or the "immoral." Posters from the period depict the Grim Reaper hovering ominously over a community or population. The best that the science of that time had to offer, the miasmatic theory of disease, mistakenly held that infections were transmitted by "bad air" or "miasma," not microbes. It was not known how likely those who attended to cholera victims might contract the disease and die—or even under what circumstances disease transmission might occur. Halfway through the nineteenth century, the pioneering epidemiological investigations of John Snow established a previously unsuspected transmission route for cholera: contaminated water.

Generally speaking, other intestinal infections are not nearly as lethal as cholera was before we developed the oral fluid therapy that transformed the disease from a tiger to a lamb. In fact, the severity of all diarrheal enteric (intestinal) infections has been lessened by oral fluid rehydration as well as improvements in intravenous therapy. Later in this book, I will describe my involvement in some of the work leading up to oral fluid therapy and the recognition of environmental enteropathy, which still kills so many children.

My story as a witness to progress in controlling enteric diseases

At this writing, I am almost 90 years old. My career in public health has so far spanned almost exactly 70 years. Going back to my childhood, my interest in the epidemiology and microbiology of infectious diseases goes back around 80 years. My work has concentrated on enteric diseases for almost 60 of those years, which apparently is longer than just about anyone else in my field. In that regard, as an emeritus professor, some consider me an elder statesman—which, of course, in the setting of diarrheal diseases, translates more fittingly as an "old fart"!

I had a special motivation for entering this field that originated even before I was born. The deaths of four of my older siblings, three as toddlers and the other in late infancy, were likely caused by enteric infections that are now readily preventable and treatable, using therapies I have had some small part in discovering and developing. As you will read, they are the angels referred to in the title of this book, and for me, they have figured prominently among the faces behind the science and statistics of my work.

The list of enteric agents is long—a wide variety of bacteria, viruses, parasites, pathogenic proteins (prions), and inorganic toxins (e.g., from industrial water pollution or toxins entering food during manufacturing processes)—but I will concentrate in this autobiography on those for which I have had personal experience. In my courses, I hasten to point out the most important cause of foodborne diseases is food itself, which causes obesity in people with poor diets, sedentary lifestyles, and genetic predispositions. However, the topic of obesity is the purview of others, and so I will not cover it here.

The defining characteristic of enteric diseases is exposure to the causative agent through oral ingestion followed by absorption in the digestive tract. Each enteric disease outbreak has its own story, from which we can learn any number of unique lessons. Cholera has often been considered the prototype of enteric illnesses, and since it has figured prominently in my career, its story will be the one around which I will interweave the story of my life in this book. However, I also want to share lessons I have learned in helping to manage other enteric illnesses. I will devote a separate chapter to botulism, an illness caused by a bacterium so different from cholera that it provides an opportunity to review succinctly the broad range of issues covered in this book from entirely different perspectives.

However, all of my stories converge on a single theme: how humanity has risen to the challenge of epidemic diseases to save millions of lives, change the way we live, and alter the course of history. I am privileged as a witness to those remarkable achievements to tell some of these fascinating stories and describe that noble theme from the historical perspective of my long life and career.

Now: a disease under control—but presenting new challenges

With proper awareness and resources, even the worst-case enteric disease, cholera, is no longer an automatic death sentence, even in the most primitive settings with no medical facilities or trained healthcare providers. A simple therapy—one that, in principle, could have been introduced at any time, even when cholera was first encountered—has saved many tens of millions of lives since the mid-twentieth century that would otherwise have been lost to acute enteric infections. That same treatment is applicable to a wide range of infectious diarrheal diseases, without need for a definitive diagnosis of the specific causative agent, and will continue saving lives in perpetuity.

But now another problem has been recognized: even though people readily survive acute enteric infections through that treatment, a history of repeated episodes caused by poor sanitation can exacerbate malnutrition, interfere with physical and cognitive development (especially in children), sap energy and dull the senses, reduce muscle mass, and decrease productivity (especially in adults). It can also lower immunity, which contributes to the vicious cycle by increasing the frequency of acute enteric and respiratory infections. These problems not only have serious impact on the health of people in developing countries but also on their regional and national economies. Treatment of these illnesses is not enough. We must also emphasize prevention, for instance through improving the sanitary conditions that inherently create an environment conducive to bacterial transmission. Prevention must also include the maintenance of newly installed as well as extant water and sanitation infrastructures.

What happened?

How did humanity rise to the challenge posed by epidemics of enteric illness? When Isaac Newton was asked why he was able to see so much farther than other physicists of his day, he replied, "Because I have stood on the shoulders of giants." The process behind the progress in public health has required the enormous ingenuity and creativity of many generations of brilliant scientists. By the time I was entering my career, my mentors and their colleagues were already standing on the shoulders of the giants before them. The pioneers of public health slogged through the hardest times to create an opportunity for my generation to make a rapid series of breakthroughs. Throughout that entire process, the emergence of a culture of public health has made these advances possible— one that has promoted the growth of knowledge, a perspective for learning from mistakes, methodologies for investigating disease outbreaks, a framework for compassionate service, and a community for internal support that fosters leadership.

The pioneers in our field lived and worked in times of great terror and confusion, but kept their heads to develop simple, straightforward ideas that provided the public health workers of my generation the foundations to implement great breakthroughs that they envisioned. Despite their great vision, they could not have imagined the many diverse ways their ideas would be amplified, modified, and applied, or the enormous effects they would have on human civilization. In a manner of speaking, those foundations introduced the safety nets that provided societies sufficient freedom from catastrophic illness to promote innovation; the scaffolding for towering skyscrapers from which the "telescopes" of epidemiology could untangle complex events on large social scales; greater impetus for developing the "microscopes" that have deciphered the inner workings of life and causes of disease; the substrate for developing "computers" adapted to forecasting and planning; and the essential infrastructures that quietly keep large cities functioning. All these amazing achievements have, in turn, fueled the scientific, technological, and economic engines that have propelled human progress for over a century and a half.

Scientists bestow their highest compliment for simple, straightforward ideas that resonate with their applications—they call them "elegant." With so many combinations of possible treatments to try—and no reassurance whatever that any would work—finding such elegant solutions required that countless scientists devote their careers and work together to wade deeply into the underlying science, reach countless eureka moments, understand the population dynamics of epidemic diseases, and systematically refine new technologies appropriate for the available resources. The seriousness of cholera epidemics justified that enormous sustained effort over many years. The simplicity of treating cholera and other enteric infections is analogous to the simplicity of the electric light bulb—which became the cartoon symbol of profound inspiration from the moment Thomas Edison invented it—and has had similar impacts on our way of living and our quality of life.

There is a reason why public health has been at the forefront of these developments. The seriousness of deadly disease outbreaks stops all other discourse in communities, supersedes all other motivations, and demands intense focus to determine causes, stop the epidemic, and prevent further occurrences. To give one example timely at this writing, the Ebola outbreak, initially local in West Africa but that spread globally, underscores the point, as it brought together a number of local as well as global organizations to control what evolved as a pandemic. In such situations, the usual impediments to progress

21

in our contentious, competitive, bickering society fall by the wayside. What is left is a space for motivated, idealistic, compassionate people to do the right thing, help others, solve problems, and make a better, safer society.

I consider myself blessed to have witnessed these events in enteric disease epidemiology long enough to appreciate some of the emerging trends and patterns in this branch of public health, which developed one innovation that is among the top 10 lifesavers in human history (oral rehydration as a simple treatment for enteric infections) and is expanding access to one other such innovation with comparable or greater potential for disease prevention (water chlorination or filtering). The magnitude of the impact of these innovations is awesome [1]. When cholera reemerged in the seventh pandemic, I was incredibly lucky to be the junior member of an investigative team having a mandate to clarify its pathogenesis through the use of modern scientific tools. Also during that investigation, I observed and elucidated a chronic condition, now called "environmental enteropathy," that is caused by years or decades of repeated milder enteric infections. I trained under some of the most inspiring mentors who were widely recognized as the best in their fields. Over the course of my career, I have developed many close friendships and working relationships with gifted young epidemiologists who have taken our field far beyond my own modest capabilities. I am both proud and humbled that my studies of cholera pathogenesis in some way contributed to what has been called "the most important medical advance of the twentieth century" (the simple treatment mentioned above) and that my early descriptions of environmental enteropathy helped motivate development of new preventive strategies and technologies having perhaps even more impact and potential for the twenty-first century.

Even though modern scientific and technological advances make the accelerating changes of our times increasingly apparent, the long course of my career has peppered my viewpoint with innumerable stories having rich personal meaning. I have experienced firsthand in many, many ways the wonderful cultural milieu that makes public health such a rewarding career.

Few scientists of my generation have been fortunate enough to see the sweep of their professional fields laid out before them as a personal perspective. I have derived a functional and operational perspective by virtue of having participated professionally in most of the activities involved in the field of public health—as a science, medical practice, community, and academic infrastructure. Having lived longer than anyone else I know among other scientists, practitioners, mentors, colleagues, students, and professors, I am in a position to reflect on our shared scientific culture with a kind of anthropological perspective. And having been an avid student of history since my childhood and having had mentors with a keen awareness of our past scientific foundations, I have connected the events in my own time with the historical sweep that preceded it. In this book, I illustrate these with anecdotes from my own career.

I consider one of the greatest benefits of my professional longevity to have seen science, culture, and history come alive through my own experiences, relationships, and observations. For me, public health, the scientific and medical field that studies the health and lives of populations, has taken on a life of its own. I hope you enjoy the themes, perspectives, stories, and inspiring personalities that I will share with you in this panoramic overview of my life and career.

References

1. Fewtrell L, Kaufmann RB, Kay D, Enanoria W, Haller L, Colford JM, Jr.: **Water, sanitation, and hygiene interventions to reduce diarrhoea in less developed countries: a systematic review and meta-analysis**. *Lancet Infectious Diseases* 2005, **5**(1):42-52.

PART I: FORMATIVE EXPERIENCES

Chapter 1: My Early Experiences

At this writing, my brother Frank was writing a book about our Gangarosa family. When completed, it will be a remarkable epic weaving together the stories of my siblings, starting from before the turn of the 20th century and following through World War I (WWI), the Great Depression, World War II (WWII), and the post-WWII era. In my book, I only touch upon the family history relevant to my own career.

My family would have been a family of 13: I was the 12th, the second to last. The first five of my siblings were born in Sicily. However, only the first one of the five survived. After my family immigrated to the United States in 1913, the remaining eight children were born. Seven survived; only one died.

My earliest role models

My mother, Carmella Bellassai Gangarosa, was an affectionate person, a pillar of strength, and a remarkable woman overall. She was born into the Bellassai family in a village, now the city of Comiso, in the province of Ragusa in the eastern part of the island of Sicily. They were a family of means, their wealth accumulated from careers dating back at least several generations in trades relating to cattle hides. Her father and brothers were shoemakers and manufacturers of luggage and rugs. My mother, in contrast, aspired to become a primary level schoolteacher. Although she completed the six years of schooling required to teach at this level, my mother never realized her goal because she married soon after completing her studies. However, her background gave her an exceptionally keen interest in the education of her own children. Report-card time was an important event in our lives. When we brought home report cards that showed good grades, my mother became animated and complimentary. In so doing, she set a goal for us, a standard of performance that we were expected to achieve. We worked hard to get good grades because it pleased her. Her gratification was the only reward we required.

My oldest brother, Sam, the only survivor of my first five siblings, reinforced these high academic standards for our family. He became an esteemed scholar, earning a JD and three masters degrees and making a distinguished career in engineering and mathematics in academia [4]. He retired as Professor of Mathematics at Ohio Wesleyan University. Both my mother and Sam encouraged us to see education as the most important pathway to a better future. We became a family of academic achievers. I learned much from both of them—information not in textbooks—about the meaning of family, family standards, morality, and commitments to both family and country. They became my first role models.

The story of my mother and her family

I remember my mother as a loving and caring woman, proud of her family and of her newfound country, and a social person. In addition to being kind and outgoing, my mother was also smart,

---

[4] Sam had five academic degrees in total: an A.B. (1931) and an M.A. (1932) from University of Rochester, an M.S. (1936) from University of Michigan, and an M.P.L. (Masters of Patent Law; 1948) and a J.D. (1947) from the John Marshall Law School in Chicago. He held various positions in engineering and mathematics throughout his career, including faculty appointments at the Rochester Collegiate Center and Ohio Wesleyan University, product development at Dominion Electric Company, and consultancies in math and law. He was also a patent-holder and a contributor to various scientific articles in mathematics and other fields. Sam was a member of numerous societies: Mathematics Association of America, Chicago Bar Association, Alpha Phi Kappa, Kappa Phi Kappa, Delta Omicron Phi, and Phi Mu Alpha.

well informed, and an avid reader; she was particularly interested in current events. We had access to newspapers only when newsboys sold them at street corners, shouting "Extra, extra, read all about it," regarding salient news events, such as the Nazi occupation of the Saar and other incidents leading to World War II. We could not afford a newspaper subscription, but one of my older brothers would sometimes bring home one of these "extras," or my brother Frank would save a copy left over from his newspaper route. In the late 1930s, we had a radio that helped us keep abreast of the news.

My mother spoke occasionally of her brothers and sister in South America. I recall her joy in receiving letters from them and from relatives still in Sicily. Since all my mother's siblings were, by contemporary standards, well educated, they were literate in Italian, and sent letters in this language[5]. She would often read these letters to us in the original Italian, and then use her broken English to explain what we did not understand. Although she could read English, my mother spoke the language with a marked accent. Despite this, she did not hesitate to engage English-speaking people in whatever social setting.

I was intrigued by my mother's stories of her siblings in South America. She mentioned they had emigrated from Italy in the same year as our family, 1913, and I noted her melancholy that she was not likely to ever see them again. Although she spoke of different aspects of her immigration story, I do not recall her mentioning her brothers' immigration to Paraguay and her sister's settling in Argentina. It was many decades later, after she died, that I learned the story of their immigration from my Paraguayan cousins. I met them in Asunción, the capital city,

---

[5] Many Sicilians at the time were not literate in their mother tongue, as its written form has not been standardized and is typically used only by poets!

during a cholera consultation for the Pan American Health Organization (PAHO).

It was the eldest of my Paraguayan first cousins, Celestino Bellassai, who told me this story. According to his account, several families on my mother's side had planned to travel together from their homes in Comiso to Palermo by rail and then by ship to "America," which, he said, they saw as one place. He confirmed the year of their emigration, 1913. In his narrative, something happened in Comiso to one of the Bellassai relatives not included in their travel plans—perhaps a death—that made it necessary to change the siblings' plans to travel together. Instead, their plan B was that my parents would proceed to Palermo, to travel first to this place called America, and that the others would take the next boat embarking from Palermo to that same America. However, the second ship, on which my mother's siblings traveled, was routed to Buenos Aires, where they traveled by train to Paraguay. It was late in their planning that they realized that they would not even be living on the same continent, and would likely never see each other again.

I mentioned this story to my brother Sam, whom I visited in Detroit several months before he died at the age of 94. Sam was only 7 years old at the time of the immigration, so he did not know of this rendition, but he thought this Paraguayan account was unlikely for several reasons. First, he argued, the Bellassais must have known that their final destination would be an area where they would be able to use their skills with leather. And secondly, they likely had a sense of geography, because they came from a family of means where most, including my mother, had been educated. So, I cannot be sure whether the Paraguayan version of the family immigration history was correct, but it is an intriguing story that seems plausible.

During that same visit to Paraguay, I met several other Bellassai cousins who were successful business entrepreneurs in the leather industry, and others who were doctors, lawyers, bankers, and businessmen. What they had in common with their North American Gangarosa cousins was advanced education, including doctoral-level professionals. A commitment to education was the common denominator on my mother's side of our family.

My family's life in Italy before I was born

During my adolescence, I sometimes asked my mother about my four siblings who had died very early in childhood before I was born. When I first discussed these deaths with my mother and for a long time afterward, I wondered what the circumstances were.

I raised this question again when I visited my oldest brother Sam who, at age 94, finally shed some light on the family's home environment. Despite his age, he recalled the family's home setting during the years of our siblings' deaths. From his account, and information I got from an elderly "zia"—my mother's niece who had visited this home and was familiar with its conditions—this is what I have surmised. I am quite certain that the family had access to water of good quality from the deep well known as the Fontana Diana in the center of Comiso. My father had donkeys that he used for his work as a stonecutter and sculptor. Sam mentioned that, while he and our mother often carried water from the fountain, the donkeys carried most of the water the family needed. Before going to work in the morning, my father would fill small barrels of water from the fountain, and donkeys would carry these to our family's home. He left the water containers at the lower level of the home next to steep stairs leading to the kitchen area of the upper floor. The kitchen that Sam described was in fact a food preparation area without

31

running water. My father would, on occasion, carry water there from the lower level. However, most of the water was carried by my mother, lugged up the steep stairway to the upper level.

My parents sheltered their donkeys, along with chickens and ducks, on a dirt floor in the lower level beneath the living quarters of their house. It seems reasonable to conclude that the animals they owned created a veneer of feces conducive for flies and vermin known to carry intestinal pathogens. By the several transmission routes that were likely, these pathogens must have had easy access to the water carried and stored in the kitchen, and the food prepared there, especially at a time when screened doors and windows were unknown. Although the quality of water from the well was most likely good, the means of conveyance and the conditions of storage and use for food preparations could easily have led to contamination. Very likely my mother did not have enough water to cope with the extra needs of caring for her young children. Because water is heavy, too heavy for a frail pregnant woman to carry vertically up steep steps multiple times per day in large quantities, she also probably had to ration it. My four siblings who died, three as toddlers and the other late in infancy, were at ages when they would have been weaned—thus removing the immunological protection they would have had from maternal antibodies present in breast milk, while at the same time exposing them to new potential sources of contamination as they were introduced to other food and drinks. In summary, I think it likely that my siblings died early in childhood from a combination of water-related diseases transmitted by hands and vermin from a much-soiled environment. This probably resulted in intestinal and/or respiratory illnesses. In support of the latter, Sam explained that during the cold winter months, fireplaces were smoky, and likely contained soot and irritants known to be especially harmful to infants and children.

As an adolescent, I spoke occasionally to my mother about these four very young children who died in Sicily. These memories were still painful to her, sometimes causing tears to well in her eyes as she reflected on them. I sensed she had deep concerns as to whether she had caused their deaths, that she was replaying worries about whether she should have, or might have, done something different to prevent their deaths. She lamented there was no one who could soothe the pangs of her conscience and reassure her that it was not her fault, that it was the cruel reality of her environment in which children were extremely vulnerable and preventive measures did not exist. When I asked her, my mother was not able to identify the diseases that caused their deaths. She remembered they had respiratory and intestinal symptoms; in regards to the death of her only child who died after the family moved to this country, Nuncio, my mother mentioned the word "tussaforte," which means "whooping cough." Tragically, her family doctor reinforced her feelings of guilt. He chastised her on the occasion of the death of one of those very young children, asking, "Why did you take her outside when it was still cold?" His question implied that the death was caused by something my mother did or failed to do, by something that she should have known to do, or not to do. It pained her that her doctor faulted her. She mentioned that even her family and my father's family raised questions that made her feel guilty about the children's deaths. While it was not uncommon for infants and toddlers to die in that era, it seemed out of the ordinary that four in a row should die given the circumstances of a well-providing husband.

It was clear that the consecutive deaths of four of her children at very early ages weighed heavily on my mother for her entire life. It is beyond comprehension to imagine her grief, her depression, her feelings of rejection, and the way that anguish compromised her quality of life. In the midst of this sea of despair, the only support she remembered was from her priest. She recalled his reassuring words, "Ma, adesso sono angeli" (But, *now* they are angels). Her priest rationalized these losses by ascribing a purpose for their deaths. His words gave her comfort. She believed him—she had to believe to make life tolerable!

The promise of America

As if in response to my mother's prayers, a letter arrived around that time that was to change her life, and profoundly affect the lives of our family including those of us still unborn. The letter was from my father's brother in the United States. His timing was perfect. My mother knew she was pregnant with her sixth child. She must have wished passionately that her new baby would live and be healthy, survive childhood, and reach adulthood. She immediately saw that this letter just might make this possible. The letter raised her hopes that her unborn child would be born in another land under conditions that might be more conducive to a healthy life. That unborn child was my brother Joe.

It must have been an exciting day in 1913 when my mother received this letter that included documents enabling the family to move to Niagara Falls. My father's brother, Giovanni (John), made these arrangements. The three of them, my parents and the only remaining child, my brother Sam, who was about seven years old at the time, made the voyage to America to start a new life.

My mother came to love this country, a bonding that contributed to her commitment and resolve to remain, and to keep her family here for the future she envisioned for us. She and I had several conversations about her memories from when she first arrived in this country. I asked, "What do you remember of your new

34

home in America?" Her response without hesitation was, "a sink." I did not understand at the time, but in retrospect she was referring to her relief, indeed surprise, that she had access to an unlimited supply of safe water at her ready disposal in her kitchen. It is a metaphor of her life, and of the lives of her children unborn at that time, that this happened in Niagara Falls, New York.

My father's experience of America

In contrast to my mother, my father was not literate and was not able to grasp the need for or potential of education. He was educated in his craft as a stonecutter and sculptor, but he could not read or even write his name. Although he was intimidating because of his loud and angry voice, he was kind and showed his affection to those of us who were born in this country[6]. He was not a person who gave kisses or hugs, as both parents are inclined to do in modern generations. As I grew up, I recognized that however subdued his affections, he loved us.

When my father first arrived in this country, he had a good job as a stonecutter building curbstones by hand for urban roads in Niagara Falls, NY. This job paid well through the World War I period. The family saved a modest sum when my father was employed during WWI. Unfortunately, they had poor management skills and even worse financial skills. My brother Sam shed light on some anecdotes to underscore the problems they faced in the early years after their arrival. He mentioned

---

[6] My father's relationship with Sam was somewhat more complicated. Sam had to play the role of my father's interpreter, a responsibility that often conflicted with Sam's responsibilities at school. This was a source of friction in their relationship that did not exist in my father's relationship to his other children, since by the time we were in school, he had already left the workforce and no longer needed us to interpret.

that my father was so concerned about his job that he awkwardly ingratiated himself by buying groceries for his boss. He also was a victim of a scheme targeting recent Italian immigrants who had well-paying jobs. Sam referred to those who perpetrated this scheme as "financial sharks," because they preyed on such immigrants by leveraging their affection for Italy and the war effort to market Italian War Bonds. Those bonds were offered with teaser rates to give buyers the impression that they were getting a good deal while supporting the war effort and helping America and their native Italy—all in the same package. He mentioned the teaser rates were applicable for a short period of time, after which owners received less as the value of bonds decreased. Finally, my parents lost everything they had invested in these bonds on Black Friday—the day of the colossal market crash of 1929, the beginning of the Great Depression. It was the entirety of what they had saved. This loss contributed greatly to the hardships my family endured during the 1930s.

We had language problems we did not recognize at the time. My father was the most affected. He was past 40 years of age when he arrived in this country. In Sicily, he had been at the top of his guild, a leader despite his lack of schooling. In America, he was not able to adapt to changing jobs. When he arrived in this country, he relied first on his brother to interpret. The following summer, he had my brother Sam, who had picked up English but was only about eight at the time, accompany him to work and interpret whenever my father was asked to meet with his supervisor. At that time, his company needed him, and he performed well at his job—one that few could do—so they kept him despite his language barrier. His tongue, and my first language and mother tongue, was Sicilian. At home, we spoke in the Sicilian dialect whenever my father was involved. I believe that I interacted with him more than any of my siblings. He called upon me often to help with tasks around the house, I guess because I was perhaps a bit more patient and responsive. Most people called me "Eug," pronounced "yuge," but my father called me "Gee," pronounced "jee," which is closer to what I preferred—Gene. Perhaps he did so because of my affection for him.

Other immigrant families tended to face the difficult economic situation better than we did, especially when both parents were literate. Indeed, Rose's family had a bilingual environment—her grandmother had immigrated along with her parents, and continued to speak only Italian—but both of her parents were literate. Her father was a barber who had a job with an income that enabled him to buy a business of his own and to invest in real estate. They were able to manage well throughout the Depression. Even with a large household—Rose was the seventh of 10 children—Rose's family managed much better than mine. None of her siblings died until very late in life. These anecdotes certainly underscore the importance of education for disease prevention, quality of life, and indeed life itself.

Because of his inability to understand or speak English, my father was culturally disconnected from the communities of his job and new life in Niagara Falls. He was uncomfortable in the presence of "Americani"—those who spoke English. His avoidance of situations where he would be challenged to speak English resulted in social isolation. Thus, when my father's company transferred him from Niagara Falls to Rochester after WWI, his difficulties were compounded. He was not able to adapt to the new job assigned to him. I do not know if he was fired; more likely, he just stopped going to work because he could not face the reality of a work situation in which he did not fit. In any case, he was no longer employed. It was the last time he was employed except when he worked briefly as a janitor during

WWII, when any able-bodied man could find a job. After several months as a janitor, he was injured when a heavy object fell on his foot. He did not report it; I suspect he thought it was his own fault. None of us had the sophistication to recognize that it was a job-related injury, for which he might have received support during his convalescence. He stayed at home to nurse his injury and did not return to work. This incident marked the definitive end of his short-lived career.

My father had plenty of time to reflect on his situation. During the difficult years of the Great Depression, many Italian immigrants chose to return, including his brother and sister-in-law, who had originally arranged for our family's immigration. Eventually, my father decided he had to return to Italy. His social isolation had a profound impact on this decision. He knew he could get a job in his family's quarry in Comiso, where his relatives lived. It was a place where he would be recognized and respected as a master craftsman—a coveted honorific. These hopes evolved into an insistence in returning to Italy—not only for his own benefit, but also for what he thought would be the family's wellbeing. His longing for Sicily and the job he would have there became an obsession.

My father's persistent desire to return to Sicily tormented my mother throughout the decade of the 1930s. They argued often over this single theme. My father urged a return to Italy, where he could work and again be the family's breadwinner. My mother was adamant; she would not return. She recalled the difficulties she had endured in a home without indoor plumbing. She must have surmised that this was why she had lost four of her first five children. In addition, she was able to understand the ominous news from Europe in the late 1930s. She was resolute in rejecting his entreaties, but she gave him the option to go by himself. In the final outcome of this anguished struggle, my mother prevailed. Confronted by the choice between family and a good job, my father chose to stay with family, to respect the strong bond he shared with my mother and us. Had we returned, I have no doubt the five of us who were of military age during WWII would have had to serve in Mussolini's Italian army, enemies of the country my mother and the rest of the family loved.

Difficult times for our family

Even my father's artistry in his craft could not salvage his stonecutting job in the years after WWI. In the industrial era following that war, a machine was invented that could carve curbstones much faster and more economically than could be done by hand. My father's job became obsolete. The permanent loss of my father's career prospects was the beginning of hard times for our family. It also was a landmark signaling a new role for my mother as breadwinner, in addition to her traditional role as homemaker. She found a job at Hickey Freeman, a leading manufacturer of quality men's clothing. She worked as a seamstress, using skills likely acquired in her father's shoe business, where she had developed expertise in the fine stitching of leather goods. Her job at Hickey Freeman was piecework, i.e., payment based on the number of garments she sewed. It was grueling, tedious, and difficult work that paid little, but it was the only means she had to sustain a large family through increasingly difficult years. She held this job for the rest of her productive life. A workers' union she joined improved working conditions and later enabled her to retire at 65 with a pension of $12 a month. This, plus her Social Security check of $13 a month, made it possible to meet mortgage payments of $20 a month.

For my family, 1935 – 1936 were especially difficult years. The Great Depression had taken its toll. Neither my father nor my brothers living at home were employed. Only my mother had a meager income working as a seamstress, and even then only when her employer had assignments. We were very much dependent on welfare assistance, but even that was exceedingly limited. For extended periods, we could not pay electric bills. My brother Frank and I made candles for light in both summer and winter evenings when our electricity was cut off because we could not pay the bill. We took pride in helping out, artistically forming some candles so as to garner the praise of our mother.

At the time, my family lived in a section of Rochester, NY that was home to many immigrant families from Italy. Of the seven surviving children born in this country, two left home for professional work and training, leaving five of us and our parents in our small home of approximately 1400 square feet, which had only one bathroom. I slept with two of my brothers in a double bed in a room built in our attic. It had no insulation and was poorly heated. I still vividly recall the oppressive summer heat made worse with the three of us sleeping in the same bed, and the cold bitter winters (typical of Rochester) that made it necessary for the three of us to huddle together for warmth at night.

Coal was a critical commodity for heating our kitchen stove, which was the means of cooking as well as the only source of our winter heat when we could not afford to use our furnace. To get coal we often had to scavenge for pieces that had fallen from railway cars. The closest was a railway complex near a street called Portland Avenue, about three-quarters of a mile from our house. I accompanied my father and brother Frank with woven "market baskets" to collect the precious nuggets of coal along the tracks[7]. Carrying the heavy baskets all the way home was hard work for me as a child.

Our diet was sparse indeed. Protein sources consisted of milk, beans, lentils, cold cuts (especially baloney), and occasionally ground beef served as meatballs with macaroni. Sometimes we had bacalla (dried cod fish that emanated an offensive odor during cooking) or eggs. Breakfast consisted of a bowl of milk with pieces of day-old bread purchased from a nearby bakery at a discount[8]. Lunch was usually a baloney or peanut butter and jelly sandwich. Fresh fruit and vegetables were rare. We did not have a refrigerator; instead, we had an icebox with lower compartments accommodating twenty-five pound blocks of ice delivered by a peddler twice a week. We had no telephone prior to WWII. Late in the 1930s, we had a radio, and we enjoyed listening to records on an old RCA phonograph. We had about 20 or 30 records, all of which had been purchased before I was born, when my family had been in less financial stress. The only toys I remember were Christmas gifts. We did not realize how poor we were largely because of my mother. She provided us the love and warmth that sustained us through those difficult years in a way that gave us a strong sense of family.

---

[7] In retrospect, our collection of unused coal bore a striking resemblance to the scavenging described in Steven Johnson's Ghost Map: The Story of London's Most Terrifying Epidemic and How It Changed Science, Cities, and the Modern World. As Johnson noted, "Where wages remain depressed, scavenging remains a vital occupation; witness the perpendadores of Mexico City." I still recall the bitterly cold December of 1935, when scavenged nuggets of coal helped keep my family warm.

[8] It sometimes fell to me to go purchase the bread. All the unsold bread from previous days was stored together in a large container—I could barely see over the side. I had to reach over the side to choose the bread by feel, occasionally throwing back a moldy loaf!

An anecdote I recall most vividly, reflecting our difficult existence and meager resources, was the lost-glove incident of December 1935. My Christmas present for that year was a pair of woolen gloves. I was delighted. When I returned to school on the first day of the new semester in 1936, I wore my gloves—I was pleased with the warmth they provided. At the end of the school day, when I was dressing to return home, I noted that one of my gloves was missing. I looked everywhere. I diligently searched the sidewalk and paths in the snow on my return home, carefully following the same route I had taken that morning to get to school. Although it was getting dark, I retraced the path to school and searched anxiously to no avail. It was well after dark when I arrived home. Reporting my loss to my mother, I cried with deep emotion. My mother embraced and reassured me.

It seems inconceivable that we could ever have managed had it not been for the relief of public welfare. My memories of those days have made a lasting impression and given me deep feelings of empathy for those families who face similar escalating financial problems created by job loss and foreclosure, struggling with deprivation and desperation and trying to make do with less and less and still less. In those days, my mother became the de facto manager of my family's financial affairs. I was inspired by her management skills, which enabled me to manage money more efficiently and to use money to improve the quality of life for those most in need. For these reasons and others, I revere her as my first living role model.

My illness and convalescence

Just before the Christmas holiday of 1935, I started having difficulty climbing the stairs to our attic bedroom. In retrospect, I had symptoms of polyarthritis, a disease of undetermined origin that affected my joints. The symptoms persisted throughout the month. My mother was deeply concerned. Because she had to work, she prevailed upon my brother Joe to take me to the hospital. He agreed, with the understanding that he would do so after the holidays.

So, on a bitterly cold day early in January 1936, my brother Joe accompanied me—along with my brother Frank, who had developed similar joint symptoms—to the Rochester General Hospital[9]. Though I was only a boy of nine, the doctor who saw me was very attentive. He spent a good deal of time getting my history from Joe and me, and then he examined me, listening ever so carefully to my heart sounds. He left the room and returned with an older doctor and a much younger one, both of whom spent time again examining me and listening to my chest. They left the room, and sometime later my brother Joe returned to tell me I was being admitted to the hospital. His reasons were evasive and confusing, but I was given no choice. I appealed; then I cried. In retrospect, the combination of polyarthritis and a heart murmur affecting the mitral heart valve spelled rheumatic fever. Neither my brother nor anyone else mentioned the disease or explained why I needed to be hospitalized. I was emotional when he left; I found little consolation in his promise to buy me another pair of gloves.

My stay at the old General Hospital on Main Street in Rochester was for laboratory tests. After a week, I was told I was being transferred to another place, called the Convalescent Hospital for

---

[9] At that time, the General Hospital was located on west Main Street, where, as I learned much later when I was in medical school, it was established as a hospital to receive and treat cholera victims for burial on what was then the outskirts of Rochester during the first North American pandemic, which affected communities along the Erie Canal in the years 1832-1849.

Children [10]. I did not know the meaning of the word "convalescence." I asked the patient in the next bed, a boy my age, if he knew what it meant, but he did not. No one explained. The word sounded much like "lesson." I wondered what "lesson"

---

[10] Years later, in one of my many trips to Rochester, I searched for but could not find the convalescent hospital where I was hospitalized. I remembered it was on Beach Avenue, but I did not remember the street number. I presumed it had closed or had moved to another place. However, in 2014, I again returned to Rochester on the occasion of my medical-school class's 60th anniversary event. The last of several class activities arranged for us was the Rochester Medical Museum we visited on October 20. Our class leader, Dr. Dave Kluge, introduced us to his museum colleague archivist Bob Dickson. In a discussion of the history of the Rochester General Hospital, I mentioned D.A. Henderson's senior medical school thesis about the 1830s cholera epidemic in Rochester, New York. He wrote about the General Hospital site on Main Street where cholera victims were taken for burial. Quickly responsive, Mr. Dickson confirmed the story of the cholera burial site and shared another anecdote that construction of the Rochester General Hospital required removal and burial of these cholera victims to another location before construction of the hospital could begin. He was equally responsive when I mentioned my unsuccessful search for the location of the Convalescent Hospital for Children. In a flash he told us its street address—425 Beach Avenue. He explained why I could not find it—It was set far back on a wooded lot not easily seen from the street. He left the room, returning in just a few minutes with printouts that described the history of the Convalescent Hospital. This is the essence of what was recorded: Dr. Edward M. Moore founded the hospital in the summer of 1887. Deeply moved by "a rise in infant deaths and children's disease from contaminated wells, stagnant sewers and poor sanitation," he built a hospital of tents to enable sick children to benefit from the "healthful Lake Breezes" in summer months. In 1928, a more permanent building replaced the tents, enabling long-term convalescence for children up to 15 years of age. Rheumatic fever was endemic in the upstate area in the years of the Great Depression. Dr. Albert Kaiser, mentioned in the text above, provided leadership for a program for patients needing "long-term convalescent care from conditions such as malnutrition and rheumatic heart." Learning this history gave me a deep sense of appreciation for the public health visionaries of Monroe County who made possible hospitalization with complete bed rest for affected children to prevent cardiac complications that often followed rheumatic fever. I was one of those children. As we were on welfare, we got this service without charge.

had to do with my being moved to another place. My circuitous reasoning led me to wonder if I was going there to learn a lesson. And why would I need to learn a lesson? In my confusion, I wondered if, for some unknown reason, I was being punished for a failure on my part. This combination of guilt and anxiety made matters worse.

Figure 1: Infants' Summer Hospital.
From the Albert R. Stone Negative Collection of the Rochester Museum & Science Center, Rochester, NY. I recall watching from the second floor, through the third window from the left, as my mother walked from the trolley stop on Sunday afternoons. Her visits were very special for me, as they relieved my homesickness. She always brought a treat for me, carried in a small bag.

I was moved by bus with some other children to the Convalescent Hospital for Children on Beach Avenue in Sea Breeze, a suburb of Rochester close to Lake Ontario. I was told that I had to stay in bed for everything, and I was informed for the first time that this was necessary to recover from a disease called rheumatic fever that might progress and disable me in later life. Knowing why this was necessary and that I was in good hands put me at ease in my new surroundings.

It was difficult staying in bed all the time. The ward was large, accommodating about 30 beds for boys; another ward I never saw was for girls. I had the impression that most but not all were hospitalized for the same problem. We had no activities, no social program, no radios, no games, and no music. I made friends with other patients on the ward, interacting with them from our individual beds. But I was bored, lonely, and homesick.

Visitors were allowed only on Sunday afternoons. The only visitor I had was my mother, with one exception, my brother Ralph. He came on a weekday afternoon with a friend whose name I do not remember. They were allowed to visit for a short while. His friend was so moved by the circumstances of my hospitalization and complete bed rest, that he gave me a dollar bill when he left. I was deeply moved by his generosity, and the fact that I had never had that much money in my 10 years. The following Sunday when my mother visited me, I excitedly gave her the dollar bill for safekeeping. She gave it back to me the day I was discharged.

Each Sunday afternoon, I looked from my bed at the wide entrance grounds of the hospital in order to observe approaching visitors. I was elated when I saw my mother coming. She came every Sunday without exception. It required between one and a half to two hours, and two trolley transfers, on a day of the week with reduced service. Even during the worst snow and rainstorms of the early months of 1936, she made the long journey to see me. She always brought me something—a cookie, a fruit, a piece of fudge, and on one occasion a comic book that I read avidly and used to barter for other comic books and items. Once she brought me Plasticine, a kind of clay that did not harden. I enjoyed this immensely in the ensuing days, making animals, toy soldiers, airplanes—whatever I could think of. However, a particular nurse named Ms. Parsons angrily snatched all of my creations and the remaining supplies, saying that the Plasticine had soiled a sheet. I protested that the clay had not touched the sheets. I cried and pleaded for her to return it, but she was adamant. So, my mother's next visit was especially important. I was crying and agitated; I tearfully explained what had happened. I did not think she could bring me more, as those were especially hard times. But, on her next visit, she brought me another supply. It was a joyous occasion. I have vivid memories of this incident—not only the bullying of an adult who made life difficult for me and others without provocation, but even more for how thoughtful my mother was to bring me another supply at a time when even a dime was more than could be spared. To avoid another incident, I only used the Plasticine when I was sure Ms. Parsons was not on duty. The rest of the time, I hid it in the back of a bottom drawer covered with a roll of toilet paper in my nightstand. I was not the only one who came to dislike her; others found her difficult, as she was strident and angry with most of the children who interacted with her. She was a grouch!

Another vivid recollection was the Sunday supper meal. This was the only meal of the week that was not cooked. It consistently featured a serving of cornflakes and a banana with milk. It was a routine consistent with a skeleton staff. However, to me it was remarkable because it was the first time in my life I had cereal from a box. It was delicious.

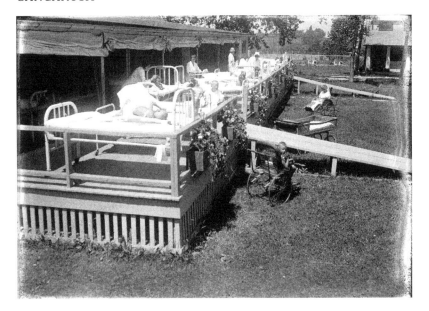

Figure 2: Children in the Sun: Rochester Convalescent Hospital for Children.
From the Albert R. Stone Negative Collection of the Rochester Museum & Science Center, Rochester, NY. Caretakers felt exposure to the sun was healthy, but they allowed only about half an hour to prevent sunburns. I recall spending time on that porch, at first in a wheelchair, and then walking about when I was transitioning between total bed rest and ambulation during the last month of my hospitalization (August 1936).

In the Convalescent Hospital, I had two teachers. Both were kind and considerate and made a lasting impression on me. One assigned math and English problems, and the other, a librarian, left history and social studies books with assigned reading. Fortuitously, one of my assigned books was Paul de Kruif's *Microbe Hunters*. Books were assigned for one week. When the librarian came at the next visit I had not read it all, so I asked if I could keep it for another week. She agreed. By the following visit I had read it from cover to cover, not once but twice. I was totally absorbed. It was so well written, so clear, and so interesting. I was extremely impressed that so many microbe hunters had made discoveries that changed our lives. I wondered about seeing invisible microbes as Leeuwenhoek had as the "First of the Microbe Hunters." I wished I would someday have a microscope of my own. I was fascinated by Spallanzani, the priest who demonstrated that life came from life and discovered the world of microbes; Pasteur, who found that some microbes can be a menace but that some of the diseases they cause can be treated and others prevented; Koch, who began his career in the practice of medicine and discovered the causes of diseases known as tuberculosis and cholera; Roux, a Frenchman, and Behring, a German, who contributed to our understanding of a deadly disease called diphtheria for which they discovered a treatment with a substance called antiserum from horses exposed to the germ that causes the disease; Metchnikoff, a Russian microbe hunter who discovered our own cells that help us fight dangerous microbes; Theobald Smith, a physician microbe hunter who discovered that diseases can be transmitted by insects and animals; Bruce, an English physician, and his wife, who used his microscope to discover the way tsetse flies transmit a microbe called a trypanosome to horses; Ross and Grassi, who proved that a particular mosquito "was the criminal in the malaria mystery"; Walter Reed, an army physician, who discovered the cause of yellow fever, but had to infect humans with the virus because only humans were susceptible; and Paul Ehrlich, a student of Koch, who discovered a drug for the treatment of syphilis that he thought would save the world. What they had in common was discovery of evidence-based breakthroughs that changed the world in meaningful ways[11].

---

[11] That this book made an indelible impression on me is evidenced by the fact that it guided me in my own career development. I have used it on many occasions in courses I have taught to help me convey the authors' and my own enthusiasm to students aspiring to careers in infectious diseases and especially in public health. At this writing, I shall be using it as a textbook in a course I

Although I had a persistent low-grade fever for the first few weeks of my hospitalization, I gained weight and felt well, so after eight months I was discharged. I returned to Public School Number 36 in the fall semester of 1936, behind a year but full of vitality and hope for the future. The following year, I was advised that I needed to have my tonsils removed because of my history of rheumatic fever, a concept championed by Dr. Albert Kaiser. My brother Joe took me by trolley for admission to the Eastman Dental Dispensary on Main Street in Rochester on a Friday evening. I waited anxiously that whole morning and was the last patient taken to surgery on Saturday morning. I recall my horror in having my nose and mouth covered for ether anesthesia. I awakened in a room with other patients with an exceedingly sore throat. I stayed in the hospital overnight and went home with Joe on Sunday. This surgery was intended to enhance my prognosis by eliminating beta hemolytic streptococcal bacteria that were seen as the inciters of relapses of the disease[12].

The most difficult times for our family

The following years, 1937 – 1938, were the most difficult for my family. My mother was fortunate to have a job because she had a unique skill—sewing seams by hand in very expensive suits—

---

teach each summer to introduce students to public health in Emory University's Pre-College Program for rising high school juniors and seniors.

[12] Although I had no known relapses, I later realized that this was no proof of the efficacy of tonsil removal. Indeed, the procedure has not been shown to be preventive in later research. At the time, evidence-based treatment was still years away. I met Kaiser years later when I served an externship as a medical student at the Monroe County Health Department, where he once served as Commissioner. He was a pleasant and persuasive person who did much to advance the cause of public health. He was also a great teacher. However, I did not include him among the role models who made a difference in my career because I had little contact with him.

but during those years of the worsening Depression, her services were needed only intermittently. So her earnings, which made up the only income for our family of 10, were cut by more than half. There were times when she did not earn enough to purchase food stamps to the full level allowed in the matching arrangement. She could manage the mortgage until it was refinanced in 1937; the interest rate was lower, but the payoff time was shorter, thus requiring higher monthly payments—$25 per month. With the arrival of the first bill for this new mortgage, my mother was shocked and dismayed. What she thought she would get by the lower interest rate was lower monthly payments. The extra $5 a month was more than she could afford; the bank foreclosed, and we lost our home in the midst of the worst depression in the history of this country. From that point on, hard times became harder times, progressing to the worst of times.

The loss of our home was a wrenching experience for the whole family. I drove my bicycle, one that I built from parts, around the neighborhood looking for "For Rent" signs. In fact, I did find the home we moved into, on a street just a few blocks away. The irony of the relief we got from welfare was that they paid the rent, $50 per month, but they would not pay the mortgage before the foreclosure—only $25 a month. The move was difficult and depressing. My mother wept. The weight allowance for the single truck-load allotment for a family regardless of size was not enough to take even essential things.

My experiences in school

I think because I had learned to study on my own while hospitalized, when I was discharged I spent considerable time in the afternoons after school reading about several topics I found interesting. I developed a keen interest in history, especially

51

global history, which served as a foundation for my future career in international health. At about the age of 12 or 13, I became an avid stamp collector and acquired a rather considerable collection of both American and global stamp issues. I was fascinated with stamps of Paraguay and Argentina, where I understood my cousins lived. I used the little money I earned as occasional allowances to buy stamps. I studied the countries that were the sources of these stamps, people and events depicted, and their value from catalogs I used.

During my adolescent years, I also had an interest in poetry. As a school assignment, I studied the history and memorized the work of several writers, most notably Rudyard Kipling. I especially liked his ballad/poem, Gunga Din. It has long interested me for four reasons: (1) Kipling skillfully mocked military and colonial policies of discrimination against the local Indian people, (2) it had an overriding theme of social justice, where the hero is the lowest-ranking person, (3) it was my first experience with the concept of social justice, which has figured so prominently in my career, and (4) it has a water theme that leverages the hero's credibility. In the six verses of the ballad, water is mentioned or indirectly implied in 12 instances.

As I advanced in my high school years, I was feeling well, indeed spunky, with no residual of the rheumatic fever that had led to my earlier hospitalization and confinement for convalescence. Benjamin Franklin High School was some distance away from my home, probably four miles—the walk required about an hour each way. I had no difficulty with this; indeed, I arrived each morning with great anticipation of the day's experience. However, walking to school during winter months was stressful because of the bitter cold. Some students rode a bus during the winter months, but we could not afford even the nominal nickel for the trolley fare.

Nonetheless, I looked forward to school each day. Learning was fun. I have fond memories of my high school courses and the many dedicated teachers whose enthusiasm I remember well. And I never again lost a glove!

The courses that especially piqued my interest were Latin and Italian, I think because they were similar enough to my mother tongue, Sicilian, that learning them felt easy. The Sicilian language is an amalgamation that reflects Sicily's prominent presence in shipping routes that attracted virtually all Mediterranean peoples and made it a prime target for conquest. Starting from pre-Indo-European influences of the island's first inhabitants, Sicilian became a confusing blend of Italian, Greek, Latin, Arabic, Norman, German, French, Spanish, and a number of other European languages. As an example of the Arabic influence, we have cousins on the Bellassai side of my family whose last name is Ali. The gap between Sicilian and Italian is wide indeed. My father, who served his required military service as a private in the Italian army, had difficulty in his service because he could understand only Sicilian, and little Italian. One of my professional colleagues, Dr. David Mel, a colonel in the army of what was then Yugoslavia with whom I collaborated on shigella-vaccine studies during my tenure at Walter Reed, was fluent in Italian. I once arranged a dinner for him and a Sicilian immigrant family. The morning after this dinner, I asked him "How did it go?" He replied, "Non ho capito nessuna parola," i.e., "I could not understand a single word"! The point I make is that Sicilian, my mother tongue, is a Romance language almost as distant from Italian as Spanish is from Italian.

I had marvelous teachers, Mr. Emil Bezant in Latin and Ms. Flora Rizzo in Italian. I had two courses in Latin and three courses in Italian. I believe both were helpful in mastering English, and my coursework in all three languages gave me a strong linguistic foundation. As I mention elsewhere in this book, I was assigned to serve in Italy during WWII most likely because I had these language skills. Little did I know that this would be such a salient point in shaping my professional career—my military experience in Naples, Italy was more a public health experience than a military one, as I note in another chapter. I am sure that my knowledge of Italian got me there and was helpful in my work.

Another course that served me well was typing. At the time it was structured to meet the needs of students who envisioned secretarial or administrative careers. This was reflected in the predominantly female enrollment. To my pleasant surprise, I have found it one of the most useful skills I possess, especially now that I use personal computers so often.

I was a good student. I learned after my graduation that I was 22nd in a class of several hundred. In my last year, I was appointed to the National Honor Society. So, despite the fact that I was a year behind students who had started school with me, I had confidence in the future and looked forward to serving in the military from a sense of patriotism and the challenge of qualifying.

My first experiences of World War II

World War II was a topic of discussion in many of our high-school classes. Two very memorable events of my adolescence were the Japanese attack on Pearl Harbor on December 7, 1941 and the Battle of the Bulge in mid-December of 1944. These were among the darkest days of the war, and they had a profound impact on my family and my own life.

Everyone of my generation remembers the December 7 attack on Pearl Harbor. I was in a movie theater on that Sunday afternoon, watching *40,000 Horsemen*, an Australian World War I movie about the "last successful cavalry charge in history." When I left, newsboys were excitedly shouting the headline "Extra, extra, read all about it, 'Japs bomb Pearl Harbor!'" I recall the shock and anguish as friends and strangers reacted to the dramatic news on the streets and on the streetcar ride home. That evening and the following day, people were glued to their radios, listening intently to each bit of news regarding the devastation and the thousands of deaths among our soldiers and sailors. As the extent of the destruction of our Pacific fleet became evident, the grim situation was eloquently captured the next day by President Roosevelt in his "day of infamy" speech to Congress, followed within an hour by a formal declaration of war against Japan. New fears arose—the possibility of a land invasion of Oahu or, even worse, our West Coast. On December 11, both Germany and Italy also declared war.

In those few shocking days, World War II, which we had observed from the sidelines as a horrifying catastrophe involving other countries, suddenly drew us full force into the entire global conflict. The country was united as never before in a patriotic fervor that at the time seemed reasonable, but in hindsight was excessive. Fueled by fear of espionage, anger, and hysteria, Congressional action was swift. Japanese families on the West Coast were rounded up and moved inland to "more secure ground." This "more secure ground" consisted of what were essentially camps confining large numbers of Japanese during the war—in retrospect totally unwarranted and unnecessary.

German and Italian immigrants were not forced into camps, as were Japanese immigrants. However, some European immigrants who had records of anti-American leanings were also affected by the news of the war. My oldest brother Sam, who was born in Italy (Sicily), became anxious even though he had not been politically active and was already well into his academic career. In this period of palpable anxiety, he made a decision that affected everyone in our family—he decided to change his name in a way that emphasized his commitment to America. He began using the name Ganis instead of Gangarosa, formalizing this change legally following WWII. All of my older brothers followed suit. My mother was dismayed, as she saw this in a somewhat different light—a rejection of our Italian heritage. My younger brother and I, my two sisters, and my parents chose not to follow this path[13]. Thus, my family line at this point includes several generations of Ganis families from the children, grandchildren, and great grandchildren of my older brothers. I was disappointed that the war had caused this family rift, but I had a great deal of empathy for my brother Sam in the difficult decision he had to make at a time when national anxiety was so high and the future was so uncertain among first- and second-generation Italian immigrants. I couldn't bring myself to change my name as they did because—fortified by my mother's convictions and the rich Latinate culture I discovered in my high school Italian and Latin courses—I was proud of my heritage. In fact, I feel strongly that I benefitted from embracing my Italian heritage, as I suspect it led to my WWII military assignment in Italy.

For two years after Pearl Harbor, we received nothing but bad news about the war. Morale continued to slide as the Japanese and German forces achieved victory after victory in rapid succession. After the D-Day invasion of Normandy on June 6, 1944, the tide finally seemed to change in our favor, and Allied

---

[13] Although my brother Ralph changed his name to Ganis at this time, after the war he had second thoughts and changed his name back to Gangarosa.

forces began to penetrate as far as the Rhine River. However, the Battle of the Bulge in December 1944 marked a severe setback that made us worry if the Axis powers would regain control. The Nazi army, led by a formidable tank force that was protected from air attack by severe winter weather, broke through the Allied lines, surrounded American forces, and put them in full retreat. Again, the nation was gripped in angst. The news was grim for several days until the weather cleared and Allied air support inflicted severe losses that reversed the course of the battle.

As the Battle of the Bulge unfolded, news bulletins and radio announcers encouraged everyone to support the war effort. I was caught up in this new wave of patriotic fervor. I was 17 ½ years old at the time and giving a great deal of thought to the inevitable call to duty required of able-bodied men at age 18. In fact, I wanted to serve. My concern was whether my history of rheumatic fever would exclude me from military service. I was physically frail, but I felt well. I figured that with so much concern about this particular military crisis it might be easier for me to volunteer right away, so that is what I did.

Two of my older brothers were already serving in the army air corps at that time. Joe was a warrant officer who participated in the invasion of Africa, Sicily, and Italy. Frank had enlisted in a special pilot training program. This program very much intrigued me, and it seemed just right because I weighed only 120 pounds, a fact I knew would be a problem in the infantry, but an advantage as a fighter pilot. I decided to enlist in that same program. Probably more than any other life event, this changed my career in so many ways. The rest of this story continues in the next chapter.

A tribute to my father's work

Here I would also like to honor my father with some additional reflections.

What does one see in the seemingly inconsequential curb pieces throughout the country? What is behind the winding roads crafted for horse and buggy traffic—now used by cars and trucks? In my eyes, these hand-carved curb pieces are monuments—examples of the kind of work my father crafted with pride using hand tools. These handiworks are still evident in many places in the eastern cities of this country. In Atlanta, for instance, 6- to 8-foot long slabs of curbstone pieces can be seen besides winding roads such as Ponce de Leon Road (once the major east-west road through Atlanta) and most of the tributary roads, such as Mason Mill and Houston Mill Roads around the Clifton Road Corridor. I see these as emblematic of my father's work, which made possible my family's immigration to America. These curbs are, more broadly, symbolic of the many other immigrant families who came to this country to build our infrastructures and make this a better country. I see these as symbols of the wealth immigrants have brought to this country. While these curbstones may lack the grandeur of the Statue of Liberty, they have a similar meaning about what this country stands for—not only the opportunities immigrants seek as they wait anxiously to learn if they may enter or stay in our country, but also the value these immigrants add to our country by being here. They reflect the pride that my father had in his work, his aspirations for a career in his craft, and my mother's dream of a safer place to bear and raise her children.

A tribute to my brother Sam

In my last conversation with my brother Sam, I asked him to share with me his most vivid memories of his childhood. Of the several he spoke of, it was this story of his role in our family's move from Niagara Falls to Rochester, NY that was so poignant. At the time, Sam was about 12 years old. My father got a notice he was being transferred to work in a Rochester, NY subsidiary of the company he had served during WWI. He had to report for this job soon after receiving his notice. This presented a problem for Sam because he was determined to complete the semester with his class. My father was adamant—Sam must move with the rest of the family because he needed Sam to interpret for him in his new job. Recognizing the importance of Sam's education, my mother supported Sam's request. She prevailed, but it was a difficult decision for her because she knew my father would have difficulty in another job, as he was not literate. Nevertheless, she was undaunted in her support of Sam's education despite the uncertainty as to how the family would manage in the event that my father lost his job and we were left without a breadwinner.

The logistics of the move were complicated. My parents bought large steamer trunks for their household goods, but no provisions were made for Sam. He stayed alone in their home for several months, managing with some help from neighbors. When the semester ended, he had little money, so he could not afford a trunk or suitcase for his move. To move his personal effects, Sam used two bed sheets he spread out on the floor. He put his own things onto one of the sheets, and on the other he put what our parents had left behind for him to take when he moved. Leaving many things that did not fit, he took what he could carry in two large bundles he made by tying the ends of the sheets. He walked from the family home to the train station, hoisting the bundles over his shoulders. As the bundles were heavy, he alternately carried one to a location where he could see the other left on the sidewalk, at which point he left the first and returned to fetch the other. He continued in this way until he reached the train station, where he bought his ticket. They would not allow him to check these bundles with the baggage, so he carried them onto the train and placed them on empty seats in the trip to Rochester. When he arrived in Rochester, he repeated his earlier strategy of carrying one bundle at a time, finally arriving exhausted at their new home. I asked Sam why he didn't take a taxi. He said he only had change in his pocket—not nearly enough for a taxi fare.

This anecdote underscored Sam's early-in-life commitment to his schooling, and my mother's priority for education of her children. Encouraged by our mother in his early years, and his wife Marion in later years, Sam was successful in everything he did in his private and academic roles. With the same zeal, my mother encouraged me and my other siblings in our professional pursuits. It was because of Sam's courage and success despite awesome obstacles, and my mother's passion, perseverance, and commitment to our education, that I see both of them as my role models in my career.

Reflections

In summary, the role models who shaped my career during the years of my early adolescence were foremost my mother and my brother Sam, who set standards for school performance; my high school teachers, especially Ms. Flora Rizzo and Mr. Emil Bezant, who taught me Italian and Latin; Paul de Kruif's "microbe hunters"; and Rudyard Kipling, who leveraged the importance of water in describing an underappreciated hero. Interwoven throughout these experiences was the notion of reaching out to those less fortunate—the concept of social justice became embedded in my being.

Chapter 2: Military Service in WWII, January 1944 – August 1950: New but still distant role models

In Chapter 1, covering the period of my life from 1935 to 1944, I identified as my "past" role models the "Microbe Hunters" from my study of Paul de Kruif's classic book on the major discoveries of the microscopic world. Although these giants were long deceased, their legacies inspired me in my career development. In particular, I have cited the work of three of them, Louis Pasteur, Robert Koch, and Paul Ehrlich, in each of the courses I have taught every year for the past 50 years. These Microbe Hunters really have become my role models in ways that have shaped my career and, through my many lectures, they have indirectly shaped the careers of students I have taught and mentored. In this essay, covering the period of my career from 1944 to 1946, I identify "distant" role models, public health professionals with whom I interacted during my experiences in Italy during WWII.

Recruitment and training

At the age of 17½, I volunteered for the same pilot training program as had my brother Frank. I was extremely nervous about my physical exam. My heart was racing when the doctor put his stethoscope to my chest. After several minutes, he said, "You are okay." I cannot find words to say how thrilled I was. I wondered whether I ever really needed to be hospitalized! The Air Force Program allowed me an additional six months to complete my high school training, and I entered the service in January 1944.

I traveled by train to the reception center at Fort Dix, New Jersey. Although I arrived after the dinner hour, the mess remained open to provide supper for the newly arriving recruits. I recall that first meal very well because it was the first time in my life that I had eaten steak! As I was setting up my pay and benefits, I was given the option for a family allotment—an automatic paycheck deduction distributed to my family. I chose the maximum deduction amount of $37.50 per month, which was matched such that my mother would receive $75.00 per month. She did not know until she received the first check; it was the largest monthly income she had received since my father lost his job after WWI. After the deduction, as an army private, I received $12.50 per month; it was my largest salary to date.

My stay at Fort Dix lasted only a few weeks. It was cold. The barracks were heated only by pot-bellied stoves at each end of a long single room with two rows of cots. Cafeteria food was the best I had known. I was excited; I looked forward to the beginning of a new adventure, proud to be a private in the Army.

From the reception center at Fort Dix, I was reassigned to Keesler Field in Biloxi, Mississippi, one of the Air Force's basic training centers. The training was rigorous; it taxed me to my limit because I did not have the strength and stamina of other 18-year-old recruits. I could barely keep up, especially with the nighttime exercises and forced marches. One such forced march remains a vivid memory. After a difficult day of drilling and marching, my unit returned to barracks exhausted. Within 15 minutes, the command to assemble for a forced march was given. We were surprised, because it was raining hard. It was planned—the sergeant in charge was ordered to conduct the march "to toughen up the recruits." It was one of many seemingly senseless things we did because they were deemed military necessities.

Figure 3: EJG in Uniform, Aged 17 ½.

I volunteered for a pilot training program, soon phased out as the tide of battle shifted and pilots were no longer needed. I served in Italy in an Air Force support unit, interacting with other Army personnel in the control of typhus.

Days later, I got a severe sore throat. When I reported to sick call, a throat culture was taken. I also had a temperature, so I was ordered back to my barracks. Two days later, I was surprised to receive a message ordering me to report to the dispensary with all my gear. When I arrived, I was informed that I was being quarantined with a group of recruits who also had positive throat cultures for "strep." All of us positive for strep were quarantined in a separate barracks and markedly restricted in our activities so as to minimize chances of infecting other recruits. Another measure to minimize risk of transmission was the repositioning of beds; spaces between beds in all barracks on the base were increased to lessen the risk of transmission between strep carriers and uninfected soldiers. In retrospect, identifying strep carriers reporting with respiratory symptoms and increasing spacing of beds were two of the interventions found efficacious in studies conducted by Dr. CH Rammelkamp and his mentee Dr. Lewis W. Wannamaker [1-3]. Years later, I met Rammelkamp at meetings of the Infectious Diseases Society; I introduced him when he gave a lecture at the University of Maryland, where I was serving as the coordinator and moderator of a lecture series for infectious diseases residents and faculty there. I recall his surprise when I mentioned I was one of those recruits at Keesler during the strep outbreaks that were described in publications by him, Wannamaker, and others [4]. He certainly qualifies as one of my role models, but I had no further interaction with him after this event. Still, I admired him not only because I benefited from being in his study, but primarily because of the quality of his research in that it was evidence based. The concept served as a seed that found fertile ground in my career development.

After basic training, I was interviewed for further assignment. For the first time during WWII, the tide of war had decidedly changed in our favor. The Allied Forces had broken through after capturing the Remagen Bridge and were advancing deeply into Germany. Having established undisputed air superiority in every war theater, the Air Force no longer needed fighter pilots, so the program for which I had volunteered was terminated. Instead, I was assigned to the Scott Air Force base in Illinois for bomber crew training on the Martin B-26 Marauder. I also received firearms certifications for the .45 caliber automatic pistol, M-1 carbine, and Thompson submachine gun. After completing my training as the radio operator and machine gunner on the B-26, I was sent to Fort Bragg, North Carolina, the East Coast port of embarkation for overseas service. I had no idea what kind of work I would be doing, but I was eager to get started. I had no way of knowing at the time that I would never fly a combat mission and that my military experience would take a radically different turn.

My squadron was put on alert for shipment to the Caribbean, an area that included the Panama Canal Zone. In anticipation of "shipping out," we were confined to barracks. To make sure we would be available when the command was given, we waited, and waited; days passed with no action. We had little else to do but wait some more. We played cards, listened to the radio, and sat around day after day. One of the days was payday, and I lost nearly all my month's pay in a poker game, about 10 dollars. It was my first and last time gambling, I have never played for money again, even on trips to Las Vegas. In the second week of this waiting, I was so bored that I decided to risk leaving the confined area. So, late one afternoon, as the light was already fading, I walked some distance to attend one of the movie theaters on the base, some distance from my barracks. I watched a double feature and then headed back to my barracks. It was already very dark. The streets were poorly lit, street names were not marked, and all barracks looked exactly the same. Without landmarks, I could not find my way back. Finally, after hours of searching, I saw a light in a barracks; it happened to be the headquarters barracks. I went inside to ask for help and directions. I was surprised to learn that my squadron had shipped out that very afternoon. To my consternation, I was informed I was "absent without leave" (AWOL). My gear had been moved to the headquarters barracks when my squadron shipped out that afternoon. I was temporarily given a bed in a nearby barracks for the night. I was restricted to that barracks and informed where and when to report for court martial the next day. At the hearing, a captain asked why I had disobeyed orders. I had no excuse and admitted I was wrong. The AWOL charge was recorded and still remains on my military record. I was given one week of punishment at hard labor. I had the messiest jobs in the mess hall. Those were the longest and most difficult days during my military training, doing double shifts for a full week. At the end of my punishment, I was reassigned to another squadron awaiting assignments to replace servicemen overseas. My overseas shipment was about a week later; to my pleasant surprise, my squadron was alerted for duty in Europe.

A new challenge

I traveled to Europe in a troop ship in very stormy weather. Nearly everyone got sick. However, we were lucky in that, by then, remarkable advances in anti-submarine warfare and intensive bombing of fortified naval bases had essentially neutralized the threat posed by German U-boats. Earlier in the war, torpedoed ships were almost invariably left behind, and everyone on them would perish. However, at the time that we crossed the Atlantic, the U-boat fleet had been virtually decimated.

We arrived in Cherbourg, France, and I continued my journal by rail to Naples, Italy. What a nice fit with my past experiences! I suspect that someone who had a role in assigning replacements must have seen my record, which showed my three years of

Italian and two years of Latin in high school. This is most likely the reason that I was assigned to a logistical support squadron in Naples. I was ecstatic.

I had no training in supply and logistics. My military training and skills were irrelevant to my new position. I replaced a soldier whose wartime experiences had earned him the necessary points to return to the States. He briefed me during an orientation lasting just one day. The second day, I was with a guide who showed me the area and scope of my responsibilities and details of what I was expected to do. I also received a tour of sites I was expected to know, culminating in a visit of the site of destruction of the city's water and sanitation infrastructure. The year before, the retreating German army evacuated the city in anticipation of advancing Allied Forces. Nazi decision-makers had decided they would use Naples to send a message. They wanted the Allies to regret their attempt to invade "Fortress Europe," so they created a situation that would generate enormous costs and a logistical nightmare for the Allies—they destroyed the Naples's water and sanitary infrastructures. It was a calamity of monumental proportions. Suddenly, one million inhabitants were left without water and sanitary facilities, just as the cold winter months approached. The disaster and the reconstructive effort are described in the book *Naples '44* [5].

Outbreaks of water-related diseases followed. Civilians had to search for water from whatever source they could find. Most of such sources were contaminated. This led to the spread of diseases that were both waterborne and water-related, i.e., diseases that were transmitted via water as well as diseases that were caused by water scarcity, as civilians had to ration what little they could find. Dysentery is one such disease.

Typhoid, which struck many, is a classic example of a

waterborne disease, resulting from ingesting contaminated water. The word "typhoid" has the Greek ending –oid, which means "like," i.e., a disease with clinical manifestations and high mortality similar to typhus.

Typhus was the most serious of the water-related diseases, caused by the lack of water for personal cleanliness. Bathing was a luxury that few could afford during the cold winter months. Under such conditions where personal hygiene is infrequent, the body louse finds its ideal nesting place in the seams of underclothes, where it is warm, hidden, and close to its food supply. At night it ventures out of its nesting place for its blood meal. As the louse sucks blood, it also defecates. The enzyme it uses to facilitate insertion of its sucking apparatus is irritating, much like a mosquito bite. The irritation causes the bitten person to scratch the site upon which the louse's feces had been deposited. This process of scratching introduces the infectious agent, *Rickettsia prowazekii*, into the bloodstream, a process called autoinoculation. One to two weeks later, symptoms manifest. The disease is called louse-borne typhus fever, and it is a severe illness. Although the Nazis did not use bacteriological warfare agents in WWII, this man-made disaster they created was an indirect form of biological warfare. In Naples, in 1944 – 1945, it was seen as a newly emerged infectious disease. In fact, it was an old disease that became a new and serious threat[14].

---

[14] Two major factors had contributed to the decline of typhus in the industrialized world. Firstly, the Industrial Revolution had enabled the mass production of machine-made underclothing, which had much tighter seams than hand-sewn garments and was thus less hospitable to the body louse. Secondly, the advent of indoor plumbing enabled more-frequent personal hygiene. In wartime Naples, this second factor broke down, and the body louse was able to thrive where it wasn't being washed away by regular bathing.

To deal with the crisis, the Allies convened a group of scientists they designated the "Typhus Control Commission." To prevent transmission, the strategy was to administer DDT in powder form, using a bellows to aerosolize the insecticide between the underclothes and outer garments of people at risk. This would kill the body louse that carried the infectious agent. News media of the period showed people lined up to be deloused during this disaster, similar to scenes of the delousing of Jews and political prisoners whom the Nazis had forced to work in concentration camps. Nazi soldiers were not at risk because they were able to bathe and change their underwear frequently.

My new role was not directly related to the typhus outbreak. I had the title of Quartermaster Supply Technician, Military Occupational Specialist 821, and most of my duties dealt with military supply and logistics. My job required maintenance of supplies, storage, inventory, resupply, and distribution to points in need; I often traveled between Naples and Rome. I met some of the staff involved in the typhus control effort, including several that I came to admire. However, I had no assigned duties concerning the typhus problem, except for ad hoc needs the typhus team requested through higher channels. Nonetheless, the problem intrigued me. Though typhus is not mentioned in Paul de Kruif's *Microbe Hunters*, reading this book gave me a foundation of basic knowledge to build on. I understood that a wide range of microbes caused diverse diseases, and that interrupting transmission required different strategies specific to the pathogen. I recalled that some of the Microbe Hunters had discovered the role of insects in disease transmission, notably Bruce's work on the transmission of trypanosomes by tsetse flies. That gave me the background to understand the concept of an insect vector, such as the body louse that transmits typhus. I read what I could find about typhus, especially circulars that the Commission prepared and distributed to citizens of Naples, as these flyers were written in very basic Italian I could read. In search for even more to read, I found the story of Charles Nicolle, the person who discovered that the body louse transmits the disease. This story would be replayed many years later, as I was preparing for my Bangkok cholera field trip. My experience in the typhus outbreak in Naples was the acorn for the interest that has germinated through the rest of my career.

I was so enthralled with the reconstruction work that I decided to seek a job after the war with the just-formed United Nations Relief and Rehabilitation Administration (UNRRA). I filled out an application to work in Italy after my military discharge. I submitted it, but while my interview was pending, I realized this would be a mistake; I needed to advance my education. The act of applying made me realize what I really needed to do. College became my new goal.

Wrapping up my service

During my service in Italy, I had advanced rapidly in rank four pay grades, from private to staff sergeant. I was deeply touched that my superiors valued my services and rewarded me for my dedication and commitment. My pay increased, nearly all of which I saved with the intent to buy a home for my family. My mother's letters expressed her thanks for the allotment I had arranged. I was gratified to know that the allotment had made a difference in my family's quality of life. This was my first taste of giving, and the unexplainable satisfaction and sense of gratification that it provides. This habit continued later in my professional career, through the several endowments that my wife and I have created.

As my service was wrapping up in October 1946, I learned that Army personnel were entitled to purchase unneeded army equipment. I went to Leghorn (Livorno) to purchase a used Jeep. I found one in good condition; it had only one bullet hole, just below the windshield on the passenger's side. I could only imagine someone who had been killed by sniper fire. It cost $200, a lot of money at the time, but I knew it would serve me well when I got back home. I drove it back to Rome and parked it at the villa on Antonio Nibbi, the Squadron Headquarters that was my home for the last several months of my service in Italy. In November 1946, I had earned the necessary points to qualify for repatriation. I had the Jeep painted blue and serviced, and the bullet hole repaired, and drove it back to Leghorn and onto the ship that took me back home to my family.

It was late afternoon when the ship departed, and I looked back for hours as the port and shoreline faded from my view. I left with a feeling of accomplishment. Especially poignant are memories of my Italian friends I worked with in the reconstruction of Naples. In my courses, I still share anecdotes of my typhus experiences with my students.

My military service in Italy was unique because of the timing of my arrival as hostilities were concluding. Instead of the usual soldier's combat role, I had a peacetime role, helping with reconstruction and improving quality of life. I did not recognize it at the time, but in retrospect, it was my first taste of public health, and members of the professional staff of the Typhus Control Commission were my first public health role models.

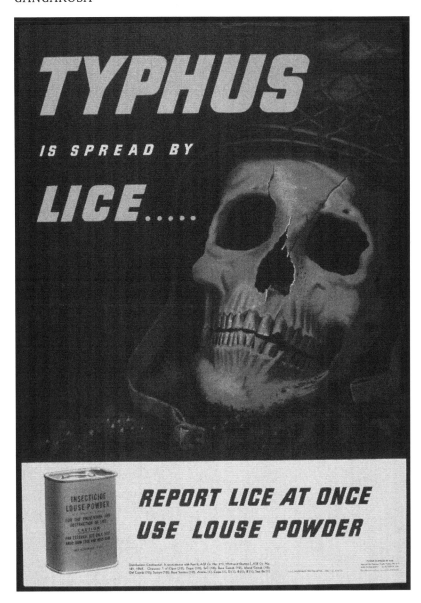

Figure 4: Typhus prevention poster.
Typhus was one of many water-related diseases that affected Naples after the destruction of the water and sanitation infrastructure. The typhus epidemic was spread through body lice. Posters such as these warned soldiers and citizens about the dangers of the disease and how to prevent its spread through the use of louse powder (DDT at the time).

Back stateside—my college experience

In November 1946, I was formally discharged from the military service. My goal was to go to college and eventually study medicine. However, my first commitment was to my family—my mother; father; a sister, Josephine, who was learning-impaired following childhood measles; and two brothers, Frank, who had recently been discharged from the army air force, and Louis, a teenager at the time. Since my military allotment, which had been essential to them, was no longer available, I felt the need to ease their financial burden. Thus, I decided to buy a home for them using money I had saved during my military service for the down payment. Recalling the trauma my family experienced losing our house during the Depression, I made it my highest priority to provide them with the security of a permanent home. To qualify for a mortgage for the balance of the home loan, I found a job as assistant manager of a bakery in a grocery store (one that I had worked in prior to my service). I purchased a side-by-side duplex such that the rental income from the adjacent dwelling could help pay down the mortgage.

Since I was working full time, I started my college career taking courses in the late afternoon and evening hours at the University of Rochester. As I couldn't be a full-time student, I enrolled in the University of Rochester's extension service, designed for students who worked full-time and commuted to campus. I took courses on the University of Rochester's satellite campus between Alexander and Prince Streets, instead of on the main River Campus where full-time students took their courses. My GI bill entitled me to course tuition and books equivalent to four years of college credit. I was highly interested in a career in medicine, and so I decided to pursue a general studies curriculum that met the requirements for medical school.

73

In the summer of 1947, I registered for my first college course, physics. It was a near disaster. Within the first week of class, it became evident that I did not have insight into the problems. I considered withdrawing, but I was too proud to acknowledge defeat. I was not as well prepared as my peers because I had lost a year of schooling during my long hospitalization and convalescence (mentioned in Chapter 1). This was a problem that I had created when, at 17 ½ years, I volunteered for military service air cadet training, which required completion of high school. In order to catch up to graduate with my peer class, I had to take an overload of courses in excess of what was usually allowed—two semesters worth of coursework in my last semester! I was a good student, and I did well in all my high school courses, but in physics I was only able to take the first of the two-semester course sequence. Because of this, I barely passed the New York State accreditation exam. However, my weak foundation in physics did not become truly evident until that first week in my college physics course. Furthermore, I had not taken calculus, a course highly recommended, and I was working full time. This was a recipe for near disaster, culminating in my getting a C minus as a final grade in a course required for medical school acceptance.

Undaunted by this poor showing, I was determined to prove to myself that I could excel academically. So, in the fall semester of 1947, I registered for a full academic load working only part time in my job at the grocery store. I finished that year with a nearly straight-A average. I knew I could.

Reflections

In summary, during this period of my life, my career was shaped by "distant" role models, people I did not know well, who were dealing with the control of typhus in Naples. I happened to be there, and casually interacted with them during my military service. My interest in the disease led me to discover another long-deceased scientist whose life intrigued me, Charles Nicolle. His scientific work subsequently came back into focus at the beginning of my Bangkok cholera experience in 1959. The work I did in Naples proved to be akin to a public health experience, as it dealt with assistance in reconstruction and improving quality of life. These experiences provided me a perspective of community that, in retrospect, shaped the rest of my professional career.

References

1.   Wannamaker LW: **Control of group A streptococcal infections and their sequelae.** *Lancet* 1955, **75**(5):197-214.

2.   Rammelkamp CH, Wannamaker LW, Denny FW: **The Epidemiology and Prevention of Rheumatic Fever.** *Bulletin of the New York Academy of Medicine* 1952, **28**(5):321-334.

3.   Dingle JH, Rammelkamp CH, Jr., Wannamaker LW: **Epidemiology of streptococcal infections and their non-suppurative complications.** *Lancet* 1953, **1**(6763):736-738.

4.   Wilson OG: **An outbreak of sulfadiazine resistant streptococcus infection at Lowry Field, Colorado.** *J Infectious Diseases* 1946, **78**:147-152.

5.   Lewis N: **Naples '44.** 1st American edition. Pantheon Books; 1978.

PART II: MEDICAL TRAINING

Chapter 3: Medical and Graduate school, 1950 – 1955: Meeting real-life role models

Preparing to enter the next stage of my life

In the summer of 1947, I decided to accept a full-time job as an orderly at what was then the Highland Hospital. My thinking was that it might help me in applying for medical school, and in any case the experience would certainly help me become a better doctor in the future. It actually paid less than what I had been earning at the bakery, but it seemed to be more relevant. My job required many patient-related tasks, including taking vital signs, assisting nurses in administering intravenous fluids and monitoring post-surgical patients, prepping patients for surgery, bathing bedridden patients, and the two most menial jobs—emptying bed pans and urinals, and prepping bodies for shipment to the hospital morgue and other destinations. It was a job that showed me medicine from the perspective of the hospital caregivers, working with patients, interacting with nurses, doctors, and supporting staff. I worked at this for about a year while carrying a reduced academic load. In 1948, I resumed my college studies in the extension school, taking a full academic load. I continued working part time. I was reenergized by As in all courses taken in that year.

The year 1949 was a momentous one for me. In that spring and summer, I continued taking college courses. One weekend early that summer, I was at home studying when an unexpected visitor came to my home, a neighborhood friend whose family lived across the street from the home we had lost during the

Depression. His name was Sam Salamone. He had come to invite my brother Frank to a picnic the following Sunday. As Frank was not at home, Sam invited me instead. I had no plans, so I accepted. It would be another turning point in my life.

It was at that picnic that I recognized Sam's sister Rose, another childhood acquaintance. I knew her casually, as our families grew up together and we had all attended the same primary and secondary schools[15]. I very much enjoyed my visit with Rose; in fact, after the picnic, I realized I had fallen in love with her. During the following week, I went to her home to ask her for a date. She accepted. We courted, and after a few months, I proposed, as I saw her as the person with whom I wanted to spend the rest of my life. I have often wondered *what if* I had not been home that afternoon that led me to Rose, whom at this writing I have loved for over 65 years of marriage. I jokingly mention that if Frank had been home that afternoon, he likely would have attended that Sunday picnic, and perhaps have married her; so, she might have been my sister-in-law instead! It was one of many "*what ifs*" that have profoundly impacted my life, and indeed the lives of all of those whose stories have been intertwined with mine.

Applying to medical school

Earlier in this same year, I had started applying for a medical school admission. It was a daunting and grueling process. I had no typewriter; every communication and application was handwritten. But what made it especially distressing was the competition. A flood of applications came from highly qualified

---

[15] In fact, two of Rose's brothers also attended the University of Rochester at the same time as I did. Though we did not have any classes together, we graduated in the same year.

WWII veterans who, like me, had recently been discharged. Most of my close veteran friends were also applying to medical school. Most had strong academic records. They were a highly motivated and a highly competitive group. Applicants who had not served, although younger, were even more anxious and also keenly competitive. I really did not think I had a chance, especially because of my one poor grade in college physics. I fretted about this because I had heard that a poor grade in a required course was a disqualification for consideration for medical school. Still, I was hopeful and determined to try because despite my near-failing grade in physics, I had raised my overall grade point average to 3.4/4.0. With this grade standing, I met the criteria to graduate *cum laude*. This added boost encouraged me and strengthened my resolve. I also had strong support from my pre-medical advisor in whose required course, chemical quantitative analysis, I had earned an A. I also had As in all other required pre-medical courses except physics. So, with some trepidation, I applied to 6 medical schools in my senior year of college in the fall of 1949. My first choice and realistically my only option was the University of Rochester. I had come to this conclusion because I had no financial support whatsoever. Leaving home for my education was simply not feasible. I had used all of my military savings to buy the home for my parents. I was fortunate that rent paid by tenants in the adjoining (side-by-side) home covered my mortgage payments. Despite this help, my parents barely had enough to meet their own expenses. For my educational advancement, I was entirely dependent on my veteran's benefits, made possible by the GI bill. Without this support, I could never have afforded a medical education, or for that matter, any education whatsoever.

Late in the application process, I was thrilled to receive a letter from the Dean's office of the University of Rochester. It is still one of my most cherished memorabilia. I was invited for an interview. I spent a day at the university with one interview after another. I was blown away by having the chance to interview with a Nobel laureate, Dean George H. Whipple[16]. He was an awe-inspiring person with a commanding presence. He was polite, almost self-effacing, gentle in his manner, and kind in his demeanor. He easily won my confidence. I was pleased and intrigued that he asked me if I had ever been hospitalized. He listened with interest as I recounted my hospitalization and convalescence for what was diagnosed as rheumatic fever when I was nine. I mentioned that this experience had given me an appreciation and a unique perspective of problems arising from an illness requiring hospitalization. He asked me to clarify, "In what way?" I replied that my hospitalization had given me confidence that I would be more sensitive, purposeful, attentive, and compassionate in my interactions with sick people, especially hospitalized children. I shared with him my anxieties in being separated from parents and family. I believe he was impressed. He was also intrigued by my army service. I noted that my service was unlike most because I had the opportunity to participate in reconstruction. I felt good about the interview; I thought I had improved my chances of being accepted. Indeed, just before the year-end holiday season of 1949, I received my letter of acceptance. It was a happy and memorable day.

Later that same year, as Rose and I were planning our marriage, her grandmother fell, broke her hip, and died a few days later. They had enjoyed an especially close relationship. The shock of this episode led us to postpone setting a date for our marriage.

---

[16] In fact, Whipple personally interviewed every member of our class. Later, when I served as Dean at the Faculty of Health Sciences of the American University of Beirut, I tried to pattern my interviews of graduate school applicants as I remembered mine with him.

Some months later, we picked August 19, 1950 as our wedding date. Medical school classes started a month later.

Our home life in those early years

Up until this time, Rose had been working as a piano teacher at her studio (which her father had built in their back yard), in nearby high schools, and at Nazareth College, where she had been the first piano performance major. [17] When I started medical school, she found a job at the university's Strong Memorial Hospital. We commuted together in the military surplus Jeep I had purchased in Leghorn, Italy. My brother Frank had helped me build a wooden enclosure for the Jeep. It served its purpose of providing protection in the worst weather. Only in retrospect, as I write this, do I realize how dangerous that vehicle was, how many risks I had taken. We drove in rain, snow, and the mixture of both that made commuting so hazardous in Rochester winters. We had to drive in the early morning hours and at dusk when traffic peaked. We had no seat belts; they had not yet become standard equipment. Military Jeeps were unstable and prone to skid, occasionally turning over; the wooden enclosure would have offered no protection. Rose was patient despite the inconveniences. Because she was barely 5 feet tall, she had difficulty climbing onto the passenger seat. We kept the Jeep through most of my first year of medical school, but the situation got worse when she became pregnant. So, I decided to sell the Jeep. With the proceeds, I bought a larger car, a pre-war sedan about 10 years old. Despite its age and many "disabilities," it was reliable. The confidence I had in it was underscored when Rose was carrying our daughter Peggy. At term, I rushed her to the Strong Memorial hospital as midnight

---

[17] Indeed, Rose was a skilled pianist. She had taken piano lessons since she was nine years old, and later attended Eastman School of Music.

was approaching on December 31, 1952, which happened to be her birthday. Her mother accompanied us in the car. We got to the hospital just in time, as Rose had a precipitous delivery in the emergency room corridor before even being transferred to a regular bed. Peggy was born there in the corridor, early that January 1st morning of 1953. She was the first baby born at the Strong Memorial Hospital in that year. I was fortunate that nothing happened on our way to the hospital because the three of us were alone in the car, it was snowing, streets were slippery, and I had no way of communicating if Rose had needed help. We kept this car through the remaining years of my medical school and the year after graduating from medical school. It set a precedent as to how long we kept our cars—about a decade and 100,000 miles for each.

We lived about 10 miles from the medical school in a second-floor apartment. Rose's father owned the house and generously permitted us to live there without paying rent. We only paid for utilities. Rose was handy, frugal, and kept a pleasant and attractive home. We lived simply and comfortably. We sometimes entertained family, friends, and classmates. Rose was the seventh of 10 children, all of whom had long, healthy, and happy lives. They were a close and caring family who celebrated holidays together. Easter, Thanksgiving, Christmas and New Year's events were joyous and memorable. Even outside the holiday season, Rose's family members often invited us to their nearby homes (Rose's sister Florence lived with her family on the first floor of our apartment) for meals, and sent us home carrying leftovers. Rose's family were loving, considerate, and generous people who reached out to us in so many ways. Their generosity went a long way in making it possible to manage on a minimal budget.

We have fond memories of those days and often reflect on how fortunate we were and how grateful we still are for their help. It was in this supportive environment that I attended medical school.

Memorable medical school coursework

All of my professors were outstanding scientists, great teachers, and helpful mentors. My learning experiences made each day an exciting adventure. The curriculum was rigorous. I am sure it was the dismal experience I had with my first college course, physics, that transformed me into a studious, determined, and serious student. Each day I studied many hours, often into the early morning. The school had a policy of not returning exams so as to deemphasize grades and to minimize competition among students. We were a close-knit group. We worked well together and enjoyed each other's company. Many were veterans with varied war experiences. I was among the most fortunate; because I did not have combat experiences, I had no horror stories or military adventures to tell. To the day of this writing, we still value time together in class reunions, which most of us attend at least at five-year intervals. We take pride that our relatively small class contributions made possible the university's largest class endowment. We have many younger honorary class members whose tuitions were funded by this endowment.

Our class was small relative to most medical schools. At a time when most medical school classes exceeded 100, our class enrolled only 66. Only one, Paul Dobosz, did not graduate with us. His death in an auto accident likely could have been prevented if seat belts had been invented. At this writing, 38 of us remain of the original 66. We are all octogenarians, most with frailties consistent with our ages, many still leading productive and enjoyable lives. I believe I am the only one still actively teaching; I teach two courses each year in my role as emeritus professor. I find it enjoyable and challenging to do mental gymnastics with students who seem to be sharper each year.

I began medical school with great anticipation. In the first meeting of our class, Whipple assured us that we were selected with the expectation that we would all graduate. He explained we would be monitored, but that we would not know our grades. We saw it as a policy to minimize the importance of grades so as to foster learning for the sake of learning. He inspired us and filled us with enthusiasm and expectations of what was to come. He engendered in us a sense of pride, an *esprit de corps*, and a deep sense of responsibility. It soon became abundantly clear that the bar was high and the curriculum was rigorous. Hard work was necessary and expected.

I found every lecture in every course interesting. I was fascinated with the subject of each lecture. The professors who taught us brought with them rich professional experiences in their respective fields. I have vivid memories of Dr. Edward F. Adolph discussing the physiology of heat exposure from his research experiences in North Africa during the war, and of the anatomy professors teaching us amusing ways to remember complex anatomical structures. To this day, I recall the names of the bones of the wrist by the mnemonic, "Never lower Tillie's pants—grandmother might come home," as the name of each bone begins with the first letter of each lyric. They were all great teachers. Here, I record what I remember most about those who contributed the most to my intellectual growth, the teachers who in fact became my mentors.

In my first year, the teacher who had the greatest impact on my career was Dr. Karl E. Mason, my anatomy and histology professor. In addition to teaching these courses, he assumed another task, improving our writing skills. He was the first in my medical career to emphasize how critically important were our writing skills. He returned our written answers to questions he asked and had us rewrite our answers using fewer words and more precise wording, repeating this process several times, each time challenging us to weigh more carefully each word for precision. I believe that all of us thought we were pretty good writers from the beginning. However, we realized through these exercises that we could do better with each rewrite. In the years that followed, I put these skills to use in many courses I taught, every report I wrote, and as I approached faculty status, every draft of each manuscript I wrote for publication. Most of my mentors in later years were also zealous about writing skills, and I benefitted from each of them. But, in retrospect, I appreciate most Mason giving us this learning experience early in our careers. In the two courses I still teach at this writing, I use Mason's model to get students to become better writers.

My second year was the most enjoyable and memorable of my medical school experience. Two courses had a profound impact on my career. My pathology course was especially notable. It was taught by Whipple; in fact, ours was the last course he taught before his semi retirement. I have no doubt that if my classmates had been asked which medical school course and professor they liked most, they would agree that it was pathology and Whipple. He was a master of the Socratic method. He engaged us in thinking through pathogenic processes, the evolution of diseases. He impressed on us his belief that understanding the pathogenesis of diseases was the key to treatment. I can see him now at the autopsy table with a diseased organ in a tray or in his hand, calling on us individually as to what we understood about the progression of the disease, the resulting impact on function, and disease symptoms. He had many anecdotes to underscore his teaching. I think he was the best teacher of all my medical school years. His emphasis on pathogenesis helped me most in a later chapter of my life when I had the fortuitous opportunity to study and define the pathogenesis of cholera (see Chapter 6). His administrative skills as dean also impressed me.

A second course that had an even greater impact on my career was bacteriology, a survey course taught in the Department of Bacteriology and Preventive Medicine. From the beginning, the term "Preventive Medicine" in the department title intrigued me. I was also surprised and pleased to learn that Dr. Albert D. Kaiser had a faculty position as Professor of Child Hygiene. His name meant something special to me because I recalled that he had had a leadership role in the preventive program for rheumatic fever when I was hospitalized for that disease as a child. I do not think that he lectured in the bacteriology course, but at department faculty events, I introduced myself and spoke to him. The three general divisions of the department were bacteriology, immunology, and parasitology. All the lecturers were superb, especially Drs. Herbert R. Morgan, John H. Silliker, Henry W. Scherp, and Albert L. Ritterson. What I learned from them fit well with my earlier experiences, first in reading Paul de Kruif's *Microbe Hunters* during my hospital convalescence and then my WWII experience in Italy (see Chapter 2). Morgan was a student protégé of Hans Zinsser, a professor and Chairman of Bacteriology at Harvard Medical School. Several times, Morgan cited teaching points from Hans Zinsser's book *Rats, Lice, and History.* Zinsser's book made for riveting reading, focusing on typhus among other infectious diseases that decimated armies and populations in ways that "changed the history of the world." Although I had not personally seen typhus, it was the focus of the control program in Naples, Italy and my first disease interest, dating to 1945.

Figure 5: Dean George Whipple Teaching Pathology.

Our class of 1950 was particularly fortunate as this was the last year that Dean George Whipple taught pathology in the medical school. He had a dynamic way of linking pathological changes with physiological and clinical findings. Of all the instructors that I ever had, Dean Whipple was the most memorable.

Dr. Henry Scherp lectured on immunology in a way I found very interesting, no doubt because of my reading of *Microbe Hunters* years earlier. Some of Scherp's colleagues had studied with mentors in the laboratories of Robert Koch and Paul Ehrlich in the late nineteenth century and in the first two decades of the twentieth century. Scherp noted that the Koch laboratories were the premier place for international graduate study and work opportunities for students in bacteriology during the pre-World War I era; the situation changed abruptly in 1914 with the onset of WWI. He lectured on historical immunological breakthroughs in those laboratories—most memorably his observations of Paul Ehrlich. As Scherp recounted, while Ehrlich was in Egypt recovering from tuberculosis, he recognized a state of immunity in a family suffering from venomous snakebites. The father, who had been bitten before, survived, while several of his children died or had severe disease. This narrative continued in Berlin when Ehrlich returned to work with Emil Behring. Ehrlich observed that a hyper-immune serum could be produced by injecting horses with progressively increasing doses of diphtheria toxin. The two scientists deduced that this hyper-immune serum could be used to treat diphtheria. It was the first-ever efficacious treatment for the disease. Scherp also told of Paul Ehrlich's discovery of a drug to treat syphilis. This drug was prepared from arsenic that was attenuated by coupling with an amino acid; it was the 606th iteration of such molecularly modified combinations, and the first one found to be suitably safe and effective against the spirochete that causes syphilis. This drug was named Salvarsan because it was seen as the "salvation of mankind." It was viewed as a miracle drug that had the potential to control the disease via mass treatment[18].

---

[18] I happened to be watching an old movie some years later and recognized that Scherp's anecdotes are told in the movie "Dr. Ehrlich's Magic Bullet," which I

The anecdote I remember best, because it has been so relevant to my professional interest in enteric bacteria, is the story Scherp told of the first serotyping system for *Escherichia coli*, a classification based on the somatic or "O" antigens and the flagellar or "H" antigens that these and so many other enteric organisms share. He noted that the pioneer bacteriologists in Koch's laboratory recognized that some bacteria grew by spreading uniformly like a film over an agar plate, while others formed separate and distinct colonies. They compared the appearance of the agar plate films to what one sees when exhaling forcibly on a cold windowpane. The relevant German word is "Hauch," meaning breath. These scientists recognized that this spreading phenomenon is due to the presence of flagella that enable some bacteria to swarm. Bacteria with this swarming property, linked to their flagellar antigens, are designated by the letter H. The O, or somatic, antigen comes from another German word "ohne," meaning "without," i.e., without flagellae. New strains are named according to this German serotyping scheme, with sequentially assigned numbers following O (for somatic antigens) and H (for flagellar antigens). Thus, the numbers in *E. coli* O157:H7 refer to the somatic or O antigen 157 and the flagellar or H antigen 7, that distinguish this particular strain from other *E. coli*. Strains are also identified by the place where a

---

have used from time to time in courses I have taught. The movie stars Edward G. Robinson as Paul Ehrlich. It was produced in the late 1930s at a time of ever worsening anti-Jewish pogroms. Choosing Ehrlich underscores to the viewer the many scientific contributions of one of Germany's most prominent Jewish scientists. Robinson, himself a Jewish immigrant, relished this role portraying a great global humanitarian scientist, as it served to emphasize the many contributions Jews made to the German people and to world citizens in an era when Jews were losing respect due to the disinformation of Nazi leaders. Robinson's role in this part was quite a departure in his acting career, as he previously was featured as the "bad guy" in gangster acting roles. He was keen to take this new role to counter the image of Jews depicted so despicably by the Nazis.

particular strain was first recognized, as for example *Salmonella waycross*, first isolated from a specimen from Waycross, Georgia; or by the strains association with a particular host such as *Salmonella typhimurium*, a strain associated with rats.

John Silliker's lectures of the enteric (intestinal) pathogens were outstanding. His research and professional background prepared him well to lecture on salmonellae and shigellae, the principal pathogens of this group. He also had a background as a food scientist. He had experiences in WWII outbreaks of salmonellosis among British residents who had eaten American-made dehydrated egg products imported from the United States during the Battle of Britain. He shared with us the story of how salmonellae were named, not after Theobald Smith, the scientist who first described the prototype strain, but rather after Smith's supervisor named Salmon who, in clearing the manuscript for publication, put his name on the manuscript as first author. Thus, by tradition in naming newly discovered bacteria, Salmon was recognized as the scientist who first discovered salmonellae. Silliker facetiously commented that the name would otherwise have been Smithellae and the disease smithosis. He also told the story of the discovery of shigellae by the Japanese scientists, Kiyoshi Shiga, a Japanese student protégé of Robert Koch.[19] Of the enteric diseases, typhoid stands out in lectures by both Morgan and Silliker.

Dr. Al Ritterson was an outstanding parasitologist with unique teaching skills. His lectures on the life cycles of the parasitic pathogens were memorable. What he taught fit well with another past experience—a course I took in my basic military

---

[19] I have sometimes mentioned these anecdotes when I lecture in courses, always giving credit to Silliker. In fact, when I was preparing to write this chapter, I discovered I still had my notes from his course!

training in Biloxi, Mississippi that was focused on preventing so-called tropical diseases. Most of my WWII military classmates were assigned to units in South Asia where these diseases were prevalent. Until this medical school course, I did not really understand how the topics covered in my earlier military training course related to my experiences in Italy. Finally, everything started fitting together. The course meant a great deal more to me because of my related past experiences. My second-year bacteriology course had the effect of whetting my intellectual appetite. I eagerly read more, such as Zinsser's book (recommended by Morgan). This book highlights stories of historical developments that rang distant bells for me, such as the role of lice in the transmission of typhus as described by Charles Nicolle, one of my previous literary role models. The combination of curriculum content and inspiring teachers heightened my desire for even more. In retrospect, the experiences of this course primed my career appetite for professional opportunities yet to come.

My clinical years and a valuable externship experience

My third and fourth years were in clinical rotations, learning physical diagnosis and various specialty disciplines. I have little memory of these assignments, but I found all of them interesting—particularly pediatrics, internal medicine, and infectious diseases. I especially enjoyed attending infectious diseases rounds and meetings. My most memorable experiences during those years were an externship with the Monroe County Health Department in the summer between my third and fourth years, and my numerous nursing assignments tending to polio patients in need of respiratory assistance.

Two summer externships were offered in the Monroe County Health Department by the Department of Bacteriology and

Preventive Medicine. These honored Dr. Albert D. Kaiser. I was fortunate, being one of two accepted in the summer of 1953 – 54. Another classmate, Robert F. Willkens (Bob) was the other classmate accepted. Our supervisor was Dr. Margaret Rathbone; she served as Commissioner of the Monroe County Health Department, where she had succeeded Kaiser. As noted above, he touched my life profoundly because he was a rheumatic fever crusader. He founded the Convalescent Home for Children, where I had been hospitalized for this disease 17 years previously when I was nine. In fact, I was one of those included in his Rheumatic Fever Control Program. Kaiser was also a strong advocate of removing tonsils of children diagnosed with rheumatic fever, thought to decrease the risk of infection with beta hemolytic streptococci, thereby diminishing chances of relapse. On the basis of this clinical recommendation, I had a tonsillectomy two years after my hospitalization. Kaiser had retired long before I started this externship, but he remained a dominant figure in the Health Department and was highly respected for his continuing services in the Department of Bacteriology and Preventive Medicine. His portrait featured prominently in Rathbone's office.

Bob and I met Rathbone the first day we began our externship assignments. She welcomed us, outlined the administrative structure of the department, and explained how a local health department functions. She described several specific long-term programs in progress and asked us to evaluate one of these programs as our required externship project. This assignment called for a written report and a final presentation summarizing our assessment. She asked us to work together "as is often required in public health practice." The program that appealed to both of us, especially to me, was an evaluation of the county's multi-year rheumatic fever control program. We looked over program data and finally decided which aspects of the program we were to evaluate independently. Rathbone concluded by advising us to assimilate our assessments into a consensus report.

Through May and early June, we were deeply immersed in assessing data relevant to our rheumatic fever topics. Suddenly, in late June, a surge in clinical cases of polio was reported in the county. We were asked to put our project work aside to support polio-related activities, because we were in the midst of one of Rochester's worst epidemics. In the 1950s, prior to the introduction of the vaccine, polio was a highly endemic disease throughout the country, with epidemic peaks during summer months. In Monroe County, the number of cases surged throughout the month of June and well into July. It had become an epidemic emergency.

Each morning we were briefed by members of the Department on the evolving surveillance data and activities in response to the outbreak. We participated in drafting notices and getting information to the public, cautioning the population about measures thought to be important such as sanitary precautions and avoiding public gatherings. I learned a lot about public health communications while attending meetings with news media professionals.

Late in July with the epidemic still peaking, Bob and I were asked to participate in an immunization program in the southern tier of New York State. This was an ongoing study to evaluate the efficacy of immune serum (gamma globulin) in preventing transmission, especially in an epidemic situation. This work was spearheaded by Dr. William McD. Hammon, Professor of Epidemiology of the University of Pittsburgh.

On Friday of the last week of July, Bob and I drove to a designated community in New York State's southern tier. The next morning, we were briefed about the study protocol and our role in it. Each of us worked in a different location with a nurse and two assistants. News media had already briefed the public about the immune serum program, given instructions about how the public could participate, and advised of the location of designated schools and the time to assemble, i.e., at 8:00 A.M. on that Saturday morning. At each school, signs provided directions to school gymnasiums, where people gathered. I was amazed how responsive people were. They queued in long lines; hundreds showed up, underscoring community apprehensions and a desire to prevent getting the disease. Team members recorded names and instructed participants to go to specified rooms. As they entered, they were given an identity badge and asked to sign an informed consent form. They were weighed and then waited in schoolrooms until they were called as family groups. They moved together into another room where syringes were loaded with immune serum in amounts corresponding to the individual's weight. Each syringe was labeled for the intended recipient. We injected adult participants in the deltoid muscles and young children and infants in their gluteus muscles. We were careful to discard used syringes. I had a bad experience that left a vivid memory—it involved a rather heavyset teenager whose dose was about 7 milliliters. Immediately after I injected the serum, he collapsed. He was unconscious. I was frightened and concerned that I had done something wrong. Help arrived after a few minutes as the boy was coming out of a faint. We had cots for just such emergencies. He rested there as we monitored his blood pressure. Within the hour, he asked to go home; his blood pressure was normal, so we released him with instructions about follow-up if needed. Our teams administered immune serum for two days to hundreds of people. Some teams remained in the community to follow up. Bob and I returned to Rochester early the following week.

Data from this large field trial (described in detail in a much later paper) demonstrated that immune serum protected against polio [1]. The study was an important contribution, as it demonstrated the important role of immunity in this disease. It paved the way for the subsequent field trials of the inactivated vaccine (Salk) and subsequently the live attenuated vaccine (Sabin). After the first national Salk trial the following year, manufacturers provided vaccine in quantity to control the disease. One important untoward incident occurred: In what has since become known as the Cutter incident, a lot of vaccine was prepared with a vaccine strain not adequately inactivated. This live vaccine caused many cases of polio. Because the cause of this outbreak was not known, confusion reigned and the vaccine itself was suspect. The entire program was halted. News media featured alarming stories, often distorting and sometimes exaggerating the investigative findings. At the center of this was the Epidemic Intelligence Service (EIS) of the Communicable Diseases Center, now known as the Centers for Disease Control and Prevention (though it has retained its designation as "CDC"). I was very impressed to learn that physicians were trained at CDC to be epidemiologists, and that these epidemiologists were now responding to an outbreak. The events of the outbreak and its investigation were fascinating to me. I was reminded of outbreaks in Naples during the typhus control work in the wake of the destruction of the city's infrastructure when I was serving there. It was also the first time I heard the name of Alex Langmuir, the chief of the investigating group. I was amazed by how quickly they responded and how rapidly they found the true cause that exonerated the vaccine. Their work made possible a quick resumption of the vaccination program. In the years that followed, Sabin's vaccine, an attenuated live vaccine, became especially useful in the developing world: fecal excretion of the attenuated virus allowed its transmission (via contaminated food, water, fomites) to the contacts of vaccinees, thus enhancing their immunity and spreading the benefit of the vaccine. The availability of these two vaccines gave people a choice of vaccine for themselves and their families. My children were vaccinated with the Salk vaccine in 1955. I marveled that this awesome disease had been controlled so quickly by a public health program relying on vaccines. The momentum of the control effort was impressive. The fearsome tragedies of yearly epidemics came to an end. These successes sparked interest in a global eradication effort with success in most countries. At the time of this writing, only residual foci persist in just a few countries, and the eradication effort is still a work in progress.

Late in July of 1953, I completed my part of the rheumatic fever assessment. Bob and I met to assimilate our data into a single report. We submitted it to Rathbone. She scheduled a meeting of her group to critique our report, which was distributed in advance. I had hoped that Kaiser would attend. I very much wanted another chance to speak with him because, even though he had retired, it was widely agreed by those in the department that he still provided leadership for the program. Unfortunately, he was not able to attend. It was my first experience giving a presentation to a group of scientific peers who we knew would critique our observations. Our presentations went well, and their critiques were constructive. We documented the decline in incidence of the disease during the decades of the program. In the discussion, we were asked why the disease was waning. We acknowledged data were not available to explain why. The decline was consistent with an improving economy during the war years and in the economic boom that followed, but we could not prove that this was the cause of the decline, or give any other reason for what we observed. We also reported on the program initiated to remove tonsils of children who had been diagnosed with rheumatic fever. I was personally interested in this topic, as I had been one of those children. We had to conclude that the rationale for removing tonsils did not have a scientific basis, and there was no evidence of benefit. The discussion piqued my curiosity because I did not know the answers to questions as to which methodology would have made it possible to test these hypotheses. The experience of assessing the data, preparing and giving a presentation to a professional audience, and getting their critique played a role in getting me to think like an epidemiologist.

Later in July and into August of 1953, I learned that the Strong Memorial Hospital had requested the services of senior medical students to assist in the nursing of polio patients who suffered from respiratory failure requiring the "iron lung." I accepted this challenge. I worked rotating shifts of 8 hours for two weeks before classes started in the fall of 1953. During the fall semester, I worked weekends until late fall. Initially, I was somewhat concerned about contracting the disease, even more so of carrying it to my family. However, scientific information known at that time left me with the assurance that polio is an enteric disease transmitted by the fecal-oral route. I had learned about preventing transmission of enteric pathogens from Silliker in my second-year bacteriology course. To teach students about the transmission of enteric diseases, he used a mnemonic called the 5 F's. Transmission occurs in routes that involve feces, fingers (hands), food, fomites (inanimate objects capable of harboring infectious microorganisms), and flies. I felt confident I could prevent transmission to myself, family, friends, and contacts by taking extra precautions like washing my hands thoroughly and often after each exposure, at the end of each shift, and when arriving home. As far as I know, none of the many medical caretakers who worked with acute polio patients acquired the disease. For me, it was my first enteric disease experience.

The iron lung was a closed cylindrical device into which patients were sealed with only their heads showing. It had a motor that created negative and positive air pressure inside the enclosed space. These changes in pressure allowed the expansion and contraction of lungs, simulating normal breathing. Portals on the sides of the machine enabled caregivers to insert our arms to provide nursing services. Standby generators were essential to provide an electrical source during power outages (most often resulting from weather conditions). No such storms occurred during my shifts, but I did hear of a power outage due to a storm that occurred during a different shift. We were drilled on how to deal with these events because attendants had only a few moments to switch from hospital electrical sources to standby generators to ensure patients' breathing would not be compromised.

At this writing, one of these machines is still in the permanent collection of the David J. Sencer Museum at CDC. A short video tells the poignant story of a young man permanently impaired who was sustained by this machine at night and by a portable respiratory machine during the day. These devices enabled him to function as a successful stockbroker. The story is a reminder of the many tragedies that were so common in the pre-polio-vaccine era. An enlarged wall photograph in the museum shows a large room with many of these functioning iron lungs from those tragic summer epidemics. It is a reminder of how much we owe to those who discovered, developed, tested, and used these vaccines in programs that have almost (at this writing) eliminated this scourge.

The D.J. Sencer Museum also tells the story of the March of Dimes program, started to honor Franklin D. Roosevelt, who had been crippled by the disease. As a young teenager, I recall attending my neighborhood movie theatre, the Dixie, which turned on lights to pass out collection boxes to collect dimes during intermissions of the usual double feature. To this day, the March of Dimes seeks contributions to control crippling diseases, especially birth defects. It is one of the many not-for-profit organizations Rose and I still support at this writing.

More recently in my career, I had the great opportunity to collaborate with a colleague and EIS alumnus, Dr. Stan Foster, in writing a tribute to Dr. Alex D. Langmuir to celebrate his life. Our chapter noted the Cutter incident among many other highlights of Langmuir's amazing career and role as the father of American epidemiology and a pioneer promoting international epidemiology. It was published as a special tribute in the American Journal of Epidemiology, and entitled "Passing the Epidemiological Torch from Farr to the World Legacy of Alexander D. Langmuir" [2]. Both Foster's and my own career were in the footsteps of this great teacher, as were the careers of so many others that each of us had mentored.

Summary and reflections on medical school

I enjoyed my medical school experiences immensely. The University of Rochester and my faculty role models gave me the opportunity to develop strong foundational skills that have served me well in my career development. Those role models and mentors helped me build on my past experiences. They helped me expand my knowledge and skills. They inspired me. They gave me confidence to function as a medical professional. I felt able and eager to take advantage of whatever opportunity arose. I was ready for whatever challenge.

My externship was a unique opportunity in public health and preventive medicine. The challenge of being involved in a polio epidemic was my first field experience functioning as a public health professional. My public health externship at the Monroe County Health Department was especially instructive, as it provided me my first taste of epidemiology in public health practice. My participation in a field trial of polio immune serum was a landmark experience for me. The opportunity to engage in the treatment and convalescence of polio patients during the polio epidemic of 1953 was another highlight of my school experience. The sum of these experiences resonated with my previous experiences guiding me to a career in public health.

I met Kaiser during my medical school years at events sponsored by the Bacteriology and Preventive Medicine Department. He and Morgan had a close working relationship. He was highly esteemed. At one event, I introduced myself and talked to him briefly about his two programs in which I had been personally involved as a patient. Until that time, I had not fully appreciated how much my personal experiences—convalescence from rheumatic fever, my tonsillectomy, and externship in the Monroe County Health Department—had originated from programs he had spearheaded.

Other events in the Department of Bacteriology and Preventive Medicine featured prominently in enriching and leading me to a career in public health. These included a series of lectures and conferences in the third and fourth years; a third-year program, Preventive Medicine I (an introduction to the role of the practicing physician in the field of preventive medicine and public health); and a fourth-year program, Preventive Medicine II (focusing on epidemiology, control of communicable diseases, sanitation, and related topics). I attended each of these, and at the conclusion of the fourth year noted that I had not missed a single day of classes in all four years.

Graduate school

At the time, opportunities to pursue post-doctoral training in public health did not exist in Rochester. Getting this training in another city was also out of the question, as I did not have the means. It was for this reason that I decided to choose an additional graduate year in academic training in bacteriology at the University of Rochester. It had been a tradition at the school for students to take an additional year of training between the second and third year of medical school. This timing had not fit well in my circumstances, so I looked for my own surrogate for such training. I found it much more convenient to apply for a fellowship while most of my classmates were applying for internships. I was fortunate to be awarded a fellowship that provided support. I enrolled in the University of Rochester's Graduate School to earn a Master of Science Degree in Bacteriology. My master's thesis was a study of cellular immunity in tuberculosis. I took other advanced courses, including one in parasitology with Dr. Al Ritterson. I look back on it as among the best courses taught in my five years at the University of Rochester. I received my Masters degree in this Department of Bacteriology and Preventive Medicine in June of 1955.

I remembered from my readings and teachers that the army had nurtured some of the greatest public health pioneers. I especially remembered and was inspired by stories of Walter Reed and William Gorgas, two of my foremost literary heroes. I knew that the army had an outstanding hospital, the Walter Reed General Hospital; and a research center in public health known as the

Walter Reed Army Institute of Research. I aimed high because I was confident in such a future.

References

1.   Rinaldo CR, Jr.: **Passive immunization against poliomyelitis: the Hammon gamma globulin field trials, 1951-1953**. *American J Public Health* 2005, **95**(5):790-799.

2.   Foster SO, Gangarosa E: **Passing the epidemiologic torch from Farr to the world. The legacy of Alexander D. Langmuir**. *American J Epidemiology* 1996, **144**(8 Suppl):S65-73.

Chapter 4: Internship at Tripler Hospital and Combined Services Medical Course

As I neared the completion of my graduate training in the Department of Bacteriology and Preventive Medicine at the University of Rochester in mid 1955, I turned to planning the next step in my formal medical training, an internal medicine residency. The application process was somewhat similar to the process for admission to medical school. The real question for me was where could I get a quality medical residency that would pay enough to support my family of four—soon to be five! At that time, the best residencies paid little, in fact far less than I could even consider. I was pleasantly surprised to find that the military services had excellent residency programs. The prospect of a military residency appealed to me because of its reasonable salary and reputation for quality. My productive and enjoyable experience in the military, providing logistical support for the reconstruction of Naples during World War II, greatly enhanced my motivation to continue my medical career in the army. By so doing, I would also receive significant medical, insurance, and retirement benefits that would further help with my family's financial situation.

With all of the above considerations in mind, I applied for an army medical residence program. This program provided a commissioned rank during a rotating internship followed by three years in a residency program. I had internal medicine in mind as the most compatible with my evolving interests in infectious diseases. My first choice was Walter Reed in the

District of Columbia, but that particular program had filled. I was matched with my second choice, Tripler General Hospital on Oahu, Hawaii. I was pleased because it had other professional advantages, namely the fact that it was not just an army hospital; the hospital was staffed with expert physicians from various military branches. It had the widest referral area for medical conditions covering military facilities from the vast Pacific region. Having endured bitterly cold winters in Rochester, NY all our lives[20], both Rose and I found the prospect of living in Hawaii to be highly appealing.[21]

---

[20] We did not know until many decades later that Rose was heterozygous for thalassemia, i.e., she had inherited the thalassemia trait from her father's side of the family. The thalassemia trait, also called thalassemia minor, inhibits correct formation of hemoglobin proteins. These malformed hemoglobin molecules are unable to bind oxygen normally, leading to reduced numbers of healthy red blood cells in the body. The resulting deficiencies in tissue oxygenation lead to a persistent state of anemia. Symptoms are mitigated in patients who, due to other genetic variations, are still able to produce functioning fetal hemoglobin, which normally disappears during the first months of life. We suspect that Rose may be one of those lucky few, given that her symptoms have been relatively minor. Thalassemia was a deadly tradeoff in Sicily during her ancestors' time. A child born with thalassemia genes from both parents has thalassemia major, which was invariably fatal within a few years (though in modern times, blood transfusions have been able to extend life into adulthood), but a person with only one gene was less susceptible to malaria, which couldn't attack malformed hemoglobin as effectively. The downside Rose experienced in Rochester from the thalassemia trait was a Raynaud's like phenomenon—a painful partial shutdown of peripheral circulation during cold weather. So, Rose found the prospects of shirtsleeves weather all year round very appealing!

[21] Rose's mother, on the other hand, was somewhat apprehensive. At this time, 1956, Hawaii was still a territory of the United States, and she was concerned that the child that Rose was carrying might not be a U.S. citizen. We reassured her that was not the case, and invited both of Rose's parents to come visit us when Rose was about to deliver. Rose's father was so impressed with Hawaii

I decided to accept the assignment as the first year in my four-year postgraduate medical training. I was also informed that I could request the Walter Reed residency program in internal medicine after completing the internship year.

I contemplated my internship eagerly, but I was worried because I had been away from the clinical environment during the year I had spent in the post-graduate master's program. Except for the clinical rounds in infectious diseases and weekly medical and pediatric grand rounds, I had no hands-on clinical experiences with patients.

The challenges of internship life

The internship was a rigorous schedule with four three-month assignments. These were in surgery, internal medicine, pediatrics, and an elective in dermatology, in that order. I was unlucky in that I was scheduled to begin with my surgical rotation. It was the most demanding in terms of time required at work, leaving little time to study and even less time for family life. It had also been my least favorite subject in medical school.

The surgical internship scheduled an initial eight-hour shift from 8:00 A.M. till 5:00 P.M., an on-call shift for overnight emergencies from 5:00 P.M. to 8:00 A.M. every other day, and, when on evening call, no time off before starting the regular shift the next day. It required a total of 32 consecutive hours at the hospital every other day, often without time to sleep[22]. I was challenged

---

that he recommended investing in real estate there. Had I had sufficient assets to do so then, I would be extremely rich now!

[22] Nowadays, comparable to guidelines that require professional truck drivers to get adequate rest between work shifts, strict rules prevent interns and residents from working in a state of extreme sleep deprivation. Common sense argues, and long experience subsequently proved, that exhausted physicians

both physically and mentally, especially on those evenings when I served in emergency rooms and assisted with various traumatic injuries in unscheduled surgeries. Gruesome injuries were common in this pre-seatbelt era, especially given that many cars had fixed spear-like ornamental metal projections on their hoods. Those distinctive features badly mangled the bodies of pedestrians and vehicle passengers involved in accidents. I recall one evening especially vividly—sailors from a Chilean naval vessel were involved in a serious bus accident resulting in severe injuries. For me, it was a grueling all-night session with rotating surgical teams.

Those kinds of experiences taxed interns to their limits. After one such 32-hour work session, I arrived home to find Rose and our children anxiously waiting for me to drive them to afterschool activities and shopping errands. I was sleep deprived, but I didn't want to disappoint them, since we only had one car and Rose didn't drive much, so I proceeded to deliver my family to their various activities. While driving at moderate speed, I fell sound asleep and drove off a road. As I went off the pavement, the jarring motion of the car awakened me, and I realized in horror that my car was out of control. Fortunately, the ground was level, and with great difficulty, I was able to bring the car to a safe stop. I was shaken. I had just avoided a

---

are much more likely to make serious treatment errors, so such policies have been enacted in large part to protect patients. No such protections for physicians-in-training and their patients were in place during my internship and residency. At the time, medical leadership felt that subjecting fledgling doctors to the most rigorous conditions would prepare them for worst-case scenarios they might encounter in practice, like battlefields or natural disasters. We are now more inclined to recognize that such practices, besides being a kind of professional torture, greatly curtailed time available for reading medical literature, interfered with a young physician's development of clinical experience, and ultimately impinged on patients' rights to the best medical care.

serious crash. It was a close call, another "what if" situation that could have been the end of my career and even the end of my family, as we were not protected by seatbelts. We learned from this startling experience—no more driving after such all-night work sessions.

New mentors and role models

I was fortunate in having a particularly outstanding mentor, Colonel Elmer J. Pulaski, with whom I developed a warm collegial relationship. At the time that I met him, Pulaski was already well into a long, productive career. His collaborators were among the leading infectious disease experts of that era, and included the renowned Max Finland from Harvard. Beginning in the late 1930s and extending through the WWII era, Pulaski focused on infections associated with traumatic injuries, use of antibiotics in treatment, and use and misuse of prophylactic antibiotics. He even performed the earliest clinical studies of the efficacy and limitations of streptomycin and tetracycline. Pulaski had a special interest in microbiological issues, especially gastrointestinal pathogens that evolved from normal intestinal flora. He and I connected over this topic—already a strong interest of mine as well as over many others. Pulaski also knew well those who had served as my faculty mentors in my master's thesis. He was someone who profoundly influenced the direction of my career development and who helped me establish my niche in gastrointestinal pathophysiology and microbiology. Because I was so interested in and impressed by his work, I dedicated time outside the grueling surgical schedule to read relevant literature—especially his research—that prepared me for his rounds and lectures. I presented my cases with confidence and used published articles, including his work as relevant. I had the impression that he was pleased by my performance. I believe that my relationship with Pulaski had an impact on my being selected for the prized medical residency at Walter Reed.

In my pediatric rotation, I found a second outstanding mentor, Colonel Ogden C. Bruton. Without doubt, he was the best-known clinical scientist serving at Tripler General Hospital during my tenure. His claim to fame was his recognition and description of the first cases of infantile agammaglobulinemia, a congenital condition characterized by the inability to develop critical antibodies necessary for life. After recognizing the deficiency, he found a way to treat these infants with concentrated gamma globulin, a blood product that he and his colleagues prepared. This treatment enabled children to grow normally and live normal or near-normal lives. Bruton's work was a landmark leading to work by other scientists who discovered a spectrum of congenital and acquired immunological illnesses. Cases from military families throughout the Pacific catchment area were referred to Tripler Hospital just because he was there. I was assigned a few of these cases. I studied his work and other relevant literature to prepare for case presentation in his rounds. In this way I got to know him well, and we became close friends and colleagues. Bruton was generous with his time for those of us who were in the "Tripler family" (those of us training at Tripler). In fact, not only was he my professional mentor, he also served as our family pediatrician. Bruton was especially helpful after our son Gene Junior was born, as Gene suffered health problems during early infancy, including a prolonged and frighteningly life-threatening encounter with pneumonia.

A vacation and a scare

After having completed six months of my internship, I was entitled to take leave. At this time, ours was a family of five, and the infant Gene Jr. was under Col. Bruton's care. One of the most popular places for such vacations was a military recreation area in the Hawaii Volcanoes National Park on the island of Hawaii. We had signed up for this vacation before Gene Jr. was born. We were looking forward to this respite, but in the early weeks of Gene Jr.'s life, he developed a respiratory infection that progressed to a lower respiratory illness. Although his condition had improved several weeks later, he still had symptoms. We were deeply concerned by our baby's incomplete recovery from this infection.

Bruton was not on duty when we arranged a follow-up appointment with another pediatrician. The baby seemed to have stabilized his respiratory illness at the time of the appointment. Out of concern for the baby's health, we asked the pediatrician whether we should still go on our planned trip. Without hesitation, he assured us it should be okay. So, in the next few days, we made our final preparations for the seven-day vacation. With great anticipation, we left our apartment with our car fully packed for the trip. We drove to Pearl Harbor to the designated pier and ship.

The ship was a World War II surplus Landing Ship, Tank (LST), a class of vessels that made a huge contribution to winning the war—but certainly not because of their elegance or comfort! The LST was conceived to deliver valuable tanks and trucks to combat zones and back. When it became apparent how many heavy vehicles these ships were transporting to combat zones, Winston Churchill remarked, "The destinies of two great empires seemed to be tied by some goddamned things called LSTs." Goddamned things indeed, as we found out! LSTs were designed for one purpose: to deliver as many tanks as possible right onto a beach in an amphibious landing. To achieve that critically important function, every other consideration was sacrificed. The shape of the LST predisposed them to instability in rough waters, and as they weren't originally designed to carry passengers, there were certainly no niceties to the interior[i]. To put it mildly, the ride in an LST was certainly not up to the standards people currently expect in sea cruises. Indeed, this experience was memorable as the worst "cruise" we've ever taken!

Of course, we didn't know all this when we planned our vacation to the "Big Island." To the contrary, we were delighted that sea transportation was provided free by the U.S. Navy because of my active military status. After arriving at the pier, I followed signs directing me to drive the car to an assigned place and parked it there in the hold of the ship. On foot, we then followed other signs to find our ship quarters. What a surprise! These were not individual rooms; rather they were large cargo spaces with hammocks. These spaces had been converted into two separate areas, one for men and older boys, and the other for women and small children. It came as a shock that we were going to be separated, but it was too late to change our plans.

The interisland waters during these fall and winter months were rough and notoriously turbulent. Indeed, just shortly after the ship departed from shore, we found ourselves in a storm. We had supper together, but none of us was hungry, as we were beginning to feel unsettled by the motion of the ship. In fact, we had started to feel nauseated even before leaving the dock, due to the overwhelming diesel fumes, which permeated the entire ship. This awful smell surely aggravated our seasickness and, worst of all, exacerbated the baby's respiratory condition!

After supper, we went to our separate designated areas, where we had no privacy and little opportunity to socialize with anyone. Rose was alone with our four-year-old daughter Peggy and the infant Gene Jr. She had to carry our baby and baby supplies up and down extremely steep stairs that had certainly not been designed for use by civilian women and children. Rose managed by cradling the baby in one arm, bracing him in the other—upon which she was also carrying baby supplies, and having Peggy hold onto her elbow as she went from one level to the next. Fortunately, with Gene being just a month old, he was not very heavy. Peggy, though too young to really help, was cooperative and characteristically fearless. It was quite difficult for Rose without me.

The next morning, Ray and I were not feeling well when we arrived for breakfast in the dining area, where we were to meet Rose and the other children. Hardly anybody attended that breakfast meal. Even the crew members who were serving food looked very nauseated—which probably didn't encourage the few people who were not already ill to eat there! Ray had little interest in food, so I asked him to go on deck to help his mother, whom we expected momentarily. In fact, she and Peggy were seasick, as were almost all others on the ship. The trip was a prolonged nightmare, especially for Rose and the children, who were suffering from rather severe seasickness. The voyage lasted two days (36 hours actually at sea) before we thankfully docked in Ililo, the largest city and port of the Big Island. Disembarkation was a confusing and difficult process, especially since we were still sick and exhausted from the long and difficult voyage. It was not a propitious beginning.

We were assigned to a small rustic cottage, as were other families with small children. It was a long walk to our quarters, but we slept well that night. In the morning, we dressed, had breakfast, and got ready for the many scheduled events at the National Park. For several days, we walked many miles with our children, covering difficult paths and mountainous terrain. Most memorable was our trip around the island on what was then a one-lane road. This included a stretch on the so-called "saddle road," on which we traveled for hours until we encountered a fork in the road—with no signs! We had to make a guess as to which way to go. We still reflect on how stressed we were on that trip. The car's gas indicator showed we had only a quarter of a tank left, and we had no idea where we would find the next gas station. We drove hours on a single-lane road over a vast lava-covered area with hardly any foliage and no indication of where or when we could possibly get fuel and find a place to stop so that we could feed and change the baby. Late in the afternoon, we were much relieved to finally approach the suburbs of Hilo.

The highlight of the trip was the volcano Mauna Loa, which is considered active even as I write this. It was a sight we will long remember. At the time, we saw lava bubbling, steam rising, and sulfurous gases emerging as we looked down into the volcano caldera. We spent a couple hours there with a knowledgeable tour guide from the National Park Service. On a later (and more luxurious!) cruise back to Hawaii, we actually saw lava flowing downhill from the volcano toward the ocean.

By the end of the week we were physically spent, and on top of that, stressed because baby Gene's respiratory infection was essentially unchanged. On the day before we were to return, his symptoms worsened, causing us more concern. On the last day, we were eager to get back as we drove our car onto the ship for the return voyage from Hilo. It was again a rocky voyage with rough seas, and our experience was made even more stressful by the baby's worsening condition during the trip. When the ship arrived in Honolulu, I asked for and got priority to disembark. We were among the first to drive our car to the pier. I found a pay phone and called ahead to the emergency room, as the baby's illness at that point had us extremely worried. We headed directly to the hospital. Col. Bruton was on service when the baby was admitted to the pediatric intensive care unit. On admission, Gene Jr.'s respirations were labored, and his chest muscles were retracting with each breath, an indication of severe respiratory distress. He was placed in a misted oxygen tent for the next several days, treated with another antibiotic, and given a bronchodilator drug. I spent many hours in the evenings and early mornings at the baby's bedside. Several times Bruton came to examine Gene Jr. and to reassure me. The baby's recovery seemed slow, but after a week he was discharged to home care.

Baby Gene's prolonged illness and the administration of antibiotics over an extended period of time led to a fungal infection of his ear canals that persisted for many years. Gene Jr. got the best of care, as Pulaski and his colleagues had actually pioneered studies of the growth of opportunistic organisms during and following antibiotic treatment. This infection followed Gene into early adulthood. I irrigated his ear canals with a special antifungal solution almost monthly until he was a teenager. Gene Jr.'s physical growth was also impaired; it proved to be a source of frustration for him until a growth spurt he had in his mid-teens. When he volunteered for Navy service at the age of 18, he was the tallest of our children and in great physical condition.

Other rotations

My next rotation was in internal medicine. What impressed me most was that several of the senior staff had spent most of the war in Japanese prisoner-of-war camps. They were outstanding internists. Although none were distinguished research scientists like Col. Pulaski and Col. Bruton, they were wonderful teachers and seasoned clinicians. They had been forced to practice medicine in the worst of circumstances under the harsh treatment of the Japanese. It was an experience that served them well under relaxed peacetime conditions. I learned a great deal, and their lessons were underscored by the many war stories and clinical accounts they shared with us. The work schedule was also rigorous, but nighttime duty was not nearly as busy and stressful as it had been on my surgical rotation; on most evenings, I found time to sleep while on call for medical emergencies.

My last rotation was on dermatology, which I enjoyed because my teachers were knowledgeable and my on-call duty was from home. In fact, in the three-month rotation, I had only one emergency call, a patient evacuated by helicopter from a ship at sea because of desquamating dermatitis. It was fortunate that this last rotation provided me time to focus on my residency application. I wrote many drafts of my essay, trying to tell my story as to why I wanted a residency in internal medicine at Walter Reed Army Hospital. I think that my ability to speak to the historic role of Walter Reed giants in the history of medicine benefitted me both in my essay and in my interviews. I was also fortunate to have strong support from both Pulaski and Bruton. Their recommendations carried some weight in the highly competitive Walter Reed positions. It was another memorable day, comparable to the day I received my letter of acceptance to the University of Rochester Medical School, when I received notice that I had been accepted for the residency at Walter Reed. This notice was accompanied by orders to proceed to San Antonio, Texas to take the Medical Physician Training Program, a three-month course to prepare physicians for various roles in military medicine.

Life outside the hospital

Despite the many hours of nighttime duty, especially stressful during my surgical rotation, I found my internship year a most productive and memorable experience. Even at the time of this writing, Rose and I have myriad pleasant memories of Hawaii. On many weekends, we enjoyed day and evening trips with our children to various places of interest and marvelous beaches. The natural beauty of the island was utterly unforgettable. The newly and elegantly constructed Tripler Hospital was positioned atop a hill overlooking Pearl Harbor. It had only recently been completed and staffed. The hospital was built during the Korean War with the expectation that it would serve as a tertiary treatment center for battle casualties. It was designed to facilitate evacuations of casualties by its proximity to the airport and the harbor. Its coral pink facade, whose color and design the Military Governor of Hawaii borrowed from the Royal Hawaiian Hotel in Waikiki, was chosen to be distinctive and easily recognized from the air by helicopter pilots. In fact, next to the apartment where we lived was the helicopter-landing site, where our children often played. During lulls, the helicopter pilots would show the controls to children who lived nearby, including Ray and Peggy. We lived in quarters D in an apartment complex for intern and resident families on a hill with a beautiful view of Pearl Harbor and the city of Honolulu. In undeveloped land above the apartments was a heavily wooded area where hunters stalked wild boars.

At that time, the old Tripler hospital was still standing halfway between the then-new hospital and Fort Shafter. It was the place where Pearl Harbor casualties had been treated. I learned later that one of my subsequent mentors, Dr. Abram (Bud) Benenson, an army captain at the time, had triaged and treated sailors and soldiers injured by Japanese bombs and torpedoes on that fateful

Sunday in 1941. We could still see oil slicks rising from the depths, emanating from the sunken battleship Arizona, which was lying on its side. Damage to the port still existed, and work to repair war-damaged ship sites and buildings was still in progress. One of the Japanese submarines that had evaded the port's defenses was still evident on the beach. The area around the hospital was almost rural, with just a few housing developments. Much of the island had not yet been developed. In our visit to this site decades later, this beautiful green semi-rural area had been transformed into a densely packed urban suburb of Honolulu. Seeing these changes made us appreciate even more the beauty we knew of the island when we lived there.

Being in Hawaii so soon after the war, we could still see the scars of war in Pearl Harbor, and I felt a sense of honor and appreciation that I had my first year of medical residency at this historic place. This was reinforced by being quartered so close to where the action had been, meeting people who had served at the old Tripler hospital, and working with physicians who had been prisoners of war just a few years earlier. The experience also bolstered my patriotic feelings. Though I was humbled by the fact that I had played a lesser role than those who served in combat, I still felt pride in having served in that war. My supportive role in the last year of the war was a stark contrast to the experiences of those who fought and died at Pearl Harbor and on so many other battlegrounds. These sights and reflections made me realize how lucky I was to have had a constructive non-combat role.

San Antonio—an unexpected experience

In the summer of 1956, army physicians who had completed internships were required to take a course before starting their residency training. I was reluctant initially, as it seemed that this was not the best use of my time. Nevertheless, it was a rigid army requirement. I was resigned to make the best of it, but I certainly did not have high expectations.

About a week before our departure, I drove our car to a pier in the port of Honolulu for shipment to San Francisco. It was difficult to get around without a car, but we managed all right that last week. Around the beginning of July, we flew from Honolulu to San Francisco, picked up our car, and departed as a family to San Antonio. Crossing the California desert in the heat of summer was a miserable experience. Our car was a light four-door sedan that, like almost all cars at that time, had no air conditioning and no seat belts. The day before the trip, we purchased window fans for the back windows that were supposed to provide some cooling. These did not have the desired effect—the temperature in the cabin must have been in the mid-90s. Nonetheless, they gave us some reassurance that we had at least made our best effort to provide the best possible comfort for baby Gene. In that era before infant car seats, we wedged the baby's crib securely between the two back seats, flanked by Peg and Ray, who took turns fanning and playing with the baby during the long drive through California on the road to San Antonio. We left San Francisco at an early morning hour, drove about seven hours, and stopped at a motel to rest in the early afternoon to avoid traveling during the hottest part of the day.

The next morning, we got up very early and left at 6:00 A.M. to continue our journey. Just after we crossed into Texas, I was driving through El Paso when I slowly crossed an intersection as the traffic light was turning yellow. A policeman in an unmarked car turned on his siren and indicated that I should follow him. He led us for nearly an hour, taking us quite a distance out of our way. By this time, we were out of bottles for the baby, and he was beginning to cry. Since the police car was unmarked, I started to wonder if the policeman was even legitimate, and where he might be leading us! Finally, he stopped us at a house that looked like a doctor's office, but was (ostensibly!) a courthouse. In an extremely short trial of less than 10 minutes, the officer accused me of the offense of "scattering the pedestrians." I pleaded "not guilty," explaining that there had been no pedestrians in the intersection. However, the judge believed the officer and levied a fine in the exorbitant amount of $50. Fortunately, we had enough in travelers' checks to cover this amount, and with the baby crying, we did not want to delay any further. We paid the fine, found a store to purchase infant formula and diapers, and went on our way. Of course, we hadn't anticipated that long delay, and San Antonio was still very far. However, we had already made plans and needed to get the baby settled, so I drove straight through the night. We arrived in the early morning hours. When we got to the Brook Army Medical Center in San Antonio, we drove to a designated office for assignment to family quarters just off the military base. We were in a virtually empty bungalow until our household shipment arrived from Honolulu soon after. We settled in for the duration of the six-week course.

The course, which met for six hours each day, had several themes. The one I recall most vividly was that of infectious diseases of military importance, those that had played a role in shaping the history of the world. Core faculty taught most lessons, with supplementation by visiting guest lecturers. I remember little of the curriculum except the contributions of two distinguished guest lecturers. They were James H. Steele, a Public Health Service Commissioned Corps veterinarian, and his colleague Karl F. Meyer, at the time an emeritus professor of the University of California at Berkeley. During a two-day period, they lectured on the zoonotic diseases. They were the most memorable guest lecturers in the course, due to their incredibly interesting professional experiences, which they embellished with compelling anecdotes. Among many topics, I was particularly struck by their presentations about salmonellosis, which reinforced what I had learned from John Silliker two years previously. Their personal involvement in many of the field studies they presented made for riveting storytelling. I found especially interesting that they had conducted their field studies with what was then the Communicable Diseases Center, the predecessor organization of the Centers for Disease Control and Prevention (CDC). During breaks, I made my way up to the front of the room so that I could speak with them, ask questions, and get them to expand on points they had made. In retrospect, this was one of my earliest introductions to contemporary outbreak investigations, the CDC, and the U.S. Public Health service, which was another uniformed service besides the ones I had known— the Army, Navy, Marines, and Coast Guard.

Next steps

In planning for my next assignment at Walter Reed, I realized the trip to Washington would be a difficult experience for my family. It was a hot summer. The trip would be tiresome and uncomfortable for them. Another consideration was that I would need time free of family concerns to find a place for all of us to live in the Washington, DC area. So, Rose and I decided that she and the children should fly to Rochester, NY, where they could stay with Rose's parents while I drove alone to DC. On the second-to-last day of the course, they flew to Rochester. I left San Antonio the following day.

Reflections

Despite my earlier concern that the course in San Antonio would be a waste of time, my assessment at the end of the six weeks was different. I had benefited considerably, primarily because I had discovered two heroes, Drs. Steele and Meyer. I did not see them as mentors at the time because our experience together was so cursory. However, they had a strong impact on my thoughts for the future. As they spoke, I realized that these two men were part of the recently formed Epidemic Intelligence Service (EIS) at CDC, to which my classmate D.A. Henderson had recently been accepted. I appreciated the opportunity to learn from contemporary "Microbe Hunters" like those described in Paul de Kruif's book. Through this experience, my knowledge of, interest in, and focus on infectious diseases were sharpened. I was more inclined than ever to see the shape of my career in public health and the place of my career at CDC. In the months and years that followed, I had other occasions to attend their lectures in other venues, giving me the opportunity to learn more about their work and the organization that made it possible. Overall, meeting and learning from Steele and Meyer profoundly changed my initial skepticism about the value of the military course, which was indeed a worthwhile experience. Later I worked closely with Steele, and he became one of my mentors at CDC. Looking back, I am extremely grateful that my early military experiences in the war, medical school, internship, and other training gave me such a sound foundation that complemented so well my subsequent career experiences.

PART IV: PUBLIC HEALTH PRACTICE

Chapter 5: My Experiences at Walter Reed Hospital and Walter Reed Army Institute of Research

I have decided to combine into one chapter my experiences during my Walter Reed Hospital residency followed by those during my Walter Reed Army Institute of Research tenure because these were linked training experiences. In both, the themes of clinical medicine, microbiology, parasitology, pathophysiology, and epidemiology figured prominently. Indeed, my Walter Reed experiences tie into so many other experiences in my career.

As a boy, I read the chapter in *Microbe Hunters* describing Major Walter Reed's discovery of the transmission of yellow fever. Even though I was but a child in a convalescent home, that was truly the beginning of my professional career in public health. The opportunity Walter Reed provided me came from that earlier enthusiasm. Through my Walter Reed experience, I was able to nurture a niche interest in enteric diseases, a topic in which I have since developed considerable experience.

At the Walter Reed Hospital, I had clinical training in the medical specialty of Internal Medicine. This was followed by a science-based experience at the Walter Reed Institute of Research (WRAIR). At these institutions, I had the opportunity to work with exceptional mentors—Garland Herndon and Bill Crosby at Walter Reed, and Sam Formal and Ross Gould at WRAIR. It was from these experiences that I made the transition from clinician to research scientist—a transformation that opened doors for me as an epidemiologist, research scientist, academic teacher, and public health practitioner.

Walter Reed Hospital: Recognizing and investigating two hospital outbreaks

Walter Reed was a referral center for the most difficult cases among army personnel wherever they served, and provided the widest range of medical services including primary care for active duty and retired military. There was keen competition among army career physicians for assignments to teaching positions at Walter Reed Hospital, and the residency-training program had a long tradition of excellence. Competition for this training was intense, and I was fortunate to get a position for a three-year residency in internal medicine from 1956 to 1959.

I had memorable clinical experiences caring for a number of general officers whose names I recognized from news media accounts during the war years. These famous people included President Eisenhower, whom I met during clinical rounds during one of his several hospitalizations when I was a junior resident. However, the most salient events during my Walter Reed experience involved me somewhat by coincidence—two outbreaks on wards where I had been assigned.

The first of these began as a cluster of cases of bacteremia among elderly patients on the ward I was assigned to for one of my residency rotations. I was surprised on rounds one morning when I noted that several patients who had shown no acute symptoms when admitted had then developed high fever and shaking chills within a day or two after their admissions. I speculated that these symptoms must be due to a common exposure. Each patient had developed these symptoms following their initial clinical work-up, which included the collection of blood samples for assorted laboratory tests. It seemed reasonable to suspect that their newly developed symptoms were linked to having their blood drawn, as none of these recently admitted patients had received medications by injection, and I could think of no other common exposure. Thus, the possibilities for the responsible exposure were narrowed to either what was used to disinfect the skin for the insertion of needles, or the needles themselves that were used to draw blood specimens.

I consulted with a colleague, Captain Frank Malizia, who supervised laboratory workers. He noted that patients on other wards had also developed the same symptoms, which were compatible with bacteremia, i.e., the presence of bacteria circulating in blood. These wards had submitted patient blood samples to the laboratory requesting tests for bacteria. As those cultures were incubating, he saw an early indication of growth compatible with what we had diagnosed as bacteremia.

At the top of our "to-do list" was checking, in each affected ward, the containers where gauze pads had been kept immersed in disinfectant solution for use in cleaning skin areas before venipuncture. Malizia and his laboratory staff collected and cultured gauze-pad specimens from each of the affected wards. The next day, growth was seen both from the patient-blood cultures and from the gauze-pad specimens that had been immersed in the disinfectant solution.

Malizia investigated the hospital central supply laboratory from which the disinfectant was distributed to the clinical wards. This same disinfectant had been used for some time in our hospital and was a commonly used disinfectant in other hospitals as well. When Malizia cultured the liquid solution of disinfectant from this central distribution point, he found it to be contaminated with a number of gram-negative organisms. Coliform bacteria were in fact capable of growing in the solution! He also found higher concentrations of organisms in the gauze-pad specimens—indicating that these contaminating organisms were multiplying in this supposedly disinfecting solution. He identified the organisms isolated from the blood cultures as *Aerobacter cloacae.* We believe this is the first time this commonly used hospital disinfectant was found to be contaminated in a hospital setting, causing an outbreak of bacteremia among hospitalized patients.

We wrote up this outbreak investigation for publication, and were pleased to learn that it would be accepted in the prestigious *New England Journal of Medicine* with few edits [1]. Our article has been frequently cited in the literature. At the time of this writing, the name of the organism is *Enterobacter cloacae,* a fact I learned from Dr. John (Jim) Farmer, a prominent expert on enteric pathogens with whom I had the good fortune of a long association, including many collaborations on outbreak investigations while we were both at CDC.

In the second year of my medical residency, I discovered another hospital outbreak. It was an outbreak of a blood condition called thrombocytopenia, the destruction of platelets. This turned out to be caused by an antibiotic drug called ristocetin. The outbreak occurred during my assignment to the hospital's Metabolic Unit. Garland Herndon was the physician in charge of this unit. Because the problem involved a blood component, he referred me to the hospital's hematologist. Working with these two scientists was a transforming experience in my career.

I met Herndon on the first day of an elective rotation on the Metabolic Research Ward where he taught the importance of the body salts—such as sodium, potassium, chloride, and bicarbonate—known as electrolytes. He was the senior medical officer, a lieutenant colonel, and the person in charge of the Metabolic Research Ward. At the time, I was a captain, but from the beginning we were professional colleagues of equal stature. He did not need rank to win respect and confidence. During a three-month rotation, Herndon had a profound impact on my career development. Residents met with him twice each day. Clinical rounds started at 7:30 A.M. An informal brown-bag luncheon provided opportunities for discussions of medical topics and presentations of journal articles assigned during rounds. I was impressed with Herndon's vast knowledge and how well he orchestrated these discussions. He was a master of electrolyte metabolism, as many of the patients we saw were those with chronic problems often associated with electrolyte imbalances.

During my rotation with Herndon, a number of patients on the medical wards developed thrombocytopenia (a dramatic reduction in the numbers of platelets crucial in the blood-clotting mechanism) during treatment with a new antibiotic drug called ristocetin. This drug was given intravenously to patients who had life-threatening septicemia, i.e., microbes that had entered and circulated in the bloodstream. To see what these patients had in common, I prepared a hand-written spreadsheet listing patients, their laboratory-test findings, and drugs administered during their hospitalizations. From this chart, I recognized that the severity of the thrombocytopenia increased with the number of injections of the drug, i.e., it was dose-dependent. These findings raised concerns that this drug might be the cause of this problem. I presented my findings to the group. Herndon agreed this was an important observation. He arranged a consultation with a senior staff physician, Colonel William H. (Bill) Crosby, the director of the Hospital's Hematology Department.

Crosby suggested a rapid test of the drug in rabbits to determine whether the phenomenon could be duplicated. In fact we did see the same effect—platelet counts dropped rapidly after the drug was administered intravenously. We reported our data to scientists of the Food and Drug Administration and the company that manufactured the drug. Crosby then arranged for me to work with his senior technician. Together the three of us prepared a protocol to study platelet functions after exposure to the drug in vitro. During the next several weeks, we collected data confirming dose-related toxicity. We presented these findings in a national meeting of the Infectious Diseases Society of America, attended by FDA and scientists from the company that manufactured ristocetin. Our previous briefing of company scientists led the company to recall the drug. Because of our findings, hematology specialists found a useful role for the drug in studies of platelet function. To the day of this writing, the medical literature features reports of these findings.

My involvement with these studies continued well after my rotation ended, as I worked to prepare our data for presentation at a national medical conference, and for publication. My three-month rotation on Herndon's unit became a year-long association to prepare our publication. Although I had published previously, I had not experienced such painstaking work guided by such a skillful writer and mentor. I was initially overwhelmed by his extensive edits on my drafts, but from this experience I became a better writer and scientist. His mentoring was essentially a truncated course on the presentation of scientific data and writing standards expected for publication. When the manuscript was finally submitted, the journal accepted it with only minor edits. I was thrilled and grateful that this, my first study in clinical epidemiology, was published in one of the most prestigious journals, the *New England Journal of Medicine* [2]. Other publications describing the laboratory corroboration of the clinical findings related to ristocetin and thrombocytopenia soon followed [3, 4]. I believe that my experiences investigating and writing up these two outbreaks showed colleagues and other mentors that I had some potential in public health.

Garland Herndon: a standout mentor

I remember Herndon as a pleasant man, easily approachable, easy to work with, and rigorous in his scientific standards. He had a commanding presence, and he spoke with conviction. Everyone respected Herndon because he had the virtues of a great leader. He was superbly trained in his specialty of internal medicine, a consummate physician committed to his residents, staff, and patients alike. His enthusiasm was infectious, and he had a great sense of humor. He set a very high standard of excellence—for himself as well as for others he worked with.

One coincidental benefit to studying with Herndon was mastering electrolytes. He was one of the army's experts on this subject—indeed a national expert. Many patients hospitalized on his ward had electrolyte imbalances secondary to chronic illnesses admitted for metabolic treatment or studies. Dealing with these clinical problems served me well in my 1959 Bangkok cholera experiences, because cholera patients lose salts critical to life. That story is recorded in other chapters of this book.

My experiences with Herndon were also my introduction to Emory University. During routine lunch meetings with Herndon (who had the habit of taking lunch with his residents when possible), we learned that he was considering leaving the army to accept a faculty position at Emory. In 1958, Herndon briefed us that he was being "courted" by Emory faculty[23]. He spoke highly and enthusiastically about his Emory contacts and opportunities they discussed with him. Knowing that Herndon was about to accept an appointment in the Department of Medicine at Emory sparked my interest in the school. For this reason, I trace my Emory heritage to my association with Herndon.

At our luncheon meetings, Herndon would also discuss his long association with Robert Woodruff during the years that he was a medical student and resident in internal medicine at Emory. He spoke fondly of Woodruff, who called upon Herndon and other Emory residents to assist him in providing the best available healthcare for workers on his farms in South Georgia. I had the impression that Robert Woodruff saw Herndon as an exceptional doctor and a perceptive advisor. When Herndon informed us that he was considering leaving Walter Reed to Emory, he did not specifically mention the relationship evolving between Woodruff at Emory and what was then the Communicable Diseases Center, the forerunner of the Centers for Disease Control and Prevention (CDC). I have no doubt that the unique partnership between Herndon and Woodruff had a profound impact on Emory's emergence as one of the world's great international universities. It is my belief that this friendship made possible the global recognition of Emory's Medical School and the Rollins School of Public Health.

President Laney was exactly on target in his July 21, 1984 eulogy of Herndon with his simple yet eloquent assessment: "He cared,

---

[23] Indeed, President Laney also records Herndon's recruitment in 1958, as does of Dr. Charles Hatcher, Jr. in his book, *All in the Timing*. According to Hatcher, it was Dr. Willis Hurst who recruited Herndon to Emory's Department of Medicine.

he showed that he cared, all knew that he cared, and...this may have been the most important ingredient in his medical bag...Garland [Herndon] possessed those qualities in abundance that make a great and good man, a great and good doctor. He was a wonderful role model for students, with his keen perception and trained powers of observation, linked to compassion and warmth. In him, medicine was manifest as both science and art. Everybody who knew Garland loved him." This was the man I was most fortunate to have served with, the mentor who had the most profound impact on my career during the years of my clinical training. [24] Many others benefitted from Herndon's impact and legacy—students, faculty, and staff. I know for sure that I did not receive special treatment from Herndon. He treated every resident the same way, and his exemplary mentoring skills benefited all of his students alike. I was only one of many thousands who benefited during his decades serving as an army medical officer and as an academician.

Mentors at the Walter Reed Army Institute of Research

The feedback I received from Herndon and other mentors during my residency training inspired my interests in epidemiology. I also believe that this contributed to my acceptance at the Walter Reed Army Institute of Research (WRAIR), where I was able to serve with the army's most distinguished scientists. This arrangement enabled me to complete my payback service (conditions of contract agreement to serve at the convenience of

---

[24] Emory paid tribute to Herndon in other ways summarized in President Laney's insightful eulogy. He wrote, "...he received much deserved recognition for his immeasurable role in the development of the Woodruff Medical Center. He was awarded the coveted Woodruff Award of Dedication, and an endowed Chair was established in his honor, the E. Garland Herndon Jr. Chair of Internal Medicine. The medical alumni of Emory also honored him with their Distinguished Medical Achievement Award."

the government for time spent in army residency training). Serving at WRAIR after my residency was most fortunate because many of my colleagues who completed army residencies at this time were assigned to Southeast Asia where the clouds of the Vietnam War were gathering. At WRAIR, I also met several important collaborators and mentors.

One distinguished WRAIR scientist to whom I am deeply indebted is Dr. Sam Formal, a prominent scholar known for his milestone research on issues relating to microbiological mechanisms of bacterial intestinal infections. Formal was the head of a center of research excellence in diseases of military importance (especially enteric diseases). His research collaborators spanned an international network that included scientists at the University of Maryland, a connection that I later leveraged when assigning Epidemic Intelligence Service (EIS) officers to work on shigellosis[25]. Another connection that later featured in my career was Dr. Bud Benenson, Formal's supervisor at the time who later assigned me to Bangkok and also played a role in my experiences in Pakistan (experiences described later in this book). The research done in Formal's group enabled the development of typhoid vaccines still featured prominently in the prevention of that disease. It is through Formal that I met Dr. David Mel, another scientist with whom I had occasion to work closely.

---

[25] Alex Langmuir, then head of EIS and a mentor of mine, was so impressed with Sam Formal's international network and its potential linkages to CDC's efforts in controlling enteric diseases in high-risk civilian groups in the U.S., that he readily approved the assignment of two subsequent EIS officers to study shigellosis at the University of Maryland.

Mel's work at the time focused extensively on shigellosis, a major issue during that time, especially for military groups[26]. Mel's team in Belgrade developed and tested live attenuated shigella vaccines that demonstrated a high degree of efficacy in military groups [5-7]. Because of the historical importance of shigellosis, manifested as bacillary dysentery in past military campaigns, their collaboration was very important to military scientists, and their continued work was supported by the Armed Forces Epidemiological Board [8, 9]. I had a role in this both as a research scientist and as a point person in the administration of these resources. I served in this role during several chapters of my career—at WRAIR, in my role at the University of Maryland, and when I joined the Epidemic Intelligence Service (EIS) at CDC (the latter two described in later chapters of this book).

Many years after my WRAIR experience, my associations with Mel and Formal continued, and my collaborations with Mel took me and my colleagues to many countries. In particular, when I was head of the Enteric Diseases Branch at CDC, Mel and I consulted together in World Health Organization (WHO) assignments. The most memorable consultations were with the Pan American Health Organization (PAHO) in several countries of Central America during the Shiga-dysentery pandemic of 1968 – 1973 [10-16]. In one of the meetings of assembled members of ministries of health and academicians in Guatemala, Mel gave an extremely impressive presentation of his research. He was polished in English (not his native tongue, as he was Polish by

---

[26] At the time of this writing, shigellosis is no longer the public health threat it once was in our country through the 1960s and 1970s. This is due largely to changes in public policy that ended the mass institutionalization of mentally impaired persons. These institutions had previously served as reservoirs for the disease, given poor hygiene and sanitation. Improvements in hygiene and sanitation elsewhere, most notably the promotion of hand-washing in child-care centers, have substantially controlled shigellosis.

origin), and also able to lecture in Russian, French, Italian, and Slovakian.

All of us associated with Mel have very fond memories of him. He had not only an outstanding professional career, but also an extraordinary personal history. Mel was born in Poland, but left the country in 1938, shortly before World War II started, to attend university in France. He then went to Italy to pursue a medical education; however, upon his graduation, he was arrested. Mel spent most of the years of WWII in an Italian concentration camp. Fortunately for him, these camps did not perform mass executions of Jews. In the camp, Mel met his wife—she was from Slovakia, which at that time was part of Yugoslavia—and learned her language. Their camp was liberated by the British 8th army in their advance on the eastern side of the Italian peninsula. Mel tried to enlist in the British army, but was not accepted—he believed because he was a Jew. He found a way to instead enlist in the Yugoslavian army, where he served with the partisans through the remainder of the war. Afterwards, he rose in rank to colonel and served in Belgrade in a Yugoslavian institution somewhat comparable to WRAIR. When Mel went back to Poland after WWII, he tragically could not find any family members—they had all been lost to pogroms during the war.

Mel was a friend as well as a colleague. In one of his visits to Atlanta, I invited him, Alex Langmuir, and D.A. Henderson to our home to play bridge, which Mel had first learned during his time in the concentration camp. A few years after this bridge game, he encountered D.A. again in Belgrade during a smallpox outbreak. Mel was waiting, along with medical officials from his institute, for D.A., who had come to consult on the outbreak. When D.A. walked into the room, he greeted Mel with an emotional embrace. This immediately dissipated anxiety among Mel's colleagues—it led to a relaxed and productive meeting that

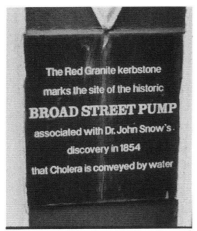

Figure 6: Plaque at the Broad Street Pump.

Dr. Ross Gould, my first epidemiology teacher (at Walter Reed Army Institute of Research [WRAIR]), was assigned to London as the Allied Army gathered for the invasion of Europe. He was able, using information from Wade Hampton Frost's introduction to John Richardson's *Snow on Cholera*, to identify the location of the Broad Street Well. Gould then worked with the British Ministry of Health to author and place the plaque, which at the time of this writing can still be found at 40 Broad Street, London.

helped in controlling the outbreak. Mel was small in stature but a giant in his profession. He enriched our lives and our global community in more ways than I can describe here.

My professional life was also advanced by another Walter Reed epidemiologist, Dr. Ross Gould. In fact, my first formal training in epidemiology was in Gould's course. In class exercises, he taught us to calculate rates using McBee cards—our data storage and analysis technology in that pre-computer era. This course was also my first introduction to John Snow's epidemiological studies of cholera—a shared interest that I have expanded on throughout my career. Gould told the following story. As the Allied Expeditionary Forces assembled for the invasion of Europe during Gould's WWII service, he was assigned to London. He found himself surprised to realize that so few knew about Snow's cholera investigations there. So, in his spare time, Gould rediscovered the location of the Broad Street Pump using Snow's spot map and descriptions. Gould worked with the British Tourist Bureau to show them the site, and he arranged with them to place a plaque at the location of the Broad Street Pump and in a nearby pub (at the time, an inconsequential place, but known as the "John Snow Pub" following Gould's intervention). To the day of this writing, I use slides in my PowerPoint presentations depicting the iconic symbol of John Snow at the pub entrance and the plaque that tells the story of the cholera outbreak that changed history (see Figures 6 and 7). Inside the pub, a large book ledger was kept where cholera students signed as they visited or transited through London.

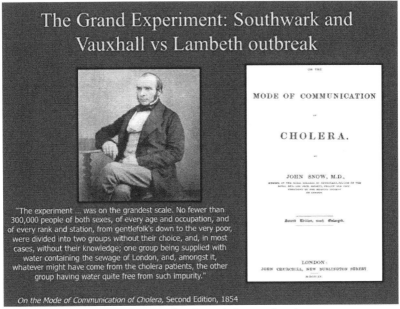

Figure 7: Lecture Slide on John Snow's Investigations.

John Snow's best-known epidemiological work covered the Broad Street cholera epidemic. However, he did not have a control group for that study, as survivors fled the area. The Southwark and Vauxhall company outbreak is Snow's most precise epidemiological work because he was able to calculate rates of disease for exposed as well as unexposed populations. To complete this work, he walked door-to-door to identify affected homes; work of this type exemplifies "shoe-leather epidemiology," or on-the-ground outbreak investigation.

It became a rich piece of history in its own right—a record of those who honored John Snow and had contributed in some way to the control of this disease. When I signed it myself, I noted the signatures of Ross Gould, Robert Politzer, Alex Langmuir, and a number of my EIS colleagues who had visited the pub and recorded their names and affiliations in the ledger. Over the years, as I visited the pub several times, I saw the names of still other "students of cholera" in this record. Unfortunately, when the pub was sold some years later, the new owner discarded the ledger, not knowing its special significance.

While at WRAIR, I also served on the Armed Forces Epidemiological Board. Through this association, I met Dr. Fred Soper, another giant in public health. I had in fact encountered Soper years earlier in Naples, while he was leading the Typhus Control Commission, although I did not meet him personally. The typhus control effort is described in more detail in an earlier chapter. It wasn't until I was in Dhaka, Bangladesh, working on cholera, that I met Soper for the first time. At that point, he was the director of the then-named SEATO (Southeast Asia Treaty Organization) Cholera Research Laboratory, where I was consulting. That laboratory is now known as the International Center for Diarrheal Diseases Research, Bangladesh (icddr,b).

Our home life in Maryland

During my time at Walter Reed Hospital and WRAIR, Rose and I lived with our children in two different bungalows in Wheaten Woods, Maryland. In 1957, I came to Washington, D.C., from San Antonio, where I had just finished a six-week military medical course. Rose and the children were in Rochester with Rose's family for a short time, so that I could find us a place to live and get settled. I arrived in an area called Wheaton Woods, which I had learned was fairly close to the hospital. I checked into a motel close by and called Rose. We were worried about where we would live—we could only afford to rent, and we felt that this limited our options.

Early the next morning I drove to Walter Reed Hospital. I was so impressed was to be in the same place where my literary hero had worked and for whom the hospital was named. I got directions from a receptionist to a bulletin board where rentals were listed. I noted an ad for a three-bedroom home with a brick exterior located about 12 miles from the hospital in the Wheaton Woods area. I called the owner, who agreed to meet me at the residence. When I arrived, he was there with the key to show me the layout. As he lived close by, he left and agreed to return in half an hour. The home was immaculate, with seasonal flowers around the outside and a carefully manicured lawn. The rent was $150 per month, just at the top of what we could afford. When the owner returned, I paid him in cash for the first month's rent and gave him a retainer to cover any damages when we left. I also spent some time visiting with him, and learned that he and his family were also neighbors and good family friends of Dr. Howard Noyes, whose name I recognized as a collaborator of Colonel Elmer Pulaski, my internship mentor. Little did I realize that Noyes would be a professional colleague and that the Noyeses and the Gangarosas would become life-long friends.

After this transaction, I returned to my hotel room to call Rose. She was thrilled with my description of the house. This became our home for the three years of my residency, and we enjoyed the neighborhood immensely. Our neighbors were friendly couples with young families. We interacted socially, participating in neighborhood potluck picnics from time to time and joining a bridge club. Our children had numerous playmates and school companions. I joined a car pool so that Rose would have a car to tend to her needs and the needs of our school-aged children.

We have fond memories living in this home except for one incident. Rose had severe nausea during each of her pregnancies every day for nine months. Her only relief came on the last day of each pregnancy, when our children were born. In the second trimester of her fourth pregnancy, I brought to her attention a new drug that had recently come to market touted for nausea associated with pregnancy. She had little relief with the lower dose recommended initially. However, when she increased the dose to the maximum recommended on my advice, she developed severe nausea and severe bulbar neurological symptoms—a reaction characterized by anxiety associated with uncontrolled gagging when she swallowed. We became extremely worried when fetal movements ceased. Rose miscarried in the early morning hours about 24 hours after the last dose. We called a neighbor who came to help as I drove Rose to the emergency room. She was admitted, the placenta was removed, and her symptoms diminished after several days. This tragic incident weighed heavily on me, and to the day of this writing I deeply regret the loss—it was my fault.

The drug that caused Rose's miscarriage was chlorpromazine, marketed as Thorazine. Although chlorpromazine is now prescribed during pregnancy only with extreme caution (it is classified as Category C, meaning that it is prescribed only when the benefits to the woman outweigh any potential harms to the fetus), at the time, there was no such guidance. I view this as a symptom of the drug approval milieu at the time. Rose and I also experienced the negative effects of this landscape during our time in Pakistan, when we suffered neurological side effects associated with the insecticide DDVP, which was used widely despite a lack of studies demonstrating its safety (described in more detail in a later chapter). Indeed, the use of this insecticide is now severely restricted due to concerns about its toxicity. The lax safety standards at that time harmed many people, including myself and Rose. I can only hope that Rose's miscarriage played some small part in informing the medical community of the potential dangers of chlorpromazine to vulnerable populations.

After my residency, we bought a nearby home in a new development in Wheaton Woods. It had an unfinished basement that appealed to me as extra space for another bedroom and bathroom for visitors. During this time, we were in the worst days of the Cold War. Our country was gripped with anxiety about nuclear warfare, especially during the days when the Russians blocked access to Berlin and reaching the city was possible only by air. Our country was in a frenzy to prepare for worst-case scenarios. Schools had drills to train students to use corridors without windows and to hide under desks. This anxiety became manifested in the architecture of the day. The Armed Forces Institute of Pathology constructed on the Walter Reed campus was built without windows and with thick concrete walls in case of an attack. The neighborhood where we purchased our home offered an optional sub-cellar room with an adjoining storage room for supplies that might be needed in such an emergency. I visited this model but decided against it, as it became clear that survival would not likely be possible in the Washington area even in such shelters. We lived in this home during the years of my tenure at the Walter Reed Army Institute. In another chapter I record how and why I resigned from the Army Medical Corps to accept my first faculty appointment at the University of Maryland School of Medicine.

Reflections

My Walter Reed experiences stand out for the excellent mentorship and the introduction to epidemiology that I received there. These mentors introduced me to still other collaborators—scientists who impacted my career in varying and positive ways. In a subsequent chapter, I tell the story of my work on cholera pathology—work made possible by my association with Bill Crosby, whose students taught me how to use his biopsy intestinal instrument, the Crosby capsule. This work allowed me to begin to nurture my niche interest in enteric diseases, a field that fascinates me to the date of this writing.

My experiences at Walter Reed fostered professional connections that have persisted for a lifetime—mentors as well as mentees. Through my Walter Reed connections, I was able to later place two EIS officers at the University of Maryland to continue work on my colleague David Mel's special interest— shigellosis. These two officers, Dr. Herbert ("Bert") DuPont and Dr. Myron Levine, built on these EIS assignments to later become prominent academics and dynamic leaders in their field. I feel that these stories truly touch on the "passing of the torch" that I wrote about with Stan Foster when honoring Alex Langmuir [17]. The experiences of Drs. DuPont and Levine exemplify how careers can be molded and nurtured beginning with EIS assignments. It is my hope that this book, in describing experiences such as these, can in fact help to recruit future EIS officers.

References

1.   Malizia WF, Gangarosa EJ, Goley AF: **Benzalkonium chloride as a source of infection**. *New England J Medicine* 1960, **263**:800-802.

2.   Gangarosa EJ, Landerman NS, Rosch PJ, Herndon EG, Jr.: **Hematologic complications arising during ristocetin therapy; relation between dose and toxicity**. *New England J Medicine* 1958, **259**(4):156-161.

3.   Gangarosa EJ: **The pathogenesis of thrombocytopenia due to ristocetin**. *Antibiotics Annual* 1959, **7**:536-548.

4.   Gangarosa EJ, Johnson TR, Ramos HS: **Ristocetin-induced thrombocytopenia: site and mechanism of action**. *Archives Internal Medicine* 1960, **105**:83-89.

5.   Mel DM, Terzin AL, Vuksic L: **Studies on vaccination against bacillary dysentery. 1. Immunization of mice against experimental Shigella infection**. *Bulletin of the World Health Organization* 1965, **32**(5):633-636.

6.   Mel DM, Terzin AL, Vuksic L: **Studies on vaccination against bacillary dysentery. 3. Effective oral immunization against Shigella flexneri 2a in a field trial**. *Bulletin of the World Health Organization* 1965, **32**(5):647-655.

7.   Mel D, Stankovic N: **[Study on the streptomycin-dependent Shigella flexneri strain for oral vaccination against dysentery]**. *Vojnosanit Pregl* 1965, **22**(6):381-387.

8.   Mel DM, Arsic BL, Radovanovic ML, Litvinjenko SA: **Live oral Shigella vaccine: vaccination schedule and the effect of booster dose**. *Acta Microbiol Acad Sci Hung* 1974, **21**(1-2):109-114.

9.   Mel D, Gangarosa EJ, Radovanovic ML, Arsic BL, Litvinjenko S: **Studies on vaccination against bacillary dysentery. 6. Protection of children by oral immunization with streptomycin-dependent Shigella strains**. *Bulletin of the World Health Organization* 1971, **45**(4):457-464.

10.   Mata LJ, Gangarosa EJ, Caceres A, Perera DR, Mejicanos ML: **Epidemic Shiga bacillus dysentery in Central America. I. Etiologic investigations in Guatemala, 1969**. *J Infectious Diseases* 1970, **122**(3):170-180.

11.   Gangarosa EJ, Perera DR, Mata LJ, Mendizabal-Morris C, Guzman G, Reller LB: **Epidemic Shiga bacillus**

dysentery in Central America. II. Epidemiologic studies in 1969. *J Infectious Diseases* 1970, **122**(3):181-190.

12.   Levine MM, DuPont HL, Formal SB, Gangarosa EJ: **Epidemic Shiga dysentery in Central America**. *Lancet* 1970, **2**(7673):607-608.

13.   Mata LJ, Gangarosa EJ, Caceres A, Perera DR, Mejicanos ML: **[Epidemic Shiga dysentery in Central America. I. Etiological studies in Guatemala, 1969]**. *Boletin de la Oficina Sanitaria Panamericana Pan American Sanitary Bureau* 1971, **71**(2):93-107.

14.   Gangarosa EJ, Perera DR, Mata LJ, Mendizabal-Morris C, Guzman G, Reller LB: **[Epidemic shiga dysentery in Central America. II. Epidemiologic studies in 1969]**. *Boletin de la Oficina Sanitaria Panamericana Pan American Sanitary Bureau* 1971, **71**(2):108-120.

15.   Mendizabal-Morris CA, Mata LJ, Gangarosa EJ, Guzman G: **Epidemic Shiga-bacillus dysentery in Central America. Derivation of the epidemic and its progression in Guatemala, 1968-69**. *American J Tropical Medicine and Hygiene* 1971, **20**(6):927-933.

16.   Reller LB, Rivas EN, Masferrer R, Bloch M, Gangarosa EJ: **Epidemic shiga-bacillus dysentery in Central America. Evolution of the outbreak in El Salvador, 1969-70**. *American J Tropical Medicine and Hygiene* 1971, **20**(6):934-940.

17.   Foster SO, Gangarosa E: **Passing the epidemiologic torch from Farr to the world. The legacy of Alexander D. Langmuir**. *American J Epidemiology* 1996, **144**(8 Suppl):S65-73.

Chapter 6: Bangkok Cholera Studies with WRAIR

My career has been shaped not only by mentors that I first encountered at the Walter Reed Army Institute of Research (WRAIR), but also by my research experiences there. In 1959, while I was finishing up my medical training at WRAIR, the first outbreak of cholera in over 10 years hit in Bangkok. WRAIR was one of the agencies that quickly responded to the crisis. The events that followed have shaped my career for over 60 years.

Controversy about the underlying mechanism of cholera

The medical literature concerning the underlying mechanism of cholera had been hotly disputed, based entirely on autopsy studies performed many decades earlier. In 1879, Rudolf Virchow concluded from microscopic studies that the intestinal wall of those who died from cholera was "desquamated" or denuded. In his study, the cells of the intestinal epithelium appeared to have sloughed off, leaving the underlying vascular tissues exposed to the intestinal contents. On the basis of this physical appearance, he surmised that the enormous watery diarrheal fluid loss was analogous to the exudation of fluids that occur with a severe burn. His findings were supported by autopsy studies by Koch in 1887 and by Fraenkel in 1892. Also in 1892, Deycke observed the same desquamated epithelium in patients autopsied within an hour of death. In 1947, Burnet and Stone claimed to find a "mucolytic" extract from cholera cultures that denuded the isolated intestinal epithelium of guinea pigs and rabbits.

However, a number of researchers disagreed with this mechanism. Cohnheim, Osler, and Goodpasture argued that the autopsy finding of a desquamated epithelium was really just a postmortem change, called "autolysis." Dutta performed an autopsy study of a large series of patients and found desquamation of the intestinal epithelium occurred only rarely. One argument was that the severe fluid loss experienced by cholera victims caused blood to become too hypertonic and viscous (or "thick"), which could compromise blood flow to the intestinal wall as the patient approached death, and thereby cause the cells to die and slough off. Proponents of this argument believed this effect did not manifest during life, and was only an artifact that occurred as death approached.

The right instrument to begin resolving the debate

To resolve these disagreements, scientists needed to perform microscopic examination of the intestinal epithelium of living patients with active cholera. At the outset of my career, the technology for flexible fiber-optic endoscopes with biopsy ports had not even been conceived. However, in my gastroenterology rotation at Walter Reed Army Hospital in 1958, I met Bill Crosby, who had invented a very elegant and much simpler method for obtaining small samples of the intestinal wall of living patients.

Crosby's biopsy instrument was a small cylindrical capsule with an opening along one side. The patient swallowed the Crosby biopsy capsule, which was on the end of a long tube with measurements along it; the other end of the tube remained accessible to the physician outside the patient's mouth. When the clinician determined from the measurements that the capsule was at the right place in the gastrointestinal tract to sample, suction was applied to the tube. This action released a small spring-loaded blade that swiped across the opening, often (but not always) cutting a small snippet of the intestinal wall surface. The clinician or researcher could then retrieve the capsule very rapidly by pulling out the tube, so the sample could be prepared and viewed essentially in the living state. The Crosby capsule is still used to obtain intestinal biopsies of adults who can't tolerate endoscopy well and young children who are able to cooperate.

Crosby invented his biopsy capsule to investigate tropical sprue, a malabsorption syndrome caused by nutritional deficiencies that causes chronic diarrhea and malabsorption with similar pathology as celiac disease [1]. In my rotation in urban Washington, DC, I didn't see any sprue patients, so I didn't get to use the Crosby biopsy capsule myself. However, I did learn how to operate it and watched some clinicians using it on their patients. I tucked this experience away and subsequently found that it placed me in just the right position at the right time to study cholera.

About that time, I read Dr. Joe Smadel's article on the pathophysiology of intestinal infections, in which he commented that the mysteries of the pathophysiology of cholera would persist until we had the chance to examine the upper intestinal tract during active disease in living patients. That comment really excited me, since I realized the Crosby biopsy capsule offered the opportunity to resolve the mystery.

An opportunity to study cholera: 1959 outbreak in Thailand

Just as I started working at WRAIR, cholera broke out in Bangkok, Thailand. Thailand's Undersecretary of State for Health, Luang Binbakya Bidyabhed (a radiologist whose nickname was "Pyn") contacted his mentor, Ken Goodner of

Jefferson University (Pyn's alma mater), to assemble a team to help control the outbreak. Smadel (then an associate director at the National Institutes of Health [NIH]) chose Bob Gordon from the NIH, Ken Goodner chose Rolf Freter and Harry Smith from Jefferson University, and Mason (then director of WRAIR) chose me.

At first my reactions were very mixed. On one hand, this was the scientific opportunity I was waiting for! I felt strongly that the Crosby capsule could be crucial for understanding how cholera causes life-threatening diarrhea. I was inspired by the story of Walter Reed himself, who put himself at risk studying yellow fever in the jungles of Panama, making discoveries that made it possible to construct the Panama Canal. On the other hand, I clearly recognized what a dangerous disease cholera could be, and I didn't want my young wife to become a widow and my children orphans. It seemed my study might put me at much higher risk of contracting the disease, since I would be doing intestinal biopsies and handling upper intestinal fluids from cholera patients—the very site where the vibrios were multiplying. I felt compelled to understand the risks that would come with this assignment.

To resolve my concerns, I consulted textbooks, but at first found very little written about the transmission of cholera. Finally, one of my mentors, Ross Gould, referred me to John Richardson's *Snow on Cholera*, a book published in 1936. Wade Hampton Frost wrote a forward to the book brilliantly summarizing John Snow's work. Hampton Frost also selected Snow's descriptions of his own epidemiological studies during the 1849 – 56 London cholera outbreaks. Snow wanted to show that, contrary to the prevailing theory of disease, cholera was not transmitted by "bad air." He found that caretakers of cholera patients seldom got sick if they did not consume the same contaminated water—the disease was not highly infectious through person-to-person transmission.

I carefully perused Snow's map and tables of the cholera outbreaks in London. They showed that the death rate for households supplied by Southwark and Vauxhall Waterworks Company was much higher than that of households that received their water from the Lambeth Company. Southwark and Vauxhall took its water from sewage-polluted sections of the Thames, while the intakes for the Lambeth Company were safely upstream from London. With this reassurance, I had some confidence that, if I was careful about what I ingested and washed my hands after handling intestinal material, I could perform the study with a degree of safety.

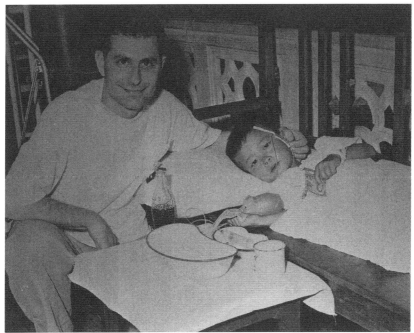

Figure 8: EJG with Young Cholera Patient, Bangkok, Thailand, 1959.
This was the youngest of 26 cholera patients from whom we obtained intestinal biopsies for our research on the pathogenesis of the disease.

Our biopsy study

While in Bangkok, I worked on the biopsy study at Chulalongkorn Hospital with my American colleagues W. R. Beisel and H. Sprinz and my Thai colleagues Chanyo Benyajati and Prapont Piyaratn. I performed a biopsy on one other patient at the Infectious Disease Hospital in Calcutta, India, who was not included in the study. We required that patients had been stabilized clinically through administration of intravenous fluid therapy and were no longer vomiting, so we could insert the Crosby capsule. We studied 29 patients with cholera and a small group of control patients who were either asymptomatic *Vibrio cholera* carriers or patients with diarrhea of undetermined origin, obtaining biopsies from different regions along the gastrointestinal tract. We performed multiple biopsies at various stages of the disease, from shortly after presentation to the hospital (as early as the first day of clinical illness) through convalescence (up to 27 days after onset of symptoms). We removed and prepared the biopsy samples between just 1-3 minutes after they were obtained, obviating the possibility of autolysis. None of the patients we biopsied had any complications. Biopsies from nine patients were sent to Walter Reed Hospital to be read by pathologists who were experts in this field. These were the patients described in our first publication about the study [2].

Our findings were remarkable. Most important, they strongly refuted Virchow's claim. Instead of seeing sloughed cells, we found that the intestinal epithelium was invariably intact. There was no evidence in any of the specimens—taken from any patient at any stage of cholera—of any pathological changes in the gut wall that remotely resembled the badly desquamated epithelium that Virchow had predicted and compared to severely burned tissue. The cells that protect the gut from contact with intestinal contents were completely intact.

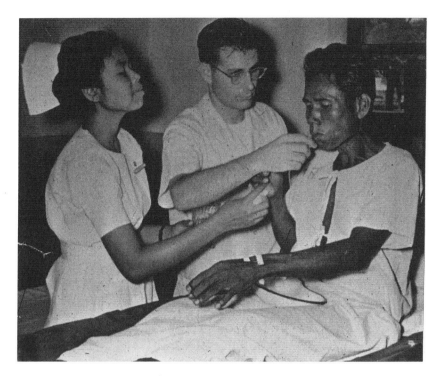

Figure 9: EJG with Older Cholera Patient, Bangkok, Thailand, 1959. This was the oldest biopsy patient (late 60s) from our study on cholera pathogenesis. Finding the intestinal epithelium entirely intact refuted the starvation therapy dictum and laid the foundation for the development of oral rehydration therapy. Note that the clothes we wore reflected the fact that transmission of cholera from patients to caretakers was not a concern.

However, we did find one perplexing abnormality in the intestinal villi, the functional units of the gut involved in digestion of food—they were atrophied and infiltrated with chronic inflammatory cells. These consistent findings resembled the malabsorption syndrome called sprue, and persisted even through convalescence. In sprue, the atrophied villi reduce the surface area available for digestion, resulting in malabsorption. We could not be sure if those findings in our study reflected (1) a

153

predisposing condition that made the intestine more susceptible to cholera, like some nutritional factor, (2) a malabsorption syndrome due to frequent gastrointestinal illnesses, or (3) residual effects of cholera. Recognizing that we had not obtained an appropriate control group to answer the question, Joe Smadel prevailed on my commanding officer, Colonel Mason, to send me back to Bangkok the next year, 1960, to determine whether the sprue-like findings were associated with cholera or preexisting conditions. We obtained repeat biopsies on some of the same patients about a year after their recovery from that bout of cholera. We also biopsied some other adult males who had not had cholera—asymptomatic family members who came with them, as well as other patients who came to the hospital for unrelated conditions. We found all the people we biopsied, both the former cholera patients and the controls, had similar abnormal pathological findings in their intestinal villi. We concluded that this pathology is not a factor predisposing to cholera. Once again, none of the people we biopsied had complications, although in one case we had temporary difficulty retrieving the biopsy capsule. Much later, researchers found that this condition of atrophied intestinal villi results from frequent acute bouts of enteric illness, and that it can cause very serious problems, especially in children, because the decreased digestive surface area often leads to malnutrition, which can cause stunted growth and long-term cognitive deficits.

Confirmation of our conclusion

Initially, my colleagues and I did not believe our results that the walls of the intestinal villi were not completely sloughed off. One of my coworkers, Oscar Felsenfeld, joked that I, as junior member of our team, had disproved long accepted foundations about the pathophysiology of cholera. With a good-natured gleam in his eye—and likely also some doubt that we may have investigated a milder form of the disease—he kidded me, "Gene, do you think you know more about cholera than Virchow?!"

Simultaneously with my biopsy study, Bob Gordon, the NIH member of our team, performed an elegant physiological investigation in Thai cholera patients showing that large molecules injected into the bloodstream did not appear in the stool. He labeled the molecule with iodine that had extremely short-term radioactivity, comparing cholera patients with normal volunteers given the same marker; he demonstrated that the cholera patients had no more radioactivity in their stool than did the controls. Together our two studies refuted Virchow's theory that fluid losses in cholera are caused by anatomical disruption of the intestinal epithelium [3, 4].

Sequel to our study

Bangkok was a wonderful place to conduct a study of cholera because of the friendly relations of our Thai colleagues and their commitment to studying the disease and solving its problems. The king of Thailand himself invited members of our team to visit so that he could express his gratitude for their efforts. As a result of this remarkable cooperation, we accomplished a great deal scientifically in a short time with a relatively small expenditure.

In 1960 – 62, the National Institutes of Health (NIH) recruited a more senior group of distinguished infectious diseases scientists to identify a study site in Southeast Asia where the cholera studies of 1959 – 60 could be continued. The group included Abram "Bud" Benenson of the Walter Reed Army Institute of Research; Drs. Joe Smadel and Robert Gordon of the NIH; Dr. Scott Halstead of the Rockefeller Foundation; Dr. Ted Woodward, Professor of Medicine of the University of Maryland, noted for his discovery of the treatment of typhoid fever; and Dr. Ken Goodner, Professor of Microbiology of Jefferson University, noted for his work as a leading expert on vibrios. They were charged with the task of identifying the site, recruiting the director and staff of scientists, and consulting on the research agenda. In planning their tasks, they asked my opinion about establishing this site in Bangkok. I, along with others, did not support this as a feasible site because cholera had been a rarity in Thailand and we recognized that our Thai colleagues would do everything in their power to prevent further outbreaks[27]. Instead, I recommended either Dhaka, East Pakistan (now Bangladesh) or Calcutta, India, because cholera was endemic in both of those sites, seasonal flooding was associated with episodic upsurges in the number of cases, and each had a distinguished university whose collaboration would ensure academic excellence in research conducted in the Laboratory. Dhaka was their choice.

The laboratory established there has indeed attracted distinguished researchers who have published extensively not only on cholera, its initial focus, but also a host of topics in so many other fields.[ii] The laboratory in which this work was done was initially named the Dhaka SEATO Cholera Research Laboratory. The name underscored the military concern about cholera by the collection of nations who belonged to the Southeast Asian Theatre of Operation (SEATO), organized as a geopolitical shield against the USSR during the Cold War. The

---

[27] Following the Bangkok team's cholera research in 1959, the Armed Forces Research Institute of Medical Sciences (AFRIMS) emerged at a different site in Bangkok as a center of excellence for vaccine trials and the study of hepatitis A, malaria, and HIV. Bud Benenson's son, Michael, played an important role in establishing and administering the research program at this center.

SEATO[28]-Cholera Research Laboratory in Dhaka was the source of many innovations in the control of intestinal infections, as we shall see. In subsequent years, I visited this laboratory and critiqued work there. At the time of this writing, it is known as the International Center for Diarrheal Diseases Research in Bangladesh (icddr,b).

Significance of our findings

Prior to the publication of our results and Gordon's confirmatory studies, clinicians sometimes treated cholera with steroids. They reasoned that, if cholera was like a burn localized to the intestine, they should administer an anti-inflammatory treatment to reduce the severity of the "burn."

Once we established that the intestinal epithelium was intact through all phases of active cholera, investigators started looking for a physiological mechanism for fluid loss. After some time, they found that *Vibrio cholera* secretes an exotoxin that poisons the biochemical molecular pump that keeps fluids in cells.

However, physicians who treated patients with severe dehydrating diarrhea outside of tertiary treatment hospitals could not wait for these involved and time-consuming biochemical studies. As it turned out, the biochemical mechanism of cholera toxin that causes fluid loss was not as important as another aspect of the disease—cholera, like other acute intestinal infections, leaves intact the body's capacity for absorbing fluids and electrolytes [5]. This observation led to the development of oral rehydration solution (ORS)—a revolution in the home treatment of diarrheal illnesses and arguably one of

---

[28] Southeast Asia Treaty Organization

the most important public health interventions of our time. It was also the launchpad from which my career evolved.

References

1.   Baker SJ, Mathan VI: **Tropical enteropathy and tropical sprue**. *American J Clinical Nutrition* 1972, **25**(10):1047-1055.

2.   Sprinz H, Sribhibhadh R, Gangarosa EJ, Benyajati C, Kundel D, Halstead S: **Biopsy of small bowel of Thai people. With special reference to recovery from Asiatic cholera and to an intestinal malabsorption syndrome**. *American J Clinical Pathology* 1962, **38**:43-51.

3.   Savarino SJ: **A legacy in 20th-century medicine: Robert Allan Phillips and the taming of cholera**. *Clinical Infectious Diseases* 2002, **35**:713-720.

4.   Gordon Jr R: **The failure of Asiatic cholera to give rise to" exudative enteropathy."**. In: *SEATO Conference on Cholera: 1960*; 1960: 54.

5.   Phillips RA: **The patho-physiology of cholera**. *Rep U S Nav Med Res Lab* 1962, **62**(1):1-7.

Chapter 7: Experiences in Lahore, Pakistan, 1962 – 1964

A career milestone

By mid-summer of 1961, I had completed my payback service for the years I was supported in my army residency program at Walter Reed. With that weight lifted, I was free to make a decision with regard to the rest of my life, and found myself delighted that several attractive options were possible.

I thought seriously about remaining at the Walter Reed Army Institute of Research. I had great colleagues and collaborators. Support for my continuing work in gastrointestinal pathophysiology was assured. Rose was pleased with our life in the Washington suburbs. Our children were happy and doing well in their schooling. I considered staying in the service because I had accumulated over half the time needed for an early retirement—between my WWII military service, my army reserve time in the years that followed, time spent in my army internship and residency, and payback time for this training, I had completed 16 years of service. But the geopolitical situation was a concern. I was a bit anxious about the growing American presence in Vietnam. Many senior Walter Reed colleagues had served in the Korea and Vietnam conflicts. Serving overseas in places of growing tensions was an unspoken expectation of medical officers completing required service obligations, so assignment to a military support unit in Vietnam was a worrisome possibility. I had already experienced month-long separations from my family during my WRAIR assignments in Southeast Asia. The prospects of even longer and more frequent family separations inherent in military duty assignments in Southeast Asia were unacceptable to Rose and me.

At this point in my career, I was already deeply immersed in the study of diarrheal diseases. Work my colleagues and I did in Bangkok had discredited the prevailing dictum that attributed the severe fluid losses characteristic of acute diarrheal illnesses to toxins that destroyed intestinal-epithelial cells—a disease process likened to what happens in severe burns. This erroneous dictum had rationalized "therapeutic starvation"—withholding oral fluids until new cells could replace those that had allegedly sloughed off. Once my biopsy study [1] and Robert Gordon's radiotracer study [2] showed that the intestinal lining cells were intact and still functional, investigators quickly recognized that therapeutic starvation was a very dangerous strategy. Success of the Navy clinical component of the Bangkok team in treating cholera patients had made it clear that mortality due to dehydration from whatever cause could be prevented[iii]. We had reached a turning point—instead of helplessness, we now felt hope that we could prevent deaths due to cholera and other diarrheal diseases.

Scientific attention turned to the simplification of treatment of diarrheal illness. My colleagues and I realized that replenishing fluids and electrolytes orally could potentially solve many practical problems. Cholera struck primarily in places with inadequate water and sanitation infrastructures, often far from hospitals. Intravenous fluids were costly, particularly in developing countries, and had to be administered by trained medical personnel. Clinicians working in the field realized that even if oral treatment could not replace intravenous therapy, it could relieve some of the burden and cost. So, even at that early stage, we envisioned that oral fluid rehydration would simplify logistics, provide greater access, and reduce costs of treatment of diarrheal diseases.

Motivated by this possibility, other investigators performed studies showing that absorption of fluids, electrolytes, and glucose across the intestinal epithelium remained intact in animals infected with cholera. Despite some initial setbacks in development of treatment[29], research continued on this topic. We knew that starvation therapy was contraindicated, and intravenous therapy was not feasible with large caseloads. Clinical decision-makers at Walter Reed Army Institute of Research (notably Abram "Bud" Benenson), the National Institutes of Health (notably Joe Smadel and Robert Gordon), the Rockefeller Foundation (notably Scott Halstead), and Charles Carpenter at Johns Hopkins took the lead in supporting and studying oral rehydration therapy. Indeed, their work constituted a momentous advancement: A Lancet editorial in August 1978 heralded oral fluid rehydration as arguably the most important discovery of the last century in recognition of its role in substantially reducing infant mortality due to diarrheal diseases since its introduction in the mid-1960s.

---

[29]In June 1962, Bob Phillips, Craig Wallace, and others at the Naval Medical Research Unit-2 demonstrated that glucose in oral fluids stimulated uptake of sodium, which was lost in high quantities through diarrhea. Encouraged by this result, they conducted a clinical trial in 1963 of oral rehydration supplementing intravenous therapy. The oral fluid contained glucose and a high concentration of sodium, while IV infusion ensured adequate hydration. The study established intestinal absorption of sodium and water; however, 5 of 40 patients died of pulmonary edema. Later it became clear that, by pushing fluids through both oral and intravenous routes, the therapy had actually worked too well, causing fluid overload and life-threatening congestive heart failure. However, at the time, Phillips was so alarmed by the results that he questioned the viability of oral rehydration therapy.

This was the professional milieu that shaped my own career, leading to my transition from a clinical orientation in internal medicine to a new focus in public health. The triggering event had been my opportunity to study cholera, which provided insight into the importance of water and sanitation, the ultimate means for controlling diarrheal diseases. Over those years, I experienced a slow-motion "eureka moment" as my early life and career development came together. I was excited to work at one of the innovation centers of a dynamic new field in which my colleagues and I shared paradigm-shifting insights, lifesaving opportunities, and "contagious" passion for water and sanitation—all of which refocused my career on intestinal infectious diseases. In this setting, I searched for a new niche in my professional life—which intersected at the University of Maryland Medical School in Baltimore, Maryland and Lahore, Pakistan.

An opportunity with the University of Maryland—my Lahore story

Those events during the years 1960 – 61 provided me with the good fortune of working with new role models who profoundly shaped my career. Most prominent was Dr. Ted Woodward. We first met in Baltimore while I was still working at the Walter Reed Army Institute of Research, right after I gave a presentation about the Bangkok studies. He introduced himself and told me of his studies of typhoid fever; only later did I learn how famous he was for developing the definitive treatment of the disease. I learned that we had a common experience—typhus control in Naples, Italy. Woodward had been an officer serving with the Typhus Control Commission assigned to Naples in 1944 – 45 after the Nazi army destroyed the water and sanitation infrastructure of the city in the days before their retreat from the advancing Allied Army. In 1945, I was assigned to an Army Air

Force Squadron as a Quartermaster Supply Technician. Both of us were in Naples in that year, but we did not meet, and I was not aware of his work at that time. We discussed those events on a flight back to the United States after a meeting in Dhaka. Sharing that experience forged strong personal and professional bonds between us that will always be imprinted in my memory.

During that flight, Woodward invited me to present my cholera studies at Grand Rounds at the University of Maryland Medical School. He followed up later with a written invitation, which I accepted. My presentation was well received. In meetings later that day, I met the impressive team he had assembled, which included Dr. Fred McCrumb, a distinguished virologist working on the measles vaccine; Dr. Charlie Wisseman, Professor of Microbiology and a much-published leader in his field of rickettsial diseases; and Dr. Richard Hornick, well known for his work on typhoid fever. I remember very well leaving with the feeling that they were interested in recruiting me. Indeed, several days later I received a call from McCrumb. He said he was calling on behalf of Woodward and Wisseman to invite me to consider an academic appointment in their two departments, Medicine and Microbiology.

The University of Maryland had recently received five academic grants from the National Institutes of Health, including one to which their group felt I would be well suited—developing an International Center for Medical Research and Training (ICMRT) in Lahore, Pakistan. Woodward's group had put a tremendous amount of work into a brilliant grant proposal for that Center, which won handily against alternatives from five other universities. Its entire focus was malaria control, which was (and still is) a very hot topic. Malaria is a mosquito-borne parasitic disease that each year infects hundreds of millions of people and kills around one million of its victims. Malaria had been eradicated from highly developed countries, primarily by draining swamps, where mosquitoes breed in stagnant water, but such intensive civil engineering projects were too expensive for use in developing countries. However, the development of highly effective insecticides, starting with DDT, created a great deal of enthusiasm that malaria could be eradicated worldwide by spraying swamplands and thereby killing mosquitoes directly. Furthermore, researchers realized that if malaria control could reduce the prevalence of human infections (i.e., decrease the number of people with the parasite circulating in their bloodstream), transmission through mosquito bites might decrease so much as to end the cycle of reinfection. As a result, shortly after WWII, the World Health Organization (WHO) spearheaded the Global Malaria Eradication Program.

Unfortunately, in the late 1950s, just five or six years after the first widespread use of DDT, mosquitoes developed resistance to that particular insecticide, putting the malaria eradication program in jeopardy. With the continued hope of eliminating that deadly killer, NIH sent a request for proposals to universities with major public health programs involving tropical medicine, especially malaria research and control, in developing countries. It was a highly coveted grant because it provided multimillion-dollar support for five years with the realistic prospect of further extensions.

It's easy to see why the University of Maryland won the competition—its plan was imaginative yet realistic, based on a solid foundation of related preexisting research, and breathtaking in scope. The Indian subcontinent was recognized as an ideal place to study malaria and other mosquito-borne diseases, in part because it was one of the first regions where DDT resistance had been identified. Furthermore, several UMD faculty were already conducting research on mosquito-borne diseases in that area[30].

The plan was based in large part on collaboration with Shell Chemicals to study a potent new insecticide and a promising new delivery system. Petroleum resin strips were impregnated with the insecticide dichlorvos, more commonly known as DDVP. The insecticide would be released slowly, so the strips had to be replaced only every few months. The strips were compact and easy to handle, thereby circumventing many of the complications of managing insecticide aerosols. No resistance had yet been noted to DDVP, so it seemed like a promising alternative to DDT.

The plan also called for installation of a state-of-the-art laboratory for studying mosquito genetics. An especially creative proposal called for genetically altering male mosquitoes to make them sterile and exploring the possibility of releasing them into the wild in overwhelming numbers, thereby suppressing mosquito reproduction through competitive inhibition of mating by fertile males. This imaginative approach had a high-energy barrier to overcome—the rapid reproduction rate of mosquitoes in the wild—but even today it captures the attention of researchers who want to manage mosquito-borne diseases with little environmental damage.

---

[30]Colonel M. I. Burney (whom everyone called "Burney") and Dr. Charlie Wisseman had already been investigating mosquito-borne arbovirus diseases in the Pakistani tribal areas around Gilgit, continuing a research program had been in place since shortly after WWII. They had established a strong working relationship with colleagues from Pakistan's army research center in Rawalpindi, which many considered a counterpart of WRAIR. Burney had worked for some time with a Pakistani colonel and physician (whom I will call "Zed") and hired him for the ICMRT plan. Burney's group at WRAIR also had considerable experience in malaria research.

I was very flattered to be offered a choice leadership position in one of Woodward's flagship programs, but I told him I wanted to think about the job offer and discuss it with Rose before making a commitment. I wasn't sure if that position would allow me to pursue the intestinal pathophysiology studies I had envisioned as the focus of my career. Rose was cautiously positive, especially in the light of concern about my being assigned to a conflict zone if I remained in the army. I expressed interest in McCrumb's invitation and asked him to continue the recruitment process.

I met again with the decision-makers at the University of Maryland, including the Medical School Dean, John Stone. All were keen to have me join the University. They briefed me about their vision for the ICMRT. They planned to recruit University faculty for assignments in Lahore, with each assignee being mentored and supported by a senior faculty person in the respective Departments. The funding for each project would come from grants obtained for studies in various Departments. I was offered joint appointments as assistant professor in both Medicine and Microbiology and a coordinating role as Director of the Center. I was assured support to pursue my own research interests, which ensured I could continue my studies of gastrointestinal pathophysiology. The offer seemed like a good fit with my career plans. I went home to discuss the offer with Rose. She was supportive and left the decision to me.

In late 1961, I accepted the offer. It was my first academic position. I submitted my request to terminate my Army commission (essentially to be released from active duty). I left with fond memories of my opportunities at WRAIR.

Beginnings with the University of Maryland

The drive to my office in Baltimore took an hour or more from our residence in Wheaton Woods. Moving was not feasible, because the Lahore assignment would require relocating within the year. For about eight months, I commuted every day. I discovered "back roads" that required less time but were a bit more stressful. Nighttime travel was especially difficult during snowfalls. One of my WRAIR colleagues hit a deer at night while driving on the same road I traveled; she was hospitalized with serious injuries. The inconvenience of these commutes and risks of traveling at night in dangerous weather led me to hasten the date of my family's departure for Lahore.

As Rose and I planned our move to Pakistan, McCrumb informed me that the new Center in Lahore would be known as the Pakistan Medical Research Center. A senior Pakistani medical officer, whom I will call Zed[31], was about to be recruited as my counterpart in the position of Associate Director, in which capacity he would have planning, service, and teaching responsibilities. He was a senior-ranking army officer with a distinguished career in the Pakistani army medical corps and as a pathologist in a prestigious army institute in Rawalpindi that was seen as a counterpart of WRAIR. He had accrued the years of service he needed to retire from the Pakistani army—an option he exercised.

Zed visited Baltimore to meet the Medical School Dean and faculty who would be playing a role in the new Center and to participate in the planning process. With McCrumb's encouragement and Rose's concurrence, I had written to invite

---

[31]Here I have given him a pseudonym for reasons that will later become apparent.

him to stay at our home. We met him at the airport, and he became part of our family during the week he was with us. My family—Rose and I and our three children—lived in a small home, but we made room for him. We found him pleasant, knowledgeable, and likeable. He clearly enjoyed staying with us, and we enjoyed having him. We had many discussions about a wide range of topics, including cultural differences and aspirations we shared for the new Center. We agreed to work together for its success. He liked that his American colleagues had named it the Pakistan Medical Research Center.

During Zed's visit in our home, I discussed with him the findings of the intestinal biopsy specimens I had obtained from cholera patients in Bangkok. He was intrigued and attentive, though a bit skeptical when I explained that all of the cholera patients treated by the navy team with intravenous replacement of fluids and electrolytes had survived. He wondered if this was an indication that we were dealing with a milder form of cholera. I assured him that was not the case because of clinical signs of cardiovascular collapse seen among patients admitted to the Navy's research ward, and deaths that occurred in cholera patients admitted to the separate hospital infectious diseases ward where I did my biopsy studies. I could sense he was not prepared to abandon the traditional explanation of the cause of the purging, i.e., the intestinal desquamation theory, which is what he had long taught in courses for army medical personnel. I saw it as healthy skepticism. In any case, it was not an issue we dwelt on at the time.

The day Zed left, Rose and I felt very pleased about our new friend. I had no concerns, accepted him as a valued colleague, and looked forward to working with him. I anticipated he would make substantial contributions during my upcoming assignment.

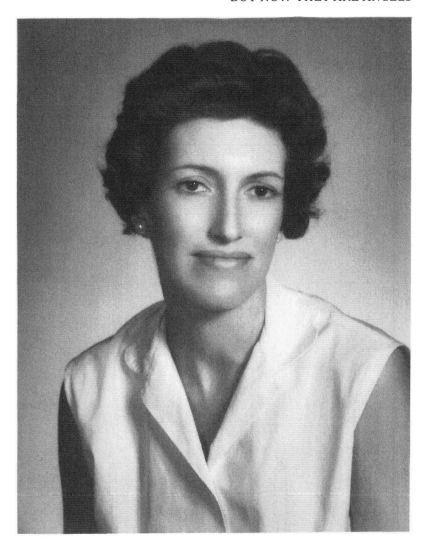

Figure 10: Rose Gangarosa, Lahore, Pakistan, 1962.
Rose was the principal of the Lahore American School, and also taught English to high-school juniors and seniors. The school still exists at the time of this writing as a thriving international school.

Zed's Baltimore visit was followed soon after by a trip I took to Lahore with McCrumb and a laboratory engineer contracted to design the Center's laboratories. The plan for the Center was to attach a new wing to the building housing the Lahore Institute of Hygiene. It would serve as an academic and reference laboratory for public health training and health activities in the Pakistan's Punjab Province, which bordered India toward the east. That disputed border was a major source of friction between Pakistan and India, and triggered occasional military clashes. The Institute also provided space for international scientists and staff who supported what was then the Malaria Eradication Program. We met numerous Institute faculty, Pakistani public health leaders, and senior scientists assigned to the Malaria Program.

During this trip, I also visited the Lahore American School to explore the possibility of a position for Rose. The school served the international community and had some Pakistani children supported by scholarships. The school enrolled several hundred children from kindergarten to twelfth grade. Most were children of executives of international companies and diplomatic families. I spoke to a senior employee of the school and provided him a copy of Rose's resume, noting that she had majored in music, minored in foreign languages, and served as Instructor in Music at Nazareth College in Rochester, NY the year we were married. He gave a guided tour of the school and asked me to fill out an application, which I did on the spot. Before I left, we spoke again on the phone and they offered her a position to teach English to high school students. In preparation for her English teaching assignment, Rose visited the Montgomery County Board of Education in the suburban Washington area where we lived and where our children attended school. Her contacts were exceedingly helpful, giving her curriculum materials for each high school grade. She corresponded with them and planned her teaching lessons long before we arrived in Pakistan.[32]

---

[32] During the time Rose was teaching at the Lahore American School, one of the high school students deliberately overturned a street vendor's cart just outside the school. As his penance, Rose made him do a book report on the novel "*The*

In early summer of 1962, we first flew from Baltimore to London, and then from London to Frankfurt. In Frankfurt, we visited the Volkswagen plant, where we picked up a minibus that we had ordered as the vehicle we would use in Pakistan. We drove our new minibus from Frankfurt through Switzerland to Rome and Naples. In our trip south through Italy, we stopped in Rome long enough for some sightseeing. We briefly visited the villa at Antonio Nibbi where I had lived for a few months during WW II when it was the headquarters of my air force squadron. It was easy to find the landmarks I remembered in Rome, which had been spared the ravage of war because it was an "open city."[33] We then traveled to Naples, but I could not find any of the places I knew from my service, because that city had experienced intense fighting and infrastructure destruction.

In Naples, we boarded an Italian passenger ship, the Victoria, for a six-day cruise to Karachi, the main seaport of Pakistan. During the voyage through the Red Sea, the ship encountered a storm so violent that it caused not only us, but also many crewmembers (as we learned later), to become seasick. The last few days of our voyage, however, were pleasant and enjoyable. When we docked in Karachi, we were met by a young couple that introduced themselves as Zed's daughter and son-in-law. They were very helpful in expediting immigration formalities and escorting us to a hotel, where we stayed overnight. We had a memorable day in Karachi where our children had camel rides and other colorful and memorable experiences. We completed our voyage to Lahore by passenger plane and were met in the airport by Zed

---

Ugly American"! This was a 1958 best seller about the impending Viet Nam War.

[33]Like Paris, Rome was deemed to be of such high cultural and historical value that all combatants tacitly agreed not to bomb the city. Thus, its architecture was largely preserved.

and a University of Maryland colleague, Dr. Merrill Snyder. Snyder had preceded me by a few weeks to coordinate the arrival of laboratory equipment even before the construction of the Center was completed. They drove us to our new residence in Fazalia Colony, a suburb of Lahore.

Home life in Lahore

At that time, Fazalia Colony was a cluster of homes in a semi-rural setting within easy driving distance from Lahore. Residents were well-to-do Pakistanis and expatriates like us who rented homes from affluent Pakistanis. Their affluence showed in the ostentatious appearance of these homes. The U.S. Agency for International Development (USAID) leased several of them, including the one assigned to us. The home we were assigned had four bedrooms on two floors, with close to 7,000 square feet of living space, compared to the 1,800 square feet in our home in the Washington suburbs.

We were surprised and somewhat uneasy at having such a large and pretentious home. When we asked, our USAID contact person explained that this home was assigned to us because I was Chief of Party, i.e., a person responsible for a contract group. Chiefs of Parties were expected to host visiting dignitaries, entertain to "show their party's flag," host prominent candidates for positions in their Party, participate in the expatriate community activities, and provide a social structure for meetings for their own staffs, expatriate dignitaries, and their Pakistani counterparts. To do all these tasks well, they would require space and servants. We had not planned for these responsibilities and were not entirely comfortable taking them on.

We soon found that, except for missionaries, almost all expatriate families had servants and ostentatious homes like ours. In all the 12 years of our marriage, Rose and I had never had a house servant, even part time. Rose was skillful in handling housework, entertaining, and cooking, sometimes for fairly large groups, and I was always available to help. The responsibilities of Chief of Party came as a shock to us, but we adjusted with the help of household servants assigned various specific roles and tasks.

Abdul was our Bearer, a coordinator and supervisor for the household servants. He had previous experience and strong recommendations from previous employers. He had a delightful personality and was extremely reliable and competent. Abdul was firm but kind and not overbearing in getting others to do their jobs.

Typically, two servants assisted the Bearer—a Hamal (porter) and a Sweeper[34], who traditionally had the lowest status among household servants. We chose not to have a Hamal; instead we had only a Sweeper to help Abdul. We hired a young man named Sardar as Sweeper. After several weeks on the job, he so impressed us by his effort, conscientiousness, efficiency, and attitude that we promoted him to Hamal, with a corresponding raise in salary and free uniforms. This was unthinkable under the caste system extant in the culture, but Rose felt it was the right thing to do. We recognized Sardar as a hard-working,

---

[34]The Sweeper's job was, as the title suggests, to sweep the floors of the household. He traditionally used only a wicker broom with no handle, necessitating an awkward, bent-over sweeping position. Once, our Sweeper, Sardar, was mopping the floor when his wet rag made contact with an electrical outlet. The shock threw him straight across the room! Fortunately he suffered no serious consequences.

intelligent young man, and so we brought a bit of American culture to our household.

Because servants were expected to present themselves properly, local tradition called on us to provide uniforms for them. Most households had a servant, called a Dobhi, who did laundry not only for the household but also for the Bearer and Hamal. Our Dobhi, a relative of Abdul named Nazir, was efficient, but when we promoted Sardar, he informed the Bearer he still considered Sardar a Sweeper instead of a Hamal and thus felt it was beneath his dignity to clean Sardar's uniforms. When Rose learned of this she said, "Very well, when you finish with the other clothes, let me know so I can wash Sardar's uniforms." That arrangement would have been even more unthinkable, so he quietly accepted our slice of American culture and henceforth included Sardar's uniforms in his laundry routine

Our cook, a man named Gulziman, was a profound disappointment. We were patient with him for months, but his dishonesty was exasperating. The quality of his work was fair, so we worked with him for a short time. However, he stole large quantities of food—and then presumptuously informed us we needed to restock items we had just bought—so we had to fire him. When he left, we actually managed better without him. Rose prepared meals by herself until she found another cook who did good work.

We also needed a gardener, called a Mali, to manage the large yard. A gardener was already living on the premises with his family from his previous employment. We did not want to fire him and evict his family, so we decided to try him. He was personable, but his gardening skills left much to be desired. I worked with him because I have always had an interest in gardening.

Like those of many other Americans, our yard was enclosed by a fence and high hedgerow and had a small enclosure at the entrance for a security guard, called a Chokidor. Chokidors protected privacy and prevented intrusions, and although they typically had no firearms or knives, they often carried a large staff to display their resolve for defending residents and property. Our Chokidor, Razha Khan, was a tall man with a warm and friendly nature. He was punctual (keeping hours of 6PM to 7AM), reliable, and cheerful. Despite the language barrier, he interacted well with our children, who came to like him a lot.

All our servants, with the exception of Razha Khan, lived with their families in quarters provided behind the house. Each had a small apartment supplied with water in one room and a toilet in another room. Because these apartments originally had no barriers to mosquitoes, we had their windows screened. We felt obliged because this was a highly endemic area for malaria. I asked USAID to do this for all servant quarters in homes they had leased for expatriate families, and they complied.

In return for their commitment to their jobs, all our servants expected us to provide health care for themselves and their families. Most employers made ad hoc arrangements for acute illnesses, but none extended themselves as we did. Because our servants knew I was a physician, they expected more from me. As I left for work in the morning, I often found the mothers holding one or more sick children who needed care. I tended to them the best I could. From the time we met him, Razha Khan had a severe cough, so I arranged for him to have a chest x-ray; it showed active tuberculosis. I purchased his medications and made him promise he would take the pills as I prescribed. Unfortunately, he would only take his medicines when his symptoms got worse. I worried the strain that infected him would become resistant to antitubercular drugs, but no matter how hard I tried, I could not persuade him to comply with his treatment regimen.

No provisions were made in my own salary for the payment of servants, for the guests we hosted, or for social events we had in our homes. It did not occur to me to make an issue of this when I negotiated my salary. I did not want to raise the question when I realized how tight the medical center's budget was.[35]

We lived with unrecognized and unexpected inconveniences and risks. Climate control was a problem during many months of the year. Daily temperatures routinely exceeded 104° F (40° C) in the hottest summer months, and reached as low as 43° F (6° C) in the coldest winter months. The rooms in our house had tall ceilings that helped cool rooms in the summer heat, an important feature because homes did not have central air conditioning, and electricity for window units was unreliable. Some rooms had ceiling fans. In the winter, we needed to wear heavy clothes and use space heaters. Most rooms had nonfunctional fireplaces that were not deep enough to hold a bed of coals. As far as I could tell, they had never been used. Besides, firewood was expensive and scarce.

---

[35]Each month my office would receive funds sent from Baltimore to a local bank for the payroll of Pakistani employees. I made arrangements with the bank to deliver the payroll to my office. One senior administrative Center staff paid employees in cash. Some months, the payroll was delayed for one reason or another, creating hard feelings among employees. On one occasion, Fred McCrumb loaned his own money to make possible a monthly payroll. Most difficult were occasions when newly arriving staff from Baltimore had unexpected needs, for which I had no contingency funds. Under those circumstances, they would have to improvise and/or rely on support from their designated mentors in Baltimore.

All of us developed gastrointestinal illnesses. One of those illnesses affected me for many weeks. Zed tested a stool sample and informed me that I had bacillary dysentery. It did not respond to treatment. I had to push myself to maintain my rigorous daily schedule. In field trips, it was difficult to find private places to relieve myself. I felt acutely embarrassed when this happened.

Most of the city's population had little or no access to safe water. Water-transmitted disease, especially typhoid fever, featured prominently in local news and in patients I saw in the three hospitals I visited from time to time as part of my work[36]—the King Edward Medical College, the Lahore General Hospital, and the Lahore Christian Hospital. We were fortunate to have a deep well for our house that functioned most of the time. However, apart from the torrential rains in late summer, drought conditions persisted most of the year. When wells failed, USAID had an emergency plan to deliver water by trucks. On numerous occasions they delivered water to our home. From time to time, Abdul informed us that nomads living in a large nearby field had come to our compound seeking water. We had no hesitation having them fill their buckets with water from an outdoor faucet used primarily to water plants and shrubs. At times, many of them came. At one point, our neighbor, a USAID administrative person, came to advise us that we should not be providing expensive water to those who were not part of the USAID network. I met with the senior administrative director to appeal this ruling in such situations. They rescinded the ban to defuse the issue.

---

[36]At these hospitals, I served several functions: I followed-up patients from our study sites (as described later) until they could return home, I occasionally cared for American patients (though this wasn't an official part of my job description), and I participated in academic medical rounds.

During the long periods of drought, families suffered from lack of water and contamination of available water. Yet the season of heavy monsoon rains presented its own dangers. Because the rains were strong enough to down electrical lines, they left puddles that presented an electrocution risk to the children from nearby nomad families, who often played in the water. These water-related problems underscored the water and sanitation experiences I had in Naples mentioned in previous chapters.

Electrical utilities were especially problematic. Electrical failures occurred often and were especially annoying when we were preparing food for social events in our home. Electrical surges also created problems. Surge protectors available at the time were often inadequate. In one incident, we were awakened in the early morning hours by our daughter Peggy's coughing and crying. I rushed to her bedroom downstairs, opened the door, and saw a plume of smoke. While removing her I saw that the wire cord of the space heater in her room was glowing and threatening to catch fire. This was the greatest risk any of our children experienced in Lahore.

Rabies was hyperendemic at this time. In those days before rabies vaccines were available, the Lahore Health Department had an aggressive rabies control program, paying bounties for reporting stray dogs and leaving bait laced with strychnine, which sadly caused prolonged and painful death. Peggy, who was nine years old, made a home in one of the corners of our compound for a pregnant stray dog she named Mama. She fed and nurtured the dog with some help from our servants, and soon afterward, Mama delivered her puppies. I warned Peggy about rabies, describing patients I had seen in hospitals, but she was too young to realize the risk. I remember a particularly poignant case when I diagnosed rabies in a German homemaker, wife of a consulate official, who had been hospitalized with the earliest manifestations of the disease. She had contracted rabies from her pet dog. I comforted her in her agonizing final hours of life in a darkened and spare hospital room. The room had been set up with no furniture and only a mattress in order to manage the uncontrollable convulsions that characterize the end stages of rabies. I recalled this incident when our next-door neighbor, a USAID senior staff person, came to our home to complain about dogs in our compound howling at night. In keeping with USAID policy, he told me he had already contacted health authorities to send rabies control technicians to remove the dogs. Having them taken away to be euthanized was a wrenching experience, especially since Peggy was so emotionally attached and felt we should have protected them. It was a sensitive issue for many years.

In those days before cell phones, computers, and e-mail, telegrams were the most reliable way to communicate across continents. Making a long-distance telephone call required a lot of patience. Telephone service infrastructures in Pakistan then were no better, and in many respects worse, than what I had experienced in war-torn Italy more than 15 years earlier. Telephone poles were routinely toppled during storms and usually weren't repaired for days. Long distance telephone calls had to be scheduled days in advance and required the assistance of telephone operators at both ends. Pakistani operators had difficulty understanding our American accents, so we had to spell out every word using the NATO phonetic alphabet—"A" as in Alpha, "B" as in Bravo, "C" as in Charlie, etc. Static made many phone conversations very difficult to understand, and quite frequently connections ended unexpectedly, so it was often necessary to restart interrupted discussions—or else to forget about them. Credit cards were not in use, and arrangements for payment were complicated. For local communications, it was often easier to travel by car to speak in person. For international communications, such as those between myself and Benenson, the Director of the Cholera Research Laboratory (located in what was then East Pakistan), we had to cope with all of the difficulties mentioned above. Communication infrastructures were further complicated by the fact that my office in Lahore, West Pakistan was separated from Dhaka, East Pakistan by the often-hostile country of India. To prevent miscommunication, after each call, the originator had to confirm salient points via telegram. This was the reality of doing research in the developing world back then.[37]

---

[37]One anecdote underscores the consequences of communication problems both locally and internationally. I was expecting Dr. Michael (Mike) Gregg and his family for a long-term assignment starting in the spring of 1964. At the time, he was a full-time faculty member of University of Maryland's Medical School. I told my administrative person to make arrangements with USAID to assign his family a home, but I did not have details of his plans. The first I knew of his arrival was his call to my home from the Lahore airport on a Saturday afternoon. I had been tending to errands that morning. I could tell from his voice he was dismayed that no one was there to meet him and no one had been available to take his calls. Within minutes, I alerted Rose and headed for the airport with my minivan. Within the hour, I met him at a designated place in the airport where he and his family had been waiting since early morning. He told me a telegram had been sent, but I had not received it. He had tried to make a long-distance call from an intermediate stop en route, but he was not successful. He had called from an airport phone several times but was not able to reach me, as I was tending to errands. I took him to our home, where Rose and I hosted him for about a week while arrangements for his home were completed. The incident distressed Gregg and me, but we soon made the best of it. It was not an auspicious start for his assignment, but it was par for the course.

The political milieu

The Partition of India in 1947 was a massive civil upheaval that resulted in the deaths of at least half a million people and the displacement of 12 million. Tensions between Muslims and Hindus in the region had existed for many centuries, and when the British granted India independence, the Muslim minority insisted on having their own country. Muslim refugees poured out of both sides of newly independent India, forming West and East Pakistan. In 1971, years after we left, what had been East Pakistan declared itself the independent nation of Bangladesh.

In retrospect, we came during an uncharacteristically calm period when a tenuous truce between India and Pakistan prevailed. A new industry, tourism, emerged, and we were intrigued by colorful brochures describing historical sites to visit. We learned more about these places from friends and colleagues who had actually taken these trips. We deferred travel vacations until our second year in Pakistan to give priority to my responsibilities at work.

In our second Christmas and New Year holiday season, we took advantage of these once-in-a-lifetime opportunities, taking our family to Delhi, where we visited the Taj Mahal. It took a whole day just to cross the border, because in the morning the Pakistani border guards made us unload everything in the car for inspection, and then after they let us put everything back and cross over around noon, the Indian border guards took the entire afternoon making us do the same thing! Nonetheless, the trip was well worth the effort. The Taj Mahal was majestic, awesome, and magnificent!

Later we visited the Swat valley, joined by our son Ray's seventh-grade teacher and her husband, the Fritschlers. Getting there was an adventure we will long remember, driving cautiously above high cliffs over a raging river, on a poorly maintained and extremely narrow mountain road, part of which had disappeared during a rainstorm. We also went on several weekend trips, especially to Peshawar, where we visited bazaars that intrigued us. We took picnic baskets on these trips. We recall how quickly crowds gathered around us when we stopped to eat—even in remote areas we initially thought would provide privacy. We collected hand-carved brass and copper works of art and beautiful rugs. We designed the patterns for two of the Oriental rugs we purchased, and watched as they were woven for us. These still feature prominently in our living room.

At this writing, tourism in Pakistan is a thing of the past because of the danger of terrorism. As it turned out, the lull we enjoyed during our stay in Pakistan did not last long.

My academic responsibilities

Soon after my arrival, the Dean of the Pakistan Medical Research Center sought out a meeting with me during which he mentioned that he would appreciate help from our new University of Maryland (UMD) group. In particular, he needed additional courses to expand the offering for the certificate program in public health. After some thought, I came up with three courses to add to the menu. The first was a course that I taught on food and waterborne diseases. A second course covered special topics in public health, and took advantage of the constant stream of visitors from the UMD, who could provide guest lectures on various subjects. For a third course, I enlisted the help of those involved in the WHO's Global Malaria Eradication Program to provide a course on strategies for controlling malaria. I found both myself and the Dean to be quite pleased with how this initiative turned out, and I was happy to be able to provide this kind of help to our neighbors in the same building.

Our work on malaria

Malaria was the research focus of the Pakistan Medical Research Center. This work benefitted from the only other external source of research funding other than the NIH-ICMRT grant that set up the Center. I spent about half of my time in support of this research.

A worldwide Malaria Eradication Program was the underpinning for the Center's primary research program. In the last years of World War II, the chemical DDT, an organophosphate insecticide, was used extensively, initially for the control of typhus, and subsequently for malaria. Since the body louse that transmits the infectious agent of typhus favors seams in undergarments, DDT was administered as an aerosol delivered by bellows between outer clothes and underwear of people at risk. Near the end of the war, researchers found that DDT sprayed on walls would kill resting mosquitoes. This was the primary intervention for the global malaria eradication effort until resistant mosquitoes were identified in the late 1950s. In 1962, when I arrived in Pakistan, leaders of the eradication program zealously began searching for alternative ways to ensure the eradication of the disease. It was in this ambience the Center entered the fray in search of methods for mosquito control that did not require DDT.

We focused on the two alternative methods that had been proposed in the grant application (described above). First, we tested the use of an organophosphate insecticide, dichlorvos, manufactured by Shell Chemicals under the trade name DDVP. The chemical was infused into petroleum resin strips for slow release over about four months, in order to kill airborne mosquitoes in enclosed places like village homes and office rooms. During the early 1960s, Shell also marketed these strips in the United States. They provided the strips used in our studies, and their scientists visited from time to time to answer questions, make suggestions, and oversee their contribution to the research.

The Center's second research project focused on genetically altering the reproductive organs of male mosquitoes to sterilize them. For these studies, conducted independently by a group of entomologists, the largest rooms of the new Center were fitted with the most advanced equipment to study mosquitoes. Our Center had the only laboratory of its kind in Pakistan for this research. WRAIR and NIH scientists collaborated in this research, but I was not personally involved.

I worked on two main projects during my time in Lahore—on the subjects of intestinal infections and malaria[38]. The topic of my own research, which consumed about half my time, was intestinal pathophysiology in young Pakistani men, studied using the Crosby biopsy capsule. I spent about half a day each week on this research during my first year in Lahore. I was fortunate that my able colleague Dr. Phil Russell took the lead in this work. Our findings were the same as what we had reported in my second Bangkok study—namely, in all of our biopsies, intestinal villi were atrophied and infiltrated with chronic inflammatory cells. The anatomical changes were identical to those seen in intestinal

---

[38] I additionally had the task of administering locally sourced funds. The Armed Forces Epidemiological Board of WRAIR provided some funding for consultants, but not for our research. In addition, some support came from so-called PL 480 Funds derived from sales of U.S. agricultural products sold to Pakistan. Country-specific currencies were available from such sales, the proceeds of which helped fund various public health projects, including our malaria research.

sprue, wherein atrophied villi result in a decrease in surface area—pathology that typically contributes to chronic malnutrition in that illness. Our publication of this study was the first description of a common pathological entity now sometimes called tropical or environmental enteropathy [3]. Sometimes environmental enteropathy is not distinguished from intestinal sprue, but in any case, both are characterized by the sequelae of malabsorption and resulting chronic nutritional deficiencies.

Subsequent studies by other investigators have confirmed our early impression that environmental enteropathy is highly prevalent in the developing world, with dire consequences. Indeed, an analysis published in *The Lancet* in 2013 estimated that, worldwide, hundreds of millions of preschool-aged children suffer from some form of undernutrition, and this contributes to nearly half of deaths of children under 5 [4]. Further, for those children that do survive, chronic malnutrition is associated with "long-term cognitive deficits, poorer school performance, lower educational attainment, and reduced adult economic productivity." [5] These articles and others describe a cycle by which poor sanitary conditions lead to repeated intestinal infections that adversely affect digestive function; combined with already marginal dietary intake and the high growth velocity of infants, this blow to nutrient absorption can be critical to infant nutritional status. To avoid what I call a pervasive "fecal veneer" on household surfaces that sets this vicious cycle in motion, many scientists advocate provision of toilets for every family, hand-washing after defecation, literacy training to promote understanding of the importance of cleanliness, and investments in water and sanitation infrastructures. This position is entirely consistent with the millennium goals of the World Health Organization [6].

I spent the other half of my time implementing a study protocol to determine the efficacy of the Shell DDVP strips in test villages. Our first step was the enumeration of the test villages, where the Shell strips would be used in homes previously sprayed with DDT, and control villages, where the only control measure would be the DDT spraying that was standard at the time. To this end, we conducted a census of small villages in the Punjab province of Pakistan near the Indian border. We identified every child in both test villages as well as control villages. During the census, we prepared slides of peripheral blood from drops of blood from one of the big toes of febrile infants. Those slides were then studied for the presence of malaria parasites. Thus, we were able to measure the incidence of malaria in infants and children under 5 years old in test and control villages.

The preliminary demographic survey was completed in about 3 months, and placement of the Shell strips followed soon afterward. Villagers readily accepted the strips when they saw large numbers of dead flies in their homes and realized that they were getting fewer mosquito bites. Surveillance for malaria parasites in slides from children with febrile illnesses progressed smoothly through the end of 1962 and into the spring of 1963.[39]

Because of extreme heat in the Punjab summer, we completed our daily trips early in the day. Except on Muslim holy days and weekends, we would work until noon. Zed met me at my home at 5:30 A.M., and from there it would take 60 – 90 minutes to drive

---

[39]In the early summer of 1963, I visited Dhaka primarily to assess the progress of studies of their oral fluid rehydration research. Progress was slow, but the scientists involved were skilled, confident, and determined. Assuming their laboratory and clinical studies would be successful, they anticipated conducting field trials. This possibility piqued my interest because our study villages in the Punjab would also have been suitable for such studies.

by Jeep to the study villages. Our Center had recruited two former army corps technicians whom Zed had trained, and usually one or both accompanied us. We could only communicate with contact people in the villages by word of mouth, so each time we completed a visit, we would schedule the next trip. This arrangement caused problems when we had to change plans or cancel trips, e.g., for mechanical difficulties with vehicles, trips for visiting scientists, and severe monsoon weather conditions. A senior village leader was designated at each study site to accompany and assist us in various ways. We offered medical treatment, so sick people—especially mothers with sick children—often waited long hours for our arrival. We brought a few medications to dispense during these ad hoc sick calls. Most of the illnesses were respiratory and gastrointestinal. Occasionally, a very sick person needed more urgent care. We had one space in our Jeep that we used from time to time to transport a sick person to the Lahore General Hospital, which was on our way back.

In the months that followed, our malaria surveillance trips became routine. We had considerable data to discuss with visitors representing NIH, the Malaria Eradication Program, and Shell Chemicals.

An incident that changed my career

For most medical conditions, Zed and I generally agreed how to treat sick villagers with our very limited resources. Very significantly, however, patients with diarrhea, especially infants, became a special source of contention. As noted above, Zed had been skeptical when we talked during his visit to Maryland about the implications of my Bangkok studies for rehydrating patients with diarrhea. He never raised the issue again, even when he had opportunities that would have been quite

187

appropriate. Therefore, I expected he would give me the benefit of his doubt on those occasions when I asked him to translate my direction to mothers whose children had diarrhea. The technicians we hired were among the students he had taught to withhold food and water, in keeping with the traditional starvation therapy for diarrhea. When we saw mothers with infants and children with diarrhea, I asked him to translate instructions to administer fluids, especially fruit juices and water, a half teaspoonful at a time. Seemingly, he dutifully translated. I do not recall seeing the same mothers in follow up trips.

For unrelated reasons, I invited Benenson (the Director of the Cholera Research Center in Dhaka, Bangladesh) for his second visit to our Center in the early summer of 1964, and he gave an excellent presentation to my staff about his team's progress on oral fluid rehydration research in Dhaka. He explained how rehydration therapy reverses the metabolic derangements associated with diarrhea, most notably the loss of sodium bicarbonate and chloride that causes vomiting, thereby enabling the body to maintain its critical acid-base balance. He spoke of various liquids that might be used in field situations to replace essential electrolytes and fluids lost in diarrheal stools. He stressed the emerging awareness among workers in this field that any fluids by mouth were better than nothing. In his closing, he reiterated that survival often depends on how much fluid mothers can give. I felt good that he had dispelled any remaining doubts on the dangerous starvation strategy. Zed and the two technicians who had been his students all attended the presentation, but none of them raised questions about oral fluid rehydration.

In the month that followed Benenson's visit, Zed and I continued our village visits. As the temperature climbed, we were seeing more cases of diarrheal illnesses, especially in infants and toddlers. As usual, I asked Zed to explain to mothers the importance of rehydrating with whatever fluids were available, and to encourage fruit juices and water in small amounts. Again, he translated my instructions at times when the technicians were present, either separately or together.

Rose and I were surprised at about 10:00 P.M. one evening when both technicians came to my residence. They politely asked if they were intruding, and we assured them they were not. Then they asked if they could come in to discuss an important matter. We invited them in and asked them to make themselves comfortable in our living room. Of course, we did not offer alcoholic drinks because they were devout Muslims, but they declined our offer for soft drinks. It was clear they had a sensitive matter to discuss, since they were nervous and fretful. Rose excused herself to create a more reassuring ambience in which we could discuss professional matters.

When the three of us were alone, I could hardly believe what they said. They took turns telling me that Zed had not translated as I had instructed when we encountered mothers with sick infants with diarrheal illnesses. Instead of telling them to treat their children with fluids, as I had advised, his instructions were exactly the opposite of what we had discussed ever since we met. He ordered them to put their babies' digestive systems at rest by withholding food and liquids, and even "educated" the mothers that vomiting was nature's message justifying starvation therapy. Of course I did not know what he was saying since I did not understand Urdu, the local language he spoke with mothers in the presence of the technicians.

I had no reason to question the veracity of what they told me. I knew they had a great deal of respect for this man owing to their many years of army service with him, but this duplicity was too much for them to accept. Zed knew and they knew I had been deceived into thinking we were providing mothers with the latest insights into treating diarrheal diseases, but Zed stubbornly insisted his old dictum was the proper therapy. The technicians had seen both arguments and had the opportunity to weigh the evidence. They were distraught to learn in subsequent visits that some of the babies given Zed's advice had died. What convinced them was that Benenson had confirmed the advice I had asked Zed to translate. So, they decided to take on the role of whistleblowers, informing me that Zed had intentionally not followed my instructions. It weighed on them that Zed continued to put these babies in jeopardy, and that some of them had died because of his stubbornness.

I shared with Rose what I had learned from Zed's technicians. Of course, I was extremely distressed that he had put the lives of infants in our charge in jeopardy. I was also upset that his actions eliminated the possibility of conducting field trials of oral fluid rehydration in our study villages. After a restless night, I told Rose I felt compelled to report these developments to my Baltimore supervisors at the first opportunity. I also felt strongly that Zed needed to be relieved of his position as soon as possible. I felt so strongly about this that I decided that if I could not prevail, we should plan to leave soon. As a matter of fact, my two-year contract, which I had planned to renew, was due to end in less than three weeks. Rose agreed that this matter was serious enough to justify leaving.

I sent my supervisors in Baltimore a telegram summarizing succinctly the enormity of the problem and requested an audience with Dean Stone to explain what had happened. My message noted I could no longer work with Zed knowing that he had compromised the lives of children in our care for whom I felt responsible.

Fred McCrumb, my immediate supervisor, made arrangements for me to return to Maryland within the week. In Baltimore, I met with McCrumb first, then with McCrumb and other colleagues, and then with Ted Woodward, who was McCrumb's supervisor. They were all sympathetic, but they had great difficulty believing Zed would do such a thing. It was hard for them to acknowledge they had made a mistake hiring a man with such a stellar reputation and record of service in the army. They scheduled a meeting for me with Dean Stone, but none of them joined me, so I felt I did not have their support. In fact, after a 45-minute meeting, Dean Stone said to me, "If it comes to Zed or you leaving, you will have to go." I left his office realizing I had no choice but to resign. And that is what I did. I just needed a propitious way to exit.

I returned to Lahore saddened by the events. Rose was fully supportive and concurred with my decision to leave. The remaining weeks were awkward because I decided not to go on field trips with Zed. I was in a difficult situation not being able to discuss this matter with Zed or other faculty because I was committed to the technicians not to reveal what they had confided in me. I sensed that they were fearful and might even be in danger if Zed learned they were whistleblowers. Despite the fact that I had done my duty in informing my supervisors, I felt guilty about this. I had no other recourse but to inform everyone that I was not renewing my contract, and I needed time to prepare for my return[iv]. After I left, I learned that none of my superiors dealt with the problem Zed had created and did not even discuss it with the staff.

Figure 11: EJG Addressing Staff at the Lahore Pakistan Medical Research Center, Upon his Going-Away, 1964.
Major General Phil Russell (first from the left) became the commandant of the Walter Reed Army Medical Center. Dr. Michael Gregg (fourth from the left) joined the Epidemic Intelligence Service (EIS) and served as the editor of CDC's Morbidity and Mortality Weekly Report (MMWR).

Our last day in Lahore was a nightmare! We did not count on visits from well-wishers, some of whom brought gifts with their goodbyes. It was clear we had not allowed ourselves enough time. Our flight was scheduled to depart Lahore at 10:00 A.M. Rose had worked the previous day, leaving only a few remaining tasks that absolutely required our Bearer Abdul's help. He assured us he would come, but he did not. We were in a frenzy making last-minute preparations without him. As we tried politely to tell our friends we had to leave for the airport, our USAID driver interrupted to inform us we absolutely had to leave in 10 minutes to arrive at the airport in time for our flight. Unexpected traffic heightened our anxiety. We arrived during the last call for boarding our flight. At the counter, we were informed that our luggage was overweight, so we would have to pay several hundred dollars immediately. This was before the era of credit cards; they would accept only cash. We did not have that much cash with us and did not have time to cash traveler's checks. In those anxious moments, not knowing what to do, and realizing the next flight would leave two days later, I saw one of our faculty in a line of arriving passengers. I quickly explained our dilemma. He fortuitously had travel vouchers acceptable for payment of the overweight luggage, which he kindly allowed us to use. It was an enormous relief when we were finally able to board our flight at the last moment. It was by far the most hectic day of our Pakistan experiences.[v]

Events at the Pakistan Medical Research Center after we left

In the time after our departure, Ted Woodward served briefly as Director of the Center, followed by Fred McCrumb, who was intended to serve an undefined term. In fact, McCrumb's tenure lasted only a few months. Later, while he visited a cholera treatment center I had set up in a hospital in Teheran, McCrumb told me what had happened. Subsequently, other Americans who had been evacuated early in the Pakistan-India war of 1964 – 65 confirmed his account of the events, adding additional details.

McCrumb's relationship with Zed was bad from the start and got much worse as the war began. Our study site was in a sensitive geopolitical area where the Pakistani and Indian armies were skirmishing and at times engaged in combat. McCrumb innocently purchased two-way radios to improve communications among the Center's study villages, and Zed promptly accused him of reporting military movements to the Indian army! These developments culminated in a crisis for

McCrumb. He was arrested for spying, jailed, and expelled from the country. It was a *force majeure* that ended the University of Maryland's role in Lahore. NIH terminated the ICMRT contract.

Our last encounter with McCrumb was in 1965, after he had returned from Lahore. He left the University of Maryland to accept a position at NIH as Director of the Fogarty Center. In this position, he had oversight responsibility for the Gorgas Memorial Research Center (now called the Gorgas Memorial Institute for Tropical and Preventive Medicine), located in Panama. When he came to visit us in our Stone Mountain home, I was surprised that he offered me the position of Director of the Gorgas Center. When he explained what would be required of me in that position, I did not reveal my hand, but I knew I did not want the job. I simply told him I wanted to discuss this with Rose. Neither of us were interested at all—she did not want to move from our newly purchased home, and I was totally absorbed and very happy with my new position at CDC. However, I was pleased and deeply touched that he had asked, because it indicated his confidence in me despite the Zed incident. Because he was such a good friend, I was also glad he was enjoying his new job and had overcome his unpleasant experiences being deported from Pakistan as a suspected spy. All of us had had great expectations for the Lahore Center, perhaps most of all McCrumb, but the Indo-Pakistan War of 1965 had abruptly brought our dreams to an end.

Within months of McCrumb's visit in our home, I learned he died of a cardiac arrest in the emergency room of the University Hospital in Baltimore. He had been working on his small farm one day when he complained of respiratory symptoms so severe that one of his sons took him to the emergency room. While being admitted, he had a cardiac arrest. Attempts to resuscitate him by cardiac massage fractured a rib that penetrated his heart.

This weighed heavily on those of us closest to him, especially Ted Woodward, who had been McCrumb's mentor for most of his short career. They were as close as father and son. McCrumb's tragic death was one of several calamitous events in Ted's life, which had included his oldest son's drowning in a swimming pool.

The program's legacy

Several decades later, in my role as Director of Emory's graduate program in public health, I interviewed and then accepted Dr. Haroon Rashid, a graduate of the Lahore Medical College, as an MPH degree candidate. He took two of my courses, and I mentored him during his MPH practicum. Impressed with his academic commitment and leadership skills, I recruited him to serve as a graduate assistant.

To write this chapter, I asked Rashid to determine what had become of the University of Maryland's Medical Research Center, which had been located just across the street from Rashid's alma mater. On September 16, 2013, he sent me an email[vi] stating that the Center had "assumed a great learning center status in Punjab province." He also described for me the various degree and research programs that were ongoing at the time of this writing. In particular, the Center "ha[d] continued mosquito research and ha[d] added many important medical and postgraduate institutes that [were] still serving the Punjab region and Pakistan as a whole."

I was heartened to hear that the Center was flourishing and had assumed such an important role in the region. I can only hope that my efforts to expand the institute's 1962 -1964 academic menu had helped contribute to some of this success. Perhaps even more, I must give credit to my colleagues at the Center for helping to lay the foundation for its expansion. Of course, I must also recognize all those who came afterwards for their role in growing the Center into an important academic public health and medical complex serving millions in Pakistan's Punjab state.

Personal reflections

My Lahore experience was my "baptism of fire" in academic public health—the first building block in a career focused on institution-building. It was challenging because I was called upon to grow an academic program with practically no budget. Compared to subsequent positions I had in academic universities, it was the most difficult of my career experiences. My research goals in Pakistan were thwarted and my tenure ended because I trusted a person who purposefully countermanded my advice in a way that likely caused deaths among infants for whom I felt responsible. I learned the importance of surrounding myself with people I could trust. Managing with scant budgets was also a hallmark of my two subsequent experiences—at the American University of Beirut's Faculty of Health Sciences, where my challenge was to reverse a deteriorating financial condition of a distinguished School of Public Health, and more recently at Emory University, where I was challenged to help transform a faltering graduate program stalled from its inception into the dynamic Rollins School of Public Health.

We had health problems during our Lahore experience. My family was at risk of rabies, a disease that was hyperendemic, at a time when my 11-year-old daughter adopted a dog that delivered puppies in a hidden place in our yard. Rose and I developed toxic symptoms from our exposures to an organophosphate product our Center was testing for malaria control. She experienced a mild short-lived illness, but mine was more troubling and lasted considerably longer. An electrical fire, with life-threatening smoke, nearly occurred in our home when the electrical cord to a space heater overheated in a closed bedroom where one of our children was sleeping. For months, I had bacillary dysentery that did not respond to antibiotic treatment. Despite these health issues, Rose and I believe our Lahore experiences were positive for us and our first three children, who, without the distraction of television, became avid readers and had educationally enriching experiences.

My research in Lahore was gratifying in a number of ways. My colleagues and I were able to build on the research of intestinal pathophysiology I had started in Thailand and India and then completed in Pakistan. Using an intestinal biopsy instrument and physiological studies, I built on the protocol that established the pathogenesis of cholera and laid a foundation upon which others invented oral rehydration therapy. In Pakistan, my colleagues and I extended previous observations to describe a condition now called environmental enteropathy. I had hoped we could have performed clinical trials of oral rehydration therapy, but others carried that torch when I could not.

Although I was not the primary investigator for the malaria research at the center, I learned several important lessons. First and foremost was to never put blind trust in an interpreter while doing scientific research, especially where lives are at stake. Secondly, as I reflect on this topic, I am again struck by the naiveté with which the DDVP research was conducted. We conducted efficacy studies blindly taking safety for granted— worrisome given DDVP's later proven toxicity, combined with the apparent lack of safe disposal of the insecticide strips. I once even saw a very young child playing with one! I am grateful that, since that time, our scientific culture has made some advancements in the consideration of safety.

Pakistan was a rewarding experience despite setbacks and risks. I learned a lot about institution-building, skills that served me well in later chapters of my career. It was also a life-changing experience—it conclusively ended my aspirations to practice internal medicine. I realized that my future was in academic public health focused on water and sanitation. That scientific field and social movement became passions that Rose and I embraced. These interests have culminated in our charitable giving in support of institutions with similar missions.

References

1.   Gangarosa EF, Beisel WR, Benyajati C, Sprinz H, Piyaratn P: **The nature of the gastrointestinal lesion in asiatic cholera and its relation to pathogenesis: a biopsy study**. *American J Topical Medicine and Hygiene* 1960, **9**:125-135.

2.   Gordon RS, Jr.: **Exudative enteropathy: abnormal permeability of the gastrointestinal tract demonstrable with labelled polyvinylpyrrolidone**. *Lancet* 1959, **1**(7068):325-326.

3.   Russell PK, Aziz MA, Ahmad N, Gangarosa EJ, Siddiqui. AR: **Intestinal Biopsies and Absorption Studies in Young Pakistani Men**. *Pakistan J Medical Research* 1964, **3**:278 285.

4.   Black RE, Victora CG, Walker SP, Bhutta ZA, Christian P, de Onis M, Ezzati M, Grantham-McGregor S, Katz J, Martorell R *et al*: **Maternal and child undernutrition and overweight in low-income and middle-income countries**. *Lancet* 2013, **382**(9890):427-451.

5.   Humphrey JH: **Child undernutrition, tropical enteropathy, toilets, and hadnwashing**. *Lancet* 2009, **374**:1032-1035.

6. **United Nations Millennium Declaration**. Edited by United Nations General Assembly, vol. 55/2; 2000.

Chapter 8: My Introduction to CDC

When I returned from Pakistan in 1964, I was again in the situation of looking for a new job. Although I had a couple of different options, a position at the Centers for Disease Control and Prevention (CDC) was the most important opportunity that opened for me. My subsequent CDC career from 1964 to 1978 was the cornerstone of my career in public health. The knowledge, experiences, and contacts I gained at CDC have proved instrumental throughout the rest of my career in academic public health.

I was fortunate to learn the essence of public health from Alex Langmuir, one of the true giants in our field. He was the founder of the Epidemic Intelligence Service (EIS), which he based on a paradigm for epidemiology and public health following William Farr's prototype of rapid response by a mutisectorial professional cadre in the investigation of outbreaks. What I learned from Langmuir is the basis of what I have taught throughout my subsequent academic career, including, at this writing, to graduate students at the Rollins School of Public Health, undergraduate public health majors at the College of Charleston, and high school students visiting Emory to explore careers in public health.

First impressions of EIS

Three people influenced me in my recruitment into the Epidemic Intelligence Service (EIS) at CDC. I first learned of the existence of the EIS some time after one of my medical-school classmates, D.A. Henderson, was accepted in 1955 and rapidly rose to Assistant Branch Chief in Epidemiology. When we were medical students, I was inspired by reading his undergraduate thesis—which contributed to his graduating with honors—about the 1832 outbreak of cholera in Rochester, NY. As it turns out, CDC was impressed by this same paper, which played a role in D.A.'s being offered a position at CDC. From D.A., I learned a bit more about the EIS—CDC's "disease detectives" who were tasked with investigating outbreaks whenever and wherever they appear! However, it was not until a few years later that I began to see CDC and the EIS as real career possibilities for myself.

The second person was a senior scientist, Dr. James H. Steele, who lectured in a military course I took at Brooks Air Force base in San Antonio, Texas in 1957. He was an impressive speaker with a dynamic personality who spoke on two subjects of great interest to me—salmonellosis attributed to dehydrated eggs shipped to the United Kingdom during WWII, and the impact of enteric diseases on the military. Dr. John Silliker, my bacteriology professor in medical school, had discussed related laboratory issues, but Steele had epidemiological expertise that raised my interest to the next level. I spoke to Steele about studies he had in progress concerning other zoonotic diseases in the Epidemiology group[40] at CDC. At the time, he served as Chief of Veterinarian Public Health Services at CDC in Dr. Alex

---

[40] CDC changed the terminology of its organizational structure during and after my time there, so I have to simplify my labels for different operational units. When I started, all the units discussed here were quite small and called "Sections," "Activities," and "Branches," but as CDC's mission in public health practice expanded, those units grew, so the Epidemiology and Laboratory units were reorganized from "Branches" to higher level "Divisions." The Enteric Diseases presence at CDC has always been at the Branch level, although at this writing, it has been subdivided into four mission-specific Branches. Since many organizational structures changed during and after my time at CDC, I have simplified substantially, and will refer to all organizational structures as "groups," except when referring to specific position titles that I held.

Langmuir's group, which included the EIS. It was the first time I became aware of Langmuir's work. I was very impressed with Steele; my encounters with him were the seed of my interest in the EIS.

Alex Langmuir was the third person who influenced my entrance into CDC. I had first met him after a talk I gave in 1960 during which I presented my cholera studies in Bangkok to the American Society of Epidemiology. During a break after my presentation, Langmuir came to the podium to introduce himself. He was intrigued with what I had done in elucidating the pathogenesis of cholera and asked me a question about the biopsy instrument. I remember that conversation vividly. As I applied for a position in the EIS, Langmuir's past interest in my work strengthened my resolve to pursue a career at CDC.

Early in 1962, I called D.A. about the possibility of attending the upcoming EIS Conference scheduled for April. He invited me to attend the conference as his houseguest. The world-class epidemiology and public health reflected in the presentations at that conference convinced me to make joining EIS a future career objective.

D.A. was intently interested in what I had shown about cholera pathogenesis from my biopsy studies, and we talked at length about the subject. Indeed, we discussed a wide range of related topics—his student thesis on the 19th-century Rochester outbreak, the Epidemiology group's support of the Dacca Cholera Lab, and his visit there. I mentioned my conversation with Emeritus Dean George Whipple during a Medical School alumni meeting in 1960, shortly after the American Epidemiological Society meeting where I met Alex Langmuir. After hearing about my cholera biopsy findings, Whipple told me that a colleague, renowned American pathologist E.W. Goodpasture [1], had investigated a 1923 cholera outbreak in the Philippines and published a paper questioning the commonly accepted dictum ascribing the purgation of cholera to intestinal-epithelial desquamation. Whipple commented that my biopsy study had rediscovered Goodpasture's findings and affirmed his conclusions. These encounters and experiences energized my interest in the EIS.

Recruitment into CDC and EIS

In July 1964, I saw no future in the Pakistan ICMRT because of the Zed incident, mentioned in the previous chapter, so I resigned from the University of Maryland to explore other options—with an EIS position at the top of my wish list. I called D.A. to ask his advice. He was supportive and said he would talk to Langmuir to explore EIS and other CDC options. After a few days, D.A. called me to tell me the window for EIS positions was closed because the required three-week annual course for incoming officers had just concluded. However, he said I could apply for the next class, which would start in July of the following year. He suggested that I consider an opening in the Laboratory Division of CDC for a Deputy Director position. He had spoken to the chief of that group, Dr. U. Penti Kokko. D.A. invited Rose and me to visit him and his wife Nana as houseguests. He contacted Kokko, who scheduled interviews with himself and his staff. Kokko also paid for my travel to Atlanta. Although it was not a position in the EIS, it fit with my special interests in microbiology and infectious diseases, and it was far better than the administrative position I had been offered in Bethesda, Maryland, reviewing applications for NIH grants. At the NIH position, there would be no future for me to pursue my interests in infectious diseases or to build on the work I had done in Bangkok.

It was not easy persuading Rose to live in the South. The prospects of moving to Atlanta did not appeal to her, because she associated the media accounts of civil rights turbulence with the city. Although I argued that this perception was not correct, she continued to urge me to consider the NIH administrative position, primarily because we were both fond of the Washington area. To make matters worse, a few days previously we had put a deposit on a home in an attractive suburb in Potomac, Maryland—an easy commute to NIH. Rose saw it as our dream house. It was very difficult to change that momentum and convince Rose to consider another option.

I prevailed on Rose to accept my decision to interview for the Laboratory Division position, and to accompany me to Atlanta so that she could see the city. Rose accepted with palpable ambivalence, at best—and with the understanding we would not withdraw the deposit on the Maryland home. In Atlanta, D.A. and his wife Nana received us warmly. We were intrigued by Atlanta—the flowering trees and lovely green forests in a city that seemed to offer so much.

Nana had contacted a real-estate friend who kindly offered to accompany Rose and her in a search of homes for sale. At the beginning of that day, Rose was candid in her hesitancy, still focusing on the home in Potomac. Her reservations weighed heavily on me.

My interviews through the day consisted of meetings with distinguished laboratory scientists. The first and final meetings were with Kokko, the Laboratory Division Chief; he said I was a good fit for the job and offered it to me. I came close to accepting it, but I hesitated, to get Rose's concurrence. So, I said I would give him my answer the next morning. I met D.A., expecting we would return to his residence. To my surprise, he informed me that Langmuir wanted to see me, and that they had scheduled a meeting for late that afternoon. So, we met with Langmuir again. Looking me directly in the eye, he asked, "Gene, have you made a decision?" I said, "No, because I needed to get Rose's input and to think about it overnight." Then he continued, "Gene, I want you to consider another offer, the job of Chief of the Epidemic Intelligence Service." I was overwhelmed! I asked him what the job entailed. He said I would be working with him in his office as his assistant, with the primary responsibility assisting with recruitment for the next EIS class, and getting to know the program. He also indicated that I could join the next EIS class starting in July of 1965. I could not ask for more! It was exactly what I wanted. So, without hesitation, I informed him that I gladly accepted, confident Rose would concur. But, on the way back to D.A.'s home, I was anxious, weighed down by the thought of what Rose saw as her dream home in Potomac, Maryland.

When I entered, I saw an expression on Rose's face that worried me. I could tell she had not had a good day. She was emphatic— none of the homes she had seen with Nana and a real estate agent were acceptable, noting they were old, needed extensive repairs, were out of our price range, and smelled moldy. Her mood changed only slightly when I told her I had accepted a different job, a job working with Langmuir that would enable me to join the next EIS class the following July. As I spoke enthusiastically about the job and the future I saw in it, she became more accommodating, knowing that my wishes were becoming a reality. But I knew I would have to convince her about a place to live. I expressed confidence we would be able to find a home as good as the one we were considering in Potomac. The real estate agent that Nana had contacted agreed to spend time with us the next day.

Rose and I spent many hours with the real estate agent the following day as we continued our search. We started in the morning looking at two older homes close to CDC, in the prestigious Victoria Estates subdivision. She was still not impressed, and was worried about prices exceeding our $35,000 limit. In the afternoon I played my trump card—I asked our agent to drive us a bit further into the suburbs east of the city to see new homes. There, in the Smoke Rise Community of Stone Mountain, we found our dream home. The name of the street, Greencastle Way, was a metaphor for the good life she hoped for.

Rose decided to support me wholeheartedly. In the years that followed, I came to recognize that we had made the most important decision of our lives, opting for a wonderful job at CDC that redefined my career, and an elegant home in the Atlanta suburbs. Rose overcame her early preconceptions about Atlanta and came to love our life together there. The sacrifice she had made in support of the job I wanted at CDC was the most important factor in my decision to return to Atlanta after our troubled experiences in Beirut, Lebanon, as I describe in a later chapter. At this writing we still live in this home with no other plans in sight. For Rose, contrary to her initial impressions, that house turned out to be her dream home.

Follow-up of the DDVP story from my Pakistan experiences

Before I started working at CDC in August 1964, I wanted to complete some unfinished business from my experiences in Pakistan. I felt that, as part of the Pakistan Medical Research Center's study of Shell's dichlorvos (DDVP)-impregnated resin strips for malaria control, I should publish a firsthand account of the side effects of my own heavy exposure to the pesticide.

In the last few weeks of my tenure in Pakistan, I had begun to have fasciculation (twitching) in many muscles of my body. Symptoms were similar to what I had seen in patients in the earliest stages of amyotrophic lateral sclerosis (ALS), or Lou Gehrig's disease. After a week or so during which I agonized about the possibilities, Rose mentioned that she too had noted fasciculations of the muscles of her face and eyelids. Her symptoms were like mine, although much less pronounced, and it suddenly occurred to me that we both shared an unusual exposure—to the organophosphate compound DDVP in the Shell strips we were testing. Significantly in retrospect, none of our three children had any symptoms that might have been related. It occurred to me that my family's symptoms depended on the degree of exposure to the Shell strips: I had the greatest exposure and pronounced symptoms, Rose had intermediate exposure and lesser symptoms, and our three children had the least exposure and no symptoms. Furthermore, Rose and I started having symptoms in the spring, presumably after higher cumulative indoor exposures during the cold winter months in Lahore.

Back then, experience with organophosphate insecticides was limited, so only acute symptoms, and not chronic toxicity, had been recognized. Thus the differential diagnosis for my symptoms was limited to one condition—amyotrophic lateral sclerosis ("Lou Gehrig's disease")—which is ominously characterized by relentlessly progressing and ultimately fatal paralysis. Since ALS was considered rare and not communicable, it seemed too much of a coincidence that two people in the same family would develop the first symptoms at the same time.

I realized from my epidemiological training and experience that the evidence was only preliminary, but in my mind, it clearly suggested the need for further inquiry. Our unusual experiences in Pakistan had incidentally led to an informal case-control study with two patients and three controls. However, the striking dose-response effect—greater exposure associated with more pronounced symptoms—considerably strengthened my suspicion. Given how much emphasis the University of Maryland's program had given to DDVP for mosquito control to reduce the enormous worldwide problem of malaria, I figured a lot of people could be exposed to the insecticide, and therefore felt further studies of its safety were warranted.

I outlined my proposal of insecticide toxicity and contacted Don Schleissmann, an EIS alumnus who had worked most of his career in mosquito-transmitted diseases, to ask who I could consult about it. He identified a colleague who was one of CDC's lead experts on malaria control and had experience with DDT alternatives such as DDVP.

Since this undertaking was not part of my new job, I did all the work at home using my own typewriter while I was off duty. I first composed a rough handwritten draft and then typed a detailed manuscript of about a dozen double-spaced pages on an original document and one carbon copy [41]. I talked to Schleissmann's colleague twice before he finally agreed to review the manuscript. I sensed he was skeptical that such insecticides could cause chronic symptoms.

I got no response from him for months, even after leaving several messages with his secretary. I realized he had a heavy work schedule that involved a lot of travel abroad, but so much time had elapsed that I sensed something was amiss. When I finally reached him by phone to ask his opinion and set up a

[41] I did this long before home computers existed, when documents existed only on paper ("hard copies").

meeting, he claimed he had not reviewed the manuscript and apologized that he had lost it, ostensibly when his office moved to a new location. He still expressed skepticism because he had never heard of such toxicity. As I hung up the phone, I realized I should have seen that—since much of his research in mosquito control involved the same kinds of insecticides— he had an intrinsic bias and was therefore not the right person to give an objective assessment.

I never did further work on the manuscript or showed my remaining copy to anyone else. The health issues were outside my expertise and job responsibilities, so I had no occasions to follow up.[42]

However, as it turned out, my concerns were prescient. Organophosphate insecticides like DDVP are now known to cause neurological symptoms, which can progress from fasciculations to death at higher exposures. Farm workers are especially at risk. Later in my career, my experiences with both sanitation and these toxicity issues proved helpful in drafting OSHA (Occupational Safety and Health Administration) regulations for comprehensive safety for temporary farm workers.

In fact, organophosphate chemicals are so widely used and have such pronounced neurological effects that exposure to them is

---

[42] For many years, I carefully preserved the carbon copy of that draft with the rest of my research documents. After I retired from CDC, I had all my research records shipped to Lebanon where I had a faculty position at the American University of Beirut. Due to shelling during the Lebanese Civil War, rainwater got in through holes in the roof of the warehouse where my household goods were stored and waterlogged all those records. The documents were essentially useless, so I had to discard all of them, including my only copy of that manuscript.

now at the top of the differential diagnosis for the once-rare symptom that I had—fasciculations. The insecticide inhibits acetylcholinesterase—the enzyme active at neuromuscular junctions and cholinergic brain synapses that suppresses synaptic transmission—the same mechanism that makes nerve gases like Sarin such deadly chemical weapons. Without normal controls on overproduction of neurotransmitters, the nervous system becomes hyperstimulated. While DDVP targets the variants of the acetylcholinesterase enzyme found specifically in insects, human neurological function can also be disrupted. The Environmental Protection Agency has almost banned the insecticide several times, and the Food and Drug Administration imposes stringent restraints on its use, including no human exposure when the chemical is aerosolized, and restrictions on indoor use of impregnated resin strips to rooms inhabited less than four hours per day. The FDA and WHO now realize the symptoms I had are a severe health threat and a natural consequence of exposure to DDVP, so the use we envisioned for that insecticide in malaria control is now banned worldwide.

In retrospect, we conducted our evaluation of DDVP for malaria control with a naiveté that would not be acceptable today[43].

---

[43] On a number of occasions, I had asked Shell scientists about potential adverse effects their insecticide strips might have on children. As products of an unfamiliar technology, the strips were a novelty in the test villages and attracted the attention of small children. The Shell officials expressed confidence in the safety of their product, and we all implicitly assumed the observed benefits outweighed the as-yet-unrecognized risks.

Despite the fact that insecticide release was temperature dependent, we were not advised to deviate from the recommended 4-month replacement schedule by season. During our research in Pakistan from 1962 to 1964, I do not recall anyone asking about safe disposal of the DDVP strips. Shell scientists collected them, but they did not warn us about environmental hazards, so I am highly skeptical that they were very attentive to those issues. However, in the absence

Public awareness and government oversight have since shifted tremendously toward far greater concern for safety and environmental issues that we hardly considered during the early 1960s[vii].

Interactions between the Enteric Diseases group and two groups of laboratory scientists

The Epidemiology and Laboratory groups were the flagships that led CDC's public health practice. In keeping with William Farr's dictum for fast responses in public health, Alex Langmuir recognized the need for committed professionals from all disciplines to be available to respond to outbreaks on very short notice, "like firemen." The Laboratory group had many distinguished scientists, but they were involved in their own laboratory reference work at CDC headquarters, and so were not generally available to get on the next flight to an outbreak investigation to provide immediate assistance. Langmuir made a persuasive case to CDC administrators to form a laboratory group under his jurisdiction to provide this capability within the Epidemiology group. Dr. John Boring, who features prominently in another chapter of this book, was initially recruited to lead that effort, and assembled an outstanding group who were ideally suited for this purpose. Thus Langmuir was assured that whenever a need arose, a professional ad hoc epidemiological laboratory team would be ready to go right away.

The Laboratory group recognized the need for rapid response in outbreak investigations and for microbiologists to participate in

---

of the most blatant environmental damage, virtually the only concern about insecticides at the time was circumventing mosquito resistance to their effectiveness.

those field studies, but could not put aside their scientists' own commitments. Therefore, they did not resent the existence of a separate laboratory group within the Epidemiology group. However, Alex Langmuir from Epidemiology and U. Penti Kokko from the Laboratory group had sparred over the process of forming two separate laboratory units, and some friction remained between them. That relationship became even frostier when Langmuir recruited me into the Epidemiology group on the very same day I interviewed for the position of Deputy Director of the Laboratory Division—after Kokko had invited me, paid for my travel, arranged a whole day for me to meet with his leading scientists, and offered me the job!

When I accepted Langmuir's offer in the Epidemiology group instead of the Laboratory group position, I felt I needed to make special efforts from the very beginning to forge a constructive collaboration. With my background, interest, and degree in microbiology, I developed close personal and professional relationships with many laboratory scientists. Fortunately, I had already established friendly professional relations with them and, recognizing CDC's best interests, everybody realized the need for a collegial working environment.

Among the scientists who interviewed me for the Laboratory Division position that I turned down were two of the most distinguished enteric diseases microbiologists, Drs. P. R. Edwards and William (Bill) H. Ewing. Edwards died within months after I was recruited in the EIS, but starting shortly after the Enteric Diseases group was established in the Epidemiology group, Ewing and I collaborated on a number of outbreak investigations published in CDC's *Morbidity and Mortality Weekly Report*. He passed away several years later, but I remember fondly our cordial and productive relationship, in which we had more than just our professional interests in common. We had served in the military in Italy during World War II around the same time but in different activities and military units. We bonded in a way that strengthened my ties with the Laboratory group, and on several occasions he was a source of expertise valuable to me and to the Enteric Diseases group.

After Bill Ewing retired, several others (Al Balows, Bud Dowell, George Hermann, John Feeley, and Jim Farmer) took over his position in the enteric diseases Laboratory group. I worked with all of them on outbreak investigations. Al Balows had expertise outside my niche in enteric diseases, but we served together as WHO consultants in various cholera control missions in Middle East countries. Bud Dowell worked primarily in botulism, so we authored several papers on that topic [2-4], while Hermann and I worked together on a typhoid outbreak [5]. John Feeley's expertise was vibrio microbiology, so he and I published together on four cholera studies [6-9] and one article identifying enterotoxigenic *E. coli*, which incorporated the gene for a toxin similar to the cholera toxin into its genome, as the primary bacterial cause of traveler's diarrhea in Mexico City [10]. My professional relationship with Jim Farmer was especially strong and has continued after our retirements as a partnership in private enteric diseases consultations. At CDC, Jim and I published three articles on salmonellosis [5, 11, 12] and collaborated on several other surveillance and outbreak investigation issues; quite recently, we collaborated on a publication on important issues for establishing causation in enteric infections [13].

During the time I was at CDC, a strong bond existed between epidemiologists in the Enteric Diseases group and microbiologists in both Epidemiology and Laboratory groups that facilitated the emergence of a strong enteric diseases presence. I believe that camaraderie and collaboration helped establish a foundation from which the Enteric Disease group grew as a strong and healthy presence within CDC for public health practice. Many years later, epidemiology and laboratory were integrated, and this has worked well over the years.

The origins of the Epidemic Intelligence Service (EIS)

Public health practice at CDC is built on three pillars—a scientific foundation of epidemiology and biostatistics, a disease control strategy based on surveillance and outbreak investigation, and a philosophy of social justice. Alex Langmuir's role models were the earliest pioneers in epidemiology—John Snow and William Farr. He based the EIS Program on three cholera outbreak investigations they conducted in London: (1) John Snow's investigation, over several years beginning in 1848, of two competing companies that supplied water to the homes of the same London districts; (2) the 1854 Broad Street Pump outbreak in the Soho district, for which Snow is best remembered, and (3) another outbreak in 1866 after Snow's death investigated by William Farr. Each of these outbreak investigations underscored essential operational concepts adopted by Langmuir for the EIS—quick responses, use of diverse professionals, and the use of rates to quantify the impacts of different exposures.

Langmuir made the point that epidemiologists use rates as specific tools for public health practice, analogous to hammers for carpenters, pipe wrenches for plumbers, scalpels for surgeons, or forceps for gynecologists. He underscored the fact that the calculation of rates is just fourth grade arithmetic: using cases as numerators, the population at risk as the denominators, and expressed per unit time. Comparison of the number of illnesses with the number of "controls" in the same exposure groups (who presumably had the same opportunity to become sick but did not) is instrumental in determining whether a given exposure was the likely source of an outbreak. A classic example is the risk of smoking based on comparing rates of lung cancer among smokers compared to nonsmokers.

EIS officers learn this systematic model of public health during a training course held in early July, within a week after they begin their service. Langmuir taught and I still teach these fundamental concepts that have always been integral to the EIS.

Alex Langmuir—a most important public health mentor

My job in Langmuir's office was challenging. He was a demanding taskmaster, difficult to work with at times, but the paragon of efficient administration—well organized and deeply committed to his EIS officers—and, above all, a dynamic leader in public health. He was a great teacher, with a charismatic, articulate, commanding presence underscored by his deep baritone voice and tall stature. He tended to dominate every conversation, but what he had to say was invariably insightful and profoundly important. The questions he asked were penetrating and lucid. During the annual EIS conferences he made frequent thoughtful and probing comments, captivating the attentive audience. He shared personal anecdotes and relevant stories that reinforced points he made. He was a gifted writer who measured every word. I wrote for him the first draft of many letters, often the third and fourth drafts as well. EIS officers complained when he rejected one draft after another of their manuscripts for publication in scientific journals and reports for the Weekly Morbidity and Mortality Reports, but his incisive critiques contributed tremendously to the quality of everyone's research and publications. I attended every professional meeting, took notes, and participated in discussions and decisions. The year I spent in his office was the best learning experience of my career. His passion for social justice was infectious, as was his zeal for disease surveillance. This year proved to be the best possible preparation for my CDC job, which lasted an additional 15 years. It also laid the foundation for my two subsequent careers—as Dean of the school of public health at the American University of Beirut; and as Director and later Division Director of Emory's graduate program of public health in its transition to the Rollins School of Public Health.

I consider myself especially fortunate that this position gave me so many opportunities to learn about disease surveillance from the master who made this expression so important in the lexicon of epidemiologists. In the next two years I was the only EIS full-time enteric disease epidemiologist at CDC, continuing to work closely with Langmuir. My experiences during that time and the rest of my 15-year tenure at CDC are the subject of the next chapter.

Alex Langmuir died in 1993. I have no hesitation acknowledging that he, out of all my mentors, had the greatest impact on my career. To pay tribute to him, the prestigious American Journal of Epidemiology devoted a whole issue to celebrate the history of his life and contributions. EIS alumni were invited to write articles to honor him. A colleague, Dr Stan Foster, and I enthusiastically responded.

In our discussions about a title for our article, we both recognized how often Langmuir cited the work and teachings of William Farr, whose pioneering contributions in surveillance are legendary. I do not believe in reincarnation, but I use the concept as a metaphor to make the point that Langmuir would have been the most likely person to emerge from Farr. Farr mentored the most influential health professionals of his day—most notably Florence Nightingale, Edwin Chadwick, William Budd, and John

Snow—all of whom measured rates in various ways to direct public health policies that evolved.

Even long after his death, Farr was the progenitor for so many other luminaries, among whom Alex Langmuir stands tall. For this reason, Stan and I used another metaphor to capture this idea—Langmuir "lighting the epidemiologic torch from the lamp of Farr; passing on this light of knowledge to the 672 EIS officers trained during his years (1949 – 1970)." Langmuir's work was continued by his EIS successors during my tenure—namely Philip Brachman and Carl Tyler—and many more after I left CDC in 1978. Through them, the EIS program has been replicated in many other nations.

I believe Langmuir had a far greater impact on the careers of public health professionals than any other person in our field. Those he mentored numbered in the thousands. They occupy the most prestigious positions in public health practice, academia, and industry. Several of Langmuir's deputies, including D.A. Henderson, Bill Foege, and Don Hopkins, have provided leadership that made possible the eradication of smallpox and, at this writing, the near eradication of guinea worm. Langmuir's students have played prominent leadership roles in every conceivable niche of public health practice and influenced every major public health policy. In our tribute, we compared Langmuir's contributions to counterpart leaders in parallel fields of medicine. We noted that he did for public health practice what Osler did for medicine, what Halstead did for surgery, and what Welch did for pathology. Among the many admirable traits the four shared were unique skills in organizing training programs that attracted the best students from near and far. In turn, each of his students cast a wide net in recruiting the best and most dedicated postdoctoral professionals.

References

1.   Goodpasture EW: **Histopathology of the intestine in cholera**. *Philippine J Science* 1923, **22**(4):413-424.

2.   Gangarosa EJ, Donadio JA, Armstrong RW, Meyer KF, Brachman PS, Dowell VR: **Botulism in the United States, 1899-1969**. *American J Epidemiology* 1971, **93**(2):93-101.

3.   Merson MH, Gangarosa EJ, Dowell VR: **More on botulism**. *California Medicine* 1973, **119**(3):65-66.

4.   Merson MH, Hughes JM, Dowell VR, Taylor A, Barker WH, Gangarosa EJ: **Current trends in botulism in the United States**. *JAMA* 1974, **229**(10):1305-1308.

5.   Baine WB, Farmer JJ, 3rd, Gangarosa EJ, Hermann GT, Thornsberry C, Rice PA: **Typhoid fever in the United States associated with the 1972-1973 epidemic in Mexico**. *J Infectious Diseases* 1977, **135**(4):649-653.

6.   Gangarosa EJ, DeWitt WE, Feeley JC, Adams MR: **Significance of vibriocidal antibodies with regard to immunity to cholera**. *J Infectious Diseases* 1970, **121**:Suppl 121:136+.

7.   Gangarosa EJ, Sanati A, Saghari H, Feeley JC: **Multiple serotypes of vibrio cholerae isolated from a case of cholera. Evidence suggesting in-vivo mutation**. *Lancet* 1967, **1**(7491):646-648.

8.   Merson MH, Martin WT, Craig JP, Morris GK, Blake PA, Craun GF, Feeley JC, Camacho JC, Gangarosa EJ: **Cholera on Guam, 1974: epidemiologic findings and isolation of non-toxinogenic strains**. *American J Epidemiology* 1977, **105**(4):349-361.

9.   Weissman JB, DeWitt WE, Thompson J, Muchnick CN, Portnoy BL, Feeley JC, Gangarosa EJ: **A case of cholera in**

Texas, 1973. *American J Epidemiology* 1974, **100**(6):487-498.

10. Merson MH, Morris GK, Sack DA, Wells JG, Feeley JC, Sack RB, Creech WB, Kapikian AZ, Gangarosa EJ: **Travelers' diarrhea in Mexico. A prospective study of physicians and family members attending a congress**. *New England J Medicine* 1976, **294**(24):1299-1305.

11. Fontaine RE, Arnon S, Martin WT, Vernon TM, Jr., Gangarosa EJ, Farmer JJ, 3rd, Moran AB, Silliker JH, Decker DL: **Raw hamburger: an interstate common source of human salmonellosis**. *American J Epidemiology* 1978, **107**(1):36-45.

12. Steere AC, Hall WJ, 3rd, Wells JG, Craven PJ, Leotsakis N, Farmer JJ, 3rd, Gangarosa EJ: **Person-to-person spread of Salmonella typhimurium after a hospital common-source outbreak**. *Lancet* 1975, **1**(7902):319-322.

13. Farmer JJ, 3rd, Gangarosa RE, Gangarosa EJ: **Does Laribacter hongkongensis cause diarrhoea, or does diarrhoea "cause" L hongkongensis?** *Lancet* 2004, **363**(9425):1923-1924.

Chapter 9: Surveillance Activities at CDC

My 15 years at CDC were marked with many extremely challenging but rewarding and diverse experiences in public health practice, including surveillance work as well as numerous outbreak investigations. The most important work I did during these years was to expand enteric diseases surveillance activities, encompassing shigellosis starting in 1965, foodborne diseases starting in 1966, waterborne diseases starting in 1971; and to provide assistance to the World Health Organization's expanding cholera surveillance programs in the 1960s and 1970s as they prepared for a global control program. I also supervised salmonella and botulism surveillance programs.

In this chapter, I will focus on my involvement with the development and oversight of surveillance systems at CDC. The next chapter will be devoted to specific experiences in outbreak investigations prompted by the findings of our surveillance tools.

The tools of public health practice at CDC: Surveillance activities and associated outbreak investigations

Epidemiology is a statistical science concerned with health and disease in populations. Thus, the essential task of the epidemiologist is to identify when a disease occurs in a population more often than would be expected ordinarily. The key statistical tool that epidemiologists use is the measurement of the occurrence of disease in terms of rates; they then assess whether these rates are above or below the endemic baseline for the disease. An increased rate of disease beyond what would be expected is called an outbreak or epidemic. Incidence is the rate of occurrence of new onset of a disease, calculated as the number of people who get ill divided by the number of people in the population at risk per unit time interval.

To detect when an outbreak occurs, epidemiologists monitor the occurrence of diseases to identify increases in incidence. The programs that perform that monitoring function are called surveillance systems. Since CDC is at the forefront of tracking down epidemics, surveillance is the first of two key aspects of its mission. Surveillance takes on many forms, both active and passive, depending on how important it is to find small outbreaks right away and how much effort we are prepared to spend looking.

The second key aspect of the CDC's mission is outbreak investigation. Once a surveillance program identifies an epidemic, by definition, more people are sick than usual, and one of CDC's primary missions is to find out why. This involves hands-on work, often referred to as field epidemiology, to help uncover potential sources of an outbreak. This will be discussed in more detail in the next chapter.

Our primitive technology

When I was working at CDC in the pre-computer era, the best surveillance programs we had provided raw data typed on paper as line listings with only the following information: patient name, age, sex, reporting state or municipality, date of illness onset, and pathogen/serotype. For the more-developed surveillance programs that I helped manage, the state epidemiologists sent reports of salmonella and shigella infections to CDC via teletype (a precursor to fax) on green paper. I spent hours each week searching these "green-sheets" for clusters of personal identifiers and/or strain. Our searches were extremely crude by today's standards—for example, I identified disease clusters at various daycare centers and at a bar mitzvah, respectively, by noticing the ages of patients and the similar apparent ethnicity of their surnames.

An even more primitive, and now completely obsolete, data storage and search technology that we used came in the form of edge-notched, "McBee" cards. I was already familiar with McBee cards from my first course in epidemiology in 1957 in San Antonio, and then I had used them while training at Walter Reed Army Institute of Research. This technology stored only the most basic information as hand-punched data entries in the edges of paperboard cards, each of which substituted for a single line listing of person, place, time, symptoms, and risk factors. To search these physical records for commonalities that might give clues in our investigation, we would insert a long, thin metal rod resembling a knitting needle, which would separate out only the cards with identical entries for that variable. Nowadays, McBee cards are affectionately called "knitting needle computers"—and are considered historical relics that are completely obsolete.

Even less-developed surveillance programs provided background information about suspected outbreaks, usually as narratives from state, territorial, or municipal epidemiologists. However, sometimes the only information we had came from newspapers, radio, or television, reporting lay impressions that outbreaks were in progress. On a few occasions, we learned about outbreaks from news reports even before local and state public health authorities knew about them!

In 1964, my first year at CDC, the entire professional staff had to attend a one-hour orientation lecture about the latest generation of computer mainframes. The latest innovation was that computers had become completely transistorized, but they still filled up an entire large room (in our case, in the basement of CDC), had a user interface only through punched cards[44], and required a large, technologically specialized staff for maintenance and operation. Obviously, those ancient computers could not perform any of the standalone functions we most often use on personal computers down to the size of smart phones— word processing, spreadsheets, calendars, etc.—and data communication between computers (the primitive precursor of e-mail) was only an area of seemingly farfetched research. Nobody imagined practical computers would be portable—it had only been 15 years since Popular Mechanics had written optimistically, "Computers in the future may weigh no more than 1.5 tons."

Alex Langmuir was not at all impressed with computers before the lecture, and his opinion did not change afterward. As he and I walked away from the orientation, he said, "Gene, this is a waste of time and won't amount to a hill of beans."

My involvement with surveillance programs at CDC

In my time at CDC, I worked primarily with six surveillance programs that fell under the purview of the Enteric Diseases group, which I describe below. They monitored incidence of (1) foodborne diseases (generally), (2) waterborne diseases (generally), (3) cholera, (4) Shigellosis, (5) Salmonellosis, and (6) botulism. I started the foodborne disease surveillance

---

[44] The machine-punched cards developed by IBM encoded information completely unlike McBee cards, as alphanumeric characters that ultimately became much more suitable for epidemiological databases. However, IBM cards almost seemed to be a step backward from a practical standpoint, since the punches were not directly related to data, feeding the cards into a reader was an additional annoyance, and computers had extremely limited capabilities for storing and analyzing information.

program in 1966, waterborne surveillance in 1971, and Shigellosis in 1965. The other three surveillance programs were already in place when I started working at CDC. The cholera surveillance program was under the jurisdiction of the World Health Organization, which engaged the CDC Enteric Diseases group (Epidemiology) as a partner and me specifically as a consultant.

Pathogen-specific surveillance

Salmonellosis, cholera, and botulism

In 1964, the beginning of my CDC tenure, I was the only and first full-time EIS officer involved exclusively with enteric diseases. Zoonotic (animal) foodborne diseases were under the purview of Dr. Jim Steele's strong veterinary group. They had been actively involved in various salmonella outbreaks—one attributed to contaminated powdered milk, another associated with dehydrated pooled eggs, and a third extending across international borders linked to a commercial cake mix product manufactured in Canada. These epidemiological investigations demonstrated the need for a salmonella surveillance program. On the strength and credibility of Steele and his group, the salmonella surveillance program was launched some time before I started at CDC.

I arrived in 1964 just in time to follow in Steele's footsteps and continue the supervision of salmonella surveillance. Steele was the most important professional mentor in my career niche in the enteric diseases. I had a close working relationship with Steele, since his office was directly across from mine when CDC was housed in a single building on Clifton Road. We often talked about salmonella-contaminated eggs and egg products.

225

Surveillance programs for cholera and botulism were already established by the time I joined CDC, and I began to supervise these programs right from the start. Findings from these surveillance programs sparked numerous interesting outbreak investigations, the most memorable of which will be covered in subsequent chapters.

Shigellosis

In 1966, I transferred from my administrative role in Langmuir's office to an operational role with responsibility for the enteric diseases. Two existing surveillance programs were already in place: salmonellosis and botulism. I initiated my first new surveillance program—shigellosis. It was a widespread disease of interest to the group known as the State and Territorial Epidemiologists, with whom I consulted closely in my planning. It was also a disease of great interest to the military. In the World War II era and post WWII decade, shigellosis was rampant during military campaigns and among recruits of all armies. Historically, it had been an important cause of disability that had impacted the outcome of military battles—a history eloquently documented in Hans Zinsser's *Rats, Lice, and History*. I was involved in this field during my Walter Reed Army Institute of Research (WRAIR) years, where Dr. Sam Formal, one of the most distinguished scientists in this field studying shigellosis, was one of my mentors. I was pleased to be able to continue this work and leverage the professional relationships I had built during my time at WRAIR.

Exposure route-specific surveillance

The surveillance program I proposed for all foodborne diseases was my most original contribution. Alex Langmuir was skeptical when I first proposed this, because surveillance up until that time had been disease specific, e.g., malaria, polio, and botulism. Despite my unorthodox approach to this program, Alex Langmuir had faith in me, hoping not only for my success, but also for an opportunity to develop a new public health tool. That surveillance system proved so useful that it was only natural to develop another one for waterborne diseases a few years later. Later, the World Health Organization (WHO) copied our approach for use in other countries around the world, and the proliferation of measurement sites and accumulation of objective data may have contributed to the movement for global safe water.

1. Non-pathogen-specific surveillance of foodborne diseases

In 1965, my second year at CDC, my primary job as an EIS officer was to build public health infrastructures that would help my group perform its missions. I saw a need for a systematic surveillance program for the entire group of foodborne diseases, and built support for its implementation in subsequent years. I envisioned extending that surveillance to include noninfectious diseases, such as those caused by natural toxins or manmade chemicals.

In the mid-1960s, that was a novel and somewhat controversial idea. Initially, Langmuir had serious reservations, because the focus of CDC's surveillance had always been on specific infectious diseases—such as malaria, polio, salmonellosis, botulism, and shigellosis. Langmuir was skeptical of what could be learned through surveillance on an extremely broad group of diseases with varied infectious and noninfectious etiologies and diverse clinical manifestations, having in common only their transmission by food. We called a meeting to discuss the pros and cons. Phil Brachman, my supervisor at the time, offered his enthusiastic support. I involved FDA and USDA scientists, who also helped promote the idea. Eventually, Langmuir agreed, saying, "Let's pilot it, see what we can learn."

In 1966, having assembled a collective mandate, I delegated the responsibility for the surveillance of foodborne diseases to Dr. George Curlin, the EIS officer assigned to our new enteric diseases group. He was thorough and enthusiastic, working full time on this project during 1966 and 1967. In 1967, another EIS officer, Bill Woodward, was assigned to assist in this effort. The three of us prepared a report published as CDC's first foodborne disease surveillance report.[1]

With increasing involvement of USDA and FDA, food industry participation, and enthusiastic approval of the State and Territorial Epidemiologists, foodborne disease surveillance expanded greatly during my CDC tenure. Laboratory procedures developed after I left CDC, like pulsed field gel electrophoresis (PFGE) and polymerase chain reaction (PCR), have made foodborne disease surveillance far more sensitive, to detect outbreaks much better, and extremely specific through molecular subtyping, to help track down their sources. Our foodborne surveillance activity served as a foundation for spinoffs that use those specific laboratory tools. For example, CDC's PulseNet was established in 1996 to provide surveillance and a state-of-the-art database for bacterial pathogens[45] that can be "fingerprinted" using PFGE [2].

2. Non-pathogen-specific surveillance of waterborne diseases

The success of the foodborne disease surveillance activity led to the natural conclusion that we should also conduct surveillance

---

[45] Subtypes of *E. coli* O157 and other Shiga toxin-producing *E. coli*, *Campylobacter jejuni*, *Listeria monocytogenes*, *Salmonella*, *Shigella*.

for waterborne diseases, especially since I had so much experience with the prototype infectious pathogen—cholera. Our experience showed right from the start that we could monitor both infectious and noninfectious waterborne diseases with the same system.

Even at the outset, there was considerable enthusiasm for starting waterborne disease surveillance from other U.S. governmental organizations, like the Environmental Protection Agency, to monitor diverse consequences of pollution from municipal sewage and industrial chemicals. In connection with their safe water programs, several international organizations, notably the World Health Organization, UNICEF, and the World Bank, also expressed an intense early interest that rapidly grew over time. In addition, commercial water providers wanted data about health risks to help with decision-making, planning, and engineering.

I had an ideal EIS officer for this task, Jim Hughes, who had a keen interest in starting a waterborne disease surveillance activity at CDC. He hadn't worked in foodborne disease surveillance, but as a member of the Enteric Diseases group, he was well aware of its six-year track record.

We got full support from CDC to initiate the program on a tentative basis without external funding. Hughes first established liaisons with interested governmental, international, and corporate entities. In quick order, Hughes got the waterborne disease surveillance activity functioning just as well as its established foodborne disease counterpart.

Interest in waterborne diseases was greatest in connection with safe water programs in the developing world. As waterborne disease surveillance became established at CDC, WHO considered our program to be a model and replicated it in numerous developing countries. This information proved especially valuable as the adverse economic consequences of enteric and other infectious diseases became more and more apparent. The improved data further documented the extent of risks of waterborne diseases, enhancing the scientific and economic basis for safe water programs.

Evolution of the surveillance systems we established

The successor to our foodborne surveillance system is called PulseNet [46], which was established in 1996. The PulseNet surveillance system casts a much wider net and uses much more refined bacteriological typing methods, enabling epidemiologists to identify widely dispersed outbreaks that may be characterized by remarkably few cases spread over many distant geographic locations. With those capabilities, CDC is able to recognize outbreaks that previously would only have been considered isolated sporadic cases, and their geographic separation can simplify finding common exposures, tracing pathogenic bacteria to their source, and recommending public health interventions with wide-ranging implications. This improvement in surveillance is made possible because CDC laboratory scientists developed a test called pulsed field gel electrophoresis (PFGE). It types bacteria by fragmenting their DNA enzymatically and then observing how the fragments migrate in an electric field. Each DNA migration pattern is so characteristic of a specific bacterial strain that it is like a biological "fingerprint," allowing public health officials to track pathogenic bacteria much the way law enforcement agencies monitor and investigate suspected criminals with fingerprint databases. Thus, techniques developed in our crude salmonella and foodborne surveillance

---

[46] http://www.cdc.gov/pulsenet/

systems are now sharper, more efficient, much more precise, and applicable to bacteriological pathogens generally. The success of the PulseNet surveillance system has encouraged its use in health departments throughout the world. Finding outbreaks by this means makes us safer at home, since outbreaks traced to travelers to and food products from disparate parts of world can now be identified much earlier and traced to sources much more efficiently. It has made possible safer food, a "win-win" for consumers and all those involved in food production. News media accounts of these outbreak investigations often come from CDC's Morbidity and Mortality Weekly Report, enabling readers to follow the progress of such investigations.

Aftereffects of our surveillance programs

Able enteric diseases EIS officers who succeeded me expanded CDC's programs for foodborne diseases and waterborne diseases, making them models for similar programs in many other countries. CDC epidemiologists have also incorporated new laboratory tools into surveillance programs that greatly enhance their ability to detect outbreaks and track down their causes, especially PulseNet [2].

I was very pleased how waterborne disease surveillance, more than any of my other projects at CDC, meshed with my interest in global safe water. Building surveillance infrastructures in developing countries provided an important tool for supporting the position and credibility of public health officials, especially for keeping national leaders honest. A routine for collecting and publishing health consequences of contaminated water seemed to be the best way to curtail the temptation and opportunity for public officials to sweep waterborne disease outbreaks under the rug to avoid short-term adverse economic consequences— and thereby ignore the long-term costs of poor water and sanitation infrastructures. Having seen this happen on more than one occasion, I hoped that shifting the focus to routinely collected objective data might counter the panoply of hysterical superstitions surrounding epidemics, instead converting outbreaks into "teachable moments" by emphasizing scientific data as the basis for rational public health decision-making by officials. I had experienced firsthand many examples when unbiased scientific presentations (including my own), had convinced public officials to support construction of sound water and sanitation infrastructures. And after all, deadly cholera outbreaks over many centuries convinced government leaders that large cities are unsustainable without investing in those infrastructures.

The synergy between these two related public health initiatives—disease surveillance and improved water/sanitation infrastructures—contributed to activism that safe water is a universal human right. A popular movement advocating global safe water started to take off around the time I left CDC. Most of my involvement with that movement occurred during my "next career"—in academic public health.

Getting a hint of what was to follow, I was excited to be invited to the International Conference on Primary Health Care held September 6 – 12, 1978 in Alma-Ata, Kazakhstan (now called Almaty). However, I was unable to attend because I had just retired from CDC and taken on commitments in my new position at the American University of Beirut. The Alma Ata Declaration was visionary in its broad definition of health (as multifaceted well-being, and not just the absence of disease), call for economic and political equality, endorsement of health as a human right, and insistence on governmental responsibility for health for all and social justice. Its emphasis on primary health care was vague and, more to the point, did not adequately emphasize more effective and less costly public health initiatives.

However, subsequent international conferences went much further in promoting adequate water and sanitation infrastructures, first in itself ("Safe Water for All by 1991"); next as part of a comprehensive approach to public health ("Health for All by 2000"); and then as a component of health, social, economic, and technological progress ("Millennium Development Goals"). At this writing, the global community is behind the schedule for most of those targets, but again, I hope objective evidence will finally convince populations and their leaders to make the required investments.

References

1. Woodward WE, Gangarosa EJ, Brachman PS, Curlin GT: **Foodborne disease surveillance in the United States, 1966 and 1967**. *American J Public Health and Nation's Health* 1970, **60**(1):130-137.

2. Centers for Disease Control and Prevention: **PulseNet**.

Chapter 10: Outbreak Investigations while at CDC—Cholera, Shigellosis, and Salmonellosis

Outbreak investigation is both science and art, requiring an intimate knowledge of the nature of the disease in question (i.e., its host, agent, and environment)—a skill pioneered by Semmelweis, Pasteur, and Koch—and strong capabilities in field epidemiology, which was pioneered by John Snow, William Farr, Alex Langmuir, and others. After disease surveillance identifies an epidemic, the outbreak investigators work closely with laboratory scientists to identify and characterize the cause of the disease.

The focus of outbreak investigation is field epidemiology, which is humorously called "shoe-leather epidemiology" because it historically (and still figuratively) required so much walking that it ostensibly wore holes in the investigators' shoes[47]. John Snow's tireless investigations were an early example. Field epidemiology involves getting immersed in the outbreak while the trail is hot, examining firsthand all the possible risk factors, eliminating those that are not associated with illness, and quickly identifying the source of the disease and its transmission process. At the site of an investigation, we investigators would collect additional information not accessible from our offices at

---

[47] One of the icons of the Epidemic Intelligence Service is the bottom of a shoe with a hole in it. I am very proud of two awards I have received from two EIS classes—a shoe with a hole drilled in its sole and a soldered metal sculpture of a stick figure man on a toilet reading a book. Those two objects nicely summarize my CDC career!

CDC, e.g., what had been ingested by people who got sick (cases) and those who did not (controls). To identify possible sources of an outbreak, we would then look for exposures that were common among cases but rare among controls [1].

I was involved in more outbreak investigations than I can count in retrospect, since each epidemic uncovered by each surveillance system would, on principle, trigger action to find the cause. However, in the setting of each surveillance program, I describe below some outbreak investigations that were particularly noteworthy.

My experience with cholera surveillance and outbreak investigation with WHO, 1964 – 1978

CDC's mandate, mission, and focus are primarily national. Thus, the World Health Organization (WHO), and not CDC, conducted surveillance of cholera because it was an international phenomenon outside our jurisdiction and so diffuse that it relied on all affected countries to report to an international organization. The two key people at WHO with whom I worked in cholera surveillance were Branco Cviejtanovic and Dhiman Barua, who were stationed at WHO headquarters in Geneva, Switzerland. I worked with them in various ways described below.

The seventh cholera pandemic sweeps across South Asia into Middle East and Europe

In the years of my CDC tenure, cholera-related activities featured prominently. The disease became pandemic in 1960, while I was working in Bangkok, as a new biotype (El Tor) emerged. The disease spread from its origin in Southeast Asia, across South Asia, into the Middle East, then into Africa, and eventually into the Western Hemisphere. At this writing it remains endemic in Haiti in the Western Hemisphere and in Cameroon in Africa, with periodic epidemics (including an ongoing outbreak in Haiti).

During my CDC tenure—the 1960s and 1970s—the Middle East was relatively calm politically. I traveled extensively in practically every country where cholera emerged as a problem, working for WHO in numerous consultations in South Asia and the Middle East. I also coordinated investigations by several of my EIS officers in outbreaks that came to my attention during my WHO consultations. The umbrella coverage of these two global institutions enabled me to travel unimpeded with my American passport and/or my WHO-issued *laissez-passer*[48]. These dual credentials provided a great deal of leverage in advocating investments through decision-makers in ministries of health in the region to promote infrastructures for water and sanitation.

As the disease spread from South Asia into the Middle East, my WHO colleagues planned a global program for cholera control and invited me to participate. In the late 1960s ad early 1970s, I worked with this group in Geneva and in other sites. I participated in discussions and planning strategies for global preparedness in countries in the path of the rapidly westward spread of the pandemic. We helped plan studies to evaluate oral rehydration therapy in disparate clinical sites. I helped prepare the surveillance plan, which underscored prompt treatment of all diarrheal illnesses and recommended stool cultures for patients seen in public health treatment facilities and hospitals. Literature we prepared for cholera workers emphasized that cholera is easily treated and that no one who arrives alive at a

---

[48] Literally, *let the person pass*. This was a document that allowed me passage throughout different countries.

treatment center should die. We noted that saving lives is important for prevention, because cholera deaths were often the cause of unwarranted fear that could precipitate inappropriate and unproductive responses in the community. In workshops for physicians and decision-makers, we emphasized this point and encouraged investment in water and sanitary infrastructures. We focused on health education, emphasizing personal hygiene and especially hand-washing for prevention. I participated in the search for a director of this program, and was pleased that we recruited the best-qualified person, Michael Merson, who was an EIS alumnus I had the good fortune to mentor in the CDC Enteric Diseases group.

I have no way of measuring what impact I may have had during my years working on cholera with CDC and WHO, but I have a good feeling about what I accomplished. Based on my influence on the construction of water and sanitation infrastructures, those may have been the most productive years of my career in terms of lives saved.

Cholera in Iran, 1964

One of Langmuir's skills was matching unique opportunities to enrich the career development of his EIS officers. One such incident affected my own career. In 1965, the World Health Organization (WHO) and global news media highlighted the spread of cholera into Iran as the pandemic spread to the west from its focus in Southeast Asia. Recognizing this might be an opportunity for me, Langmuir asked if I wanted to be involved. I had no hesitation in volunteering. He called his counterpart in the WHO to make the necessary arrangements, and in a matter of days, I arrived in Tehran on a WHO cholera team assigned to advise the Iranian Ministry of Health. My role in Tehran was to assist in the investigation of the transmission of the disease.

In the first few weeks of the epidemic, the ministry of health reported all cases of the disease to WHO as per international agreement. During this time, I participated in a study of an outbreak linked to a local water supply. However, my epidemiological consultation was cut short when the ministry abruptly stopped reporting this disease because of inappropriate and unwarranted responses in countries near and far. For example, Switzerland refused to accept Iran's mail, while Russia closed its border and banned the importation of not only foods but also Iran's chromate ore! Tourist industries suffered first, but repercussions spread rapidly to other industries locally, nationally, regionally, and internationally. Because of the economic impact of these inappropriate responses, Iranian decision-makers took drastic steps to protect their economy—they stopped reporting cholera cases. News media were excluded from their deliberations, and control measures were kept secret. In that environment of panic and irrationality, our four-person WHO team was denied information we needed for cholera surveillance and outbreak investigations. Thus, my participation in epidemiological studies ended when the Ministry of Health decided they would no longer report cholera cases. They did not want me there.

Our WHO team debated how we could continue to assist under these constraints. Because of my prior clinical and laboratory experiences during cholera outbreaks, I volunteered at the Ferozabadi Hospital—Tehran's designated cholera treatment center—to teach clinicians, laboratory technicians, and students who had some English-language skills.

Physicians assigned to the infectious diseases ward of the hospital were woefully unprepared. None had seen a cholera case. Financial disincentives aggravated the problems tremendously. All treatment, even urgently needed oral and intravenous fluids, had to be ordered by physicians, but they only worked part time, in the cholera wards, leaving in the afternoon for their lucrative private practices. As a result, patients admitted in the afternoon, evenings, and early morning hours were seen only by attendants supervised by nurses, who were not authorized to start any kind of rehydration therapy without a doctor onsite. Thus, critical lifesaving therapy for these patients was delayed for many hours until physicians arrived the next morning. Since doctors were on duty only a small fraction of the day, most cholera cases arrived when no physicians were on duty, so many preventable deaths occurred due to untreated cholera within the hospital itself. In keeping with the climate of secrecy imposed by the Ministry of Health, the number of cholera deaths was concealed from me.

My work was cut out for me. I spent 10 weeks on call in that hospital, 24 hours a day, seven days a week. I saw every patient admitted during that time. During that brief time, when I supervised the treatment of over 200 patients, four died. Two of them died on the only evening I was not present during this entire period. I felt so bad. The third was an elderly man who arrived on death's doorstep while we were starting intravenous rehydration. The fourth was an infant requiring scalp needles not available at the time. I relied extensively on the only two health professionals who spoke English with moderate fluency: a nurse who fortunately worked evenings and a physician who worked only mornings. At the end of the 10 weeks, I left regretting that I had not been allowed to help conduct epidemiological studies, but grateful for a solid clinical and laboratory experience.

Cholera in Turkey, 1971

I was in eastern Turkey assessing cholera control resources in 1972 when I learned from a Ministry of Health colleague of an outbreak of cholera in the European sector of Istanbul the previous year. He was a middle-level professional familiar with cholera in his country. He could not tell me any details of the outbreak, but confided that no cases had been reported because of concerns about intense overreactions and economic repercussions that a number of countries had suffered after reporting cholera cases to WHO. At this writing, I see the same irrational reaction to the Ebola pandemic in Africa, where political leaders and newspaper reporters who misunderstand the nature of the disease and public health measures act irrationally on their own. My colleague could only tell me one thing that he had learned as one of the investigators—the most likely cause was cross contamination in old, decaying water infrastructure on one side of the city. The outbreak was primarily in the European sector of the city of Istanbul. I am unaware of any documentation of this 1971 outbreak, except for a WHO report [2] that we have recently found that documents a high number of cholera cases in the preceding year, 1970, followed by none until 1977 at a time when cholera was very prevalent in that part of the world (Table 1). This is consistent with what I learned from my colleague.

Other countries in the region were preoccupied with the same types of extreme control measures that in fact were inappropriate for the control of cholera. These included mass vaccination with what at that time was a questionable vaccine, severe quarantine measures such as I described in my Iran experience, and embargo and restrictions of products that in fact had no relation to the transmission of cholera. At my consultations I urged country decision-makers to avoid these

241

untested and unproductive measures, and instead rely on investments in infrastructure, surveillance for diarrheal diseases to enable early detection of cholera cases, and health education, especially for journalists—whose hyperbole often caused decision-makers to overreact inappropriately—but also for the public in general. For example, some decision-makers had lost their jobs because of stories published in local media by journalists who did not understand the disease. These journalists, and many medical and even public health officials, did not recognize the limitations of the vaccines, the lack of evidence of cost-benefit ratio at that time in using vaccines, the inappropriateness of using antibiotic drugs as a cost control measure, and the relevant transmission routes—in particular, they did not understand that the disease itself is not highly infectious by person-to-person contact. This type of misinformation contributed to inappropriate reactions by local physicians, public health practitioners, and most importantly, political leaders. To me, this is one of many examples of lost opportunities that I saw in my cholera experiences in countries of South Asia and the Middle East. Initially, they were all making the same mistakes, leading to preventable deaths, potential development of a bad habit of concealing disease outbreaks, weakening the influence of public health officials, and contributing to very high and unnecessary costs from implementation of ineffective measures. [49]

---

[49] WHO Report on Global Surveillance of Epidemic-prone Infectious Diseases (WHO/CDS/CSR/ISR/2000.1)   website
http://www.who.int/csr/resources/publications/surveillance/en/cholera.pdf

Table 1: Excerpt from WHO Report on Cholera, 1950 – 1980

Country	1950-1969	1970	1971	1972	1973	1974	1975	1976	1977	1978	1979	1980
Armenia												
Azerbaijan												
Georgia												
Greece												
Iraq	227							133	96			
Iran	5,977	19,663	344	322	55	304	2,966	2,100	10,836	264	1,856	1,599
Israel	185	1	11									
Jordan	3							152	427			
Lebanon	54								30		141	
Macedonia												
Syrian Ar Republic	49	5		505			67	795	2,362		689	
Turkey	384								17			
West Ban	239	1						42	3		9	
Gaza Strij												
Ukraine												

Cholera in Italy, 1973

While I was on another consultation in Turkey in 1973, my WHO colleagues notified me that news media in Naples, Italy had reported a cholera outbreak. I had intended to stop in Geneva to report to my WHO colleagues before returning to Atlanta, but was asked instead to return through Rome so I could discuss the cholera situation with Ministry of Health officials. I briefed my CDC supervisors, Drs. Phil Brachman and John Bennett, and asked them to advise my EIS officer, Dr. William Baine, that I wanted him to participate in the outbreak investigation. I singled him out for this assignment because he spoke Italian fluently— as an adolescent, he lived in Rome while his father served as a diplomat in the U.S. Embassy.

The Instituto Superior di Sanita (the Ministry of Health) asked my two WHO colleagues, Drs. Branco Cviejtanovic and Dhiman Barua, for assistance in the investigation of the cholera problem and inquired about my pending visit. The Minister of Health, Dr. Franco Pocchiari, and his Deputy, Dr. Duccio Zampiere, knew of my travel plans and were expecting me when I arrived the following day. I was informed that Zampiere was in charge of the situation, and I dealt primarily with him after they both briefed me on my arrival. They informed me, and it became readily apparent, that they were under tremendous pressure, especially from the tourist industry and an army of local, national, and international news organizations, who saw this outbreak as a historic event. News media had been sharply critical of the Ministry's handling of the outbreak, complaining that little was being done. Unsystematic observations that were widely reported in the local news media had blamed mussels known locally as "cozze," despite the fact that no epidemiological studies had been done to test this hypothesis. I was surprised to learn that they were considering having the Italian navy destroy the

244

mussel beds in the bay of Naples, on the assumption that they were the source of contamination. I advised that the evidence was weak, certainly insufficient as a basis for action, and recommended an immediate epidemiological investigation. The Ministry did not have an epidemiological presence at the time, so they enthusiastically welcomed CDC's help in the investigation. I mentioned that an EIS officer who spoke Italian fluently was available to help. Without hesitation, they accepted. I placed a call to Atlanta to activate the plan, and Baine came on the next flight.

With the tourist industry collapsing and news media reporters demanding action, the Minister, personally concerned about the Ministry's image, succumbed to the pressure. Even as Baine was en route, an Italian minesweeper destroyed the mussel beds in the Bay of Naples with explosives. Predictably, that action dealt a substantial blow to the industry.

Baine arrived the following day. After his introductions and briefing he began his investigation. He teamed with Dr. Donato Greco, a physician who had worked in the hospital in Naples where many of the cholera cases were treated. In a matter of a few days the Baine/Greco team, augmented by bacteriologists and other professionals, completed a case-control study confirming that the vehicle of transmission was indeed the mussels. Most important, however, they showed the mussels were not contaminated in the beds where they were harvested, but rather by contaminated water from the bay that used in seafood markets to keep the mussels "moist and fresh." Their epidemiological data underscored the point that the navy's destruction of the mussel bed was costly, unnecessary, and inappropriate [3].

In the following months, the Baine/Greco team conducted other cholera investigations in Italy and Sardinia, identifying disease transmission vehicles and their sources. This investigative team convincingly demonstrated the efficacy of CDC's science-based epidemiological approach. The Ministry of Health asked for Baine to conduct expanded epidemiological training and surveillance. We welcomed this collaboration. Baine provided outstanding leadership, laying the foundation for a strong epidemiological presence in Italy's Ministry of Health.

I attended a second meeting several months later in Rome to discuss the epidemiological findings of the Baine/Greco team. Their work was so helpful and so well received that it led to the institutionalization of this epidemiological model in the Ministry of Health. This episode provided a prototype for CDC's now-famous "Field Epidemiological Training Programs." [50] The success and prestige of those programs have convinced countries throughout the world to deploy epidemiological resources rapidly when disease outbreaks occur. This public health innovation has become especially important to control diseases capable of crossing borders easily, e.g., via modern day travel.

Greco later became the country's ranking epidemiologist in what had become a large presence in the Ministry of Health. On May 2, 2001, he invited me to speak about the 1973 cholera experience at the Instituto Superiore di Sanita in Rome. The event was a memorial for the death of Duccio Zampieri, who was among the most accomplished and respected public health professionals in Italy. As I was writing this chapter I remembered and found the booklet prepared for this auspicious occasion. I paraphrase

---

[50] http://www.cdc.gov/globalhealth/healthprotection/fetp/

below how the booklet described the situation leading to the 1973 cholera crisis:

The findings of the cholera investigation published in Lancet in 1974 made it clear—that at the time of the outbreak Italy woefully lacked epidemiological resources necessary to deal with the problem. The cholera consultants from CDC and WHO— Gangarosa, Cviejtanovic and Barua—gave us the identical message: Italy must organize a group dedicated to epidemiology and biostatistics in ISS (Instituto Superiore di Sanita) to make possible quick recognition and the best and most appropriate responses to prevent such crises.

Baine's brilliant work was yet another instance of a new generation of epidemiologists successfully carrying Langmuir's public health torch to a new country.

In one of the courses taught at Emory, Dr. Robert V. Tauxe, who has at this writing a comparable position at CDC that I had at the time of these events[51], lauded Baine's accomplishments. Tauxe singled out the methodology of Baine's novel case-control study, which recruited controls from the same neighborhoods from which cases had been identified and then matched cases and controls by sex and approximate age. In the decade that followed, a number of other Field Epidemiology Training Programs were established in several countries to replicate the Baine/Greco model. The leadership for these programs came from Dr. Phillip S. Brachman, who succeeded Langmuir as Director of the Epidemiology group. During the remainder of my CDC tenure, I lectured and assisted Brachman in establishing these programs in Kuwait, Saudi Arabia, Taiwan, and Thailand.

---

[51] Deputy Director, Division of Foodborne, Waterborne and Environmental Diseases, National Center for Emerging and Zoonotic Infectious Diseases.

After I left CDC, many more were established in other countries. A number of epidemiological studies in these Field Epidemiological Programs have been equally persuasive in changing existing public practices. Given that policy decisions in the wake of public health crises are still matters of public discourse, there is a continuing need to educate the public, physicians, public health practitioners, and journalists. These surveillance programs are important in providing factual information to educate these individuals and the public.

Cholera in Portugal, 1974

CDC's enteric diseases group was not expecting the seventh cholera pandemic to extend into Europe—to the extent that we initially thought the 1973 outbreak in Italy was a fluke. Living standards in European countries were on the rise, and their water and sanitation infrastructures seemed up to the task of keeping cholera at bay. As a result, we were surprised—but not unprepared—when Portugal had an outbreak the next year. The rapid westward spread of cholera left terror and chaos that European cities had not experienced since the nineteenth century.

Paul Blake and EIS officer Mark Rosenberg responded quickly and uncovered a very unusual story—a multisource waterborne epidemic due to inadequate water infrastructures that set the stage for a superimposed point source outbreak. As cholera invaded the coastal waters through pandemic spread, its earliest manifestations were widespread community outbreaks. When Portuguese public health officials initially responded to the outbreak, they found that many community water systems were contaminated with fecal coliforms—markers for the possibility of contamination with human feces and thus the danger of other more-serious pathogens including cholera. Even more to the point, that finding led to an ominous conclusion that even water infrastructures that had not been contaminated with cholera were vulnerable now that the organism was lurking in shallow waters throughout the country.

As a result, Portuguese officials made the decision to issue countrywide water alerts that all community water must be boiled before drinking. The advisory noted that if this was not feasible, bottled water should be used. One of the most popular bottled-water providers experienced a sudden and overwhelming increase in demand for its two products—one was a carbonated bottled product, the other was the same product not carbonated. Because of this surge in demand, the company was not able to meet the needs of customers without increasing the supply of bottled water. They quickly had to find another source of water to meet this need—which turned out to be one of the vulnerable (and in fact, contaminated!) community water supplies from which public health officials were trying to protect the public! This epidemiological study showed this outbreak was quite unusual—this company's bottled water was responsible for a secondary countrywide cholera outbreak that was even more widespread than the primary outbreak. Furthermore, the nationwide epidemic was actually triggered by the chain of events set in motion in hopes of controlling the sporadic outbreaks attributed to inadequate infrastructure!

The brand name of that company's contaminated water may have induced some people to choose to consume it in favor of other brands to allay their fears—it was marketed as "Agua Santa," which means "holy water." It's a well-known fact that clinicians develop a characteristic black humor to shield themselves somewhat from the empathetic anguish they feel watching their patients suffer. As we pondered these epidemiological findings and their public health implications, that black humor, transposed into the public health arena, led someone in our group to come up with a joke for the occasion: "Do you know how to make holy water safe to drink?" "No, how?" "Boil the hell out of it!"

Our case-control study revealed that the company's non-carbonated natural water-bottled product was causing cholera, but that the same company's otherwise identical carbonated water product was not incriminated. We inferred that carbonation kills cholera vibrios, making carbonated water safe even if it comes from a contaminated source. The most likely explanation why carbonation was protective is that the dissolved bubbles of carbon dioxide make water more acidic by dissociating in aqueous solution into carbonic acid. Vibrios are halophilic and relatively uncompetitive, i.e., they are poorly adapted to environments that are acidic and/or crowded with aggressive bacterial species, instead thriving in alkaline, sparsely populated habitats. This is the reason that the infectious dose necessary to cause cholera is extremely high—the extremely acidic environment within a normal human stomach kills cholera vibrios very quickly. Consequently, medical attendants who are in contact with cholera patients seldom acquire the disease.[52]

The case control study Blake and his colleagues conducted was so exemplary that WHO asked him to publish it as a guide for other investigators. Just as Baine had collaborated with his Italian colleagues in conducting their case-control study, Blake worked closely with Portuguese public health officials [4]. Both

---

[52] In contrast, many pathogenic viruses such as the noroviruses and Ebola virus have protective exteriors that are highly acid resistant, thus greatly increasing the transmission risks to caretakers of these patients. This is why clinical staff treating people infected with Ebola virus require layers of protective clothing covering the whole body and must carefully follow many other elaborate special precautions.

studies have served as useful models to guide other outbreak investigations.

A case of cholera in Port Lavaca, Texas—the first in the Western Hemisphere arising during the seventh pandemic and initially presumed to be related to the pandemic in progress[53]

Soon after the outbreak of cholera in Italy in 1973, a case of cholera was diagnosed in the small coastal town of Port Lavaca, Texas. It occurred at a time when cholera featured prominently in the news media, with stories of the disease's rapid spread through countries of South Asia, the Middle East, Africa, and most recently a European country leading to predictions that the feared disease would soon reach America. News media accounts dramatized and exaggerated the risk in ways that affected many industries—Italy's tourism, usually at its height in August, plummeted. Anxiety created by these stories underscored the importance of a thorough investigation. Thus, our Enteric Diseases group mobilized a team of 10 epidemiologists and microbiologists to assist an even larger group of local public health officials to investigate this single case in Texas. Our investigative team was on site a single day after our notification.

Our investigation began with an exhaustive history, leading us to search, question, and culture samples from the patient's work place, household and neighbor contacts, persons who worked or had eaten with him in past days, families of recent immigrants from cholera-infected places, foods in the patient's home (including frozen shrimp he had caught), sewage from his home, and sewage from the Port Lavaca sewerage plant. However, all tested negative using a variety of culture methods. The

---

[53] This in fact turned out to be a different strain from the pandemic strain—an endemic U.S. strain occurring coincidentally at the same time as the pandemic.

investigation also included cultures and serum specimens from the crew of 13 Gulf Coast freighters that had passed through the ship channel where the patient had caught shrimp on the days prior to the onset of his illness. No history or laboratory tests from these sources were positive for *V. cholerae*.

Fluorescein dye placed in a nearby motel toilet appeared in the motel's water supply the following day. With this presumptive evidence of sewage contamination of the motel's water supply, the names and contact information of motel patrons for the previous two months (52 families, 50 of whom lived in Texas), were located. Serum specimens and stool cultures were obtained, all of which were negative. All shrimp and water samples from the Gulf shipping channel in and around Port Lavaca were also culture negative. The only positive culture for *V. cholerae* was a Moore swab sample taken from the patient's septic tank. This strain was identical to that isolated from the patient. Although this strain was of the El Tor biotype, it was not otherwise characteristic of the seventh pandemic.

The investigation did not identify the source of the patient's cholera infection and found no evidence of transmission of cholera in his environment [5]. It was after this that we came to recognize (due to the work of several investigators including Dr. Rita Caldwell) that strains of vibrio cholerae are indigenous in the Western Hemisphere in marine environments where fresh water from rivers dilutes seawater, resulting in a gradient of salinity favorable to the growth of vibrios.

Public health lessons learned in this investigation were notable. The patient was properly diagnosed and treated by a physician who had never seen a case of cholera. The patient's quick and complete recovery underscores the point that the first line of defense against cholera are physicians knowledgeable in treating diarrheal diseases—emphasizing the importance of medical training on this topic. The second line of defense is the provision to contain the pathogen in feces—though the patient was shedding the organism in the environment, the septic tank at his home prevented spread into his community. The third line of defense is a safe water infrastructure, such that even if the environment is contaminated, water for consumption has been rendered safe to drink.

Thus, this investigation corroborates what we have learned about the risk of a sporadic case of cholera. Single cases of cholera that are not the consequence of a common source of infection do not usually transmit the disease. This is because transmission does not occur by casual person-to-person contact, as *V. cholera* is highly susceptible to gastric acid and thus requires an exceedingly large dose to cause illness (in striking contrast to more acid-resistant pathogens such as noroviruses or the Ebola virus, which spread readily by person-to-person contact). Single cholera cases that are not the consequence of a common source of infection, for which the Port Lavaca case is the poster child, have simply not resulted in secondary spread in modern nations [6, 7]. This reasoning also explains why *cordon sanitaire*, i.e., strict quarantine measures, widely used in some countries, is not effective in cholera control. The scope and magnitude of the Port Lavaca investigation provided a resounding exclamation point for the concepts of cholera control that CDC had been teaching and advice we and our WHO colleagues had been advocating in our global consultations.

The Port Lavaca case also underscores the importance of outbreak investigations to prevent unnecessary and often expensive measures, as occurred in the Italian cholera outbreak, when an industry was destroyed for lack of knowledge as to the cause of transmission.

Epidemic Diarrhea at Crater Lake National Park caused by a cholera-like pathogen, 1975

I conclude my cholera stories with this last one, which was not cholera but rather a most unusual outbreak of a severe diarrheal disease caused by enterotoxigenic *E. coli*, which produces a fluid-secretion-causing toxin extremely similar to that produced by *Vibrio cholerae* [8].

Crater Lake National Park in southwestern Oregon is considered among the most beautiful of our national parks and one of the great wonders of the world. It is a 250-square mile rectangular tract in southwestern Oregon created thousands of years ago by a volcanic eruption that blew the top off a mountain, leaving an enormous crater that has formed a 2,000-foot-deep lake famous for its remarkable clarity and deep blue color. It is among nature's most beautiful places. A national park was created to enable the public to enjoy this beauty.

The high elevation of the park accounts for snow nearly year round except for about seven weeks during July and August of each year. It is during this season that the park attracted almost 3,000 tourists each day in 1975. National Park rangers and their families maintain the park throughout the year. At that time, a concessionaire provided meals and other services for tourists.

It was in this setting that an outbreak of moderately severe gastroenteritis occurred in June and July of 1975. The outbreak was recognized during the first week of July among park staff and their families. The Klamath County Health Department conducted a survey of 317 of 345 park employees July 8 – 19, revealing an attack rate of 91% with the first case occurring on June 16. No deaths or serious complications had been reported. Water samples obtained from the water distribution system on and after June 30 were contaminated with coliform organisms. On July 2, a higher dose of chlorine was added; however, although some sections of the distribution system had chlorine levels of 1 – 2 parts per million, other sections had no measurable chlorine levels.[54]

On July 9, I received a mid-morning call from the Oregon state epidemiologist requesting CDC's assistance in the investigation of the outbreak. I briefed my CDC supervisor, Dr. Phil Brachman, and he called Dr. Jeff Koplan, who had recently completed his two-year EIS assignment and was in a preventive medicine residency on the west coast. He was instructed to go to the site of the outbreak to begin the outbreak investigation with Dr. Mark Rosenberg. After that call, I asked Rosenberg, a first-year EIS officer in my enteric diseases group, to get to the site as soon as possible. Arrangements were quickly made for him to depart on the next flight from Atlanta to San Francisco. That flight was delayed in its arrival in San Francisco, causing Rosenberg to miss his connecting flight to the Klamath airport, which was closest to the park. It was already nightfall when he arrived in Klamath on a later flight, so he rented a car, drove many hours over mountain roads, and arrived at the park at 3:00 A.M. the next morning. A large group of local decision makers had already been waiting many hours for the "CDC expert" to arrive to continue their discussions as to what needed to be done to control the outbreak. They confronted him with difficult questions that he was ill prepared to answer, and with laboratory reports showing large numbers of coliforms in the park water specimens. When Rosenberg saw the laboratory reports, he gave a very concise professional opinion: "You've

---

[54] The WHO suggests a free chlorine level of 0.5 ppm to ensure adequate disinfection throughout a distribution network (via CDC http://www.cdc.gov/safewater/chlorine-residual-testing.html).

been drinking pure shit." Drs. Koplan and Rosenberg, constituting "CDC's field team," left the meeting to begin their joint investigation. They collected what information they could before a briefing with "CDC's home team," Brachman and myself, scheduled for 10:00 A.M. on July 10.

In the meantime, several news-media journalists gathered at CDC, pressing for information to clarify news accounts of this serious outbreak at the park. Television accounts and newspaper headlines of this "massive outbreak" had already alerted the public. As Brachman and I made arrangements for this conference call, my secretary came into our office to tell us that several journalists were asking if we intended to close the park, so they could report our decision in time for the evening news. This startled us. We had not yet been in touch with our field team, who had just arrived at the site the day before, and so we were not aware that closing the park was an issue at this point.

Our conference call started a few minutes later. Our field team confirmed tourists getting sick in large numbers, and informed us of control measures already taken including hyper-chlorination of the park's water system the previous day (not yet evaluated). They also reviewed laboratory data, still inconclusive given conflicting readings at different locations, and measures to inform newly arriving tourists of the outbreak and potential hazards of entering the park. The field team also mentioned the pressure from various sources to close the park immediately, and the steps being taken by another group to keep the park open.

The field team expressed their strong feelings that the park should be closed, an opinion strongly reinforced by the news media. Brachman and I did not agree, as we did not have evidence as to how the disease was being transmitted; we felt there was insufficient information to support closure. The park's community water was suspect, but we had the assurance of the lead environmentalist in the Oregon State Health Department that it was not the water. He was not available on that July 10 morning to explain his position on this. A second point was that on July 9, the Park Rangers had hyper-chlorinated the water system. Water tests after this were still pending at the time of the July 10 conference call. We all agreed on a plan to advise arriving tourists about the risks. We asked the field team to collect additional information we thought would be helpful, and scheduled another conference call the next day to review the situation. But, even before the conference call had ended, my secretary came into the office and handed me a handwritten note informing me that several journalists waiting for our decision had "a 12 noon deadline to file their reports." The last sentence of her note was, "This is a friendly reminder!" Clearly everyone was under enormous pressure.

It did not seem consequential at the time, but our field team mentioned in this first field report on July 10 that a heavy snowfall the previous day was making it difficult to get around in the park. As noted above, such snowfalls, even this late in the season, were not unusual. Late in the afternoon of this same day, July 10, the field team called back to report that a bright July sun had melted snow that had been covering an ajar manhole several hundred yards from the hotel at the rim of the crater. Investigators had previously placed fluorescent dye in one of the commodes in that hotel. From this manhole, fluorescent dye had appeared, creating a visible trail running down the hill into the creek that drained into the lake. The cover was removed, revealing a large rock that had blocked the flow of sewage, forcing it to flow upward out of the sewer and onto the ground, where it ran downhill hundreds of yards into the creek. This creek was the source of the community water supply. Clearly,

257

someone had dropped that rock into the sewer—an act of vandalism had caused this extraordinary outbreak. Having this additional information, it was clear what needed to be done. All agreed—the park needed to be closed.

At the time, the CDC epidemiology laboratory had diagnostic capabilities not generally available in most laboratories in the country. Because of the cholera pandemic noted in the stories above, CDC laboratories had developed tests to identify cholera-like toxins and cholera-like organisms. These tests revealed that *Escherichia coli* strains in diarrheal-stool specimens of park personal and visitors tested positive for a pathogen known to cause the illness in question. It was identified as an enterotoxigenic *E. coli*—so called because it carried genetic material to produce toxins extremely similar to those produced by *Vibrio cholerae* -1, the pathogen that causes cholera.

After the park closure, inspection of the plumbing system revealed "a colossal mess"—extensive accumulation of debris in the entire plumbing system and water-storage facilities. The situation was beyond repair—the entire plumbing network had to be replaced. As early warning signs of plumbing failure had been ignored in previous years, not only in this but also in other national parks, this outbreak provided leverage for funding for extensive plumbing renovations in all national parks. Political decision-makers acknowledged that money was needed not only for this park but also for many parks whose water systems were equally outdated, crumbling, and in need of replacement instead of costly ad hoc repairs (which served only as band-aids, not solutions). I cite this as another example of cholera's "legacy"— prompting needed actions that would not have otherwise taken place. Admittedly, this was not a cholera outbreak, but I take the liberty here to cite it as an example of cholera's legacy because it was a cholera-like pathogen that caused this historically important outbreak that prompted sufficient funding for lasting disease prevention.

This outbreak set several precedents. It was the first time that an outbreak required a national-park closure. It was the first time that this particular strain of *E. coli* was isolated in a waterborne outbreak in this country. It was the first time that I was called to testify before a congressional committee to justify my actions in an outbreak investigation—as to why CDC did not recommend closing the park that July 10, 1975 morning when our field team reported their initial findings including their recommendation to close the park. Ironically, that recommendation was made just hours later—that same afternoon when we learned what caused the outbreak. The discovery of the obstructing rock was an important part of the epidemiological investigation, and was the information that prompted us to act that very same afternoon.

The pressure for action in the face of such a dramatic outbreak reminded me of the situation in Rome I described above, when news media generated pressure for the destruction of the mussel beds where the incriminated mussels were harvested. It was the epidemiological evidence that made it clear that particular act was inappropriate and entirely unnecessary. I have used these experiences in my teaching to point out the importance of making decisions based on evidence, including epidemiologic evidence. In more recent years other CDC leaders have had similar experiences—as for example in the Ebola outbreak current at this writing. News media plays such an important role in teaching the public, as well as in pressuring decision-makers—the journalist who writes the story has a great impact on public perception as well as the reaction of decision-makers. Given this influence, journalists must be seen as collaborators in making important decisions. This point was cogently underscored by the brilliant leadership of Tom Frieden, CDC

Director, and Anthony Fauci, NIH Director, during the Ebola pandemic. Frieden and Fauci were able to navigate these relationships, and so journalist reports underscored their own accounts. There is a similar pressure in every large outbreak investigation.

Those of us at CDC involved in the Crater Lake investigation prepared a class exercise requiring students to mimic positions taken on that critical July 10, 1975 morning by disparate groups; this exercise is intended to underscore the point that decision-making in public health practice depends on where one sits in the hierarchy of those affected. In this outbreak, the affected groups included National Park Service personnel, the concessionaire who served the park, Oregon state health officials, CDC field epidemiologists, and their CDC supervisors in Atlanta. The exercise calls for students to be part of one of these groups; a team leader represents the group, and all meet in a simulated exercise as the team leaders debate decisions that came from each of the groups, whose differing agendas affected their own positions. After this debate, a lecture summarizes what actually happened that afternoon when critical evidence became available. The closing lecture also underscores an important point in public health practice—that hyper-chlorination is not effective when pathogens are embedded in biofilms[55]. Our publication of this outbreak helps students learn from the experiences we learned from which we now teach. We learned from things not taught in books, things we wish we had done differently, and even some mistakes [9].

---

[55] Communities of bacteria embedded in slime. Because bacteria are present in many layers and embedded in slime, they are much more resistant to antibiotics and other antibacterial agents.

Figure 12: Gift from a student.
In my lectures, I had indicated and underscored often the importance of fecal containment in sanitation facilities such as toilets or latrines. This statue is a prized memento of my teaching career.

The last cholera activity of my CDC tenure—Set-up of contingency plans to deal with cholera should it enter in the Western hemisphere

I have noted above the growing concern that cholera would spread into the Western Hemisphere as the pandemic spread so

261

rapidly and so extensively in its western progression. We watched as the disease spread from Southeast Asia, across South Asia, into the Middle East, into Northeast Africa, and leap-frogged across the African continent into West Africa, all within a matter of two decades. We students of cholera presumed it would be just a matter of time before the disease would spread into the Western Hemisphere.[56] One of the two remaining questions was, when was this most likely to happen? The other was, where was it most likely to first appear?

Roger Feldman (whom I had recruited to be my successor in the Enteric Diseases group) and I were involved in these discussions with WHO's Western Hemisphere office, the Pan American Health Organization (known best by its acronym, PAHO). Our contact person in the Washington PAHO office was Karl A. Western, a seasoned EIS alumnus with important public health participation in the smallpox eradication program and in malaria control. We and others concerned met to discuss these questions and to plan a strategy to deal with what we all agreed was going to happen. From these discussions, a plan evolved that gave priority to physician education, laboratory training, administrative training for hospital managers, and nursing education. We studied shipping lanes and air-traffic routes. We all agreed the most likely first introduction of the disease would be in the Caribbean area, and particularly in Haiti—the poorest nation with the highest infant mortality rate in the region[57].

---

[56] Although a single case had been isolated in Texas, it was later determined to be endemic rather than related to the pandemic.

[57] Infant mortality is an indicator of health standards and sanitary conditions contributing to the spread of enteric diseases.

We agreed on places to offer short courses and faculty to teach. Feldman and I taught several of these courses—in Kingston (Jamaica), Rio di Janeiro, Buenos Aires, and Asuncion (Paraguay). Our selection of places reflected our thinking at the time that the first introduction would be in eastern locations of the Hemisphere. We did not select a western city, but someone in the group thought of Asuncion, an inland place somewhat central to western cities. I had no objection to this because it happened to be a place where most of my blood relatives lived, cousins on my mother's side who had immigrated from Sicily (see Chapter 1). Furthermore, one of my nieces, Janice Massi, was a medical student in Asuncion, and she was supportive of my mission to educate physicians in the treatment of cholera (the topic of one of my lectures). In fact, when I lectured there, she interpreted simultaneously. I remember a large attendance from western cities when I lectured there in 1973.

We were correct in our predictions on one point and wrong on the other two. Yes, the pandemic did spread to the Hemisphere. We were wrong in our other two predictions—that the pandemic in this hemisphere would be sooner rather than later, and in the place it was most likely to occur first. In fact, the first introduction was in 1991, almost two decades later than we expected. We were also wrong on the place—it started in Peru, not in the Caribbean area or in eastern cities. We were pleased that the case-fatality rate among treated cholera patients was exceedingly low in Peruvian hospitals—in fact as low as I recall in all newly infected places in my experience. I have believe this was not coincidental, that it was because we had trained physicians, as a result of which they were not afraid and were skilled in treating patients with the disease. So, we think the investment we made in preparation for the pandemic paid off.

Although Haiti was not the first place affected, the disease did eventually arrive and spread there. An earthquake and a hurricane in 2010 aggravated the transmission, and at this writing the disease has affected the other country on the same island, the Dominican Republic. The disease has found an endemic focus in these two countries. However, I am optimistic because again the legacy of cholera has provided leverage for funding of infrastructure investments for water and sanitation. Time will tell if these investments will be sufficient to eliminate the disease from these countries that share space on this island.

Surveillance and investigation of shigellosis and a pandemic of Shiga bacillus dysentery in Central America

Shortly after my return from Iran, in 1966, I transferred from my administrative role in Langmuir's office to an operational role with responsibility for the enteric diseases. At this time, I initiated my first new surveillance program—for shigellosis. This was a disease of particular interest to the military, given its historical role during military campaigns[viii]. I had been involved in this field during my Walter Reed Army Institute of Research (WRAIR), and was interested to return to the disease and to the contacts I had made at WRAIR.

When I requested an EIS officer for the program, Langmuir was supportive, as he was well aware of the public health importance of the disease in both civilian and military situations. I made arrangements for the assignment of Dr. Herbert H. DuPont in 1967 to the University of Maryland vaccine development group, in collaboration with my WRAIR colleagues. This worked out so well I had no difficulty when I requested a second EIS officer, Dr. Myron M. Levine, to work with DuPont in 1970. The assignment of two EIS officers to shigella vaccine studies was an indicator of the high priority given to the shigella vaccine work.

Shigella background

Shigellosis is a diarrheal disease to which only humans, not animals, are susceptible. Three serotypes of the *Shigellae* family are the most common strains causing disease. *S. sonnei* is the most common in developed countries; *S. flexneri* and *S. dysenteriae* are the most common in developing countries. The name *Shigella dysenteriae* honors the Japanese scientist Kiyoshi Shiga, a student of Robert Koch, who first recognized and described it. The disease it causes is mediated by "Shiga" toxins produced as it attaches to and invades the epithelial cells of the intestinal cells in the sigmoid colon, in the lower portion of the intestinal tract. One of these toxins agglutinates platelets, causing them to clump and thus resulting in thrombi that block small blood vessels. This can affect any organ, but the most commonly affected organ is the kidney; this can result in a complication called hemolytic uremic syndrome, or HUS.

Bacillary dysentery due to *Shigella dysenteriae -1*, often called "the Shiga bacillus," is by far the most serious shigella infection—it can sometimes be life-threatening. The infection causes cramping abdominal pains, loose stools with small volume and often with blood, mucus and pus, fever, toxemia, prostration, and painful defecation. Severity of illness depends largely on the health of the person infected, especially age. The highest attack rates for shigellosis, including this most virulent strain, are among toddlers, who abundantly sample the fecal veneer of the environments in which they play and are also vulnerable when caretakers who fail to wash their hands after defecation prepare foods they eat.

All shigella strains are moderately resistant to gastric acid, so that the number of shigella organisms required to cause disease can be as low as 10 bacterial cells of *Shigella dysenteriae-1*, as demonstrated by M.M. Levine (Mike) in human volunteer vaccine studies done during his EIS assignment to the University of Maryland vaccine center [10]. Since this small number of bacterial cells can be easily transmitted on fomites, such as doorknobs, handrails, or pencils, the disease is highly infectious. Toddlers who attend day-care centers and those who come into contact with them are at highest risk. Other susceptible groups include those with impaired nutrition, those compromised by chronic diseases, malnutrition, or drugs; or those who are confined in institutions.

During my WRAIR tenure and my services with the Armed Forces Epidemiological Board, I met and worked with a distinguished scientist, Dr. David Mel, an army colonel for what was then Yugoslavia who had developed and conducted field trials of shigella vaccines in his country. Mel's field and laboratory studies led to the discovery of attenuated strains of shigella, enabling the development of vaccines to protect against the two leading shigella, *Shigella flexneri* and *Shigella sonnei*. Because shigellae are relatively resistant to acid, it is necessary to neutralize gastric acid with bicarbonate of soda when administering attenuated strains by mouth. This procedure ensured maximum immunity. Mel's field studies were impressive, giving protection against both strains in excess of 90% and leading to global recognition. Encouraged by Mel's work, the AFEB (the Armed Forces Epidemiological Board) began supporting shigella-vaccine research in the lab of Sam Formal, my WRAIR mentor, at around the time I joined WRAIR in the late 1950s. One of my WRAIR responsibilities was to serve as a contract officer for shigella vaccine field work in progress in Yugoslavia using Public Law 480 funds (money accrued from the government sale of surplus agricultural products). It was this funding that later helped rationalize the shigellosis surveillance program and the EIS officers for this work. These efforts led to several publications [11-14].

Levine and I traveled on several occasions (also using PL 480 funds) to observe Mel's field trials in Yugoslavia and to plan our own field studies. DuPont and Levine had documented, through surveillance and outbreak investigations, that shigellosis was a serious problem in high-risk community settings globally—in particular in institutions for mentally impaired patients, day-care centers, and community settings where workers and visitors to these institutions and daycares lived and spread the disease. At the time, we envisioned that Mel's vaccine could be especially useful in military personnel and to protect institutionalized patients where personal hygiene was difficult to maintain. Our Enteric Diseases group frequently consulted with health departments, professional staff, and administrators of institutions and in communities affected. We expected that the use of Mel's vaccine would likely prevent transmission among those vaccinated, and through herd immunity would protect visitors, employees, and nearby communities. To prepare the field testing of shigella vaccine strains, Dupont, Levine, and their WRAIR and CDC colleagues documented the characteristics of the disease in custodial institutions, protection induced using the attenuated strains mentioned above, and baseline rates [13, 15-17].

A shigellosis outbreak in Central America

As the studies above were in progress, I received a call directly from Guatemala from a person I knew well from the literature, Dr. Leonardo Mata. I was familiar with his milestone work in a cohort of Guatemalan infants who had varied degrees of nutritional impairment linked to repeated infections. His call was a request for assistance to determine the cause and means of transmission of a dysentery-like illness that local physicians were diagnosing and treating as amebic dysentery. He had preliminary laboratory evidence that this was not amebic dysentery, but rather that it might be bacillary dysentery caused by *Shigella dysenteriae–1*, the Shiga bacillus. He said he needed help clarifying this because drugs used to treat amebic dysentery were dangerous, expensive, and ineffective, and the disease was spreading quickly and widely. My two supervisors, Phil Brachman and Alex Langmuir, approved the request. I identified a Spanish-speaking EIS officer, Dr. David Perera. In the tradition of the EIS, he and I got on the next flight to Guatemala.

In Guatemala City, we documented that the disease was widespread, killing many patients, especially children. Physicians—even older practitioners—had not recalled seeing this disease. They were astonished that so many cases were occurring and that case fatality rates were so high. Mata informed us that the debate about its cause was rancorous and protracted prior to our arrival in the summer of 1969. Practicing physicians were convinced the cause was an especially virulent strain of *Entoamoeba histolytica*, a parasite linked to a somewhat similar form of dysentery but rarely seen in outbreaks. Their reasoning relied on two factors—reports of laboratory technicians who claimed seeing the unicellular amoeba under the microscope in stools of dysentery patients, and poor responses patients had to antibiotic drugs.

This was the entry point for Mata. Although he was not a physician, he was well versed in the epidemiologic fact that amebic dysentery was a sporadic disease and had never been documented in epidemics. In his laboratory, he could not identify the amoeba in question. He concluded what technicians were identifying as amoeba were in fact phagocytes, i.e., macrophages and perhaps polymorphonuclear neutrophils commonly found in bloody mucoid stools of patients with shigellosis. He cultured these stools and found *S. dysenteriae-1*. He concluded this was the cause of the outbreak. He shared this information with his physician colleagues in clinical conferences, but they did not believe a non-physician, and many had put their reputations on the line in diagnosing and treating the disease as amebic dysentery. It was at this point, in the heat of this debate, that Mata called CDC for help. It was a turning point that we were able to confirm his conclusions with our own epidemiological and laboratory findings. Practicing physicians changed their treatment strategies accordingly. CDC's credibility was an important factor.

Our investigation revealed that many communities in Guatemala and in neighboring countries were experiencing similar outbreaks. The pattern was similar—the same confusion in diagnosis, a large number of illnesses, and many deaths. We found indications that Shiga dysentery had become endemic in the region, documented in reports in various sources published in 1915, 1928, 1947, 1951 – 1952, 1955 – 1956, 1961, and 1963, but that it had appeared only in small clusters of cases, with the exception of a large and widespread outbreak in 1915. The outbreak we investigated was decidedly different in its scope and severity. In our collaboration with Mata, we collected data recording baseline dysentery rates of 34 per 100,000 in the years from 1960 to 1966 as well as a sharp increase to 240 per 100,000 in the single year of our study from October 1968 to September 1969.

Before returning to Atlanta, I called and briefed Dr. Karl Western, an EIS alumnus working with the Pan American Health Organization (PAHO) in Washington. He had preliminary information that the disease was also in El Salvador. Mata called his colleague, Dr. Max Bloch, the Director of the Ministry of

Health Laboratory in the capital city, San Salvador to suggest that he call me. Bloch invited CDC to participate in his investigation. When I arrived in San Salvador, he had in hand an invitation for CDC to participate in his ongoing investigation. After my assessment I called for another EIS officer, Dr. Barth Reller, to assist in the investigation. His investigation continued during several field trips in 1970 that recorded what proved to be the largest Shiga-dysentery pandemic on record, with over 100,000 estimated cases [18]. It included several southern provinces of Mexico, Guatemala, El Salvador, Honduras, and Nicaragua extended in time from 1968 to 1973. Hundreds of cases among travelers were also recorded in the United States during this period.

The epidemic curve Reller constructed from Ministry of Health data showed cases of dysentery in the capital city of San Salvador had increased from only 1 or 2 per 1,000 per year during the years 1964 to 1968, to 3 to 4 cases per month, reaching a peak of 4 and 5 in September and October of 1969. In 1970, attack rates initially decreased during the spring months but increased even more during the summer months, reaching a peak of 34 cases per 1,000 inhabitants. An estimated 3.4% of city inhabitants throughout the city had dysentery in July of that year! Our investigation documented transmission by water. I know of no larger Shiga epidemic recorded. The geographic distribution of cases suggested multiple waterborne outbreaks.

Impact of the pandemic on our shigella vaccine studies

In response to the investigative findings from the Central America pandemic, we and colleagues from the University of Maryland and WRAIR decided to change the focus of vaccine studies from the more commonly isolated strains of shigella to this more virulent and deadly form of shigellosis caused by the

Shiga bacillus, *shigella dysenterae* serotype O1. Levine and I presented our findings to the AFEB. Levine presented a convincing and focused proposal for a vaccination program among school-aged children using the attenuated Shiga strain developed at WRAIR. We made plans to test this attenuated strain in volunteers.

After institutional approvals and informed consent from volunteers, Levine conducted challenge studies in a Maryland institution with a protocol that also had FDA's preliminary approval. The study was designed to elucidate the pathogenesis of the disease in a protocol challenging volunteers. This was a landmark study not only because it clarified the pathogenesis of the disease, but also because it defined a dose-related attack rate showing that as few as 10 organisms could cause the disease [8]. Such a remarkably small infectious dose has also been inferred from clinical anecdotes of transmission acquired by fomites such as a pencil. This "pencil anecdote" is attributed to William Ferguson, a public health officer in Michigan in the late 1930s. He mentioned it in a meeting I attended at WRAIR in the last year of my WRAIR tenure, 1961. The story of the outbreak he investigated included a series of cases, one of which was a case of bacillary dysentery in a Western Union delivery person who went to a home housing a migrant farm family. The delivery person required a signature in his log, which he obtained from a child about 10 years old. The child was asked to sign the log for the telegram using a pencil from the delivery person, who then proceeded to put the pencil in his mouth for just an instant; a week later he developed the disease. He had not touched the boy, entered the home or eaten anything at the home. This pencil-in-mouth exposure was the only contact he had with this family. Ferguson documented that a dysentery outbreak was in progress among migrant farm workers at the time, but the telegram-delivery person had no contact with them [19].

Years later, Levine's article reporting his volunteer study corroborated this small-dose transmission in Shiga dysentery. His data are the basis for the more recent inference of low-dose transmission of the Enterohemorrhagic *E. coli* O-157:H7 that cause a similar Shiga-toxin mediated enteric disease and similar complications. Indeed, the toxin that causes symptoms in *Shigella dysenteriae*-1 is functionally the same as the toxins causing symptoms in *E. coli* O-157:H7, consistent with the hypothesis that these toxins were derived from the same genetic source.

In the years of that pandemic[58], Shiga dysentery epidemics became a major focus of our interests at CDC. Collaborating institutions included the Central American Ministries of Health, WRAIR, WHO, and a number of academic institutions. At Emory University, Dr. Edwin Farrar in Sellers's Department of Preventive Medicine identified the toxins responsible for the disease from strains we provided him from our Guatemala and El Salvador investigations. He recognized and described these toxins as related to the Shiga toxin.

In 1975, plans for the vaccine field trial were abandoned because of two totally unanticipated developments. The first was the

---

[58] The epidemic met the criteria of a pandemic, defined as an epidemic sustained in time and covering several countries or regions of the world. The epidemic in question had spread to five countries of Central America and was sustained in time over several years. During these years we were involved in field investigations of shigella vaccines in three of the affected countries, numerous laboratories at WRAIR, INCAP, CDC, and Ministries of Health in the affected countries, and international studies involving WHO in Geneva and PAHO, and in Yugoslavia. Initially Bert Dupont and later Mike Levine at the University of Maryland and Sam Formal from WRAIR provided leadership for these studies. About 12 EIS officers and many laboratory staff participated in various phases of these studies. It was a massive undertaking at the time— somewhat analogous to the Ebola virus pandemic in Africa at this writing

unexpected but very good news that the pandemic rather abruptly came to an end. Thus, the vaccine was no longer needed. I have no evidence to explain why the pandemic ended, but I have a plausible explanation—the accelerated pace of water infrastructure development in response to news media accounts of our investigative findings. The second reason we abandoned our shigella vaccine testing was the finding in the laboratory that the attenuated Shiga strain we had planned to test as our vaccine strain had reverted from avirulent to virulent, posing a real disease risk. When this happened, we turned our attention to a new surveillance initiative—surveillance for cases of Shiga dysentery among returning tourists who had visited Central America. MMWR reports and news media coverage alerted and encouraged physicians to report such cases.

As the Shiga dysentery pandemic spread during the years 1968 to 1974, we expanded our shigella surveillance to include cases of Shiga dysentery among tourists returning from any of the six affected countries of Central America and Mexico. Dr. Jack Weissman provided the leadership for this new initiative. We identified numerous cases of bloody diarrhea among such travelers. Presumably, this led to many other infections among contacts of these travelers, introducing the genes coding for Shiga toxin into the vast pool of enteric bacteria in intestinal tracts of our American community. The severity of such illnesses, especially reports of moderate to severe bloody diarrhea, led some physicians to erroneously diagnose acute regional colitis, for which unnecessary colonic surgery was performed [18, 20].

Use of church death records to conduct surveillance of Shiga dysentery

During our 1969 investigation of Shiga dysentery in Guatemala, I recognized a particularly promising public health physician in one of our collaborators—Dr. César Mendizabel Morris, a Guatemalan physician working in the Ministry of Health. I made arrangements with Langmuir to accept him in the EIS course. After completing the course, he conducted a study using a unique church database to trace the origin and spread of the pandemic. His surveillance was based on the premise that families of the deceased need a burial certificate to bury their loved ones in church-consecrated cemeteries. Lay people could easily recognize dysentery or "disentería" because of bloody diarrhea—an almost-universal finding in such cases. Thus, he meticulously recorded these deaths in official community registers. He transferred these data to a spot map showing affected communities, and delineated the geographic routes of transmission. His subsequent "time, place, and person" analysis of the pandemic provided critically important information regarding transmission.

Mendizabel's data showed the pandemic started in 1968 in communities close to the Guatemalan/Mexican border, suggesting this as the initial focus of the pandemic. It had spread from north to south and throughout Guatemala and neighboring countries except Costa Rica. In Salvador, the death rate in 1969 was 250 per 100,000, a rate as high as seen in some of the worst cholera epidemics of the century. Mendizabel showed that hospital case fatality rates ranged from 10 to 15 percent, higher than the 8.4 percent mortality in non-hospitalized patients. The unusually high case fatality rate was no doubt due to vigorous treatment by physicians for what was erroneously diagnosed as amebic dysentery. This was particularly problematic during the first year of the pandemic. A second factor was the rapid emergence of drug resistance of these Shiga strains to commonly used antibiotic drugs inappropriately and extensively used especially in the early years of the pandemic.

This study provided one of the early records of the emergence of an episome-mediated multi-drug resistance enteric pathogen. The investigation of drug resistance expanded the Guatemalan laboratory's role into molecular epidemiology. The availability of sera stored at INCAP from Mata's earlier community studies of nutrition/diarrheal diseases provided serological evidence that the pandemic had derived from a multi-decade endemic presence in the same areas.

Mendizabal's documented his work in a manuscript that he sent around for comments All of us including Langmuir were impressed by Mendizabal's epidemiological insights and use of epidemiological skills taught in the EIS course he had recently attended. With these skills, he was able to trace back to sources from the earliest cases in a community, and from these cases he documented a time and transmission link to a focus close to Mexico's border with Guatemala [21]. It was truly impressive.

Outbreaks of salmonellosis

Salmonellosis and botulism were among the earliest of CDC's enteric diseases surveillance programs, beginning in the early years of the 20th century. Salmonella surveillance included both typhoid fever, caused by a unique salmonella, S. typhi, a pathogen host-specific for people; and "non-typhoid salmonella" that infected a wide-range of animals, birds, and reptiles identified and reported to CDC from states and some of the larger municipal health department laboratories[59]. I was assisted by first one and then a second statistician. The two of them established baselines—the number of every known salmonella strain reported to CDC since the inception of the salmonella surveillance program. I summarize below a few of the salmonella

---

[59] http://www.cdc.gov/salmonella/reportspubs/salmonella-atlas/

outbreak investigations conducted by the Enteric Diseases group to underscore how such investigations led to changes in food handling practices and/or changes in public policy.

The waning of typhoid fever in the United States

In the early 1900s, a doctor named Wade Hampton Frost conducted epidemiologic studies of typhoid fever along the Ohio River. These studies demonstrated lower incidences of typhoid fever in communities that had invested in water infrastructures as compared to communities that had not, information that played an important role in the control of typhoid fever in this country. Both Frost's studies in this country and John Snow's cholera studies in England may be credited with convincing decision-makers of the importance of investments in water infrastructures, ultimately having the effect of controlling an even wider spectrum of waterborne diseases. In each case, surveillance and outbreak investigation provided the scientific basis for important public health interventions.

It was during my CDC tenure that typhoid fever essentially disappeared in the United States, but—I hasten to write in this same sentence—I take no credit for this triumph. I just happened to be monitoring it in our CDC salmonella surveillance from 1965 to 1978. I believe it happened for various reasons including the fact that the pathogen *Salmonella typhi* is host-specific for primates, i.e., only humans and other primates get this disease, in sharp contrast to the rest of the salmonellae, nearly all of which are found in a wide range of creatures from insects (which they tend to harmlessly colonize) to people. In fact, the creatures that tend to be most favored by most salmonellae are those that have cloacae[60], i.e., reptiles and birds. Besides these biological host preferences, salmonellae are remarkably adaptable in environments with other bacteria, with whom they may share genes, creating more adaptive characteristics such as drug resistance and other traits facilitating their survival in more stressful environments. *S. typhi* can develop drug resistance, but to this date, they cannot multiply or cause disease in non-human hosts. Given their host preferences, *S. typhi* have largely disappeared in sanitary places where people have safe water, soap used frequently for hand washing, and private toilets. I remember one anecdote that makes this point: early in the last century, in studies of risk factors for typhoid, women whose occupations involved washing, e.g., laundry workers, or maids who washed clothes for many hours every day, had substantially lower rates of the disease.

Due to social investments in water infrastructure, which had already controlled typhus and malaria in the United States, in addition to better standards of living and improved food-handling practices, typhoid fever virtually disappeared in the U.S. and other developed countries during my tenure at CDC. Concurrent with the decrease of cases of typhoid, other salmonellae increased. The most likely reasons for this increase were changes in meat production—cows previously grazed in fields were herded together into "cow factories," immersed in their own fecal and urinary discharges, and preferences for pets with cloacae, such as chicks and turtles, are two of the most notable factors responsible for the increase in salmonellosis. Just as the industrial revolution led to better homes, i.e., window screens and indoor toilets that eliminated malaria from this country, somewhat similar quality of life factors have enabled

---

[60] A single opening that serves for the elimination of liquid and solid wastes as well as the passing of eggs.

the control of typhoid fever. Most recent cases of typhoid fever seen in this country come from traveling to developing countries. To underscore the dissipation of typhoid, my CDC Enteric Diseases group investigated only one large typhoid fever outbreak—it was in a nearby less-developed country [20].

Epidemic of Febrile Gastroenteritis due to Salmonella java Traced to Smoked Whitefish

Recurring outbreaks of gastroenteritis associated with smoked whitefish had been documented in the New York, New Jersey, and Pennsylvania metropolitan areas in the decades prior to CDC's Salmonella surveillance program. The three largest were in 1934, 1940, and 1955, each with several deaths. Late in May 1966, our surveillance program noted a sharp increase in the numbers of isolates of *Salmonella java*[61] from these same three metropolitan areas, from background levels of less than 10 per month to over 60. We called to verify that outbreaks were in progress. As this was an interstate outbreak, CDC already had jurisdiction, but as was our custom, we asked and received an invitation to investigate the one in New Jersey that had the largest number of cases.

At the site, our investigative team found high rates of illness among guests who ate smoked whitefish at a bar mitzvah in Edison, NJ and low rates among those who attended but did not eat smoked whitefish. We documented 12 separate outbreaks of febrile gastroenteritis in the three metropolitan areas that included over 300 persons who had ingested the smoked whitefish. We discovered that the fish came from a Canadian supplier who shipped the fish in ice from an unknown source. We traced the outbreak to one of the largest suppliers of

---

[61] Now known as *Salmonella Paratyphi B var L(+) tartrate +.

whitefish smoking plants in the area, which we designated as Company A[62]. The plant had been seriously damaged by an extensive fire. Major plumbing and structure repairs were necessary from the time of the fire until the time of the outbreak. During this time, the plant's refrigeration and freezer space had been compromised. We found no indication of employee illnesses prior to the outbreak, although two employees who processed the whitefish had concurrent illnesses similar to those affected in the outbreak. Their stool cultures and stool cultures of nine other employees were positive for *S. java*. Although many denied eating the product, it was generally accepted as inevitable that all employees ate the fish while on the job. Fish produced by the company were withdrawn from the market via voluntary recall[63]. The plant ceased operations as we conducted an extensive environmental survey. No evidence was found of environmental contamination.

Fish involved in the outbreak were caught in a lake in the Northwest Territories of Canada, dressed, frozen, and shipped by truck to Winnipeg, where they were repackaged and stored until February 1966. Thirty-one cartons of fish were shipped by rail to another fish company in Brooklyn that delivered four cartons to Company A on May 24. Fish in three of these four cartons were responsible for the outbreak. *S. Java* was isolated from one fish in the remaining carton from a Company A freezer. This

---

[62] CDC's policy is to protect companies from premature publication of suggestive but not presumptive involvement in outbreaks. Once there is definite scientific evidence incriminating a particular company, there is no hesitation in revealing the name of this company when it is important in the continuing investigation.

[63] Food recalls are generally requested by the USDA based on evidence from investigations. In the event that a company refuses to comply with the recall, USDA has the authority to remove the suspected products from the market.

assessment confirmed the fish as the vehicle of transmission of the outbreak.

The next phase of the investigation involved a collaborative trace back of the fish with public health staff in Ottawa, the capital of Canada. We found that fish from two other shipments from the Great Slave Lake (the second-largest lake in the Northwest Territories of Canada), one of which did not go through Winnipeg, tested positive for *S. Java*. Fish from these shipments had been caught and processed in June 1965. One shipment was in cold storage in a company in New York City. From this shipment, a total of seven fish, each from a different carton, were cultured; two of the fish from unopened cartons tested positive for *S. Java*. Thus, this part of the investigation proved that the source of the contamination was most likely at the Great Slave Lake.

The next phase of the investigation was at the Great Slave Lake. I recall clearly, because it was snowing on that July 2, 1965 when our team landed at Hay River, in the Canadian Northwest Territories close to the Arctic Circle. The EIS course in which I was enrolled with incoming EIS officers started the next day. Langmuir taught this course, as he had during every year of his CDC tenure. With his usual flare, the course began with a telephone conference call, a report from the field of an ongoing investigation. I spoke to the class, reviewing what we had found in previous phases of the investigation and providing a description of the setting of our investigation of the source of these recurrent smoked whitefish outbreaks. The town of Hay River was located at the mouth of the river by the same name, where it emptied into the Great Slave Lake. It was the northern terminal of the MacKenzie Highway and the Great Slave Railway; thus, it was designated the "Hub of the North." One of the students found it incredible that we were conducting our investigation in the midst of a snowfall on July 4th. Later that week, our team updated our findings. Fishing was the most important commercial activity, creating a boomtown population of 3,000. The town had no sewage facilities; sewage from local outhouses flowed directly into a river. None of the various sources of water were chlorinated. Although there had been no recent outbreaks of salmonellosis, outbreaks were reported due to *Salmonella paratyphi B* in 1950, 1951, and 1952; and in 1961 another caused by a different salmonella strain. The *S. paratyphi B* finding could have been *S. Java,* as they have similar antigenic profiles. Fish was washed in water that had been contaminated. Ice collected in blocks in the winter was used to pack cartons and crates of fish for shipments to markets. Water intake hoses were located a short distance offshore, in shallow water close to the effluent drainage from the same plant. Outdoor latrines were located close to the shoreline near the water intake from the same plant. Numerous samples taken from water and lake, and ice stored at plants were cultured; all had high counts of coliform organisms, suggesting fecal contamination.

We concluded that the recurring outbreaks of salmonellosis over a span of several decades in the Canadian Lake communities and in three northeast states in the U.S. were caused by contaminated sewage in water used locally, and in ice used for packing fish for markets in the U.S. The Memorial Day bar mitzvah outbreak we investigated in New Jersey was the largest of these interconnected and multifactorial outbreaks on record. The tri-state outbreaks resulted from a combination of circumstances that favored the multiplication of salmonella at the processing plant—1965's unusually warm Memorial Day holiday, limited cold-storage space compromised by a recent fire, and food handling practices that failed to ensure lethal end-stage cooking (smoking) temperatures. The rest of the story is not recorded here—the fact that this investigation leveraged funding to correct the infrastructure problems, thus saving a budding commercial industry in Canada and improving food handling practices in the USA. It is one of many examples of how surveillance identified an outbreak, the investigation of which enabled safe water and sanitation [23].

Epidemiology of an International Outbreak of Salmonella agona.

In just two years, 1969 and 1970, *Salmonella agona* emerged as a public health problem in the U.S., the UK, Netherlands, and Israel. This strain had not been identified prior to the fourth quarter of 1969 in the salmonella surveillance programs at CDC or any of those countries prior to the fourth quarter of 1969. In 1970, three isolates were reported from human and three from animal sources. In subsequent years, the number of isolates from humans increased dramatically and peaked at 195 in 1972.

With the cooperation of state epidemiologists reporting such isolates, we started our investigation in Paragould, Arkansas, as it was a place that had reported a large number of such isolates. What we found in common was that persons who tested positive had eaten at the same restaurant A. The state health department had also found several asymptomatic employees of restaurant A who tested positive for this strain. We selected five other restaurants at random in a survey we conducted to determine how often responders had eaten at the six restaurants, what foods they customarily ordered, and whether and what kind of intestinal symptoms they had experienced in the past three months. At the time of the survey, rectal swabs were obtained from each person interviewed, and environmental swabs and food samples were collected from restaurant A. What we found was significant difference in *S. agona* infection rates of patrons and non-patrons of restaurant A and no differences in patrons of the five other restaurants. Exact food histories could not be obtained from persons who were culture-positive, since most of them had asymptomatic infections, and the dates of their exposures could not be determined. Therefore, food-preference attack-rates were determined by asking 67 persons who visited restaurant A (17 infected, 50 uninfected) which food they usually ordered. Of the eight basic food items on the menu, the infection rate was significantly higher in persons usually eating coleslaw and raw onions.

We began an extensive environmental survey to determine the chain of transmission. Chickens served at restaurant A were purchased from distributor X, who obtained them from distributor Y; *S. agona* was subsequently isolated from the cooler floor of distributor Y. Distributor Y obtained chickens from five sources. Only one of these sources, a Mississippi firm, produced a 2lb chicken, the size preferred by restaurant A. Because cross contamination of the Mississippi firm and another major supplier to distributor Y, all Arkansas poultry firms were investigated. Both firms were large, USDA-inspected poultry operations with slaughtering and rendering plants, feed mills, breeder and broiler flocks, and hatcheries. The rendered byproducts of their slaughtering operations were used in feed for their broiler and breeder flocks. All stages were investigated and specimens were taken for culture at each location. *S. agona* was found from environmental swabs at the slaughter house and from offal (the internal organs of the poultry) delivered to the rendering plant of the Mississippi firm, but we could not determine how it got there. This is a brief summary of an exhaustive environmental survey that failed to identify the chain of transmission. I go into such detail to make the point that microbiological-environmental trace-back studies are important and necessary, but they have limitations. In this study, as in others, we failed to define the chain of transmission during this outbreak by this means.

Instead of environmental trace-back, we were able to use surveillance data from multiple sources to establish the chain of transmission in this outbreak and thus determine the source of the contamination. We knew from the survey above that that feed used for poultry in the Mississippi plant contained 8% Peruvian fishmeal. *S. agona* was cultured from this fish meal on numerous occasions after 1969. One of the first *S. agona* isolates in the U.S. was recovered from Peruvian fishmeal shipped to the southeastern states in the U.S. in March 1970. After this initial isolation, *S. agona* was reported with increasing frequency. Of the first 53 non-human isolations reported in the period 1971 – 72, 83% were from poultry and poultry feeds manufactured in southeastern states—all of which had imported Peruvian fishmeal. In the same period, *S. agona* also emerged as a public health problem in the UK, Israel, and the Netherlands—all had imported Peruvian fishmeal for use in poultry feeds. *S. agona* was rarely isolated in the UK before 1970. One of the UK's first isolations was from this imported fishmeal. In the years that followed, *S. agona* became the second most common salmonella serotype reported and remained among the most common isolated from human sources in the years that followed. In Israel and in the Netherlands, *S. agona* was also first isolated from Peruvian fishmeal in 1969. Thus epidemiological surveillance date from five countries provided evidence that the chain of transmission responsible for the emergence of this salmonella serotype most likely was from the Peruvian fishmeal used almost exclusively for poultry feeds. The simultaneous appearance of *S. agona* in several countries suggests a worldwide distribution from a common product. Although importing countries had imported Peruvian fishmeal for many years, *S. agona* was first isolated in 1969 [24]. This suggests that the contamination of Peruvian fishmeal was a discrete event that occurred at approximately that time.

Back to the question of our outbreak investigation—how did the coleslaw and onions in the Paragould restaurant get contaminated with *S. agona*? This is the most likely explanation: Contaminated chickens probably did not directly cause the infection, because cooking temperatures are usually sufficient to kill salmonellae. However, use of the same table and knives for cutting chickens and vegetables and inadequate cleaning of the table or knives after each use likely resulted in cross-contamination between the cutting surface and utensils. Poor refrigeration and storage of these foods for several days likely permitted bacterial growth in coleslaw and on the onions. After the initial contamination, the lack of adequate routine disinfection perpetuated environmental contamination.

This outbreak investigation is the story of a worldwide introduction and spread of a newly recognized pathogen, *S. agona*, from Peru to Paragould, Arkansas. Once established in the food chain, it has been transmitted by many foods, causing many outbreaks and countless numbers of illnesses. This outbreak illustrates the importance of disease prevention by implementing proper kitchen hygiene to prevent cross-contamination from working surfaces and utensils [24, 25].

An international outbreak of Salmonella eastbourne traced to contaminated chocolate

Between December 4, 1973, and February 15, 1974, 80 cases of infection due to *Salmonella eastbourne*, previously a rarely isolated serotype in the United States, were reported from 23 states. An additional 39 cases were reported from seven provinces in Canada during a similar period. A telephone case-control study implicated Christmas-wrapped chocolate balls manufactured by a Canadian company as the vehicle of transmission. *S. eastbourne* was subsequently isolated from several samples of leftover chocolate balls obtained from homes where cases occurred. Investigation of the factory revealed that the contaminated Christmas and Easter chocolates, and a few chocolate items for year-round sale, had been produced between May and October of 1973. Bacteriological testing of samples taken at the plant implicated cocoa beans as the probable source of the salmonella organisms that, in the low-moisture chocolate, were able to survive heating during production. This large international outbreak, the first reported salmonellosis epidemic due to contaminated chocolate, probably would not have been detected had the serotype been a more common one (it was identified by PulseNet surveillance). The additional finding of three other serotypes in another manufacturer's chocolate, even though unrelated to any known cases, suggests that salmonella infections due to consumption of contaminated chocolate may have been common in this era. This outbreak contributed to greatly improved production standards that have largely eliminated such contamination, resulting in chocolate products now with exemplary records of safety. Again, CDC's salmonella surveillance led to the recognition of this outbreak, and the investigation that followed played an indirect role in transforming this industry [26].

Chapter summary: leveraging experiences for the public good

The theme of this chapter is what I call the legacy of cholera, but during my CDC years other enteric diseases provided leverage for changes important for the public's health. Cholera featured prominently in my career in a way that enabled me to influence decision-makers to invest in infrastructures for water and sanitation. The salmonella outbreaks detailed in this chapter were important in changing the paradigms for manufacturing practices of a number of food products. The shigella outbreaks we investigated provided leverage to control shigella outbreaks in institutions and communities. My work involving the bacillus responsible for bacillary dysentery, *Shigella dysenteriae -1* , the Shiga bacillus, provided leverage similar to cholera in promoting infrastructures for water and sanitation. The surveillance of the latter helped us understand the enterohemorrhagic *E. coli* group—a collection of pathogens that also secrete a Shiga toxin and thus cause a somewhat similar disease involving destruction of an important blood element called platelets. These new diseases became prominent in the decades after my CDC retirement, but I played a role in their control as a consultant in preparing the legislation for a new food-safety strategy called HACCP (described in a subsequent chapter). The prompt for this legislation was an outbreak at Jack in the Box restaurants; mothers whose children died in that outbreak provided the impetus for change realized in the new food safety law signed by President Clinton in 1997.

In my CDC years I came to realize how influential the book written by Paul de Kruif *The Microbe Hunters* was in my childhood. I was one of many readers captivated by stories in that book about infectious-diseases pioneers who helped conquer diseases. As I reflected on what I wrote in the stories above, I had a sense of satisfaction in describing my professional journeys—starting with typhus in WWII Naples, my professional school experiences, my army residency experiences, my WRAIR cholera experience, my University of Maryland/Pakistan experiences, and my WHO experiences—each serving as building blocks for my professional foundation leading to my CDC career.

References

1. Woodward WE, Gangarosa EJ, Brachman PS, Curlin GT: **Foodborne disease surveillance in the United States, 1966 and 1967**. *American J Public Health and Nation's Health* 1970, **60**(1):130-137.

2. Centers for Disease Control and Prevention: **PulseNet**.

3. Baine WB, Mazzotti M, Greco D, Izzo E, Zampieri A, Angioni G, Di Gioia M, Gangarosa EJ, Pocchiari F: **Epidemiology of cholera in Italy in 1973**. *Lancet* 1974, **2**(7893):1370-1374.

4. Blake PA, Rosenberg ML, Florencia J, Costa JB, do Prado Quintino L, Gangarosa EJ: **Cholera in Portugal, 1974. II. Transmission by bottled mineral water**. *American J Epidemiology* 1977, **105**(4):344-348.

5. Weissman JB, DeWitt WE, Thompson J, Muchnick CN, Portnoy BL, Feeley JC, Gangarosa EJ: **A case of cholera in Texas, 1973**. *American J Epidemiology* 1974, **100**(6):487-498.

6. Collins CM: **Importation of cholera into New Zealand 1972**. *N Z Med J* 1973, **78**(496):105-106.

7. **Cholera in an American tourist--Australia**. *CDC Morbidity and Mortality Weekly Report* 1970, **19**(4):41.

8. Sanchez J, Holmgren J: **Virulence factors, pathogenesis and vaccine protection in cholera and ETEC diarrhea**. *Curr Opin Immunol* 2005, **17**(4):388-398.

9. Rosenberg ML, Koplan JP, Wachsmuth IK, Wells JG, Gangarosa EJ, Guerrant RL, Sack DA: **Epidemic diarrhea at Crater Lake from enterotoxigenic Escherichia coli. A large waterborne outbreak**. *Annals Internal Medicine* 1977, **86**(6):714-718.

10.	Levine MM, DuPont HL, Formal SB, Hornick RB, Takeuchi A, Gangarosa EJ, Snyder MJ, Libonati JP: **Pathogenesis of Shigella dysenteriae 1 (Shiga) dysentery**. *J Infectious Diseases* 1973, **127**(3):261-270.

11.	Eichner ER, Gangarosa EJ, Goldsby JB: **The current status of shigellosis in the United States**. *American J Public Health and Nation's Health* 1968, **58**(4):753-763.

12.	Reller LB, Gangarosa EJ, Brachman PS: **From the national communicable disease center. Shigellosis in the United States. 1964-1968**. *J Infectious Diseases* 1969, **120**(3):393-396.

13.	DuPont HL, Gangarosa EJ, Reller LB, Woodward WE, Armstrong RW, Hammond J, Glaser K, Morris GK: **Shigellosis in custodial institutions**. *American J Epidemiology* 1970, **92**(3):172-179.

14.	Reller LB, Gangarosa EJ, Brachman PS: **Shigellosis in the United States: five-year review of nationwide surveillance, 1964-1968**. *American J Epidemiology* 1970, **91**(2):161-169.

15.	DuPont HL, Hornick RB, Snyder MJ, Libonati JP, Formal SB, Gangarosa EJ: **Immunity in shigellosis. I. Response of man to attenuated strains of Shigella**. *J Infectious Diseases* 1972, **125**(1):5-11.

16.	DuPont HL, Hornick RB, Snyder MJ, Libonati JP, Formal SB, Gangarosa EJ: **Immunity in shigellosis. II. Protection induced by oral live vaccine or primary infection**. *J Infectious Diseases* 1972, **125**(1):12-16.

17.	Levine MM, Dupont HL, Gangarosa EJ, Hornick RB, Snyder MJ, Libonati JP, Glaser K, Formal SB: **Shigellosis in custodial institutions. II. Clinical, immunologic and bacteriologic response of institutionalized children to oral attenuated shigella vaccines**. *American J Epidemiology* 1972, **96**(1):40-49.

18. Weissman JB, Marton KI, Lewis JN, Friedmann CT, Gangarosa EJ: **Impact in the United States of the Shiga dysentery pandemic of Central America and Mexico: a review of surveillance data through 1972**. *J Infectious Diseases* 1974, **129**(2):218-223.

19. Block NB, Ferguson W: **An Outbreak of Shiga Dysentery in Michigan, 1938**. *American J Public Health and Nation's Health* 1940, **30**(1):43-52.

20. Rosenberg ML, Weissman JB, Gangarosa EJ, Reller LB, Beasley RP: **Shigellosis in the United States: ten-year review of nationwide surveillance, 1964-1973**. *American J Epidemiology* 1976, **104**(5):543-551.

21. Mendizabal-Morris CA, Mata LJ, Gangarosa EJ, Guzman G: **Epidemic Shiga-bacillus dysentery in Central America. Derivation of the epidemic and its progression in Guatemala, 1968-69**. *American J Tropical Medicine and Hygiene* 1971, **20**(6):927-933.

22. Gonzalez-Cortes A, Gangarosa EJ, Parrilla C, Martin WT, Espinosa-Ayala AM, Ruiz L, Bessudo D, Hernandez-Arreortua H: **Bottled beverages and typhoid fever: the Mexican epidemic of 1972-73**. *Am J Public Health* 1982, **72**(8):844-845.

23. Gangarosa EJ, Bisno AL, Eichner ER, Treger MD, Goldfield M, DeWitt WE, Fodor T, Fish SM, Dougherty WJ, Murphy JB *et al*: **Epidemic of febrile gastroenteritis due to Salmonella java traced to smoked whitefish**. *American J Public Health and Nation's Health* 1968, **58**(1):114-121.

24. Clark GM, Kaufmann AF, Gangarosa EJ, Thompson MA: **Epidemiology of an international outbreak of Salmonella agona**. *Lancet* 1973, **2**(7827):490-493.

25. Gangarosa EJ, Barker WH, Jr., Baine WB, Morris GK, Rice PA: **Man v. animal feeds as the source of human salmonellosis**. *Lancet* 1973, **1**(7808):878-879.

26. Craven PC, Mackel DC, Baine WB, Barker WH, Gangarosa EJ: **International outbreak of Salmonella Eastbourne infection traced to contaminated chocolate**. *Lancet* 1975, **1**(7910):788-792.

Chapter 11: The Legacy of Botulism Surveillance and Control

Background to botulism

Botulism fell under the jurisdiction of both the Epidemiology and Laboratory groups responsible for Enteric Diseases, because its most common exposure route is ingestion. However, it is important to realize that botulism involves clinical and epidemiological issues different from those of other enteric diseases. Botulism can be as life threatening as cholera, but with entirely different disease characteristics, mechanisms, and manifestations. Not only did botulism require development of different clinical treatments, but also it mandated public health interventions of an entirely different nature—primarily focused on food preservation—but with the same kind of urgency as cholera.

Botulism nicely illustrates other aspects of epidemiology that I teach, especially for disease surveillance and control. Whereas communicable disease has been taught in terms of human illness (host), biological features of the organism (pathogen), and environment (especially in terms of distribution and mechanisms of disease), surveillance programs can focus on simple, specific properties of the pathogen's life cycle that determine its epidemiological characteristics.

For example, vibrios, most notably the cholera vibrio, die quickly in acidic environments and do not compete well against other bacteria, but they have an affinity for alkaline, slightly salty water, so migration along their main niche, coastal estuaries, has determined the course of pandemics; shigella bacteria are not killed by gastric acid, so just a few microorganisms can cause disease; salmonella have an affinity for animals with cloacae, e.g., reptiles (especially turtles) and birds; the bacterium that causes botulism produces extremely hardy spores that can survive, grow, and produce toxin in preserved foods. These biological characteristics are critical adaptations that have evolved to provide each organism a secure niche in its Darwinian struggle for survival.

However, those characteristics also determine how an organism interacts with human populations to cause disease. As such, we can link the most fundamental aspect of a pathogen's biology to the design and conduct of a surveillance program. By contrast, for surveillance programs that focus on a single organism or a group of similar organisms, host and environmental factors are fixed, and therefore only indirectly affect program planning and operation.

This simplification is extremely helpful in public health education and practice. Characteristically, a single salient feature of the pathogen determines many aspects of the way a disease spreads. For this reason, I want to tell the story of botulism because it summarizes many of the same issues that I've described for cholera in a revealingly different context.

Host factors

In the setting of human (as opposed to veterinary) medicine, the term "host" refers to a human being and "host factors" refer to ways the body works that make it vulnerable to a disease in question. Host factors are of primary concern to clinicians treating patients.

Clostridium botulinum, the bacterium that causes botulism, produces one of the most potent toxins known. Just two billionths of a gram of botulinum toxin can kill an adult. It is a neurotoxin that induces severe paralysis, characteristically within 12 – 36 hours, although longer incubation periods can occasionally result from exposure to extremely low doses. The life-threatening aspect of botulinum toxin comes from its ability to compromise the function of respiratory muscles. Treatment for acute botulism requires prompt administration of botulinum antitoxin to reverse paralysis, and assisted ventilation with a mechanical respirator to sustain oxygenation until paralysis subsides. The fact that disease onset is so rapid, dramatic, and incapacitating helps clinicians and epidemiologists to identify cases, initiate rapid lifesaving measures, and start outbreak investigations to determine the cause and prevent further illnesses.

Pathogen

The characteristics of a disease-causing organism determine how human populations contract disease from it. As such, pathogen characteristics establish a bridge between the host factors and the environment. As I mentioned, this fact greatly simplifies the issues of disease surveillance, especially as related to CDC's mission.

Clostridium botulinum is a ubiquitous microbe in soil everywhere, so it is a common contaminant in uncooked foods. The organism is an obligate anaerobe that dies quickly in highly oxygenated and/or acidic environments but survives well in oxygen-poor, alkaline media, e.g., in many kinds of canned food. Two species are now recognized as a cause of botulism. When I was involved, only three botulism toxin types (A, B, and E) had been identified in outbreaks, but more have been discovered since. Botulism toxin can be rapidly deactivated by heating, so immediate ingestion of well-cooked foods can reduce risk considerably, even though the organism can still live in its inactive form.

C. botulinum exists in two forms—as "vegetative" bacteria when environmental conditions are favorable, and as inactive but remarkably hardy endospores in environments too harsh to allow growth. Only vegetative bacteria can produce botulinum toxin, so the presence of spores alone does not necessarily make ingestion hazardous. However, if favorable conditions return, spores can germinate into vegetative bacteria, which can then produce toxin. Canned foods can effectively provide *C. botulinum* a culture medium conducive to germination and growth during storage, so even a single spore can turn preserved foods into a ticking time bomb, even if botulinum toxin is not initially present.

Sporulation provides *C. botulinum* tremendous ability to resist extreme environments that readily kill most other microorganisms, like boiling water. Water boils at 212°F (100°C) at atmospheric pressure, preventing further increases in temperature, so attaining sufficient temperatures to kill *C. botulinum* spores also requires increasing the pressure. Eliminating all spores prior to canning requires heating food in an autoclave or pressure cooker to at least 250°F (121°C) for at least 30 minutes.

Environment

Botulism poisoning can be acquired through three environmental routes, listed here from most to least common: (1) food ingestion, (2) wound contamination, and (3) aerosol exposure. Historically, when the cause was initially unknown and then control measures were poorly developed, botulism was quite common. As with cholera, attention to reducing the incidence of botulism has had tremendous impact on public health surveillance, control, and policy—as well as food preservation technologies and practices.

Botulism emerged in Western countries in the early 1800s with technologies for food preservation, especially canning. Despite the ubiquity of *C. botulinum*, isolated organisms did not pose much of a threat until the emergence of a food canning industry: (1) Without proper safeguards, preserved foods could become a culture medium for *C. botulinum,* allowing the bacteria to grow and produce toxins. (2) Development of food preservation technologies made large-scale canning economically viable. (3) With widespread exposure to canned foods prior to understanding the microbiology of *C. botulinum* in the 19th century and development of safe manufacturing practices in the 20th century, botulism outbreaks became common.

In wound botulism, the organism invades the skin—typically through traumatic injury, intravenous drug abuse, or surgical incisions—and then multiplies and elaborates toxin in damaged tissues that are poorly perfused and oxygenated. The historical advances in sterile techniques essentially eliminated wound botulism, first in surgical settings and then for trauma patients. In fact, researchers are investigating therapeutic injection of subtoxic doses of botulinum toxin type A to promote wound healing by breaking the vicious cycle of muscle spasm, pain, inflammation, decreased blood flow, and ischemia (tissue damage due to underperfusion)[1]. Wound botulism outbreaks are still reported occasionally among IV drug abusers. Finally, a rare form of botulism has been reported in laboratory workers exposed to aerosols containing toxin.

Figure 13: Karl Friedrich Meyer, 1954.
Portrait of KF Meyer (1884-1974), at the age of ca. 70 yrs. Meyer was a Swiss American scientist who made major contributions to infectious diseases of man and animals, to pathology, epidemiology, public health, laws on hygiene in the food industry, and the planning of WHO. I met him during my military course in San Antonio, Texas, in 1956.

Botulism control in a historical context

Napoleon's government, recognizing the difficulties of feeding an army, offered a large cash award to the inventor of a practical method of large-scale food preservation. Nicolas Appert, a confectioner and brewer, noted that food boiled in a jar did not spoil if completely sealed, and won the award in 1809 by implementing that method using wide-mouthed glass jars. Initially, canning was much too expensive for commercial use, but over many years, glass jars were replaced with much cheaper tin cans; can openers replaced crude, ad hoc methods for opening containers; and poisonous lead soldered metal containers were replaced with nontoxic, stamped tin cans suitable for mass production.

Louis Pasteur extended Appert's empirical observation with a theoretical, microbiological basis for ensuring safe preservation of foods: (1) in 1858 – 65, discovering that heat (through what we now call pasteurization) could be used to eliminate harmful microbes and thus safely ferment wine, (2) in 1862, disproving spontaneous generation of organisms, (3) in 1878, articulating the germ theory. Pasteur's work was the foundation for the subsequent discovery that sufficient pressure and heat could kill microbes, thus establishing a reliable method for preventing preserved foods from transmitting infectious diseases.

I was privileged to know and work with Karl Friedrich Meyer, whom I met in my military course in San Antonio, Texas, in 1956. Meyer has been called "the Pasteur of the 20th century" for his landmark research, surveillance, and collaboration with the canning industry to eliminate botulism as a health risk in canned foods. In the early 20th century, when canned foods were cheap and plentiful but manufacturing standards lax, botulism outbreaks were rampant. Furthermore, given the variable sanitary standards among home canners, botulism was an even worse problem in non-commercially preserved foods. Cultivating "victory gardens" and home canning was encouraged as a patriotic contribution to war efforts in both World Wars.

An outbreak of botulism in canned olives in 1919 threatened the economic viability of the canning industry, which turned to the George Williams Hooper Foundation. As the first health-oriented institute housed within a university (the University of California at San Francisco), the Hooper Foundation[64] has been a powerful force in public health due to the visionary leadership of its directors. The first director of the Hooper Foundation, starting in 1920, was George Hoyt Whipple, who, you might remember, was my pathology professor in medical school in the late 1940s. At the outset of his affiliation with the Hooper Foundation, Whipple was Dean of the UCSF medical school and continued research he had started at Johns Hopkins on liver metabolism and its relation to blood formation, for which he shared the 1934 Nobel Prize in Medicine and Physiology[65]. At the request of the National Canners Association, Whipple hired Karl Meyer, who subsequently became Director of the Hooper Foundation for 33 years following Whipple's departure in 1921 to become the first

---

[64] Mrs. Sophronia Hooper donated the endowment that established the Hooper Foundation on March 7, 1914 in memory of her husband George Williams Hooper, a lumber merchant and philanthropist.

[65] The most dramatic result of George Whipple's research was his demonstration that raw liver was a simple way to treat anemia, even including pernicious anemia, which previously had proved fatal within 1-3 years. Whipple's observation inspired George Minot and William Murphy to identify the therapeutic factor in raw liver, isolate vitamin B_{12}, and thus cure pernicious anemia. All three men shared the Nobel Prize in Medicine for discovering a simple cure for a previously fatal disease of unknown etiology.

Dean of the newly founded University of Rochester School of Medicine and Dentistry.

Figure 14: George H. Whipple.
Nobel Laureate George H. Whipple was the first director of the George Hooper Foundation. He later became the Dean of the University of Rochester School of Medicine and Dentistry, where he was also the Chairman of the Department of Pathology and my professor in that subject.

Meyer supervised a botulism surveillance program extending retrospectively from 1899 as well as prospectively. Even more important, he helped the canning industry develop a system of tiered backup processes for sterilization in high temperature/pressure industrial autoclaves, meticulous quality control, detailed documentation of manufacturing conditions, factory worker training, and food lot tracking. As a result, with the exception of the years of the Second World War when exposure to home-canned foods increased, the incidence of botulism decreased steadily.

The virtual elimination of botulism risks from commercially preserved foods was a remarkable achievement of Meyer's leadership, for which he won the 1951 Lasker Prize. Many years later, in events that tangentially involved me (see Chapter 12), the food preservation system that Meyer's methods were extended "from farm to fork" as HACCP (Hazard Analysis and Critical Control Points) regulations and procedures. I feel that Karl Meyer did for botulism control what John Snow had done with cholera and Wade Hampton Frost with typhoid[66]. In that regard, the 1919 botulism outbreak due to California canned olives was Karl Meyer's Broad Street Pump.

The monumental work done at the Hooper Foundation at the University of California School of Medicine was commemorated in a 1938 mural commissioned by Franklin Roosevelt's New Deal and painted in a prominent building on the foundation campus, Toland Hall, by artist Bernard Zakheim, who was a student of

---

[66] Meyer's achievements and contributions to the canning industry were described as "no less than monumental": "Since 1919, the Hooper Foundation was largely if not solely responsible for the investigation that led to the control of botulism in the commercial canning industry." [LaDou, Joseph. "The Hooper Foundation." http://history.library.ucsf.edu/hooper.html]

Diego Rivera. This mural emphasized the landmark achievements of Whipple and Meyer (among a few others), with recognizable portraits of both: Meyer to the right, standing in front of a cupboard with canned foods and holding a chart entitled "Botulism" showing bell jars for food preservation, and Whipple on the left, working in front of a poster announcing his 1935 Nobel Prize with a distillation apparatus for isolating vitamin B_{12}.

My experiences at CDC with botulism surveillance and outbreak investigation

When I arrived at CDC, botulism surveillance had been in place for some time in Alex Langmuir's Epidemiology group as well as in the Laboratory group. However, it had not been assigned to any specific activity or person. The two activities were outbreak investigations, supervised by Phil Brachman, and surveillance, headed by D. A. Henderson. However, the jurisdictional lines between these activities were not sharply delineated, and even more to the point, our group was small enough that Langmuir directed many of the activities himself. After my administrative year with Langmuir, I assumed responsibility for all activities related to enteric diseases. For every botulism case reported, I briefed Langmuir, and together we planned details for all CDC responses.

Since botulism had already become a rare disease, market forces made the manufacturing and stockpiling of botulinum antitoxin prohibitively expensive if left in the private sector, so CDC's strategy was to provide the antitoxin free of charge when requested by a physician. The life-saving antitoxin was hand-delivered quickly by an EIS officer, leaving on the next flight to the patient's physician. Our target was to provide the antitoxin within 24 hours of notification, and sometimes expedited delivery via police escort from airport to hospital. We provided a trivalent antitoxin (produced by Connaught Laboratory) that covered all three types of botulism toxin (types A, B, and E) that were then known to cause illness in humans.

In addition to contributing to the care of patients affected with botulism, the assigned EIS officer quickly initiated an onsite investigation to establish how the disease had been acquired and determine what measures were needed to prevent further transmission. The EIS officer would then report to me from the field to discuss implementation and public communications. Langmuir was involved throughout.

The EIS officer at the site would also collect specimens for laboratory analysis. As previously discussed, the Enteric Diseases group strengthened collaboration with the Laboratory group while I was at CDC[67]. For analysis of botulism samples, we worked closely with V. R. Dowell, activity chief of the anaerobic laboratory. His research involved media for isolation, characterization, and identification of obligate anaerobe bacteria, of which Clostridia are the prototypes[68]. Together we collected and analyzed epidemiological and laboratory data on over 100 botulism cases.

We combined our findings with data collected from two earlier botulism surveillance activities—Karl Meyer's retrospective data

---

[67] Since I met a lot of the microbiologists in the Laboratory group during my job interview for the Deputy Director position, I was in a good position to work closely with scientists there, even though I took the job in the Epidemiology group.

[68] V. R. Dowell worked extensively with Steve Arnon and his colleagues in California, starting with a botulism outbreak I will describe below and continuing with publications on many aspects of C. botulinum.

for California extending back to 1899, and the predecessor to CDC nationwide botulism surveillance from the U.S. Public Health Service office in Washington, DC. My own contribution to this surveillance started in 1965. I was the first full-time person specifically assigned to this surveillance program at CDC's main office in Atlanta. I was very fortunate in having learned about botulism surveillance program from Karl Meyer himself in the military medical course I had taken in San Antonio in 1957 and in my interactions with him after his lectures. I called him at the George Hooper Foundation to tell him I was assuming responsibility for CDC's nationwide botulism surveillance and ask if we could incorporate his data in a manuscript we were preparing on botulism surveillance in the United States [2]. He didn't remember me, but recalled in detail the material that he and Jim Steele had taught to my class. He was very gracious with his advice and willingness to contribute the data he had collected.

We folded all these data into a single comprehensive analysis published in 1971 in the American Journal of Epidemiology, covering the period from 1899 to 1969 [2]. Since the data were selected from different sources using methods that grossly underestimated the number of outbreaks (especially during the earlier years) and almost certainly varied considerably over time, our report gave only a rough indication of trends that could not include the number of cases, but our findings were revealing. We noted fewer outbreaks of type A botulism with improved canning methods, but more outbreaks due to type E (which is more often linked to preserved seafoods, especially whale meat). The distribution of type of toxin contamination tracked spore surveys in regional soil samples. We also saw that more outbreaks were associated with preserved vegetables (e.g., beans, spinach) since vegetables were often less acidic than other commonly canned items (e.g., fruits). From 1960 to 1969,

305

there was an increase in outbreaks due to new and untested preservation methods accompanying rapid growth in the food industry. However, from 1950 to 1969, we did observe a decreased and decreasing case fatality ratio probably due to clinical advances, especially in respirators (helpful since botulism commonly affects respiratory muscles, leading to respiratory failure), and to CDC's more rapid delivery of antitoxin. The case fatality ratio, though decreased overall, was higher in adults than in children, probably because adults more often eat the canned foods that are most likely to harbor the toxin.

We also published CDC botulism surveillance data separately in three other peer-reviewed botulism surveillance reports, two clinical manuscripts dealing with the pathogenesis and treatment, and four textbook chapters [3-8].

Jim Steele saw Karl Meyer, who also did groundbreaking studies of zoonotic diseases, as his prototype for the veterinary EIS officers he envisioned. The illustrious work of those two famous veterinarians[69] easily convinced Alex Langmuir to give carte blanche for recruiting veterinarians into the EIS. EIS veterinarians have distinguished themselves in many aspects of public health during and after their CDC service.

I feel a special bond to the veterinarians with whom I have worked throughout my career, especially since my late brother Ralph was a veterinarian who worked in the Vermont Public Health Department from 1942 to 1943. Steele and I had a close working relationship during the early years of my CDC tenure

---

[69] The American Veterinary Medicine Association honors one veterinarian each year with a prize named for both of them, the Karl F. Meyer-James H. Steele Gold Headed Cane Award.

because of common interests in zoonotic enteric diseases and the fact that our offices at CDC were close together, encouraging frequent encounters and discussions in salmonella outbreak investigations in which I was the point person and he had so many professional relevant experiences. Our common interests and research in zoonotic diseases led to my being awarded honorary membership in the American Veterinary Epidemiological Society. I am proud of this citation, displayed on a diploma in my office.

Steve Arnon was one of the EIS officers I supervised during his assignment to the Enteric Disease group from 1975 to 1977. He and epidemiologists from the California Health Department investigated a pivotally important multistate outbreak of botulism in fifty-eight 3 – 26-week-old infants who had ingested honey containing botulism spores but no detected toxin [9]. Botulism transmission was not then associated with natural unfermented foods, like honey, but what made this outbreak investigation so remarkable was its discovery of a new mode of botulism transmission. Ordinarily, *Clostridium botulinum* growth is suppressed in the intestine, but when the intestinal flora is not yet developed (i.e., in infants) or has been compromised (e.g., by prolonged antibiotic therapy), botulism spores, unobstructed by competition from bacteria that normally populate the digestive tract, can find a favorable growth environment in characteristically alkaline segments of the intestine. In such settings, termed infant botulism and adult intestinal toxemia botulism, respectively, the pathogen can germinate, multiply, and produce toxin entirely within the gut. This was a historic outbreak in that it provided new knowledge that led to the discovery of the disease in infancy—at this writing, there are warning labels on many susceptible products such as honey[70].

Thus from remarkably insightful work originating from a single outbreak investigation, Arnon and his colleagues thereby identified two potentially life threatening clinical conditions, their associated risk groups, an unanticipated vulnerability in the human digestive tract to botulism infection, an unrecognized infectious disease transmission mode (via spores alone), and unusual in vivo (intra-intestinal) bacterial growth and toxin production mechanisms. Arnon was so excited and enthusiastic about discovering so many new aspects of this disease, centered around intra-intestinal toxin production, that I encouraged him to make botulism his career niche. I was delighted that he jumped at a perfect opportunity in California, the traditional home of botulism research and surveillance, to help start an Infant Botulism Treatment and Prevention Program[71], where he and his colleagues have continued groundbreaking work in the pathogenesis, treatment, and control of this disease.

The social contract for botulism control

Like cholera, botulism is a deadly and much-feared disease that altered the history of public health with new social contracts. The main difference between the social contracts for cholera and botulism were the public health roles that commercial industries played.

---

[70] Infant botulism is seen in infants usually less than two months of age who eat foods (especially honey) contaminated with spores. Infants with this syndrome have symptoms ranging from mild flaccid paralysis to sudden death. Loss of head control is a diagnostic finding.

[71] http://www.infantbotulism.org/

Water supplies and sewage systems are the social infrastructures involved in cholera transmission and control. Contamination of water and inadequate sewage disposal are typically the sources of cholera outbreaks. Of course, water and sewage companies have a commercial interest in keeping their customers safe, but the main effect of cholera outbreaks has been to make public investment in these infrastructures, regardless of their ownership.

By contrast, botulism historically was an uncommon disease until it became a consequence of commercial food preservation. In the transition period when canned foods had become popular but botulism contamination was not adequately controlled, commercial canners lost millions of dollars to former customers' fear of the dreaded disease. The 1919 botulism outbreak involving olives canned in California threatened to bankrupt the company involved. The canning industry recognized that prevention of botulism outbreaks depends on killing all *C. botulinum* spores with absolute reliability—or, as a last resort when sterilization methods fail, recalling all contaminated foods to prevent further toxin exposures. The convergence of their business interests with the public good spurred them to enlist help from the best scientist and best institution for botulism control—Karl Meyer and the Hooper Foundation.

Cholera cannot get a foothold in countries that have made a public commitment to building modern water and sewage infrastructures. By the same token, botulism is again an extremely rare disease because of the commercial commitment to food safety, as now conceived "from farm to fork," i.e., in an arc that starts with all raw materials and ends with the consumer.

For cholera, the disease came first from natural sources and spurred investment as a reaction. Cholera control has primarily involved public investment, in close cooperation with commercial contractors and utility companies. The social contract for cholera control has been between municipalities and residents.

For botulism, the disease was manmade, and demanded investment up front. Therefore, botulism control has been achieved in large part with corporate investment, albeit under the supervision of government regulation. The social contract for botulism control has been between food preservation corporations and consumers.

Cholera and botulism represent worst-case scenarios in human history for natural and manmade diseases. The control measures developed for those diseases have spilled over to prevent a wide range of other communicable infectious diseases.

The measures for cholera and botulism control have not covered prevention of all epidemic diseases. For example, control of chemical poisoning has involved more government regulation, including environmental protection, which does not fall under the purview of cholera or botulism control. As an even more extreme example, corporate and public interests coincided well with botulism control but are in complete divergence for smoking-related diseases. Thus social contracts in public health are complex and nuanced.

References

1.   Lebeda FJ, Dembek ZF, Adler M: **Kinetic and reaction pathway analysis in the application of botulinum**

toxin a for wound healing. *J Toxicology* 2012, **2012**:159726.

2. Gangarosa EJ, Donadio JA, Armstrong RW, Meyer KF, Brachman PS, Dowell VR: **Botulism in the United States, 1899-1969**. *American J Epidemiology* 1971, **93**(2):93-101.

3. Gangarosa EJ: **Botulism in the United States, 1899-1967**. *J Infectious Diseases* 1969, **119**(3):308-311.

4. Donadio JA, Gangarosa EJ: **Surveillance for botulism in the United States, 1968-1969**. *J Infectious Diseases* 1970, **122**(1):122-123.

5. Merson MH, Hughes JM, Dowell VR, Taylor A, Barker WH, Gangarosa EJ: **Current trends in botulism in the United States**. *JAMA* 1974, **229**(10):1305-1308.

6. Horwitz MA, Hughes JM, Merson MH, Gangarosa EJ: **Food-borne botulism in the United States, 1970-1975**. *J Infectious Diseases* 1977, **136**(1):153-159.

7. Hughes JM, Blumenthal JR, Merson MH, Lombard GL, Dowell VR, Jr., Gangarosa EJ: **Clinical features of types A and B food-borne botulism**. *Ann Intern Med* 1981, **95**(4):442-445.

8. Hoeprich: **Botulism**. In: *Infectious Diseases.* edn. Hagerstown: Harper & Row Publishers, Inc.; 1972: 1031-1036.

9. Arnon SS, Midura TF, Clay SA, Wood RM, Chin J: **Infant botulism. Epidemiological, clinical, and laboratory aspects**. *JAMA* 1977, **237**(18):1946-1951.

Chapter 12: Public Health Practice Outside the CDC

Although I left the CDC in 1978 for "academic" public health, I continued to be involved in the "practice" of public health through various consultations and projects. The stories below tell just two such instances, each of which involved the drafting of new legislation.

A changing paradigm for food safety emerging from the Jack in the Box outbreak

Enterohemorrhagic *E. coli* was not known in 1978 when my tenure at CDC ended. Its recognition from the early 1980s has been a public health milestone. One major outbreak brought this group of pathogens into the public eye: a 1993 outbreak of *E. coli* O157:H7. Although I was no longer a part of the CDC Enteric Diseases group, I became involved with the consequences of this outbreak and was asked to serve as a consultant to USDA. This story begins with an understanding of *E. coli.*

Most of the bacteria classified as *Escherichia coli* are harmless organisms. Students are often surprised to learn that we carry within our bodies more living cells of the *E. coli* family than there are cells of our own bodies. These bacteria reside primarily within our intestinal tract (along with other bacteria), performing important functions that contribute to our wellbeing. *E. coli* bacteria are the most common, actually constituting most of the weight of feces. Some of them are helpful—assisting in the breakdown of aged blood cells and facilitating the metabolism and recycling of these wastes. Others contribute by synthesizing helpful enzymes and vitamins. Their presence often serves as a defense barrier; as they compete for space, they produce chemicals that inhibit or kill other pathogens. However, not all *E. coli* are so beneficial.

Enterohemorrhagic *E. coli* became manifest in outbreaks during the decade of the 1980s with the first documented outbreak in a McDonald's restaurant on the West Coast in 1982. A subsequent outbreak occurred in 1993 and became known as the Jack in the Box outbreak, named for its occurrence in a restaurant chain located in Western states. This particular outbreak is historically notable because the investigation and subsequent developments substantially changed food-handling and manufacturing practices. As I had retired from CDC in 1978, I was not involved in the investigations of either of these outbreaks, but I played a role in events that followed. This is how it happened.

Manufacturing practices of beef products in the United States were totally unregulated prior to 1906, when *The Jungle*, a book written by Upton Sinclair, brought to light the appalling working and manufacturing practices in beef-processing companies in Chicago. This story was widely highlighted in graphic news-media stories, and the book became a best seller. Soon after its publication and subsequent surrounding publicity, contaminated meat products caused a large multistate outbreak of disease, underscoring how such unsanitary practices compromised the public's health. The news media coverage of this outbreak, coupled with the story presented in *The Jungle*, created such an outcry for action that a congressional hearing was held. President Theodore Roosevelt promised that every slaughtered animal would be inspected. As a result, Congress legislated the first food-production law, and the United States Department of Agriculture (USDA) was created. It called for inspectors to monitor the slaughtering process and manufacture of beef products throughout the country. The strategy for inspections was an organoleptic assessment – acting on one's senses to assess safety. In essence, it was a miasmic era approach totally lacking a scientific base. It was dubbed a "sniff and poke" method. A large number of inspectors were employed, many of whom were professional people including veterinarians assigned to beef-manufacturing companies throughout the U.S. For years, USDA products were stamped with a persistent dye touting inspected products as "Certified"—thereby conveying a false sense of safety to consumers. The Agency was long criticized for this and other practices that had no scientific foundation, but was resistant to change.

A seemingly coincidental event in 1958—the USSR (Union of Soviet Socialist Republics) launch of the first space satellite, called Sputnik—led to a profound change in the food manufacturing and serving industries. Initially, it shook up and aggravated the so-called Cold War between the West and the East. Realizing astronauts would follow in the space competition, the National Aeronautics and Space Administration (NASA) issued a request for proposals (RFP) to ensure astronauts would have safe foods for space flights. The Pillsbury Company won that contract, and from it emerged the Hazard Analysis and Critical Control Points (HACCP) strategy for the manufacturing of food products "from farm to fork." It shifted the responsibility for oversight from government to companies, placing upon manufacturers the onus to identify product hazards and the critical points for possible introduction of pathogens or toxins in the manufacturing process. HACCP also required companies to monitor and maintain records to facilitate trace-back, train their employees on food safety, and utilize microbiological monitoring to ensure the safety of manufactured foods. This strategy was widely and quickly accepted by food manufacturers who recognized that ensuring the safety of food they marketed was in their best interests. However, for decades, USDA resisted

315

changes, as they were entrenched in their own obsolete procedures.

Dr. Frank Bryan, a distinguished CDC food scientist, spearheaded efforts to bring about change largely by education of the profession and the public. He collaborated with industry on studies on food safety that showed poor or no correlations between food safety and the elements of the organoleptic strategy. After we launched the foodborne diseases surveillance program in 1965, I saw advancing HACCP as a major objective of our work and a natural strategy to help prevent foodborne disease outbreaks. However, little progress was made until the Jack in the Box outbreak in 1993. Below is the story of the transformation of the food industry.

Undercooked beef in hamburgers sold by a restaurant chain called Jack in the Box caused a multistate outbreak of *E. coli* O157:H7, with hundreds of cases and four deaths. CDC's investigation was lead by Dr. Patricia Griffin. Her epidemiological study enabled quick recognition of the cause. Her study was brilliant in its use of surveillance data and epidemiological methods. The calamity of tragic deaths that should have been avoided was the focus of extensive news coverage. Griffin played another essential role in this story. She educated the news media and the mothers whose children had developed hemolytic uremic syndrome, some of whom died. Mothers organized to deal with the problem.

The teaching of Margaret Mead, the American cultural anthropologist who featured frequently as an author and speaker in the mass media of this era, must have played a role in these events, in particular her adage, "Never doubt that a small group of committed citizens can change the world; indeed, it's the only thing that ever has." How true this was in this case!

These well-educated mothers demanded and got a congressional hearing. At this hearing, mothers tugged at the heartstrings of members of the committee in making their case that USDA's outdated strategy for food safety was responsible for the deaths of these children, and that their deaths could have and should have been prevented. At the conclusion of the meeting, the chairperson of the committee promised action. Both USDA and FDA were charged to organize committees to plan action for change. I was fortunate to be called upon to participate in one of these committees—I presume I was asked because of my past association with CDC and specifically my surveillance experience with a similar illness—Shiga dysentery, which was the focus of my attention in the Central American pandemic described above. As noted above, this surveillance documented the return of infected U.S. travelers from affected countries. Indeed, it was most likely these travelers who carried the Shiga-toxin-encoding gene to the bacterial pool of our population, thus indirectly causing the emergence of the *E. coli* 0157:H7 strain that caused the Jack in the Box outbreak.

I worked with my committee to draft the wording of the HACCP strategy into the new legislation that was signed by President Clinton in 1997. This legislation ushered in a new era, a changed paradigm for food safety requiring industry to incorporate the HACCP strategy into manufactured food. It was Griffin carrying Langmuir's epidemiological torch that set this in motion[72].

---

[72] Letter dated Feb 22, 1995 from Judith A. Segal, Director, Policy, Evaluation and Planning Office United States Department of Agriculture, Food Safety and Inspection Service, Washington, D.C.; and The Federal Register Feb 3, 1995, Part II, Pathogen Reduction; Hazard Analysis and Critical Control Point (HACCP) Systems, Proposed Rule.

OSHA Consultation while at Emory

Here I break again from chronological order to tell the story of another time when I became involved in national legislation. In my first year at Emory, in , 1983, the Occupational Safety and Health Administration (OSHA) asked me to assess published data regarding conditions experienced by agricultural workers and to assist in writing new regulations that addressed sanitation deficiencies. This assignment resonated with my personal experiences.

When I was 13 and 14 years old, I worked summers on farms picking strawberries, beans, and cherries along with other boys from Benjamin Franklin High School. We met at Avenue D and Carter Street next to Pulaski Park in Rochester, New York. A large truck picked us up at 7:00 A.M. Ten to 15 of us would climb into the back of an open truck, where we stood or sat during the daily 50 – 60 minute trip to farms south of the city. I was paid 10 cents per hour and worked eight hours each day; this amounted to $4 per week. That was big money for me—the most I'd ever made up till then. Our time was recorded from the moment when we picked our first basket of whatever crop assigned for the day. Financial incentives drove us to pick as much as possible. There were no toilet facilities, no water, and no way to wash our hands. We had an hour for lunch. I usually brought a baloney or peanut butter and jelly sandwich and a small bottle of Pepsi. The work was especially grueling during days with full sun, and I didn't have a hat. Fortunately, Rochester often had clouds. The farms were by the Erie Canal. I occasionally swam in it during the lunch break, but I didn't submerge my head because I could tell from the smell that it was grossly contaminated. In nearby fields, migrant workers picked other produce on the same farms. The truck took us back to the morning rendezvous place at 5:00 P.M. Every night, I got home exhausted. In addition to the meager stipend, the only perk was a taste of the raw fruit or vegetable we were to pick; there were no other benefits.

During the momentous activities in the MPH Program in the early months of 1983, I received a call from Claudia Thurber, an attorney from the U.S. Department of Labor. She knew of my work in the enteric diseases at CDC, and this led her to ask for my assistance on a matter relating to working conditions of migrant laborers. She mentioned that the Secretary of Labor was concerned because egregious unsanitary working conditions were compromising the health of migrant laborers. She asked if I would consult for her office in the Occupational Safety and Health Administration (OSHA), to document not only diseases but also environmental risk factors and subtler issues of quality of life of migrant laborers. She explained that her goal was to develop an evidence-based rationale for a prevention program. I was overwhelmed by both the challenge and the amount of time that would be needed. My initial impulse was to decline, but I decided to ask for some time to consider this. She agreed.

I gave the matter of the consultation a great deal of thought. I reflected on my own experiences as an adolescent picking crops as a temporary farm hand. I recalled how difficult it was to work in the summer heat with no provisions for water or sanitation. I remembered immigrant women working in nearby fields, and how I had felt strong sympathy for them as they were more affected than my high-school classmates and me by the lack of water and toilet facilities. I remembered Edward R. Murrow's video, "Harvest of Shame," depicting not only these difficult working conditions, but also the unsanitary and substandard living conditions of the migrant workers, who were often exploited by those who hired them. I had been deeply moved by that story. The challenge met a personal need as well: I wanted to be involved in more practical (vs. academic) public health work, especially on a theme involving water and sanitation. I consulted with Tom Sellers; he was supportive, but was concerned that this might create a distraction that would compromise the MPH program. I reaffirmed my commitment to the program, making it clear that if I accepted this consulting assignment it would not compromise the auspicious beginning of the work I was doing with the program. I mentioned that I would find an MPH student who might find the topic of interest as a Master's thesis; thus, the project could also benefit our program and our students. I believe that Tom found this reassuring.

Ultimately, I decided to accept. I prepared a plan with a work schedule for a limited amount of my own time that would not detract from my role with the MPH program, to which I was fully committed. I called Ms. Thurber to accept the consultant assignment. She was pleased and had no problem with my time constraints. I was pleasantly surprised that she asked me to prepare to testify before a congressional committee in September of the following year. In this effort, I had the good fortune of collaborating with Dr. Jane Seward, one of the recently recruited MPH students. We considered risks of various illnesses, especially diarrheal and respiratory, that are often caused by poor sanitary conditions. We also considered toxic exposures, particularly from organophosphate insecticides. In addition, our report addressed privacy issues, particularly for women working with men in fields without toilet facilities. We studied published documents on the subject of agricultural workers and voluminous testimony that would have to be included in a written report. I worked on this on weekends and on nights when I was not teaching. The findings of Seward's master's thesis featured prominently in our final OSHA report.

The document we prepared was one of the most important policy papers of my career. It was distributed to a congressional committee in October of 1984. It was entitled "An epidemiological analysis of data presented in evidence in the rulemaking record, Docket No. H-308, in connection with field sanitation proposal 29 DFP 1928.110." At the conclusion of the hearings, it was again edited and published in the Federal Register dated May 1, 1987[73]. Two years later, it was promulgated into law. The law set standards for three basic services employers of 20 or more migrant farm laborers must provide, maintain, and make readily accessible: drinking water, toilets, and hand-washing facilities. These regulations provided individual states with "sufficient flexibility so that they could shape provisions to fit local climatic, topographical, crop, and labor conditions."

Years later, I still value the note sent by my OSHA colleagues. It was a copy of the Federal Register that had a penned statement on the first page that read, "We couldn't have done it without you," signed by Claudia Thurber. Tom Sellers also sent a news item entitled, "Farms: States accused of violating U.S. hygiene rules," with a handwritten note noting, "Gene, You should be pleased with what your work has accomplished." This communication served as an affirmation of my decision to take on this task. My work experiences, personal philosophy, and interests in water and sanitation resonated with this effort to help disadvantaged people. I was gratified to have this academic challenge, which gave me the opportunity to mentor a graduate student, and I felt it complemented my administrative role. It was another foundation-building experience, one of the most rewarding of my career.

---

[73] It had the final title "Department of Labor, Occupational Safety and Health Administration 29 CFR Part 1928, Field sanitation; Final rule."

PART V: MY ACADEMIC CAREER

Chapter 13: Academic Public Health Amidst Chaos: My experiences during the Lebanese Civil War (1978 – 1981) at AUB's school of public health—from peril to onset of recovery

The story I write is a personal account of my years at the American University of Beirut (AUB) as the first Dean of the Faculty of Health Sciences, in the years 1978 – 1981. I inherited what had previously been a strong academic school of public health that had become financially compromised by the same civil war "chaos" described by Dr. Samuel P. Asper in his book *Care Amidst Chaos: The Story of the Medical Center of the American University of Beirut in the Early Years (1975 – 78) of the Lebanese Civil Strife*. Asper wrote about how this chaos financially drained AUB's Medical Center through costs incurred in treating combat casualties that required unreimbursed treatment at AUB's Medical Center. I explain the consequences of this same chaos on AUB's School of Public Health, and how the school emerged as an independent faculty, the Faculty of Health Sciences (FHS) [1].

Introductions to AUB

My interest in AUB was first piqued after a chance encounter with an AUB School of Public Health speaker at a public health meeting I attended at the World Health Organization (WHO) regional headquarters in Alexandria, Egypt in 1964. The meeting was on a cholera-related topic, and I was in attendance due to my role as a consultant to WHO. Since I had a shared interest with the speaker, I introduced myself during the break and engaged him on various issues. Learning of my interests, he invited me to visit AUB, and I accepted. At the end of my University of Maryland tenure in Lahore, Pakistan (see chapter 7), I scheduled a stopover in Beirut on my homeward-bound Pan American Airline (Pan Am) flight.

It was a pleasant, bright sunny day in June of 1964 when my flight landed in Beirut. I was traveling with my wife Rose and our 13-year-old son, Ray[74]. On that first day, we were tourists. On the second day, I attended a conference at the School of Public Health while Rose and Ray spent their time visiting other tourist sites of interest. I met the director, Dr. Craig S. Lichtenwalner. I was impressed—with the academic rigor of the conference, his tour of the school, and with those I met. At the end of that second day in our hotel room, the three of us talked about our experiences and impressions. We agreed that this was a remarkable place, not only for its natural beauty, but also AUB's academic standards. The next morning as we drove to the airport, Rose casually remarked, "This would be a nice place to retire." The thought was the seed for a later chapter in our lives.

History of AUB

AUB has a remarkable history. The university was founded by Christian religious visionaries in 1867. They named it the "Syrian Protestant College," reflecting the university's academic and religious mission. AUB's founding father, Daniel Bliss, articulated

---

74 We had sent our other children, Peggy and Gene Jr., ahead to the U.S. already since we were intending to make a stop to buy a car and the trip was already going to be long and difficult.

the university's concept of social justice in a dedication event in 1871: "This College is for all conditions and all classes without regard to color, nationality, race, or religion. A man white, black, or yellow, Christian, Jew, Mohammedan, or heathen, may enter and enjoy all the advantages of this institution for three, four, or eight years, and go out believing in one God, in many gods, or in no god. But it will be impossible for anyone to continue with us long without knowing what we believe to be the truth and our reasons for that belief." A few years previously, Reverend Bliss had met Abraham Lincoln and received his blessings, but not the financial support the Reverend had hoped for in this new venture in Beirut. The school changed its name in 1920 to the "American University of Beirut." The university survived the upheavals of WWI and WWII, and a school of public health was established soon after WWII.

The School of Public Health prior to the Lebanese civil war was a jewel in AUB's crown. In the early 1950s, the Medical School offered courses in public health and public health nursing. In 1955, a school of public health was established within the Medical School. The first director was Dr. Leland E. Powers, who served in this role from 1955 to 1959. In keeping with AUB's parasitological focus (driven by the major importance of this topic to public health in the region), Powers was a distinguished parasitologist and educator. His disease niche was echinococcosis—more commonly known as hydatid disease. It is a water-related disease transmitted by hands or flies and by dogs fed viscera from livestock. During his AUB tenure, Powers published an extensive bibliography on this disease that included his many landmark contributions [2, 3].

Powers defined the school's initial admission requirements for an expanding menu of higher-level academic offerings. The requirements noted that "Candidates admitted ... must have a medical degree or a university degree with a major in certain fields," i.e., must be established professionals. Some of these admitted students were veterans of military services in countries of the region during WWII. Those health professionals generally wished to pursue new careers in public health or else had already entered public health services but needed or wanted professional credentials to practice public health. AUB's diploma programs uniquely met that need. Although similar degree programs were being offered by other schools of public health at that time, AUB's reputation of excellence and its relatively easy access by air gave it an edge in attracting applicants from the region. The diploma programs initially offered required one academic year—generally nine months of course work on campus. Academic offerings expanded to include diverse certificate offerings, baccalaureate, and master's level degrees.[75]

---

[75] Certificate programs included the following: Public Health Education Certificate (PHEC), Public Health Midwifery Certificate (PHMC), Public Health Nursing (PHNC), Sanitation Certificate (SC), Certificate in Basic Lab Technique (CBLT), and Applied Laboratory Tech Certificate (ALTC). Academic offerings included the following diploma programs offered in the late fifties and early sixties: Public Health Administration for Physicians Diploma (PHAPD), Public Health Education Diploma (PHEC), Public Health for Engineers (PHEnD), Nursing Diploma (ND), Diploma in Public Health Nursing (DPHN), Post Basic Midwifery Diploma (PBMD), Sanitary Sciences Diploma (SSD), and Diploma in Basic Laboratory Technique (DBLT). In addition, the school offered the following health-related bachelor's degrees: Bachelor of Science (BS), Bachelor of Science in Medical Technology (BSMT), Bachelor of Science in Environmental Health (BSEH), Bachelor of Science in Nursing (BSN), Bachelor of Science in Biostatistics (BSB, Bachelor of Science in Medical Lab Technology (BSMLT). The School also offered five master's degree programs. The Master of Sciences in Parasitology was the first of these until the exodus of faculty experts in this field in the early seventies. The Masters of Science in Epidemiology degree was offered in 1976. Other master's level offerings included Master of Science in Population Studies (MSPOPS), Master of Science in Environmental Health (MSEH), Master of Science in Population Health (MSPOPH), and a generic MPH

No other institution in the Middle East offered so many academic options—a total of 24—to so many medical, nursing, engineering, and administrative professionals who aspired to careers in public health, public health advancement, continuing education, and mentored studies. Tuition fees and charges from these diverse academic activities enriched and helped grow the school and university. During roughly two decades following WWII, the school was academically and financially solid. It was this thriving program I saw in my 1964 visit.

My recruitment to AUB

When I next came into contact with AUB, in 1977, the situation had changed drastically. From 1975 to 1978, Lebanon was absorbed with a brutal civil conflict, with an eventual death toll of over 40,000. The impact of this conflict was felt by all of AUB, but especially acutely by the Medical Center, which bore the brunt of the effects given its responsibility for treating the wounded—many of whom refused to pay, and carried guns to prove this point! Nonetheless, the Medical Center "survived against staggering odds, in spite of artillery and mortar shelling, staff and supply shortages, water rationing, power cuts, and reduced revenues, any one of which could have abruptly terminated its operation." [1]

In the intervening years between my 1964 visit and my next experiences with AUB, I had spent time with the Epidemic Intelligence Service (EIS) at the Centers for Disease Control and Prevention (CDC), focusing on intestinal infections. During this time, I worked as an ad hoc consultant on cholera issues and other enteric infections with the World Health Organization

---

degree that was offered from 1972 through 1978—Master in Public Health (MPH) [4].

(WHO) and the World Bank as the 7th cholera pandemic swept across the countries of Southeast and South Asia and into the Middle East. I advised and assisted in planning cholera control measures with health decision makers. On a few of these consultations, I encountered AUB alumni who worked in ministries of health in the region, all of whom had positive things to say about their AUB training and experiences.

For my consultations in the region, it was necessary to make connections for flights on other airlines serving the region. Beirut was the crossroads for these trips. Transfers to other flights sometimes required hours of waiting, at times overnight. I had learned about Dr. Sam Asper and his role at AUB from news media coverage of the Lebanese civil war. During one of my 1977 consultations, I decided to make the best use of my layover time by writing to him. His response was warm and cordial; he invited me to stay as his houseguest. At the time I visited, Asper served as the Interim Director of the School of Public Health and Vice President for Medical Affairs. Over the course of that time together, we began to bond over similarities in our situations. Asper and I were both internists in academic practice, led into public health by our career circumstances. Asper unexpectedly entered public health via his role as interim director of AUB's School of Public Health. My first entrance into public health was during a WWII typhus epidemic in Naples, Italy, when I was with the U.S. Army. My experiences with cholera in Bangkok changed my career. I am convinced the most important work in my career was the influence I had with decision-makers to leverage country investments into sanitary and water infrastructures, which undoubtedly saved many lives. Asper was especially influenced by Jamal Harfouche's landmark work in infant-growth monitoring, which set a standard in pediatric practice and certainly averted substantial child mortalities. Through these different career pathways, we both became public health practitioners and advocates of social justice. It was from Asper that I first heard AUB's motto: "That they may have life and have it more abundantly." I also learned from him that AUB's mission was LIFE—improvement of quality of life.

During that visit, I learned a great deal from Asper and others about many other aspects of the university—its high academic standards; diverse professional schools teaching courses in English; its past association with the Rockefeller Institute that funded construction of the Van Dyke building for the school; and the arrangement with the New York State Department of Education for accreditation of academic curricula and degrees. He also made known his concerns about the consequences of intermittent fighting and its adverse impact on student applications from the region. At the end of this visit, Asper offered me a position at AUB. I believe that his decision to do so was driven not only by my complementary research interests, but also by the fact that I had known AUB in its grandeur when I visited in 1964. Perhaps he felt that I would be an appropriate person to help restore AUB to an era of stability.

As a WHO consultant on cholera, I attended another event in 1977 that led me to consider Asper's job offer—a meeting in Bahrain chaired by Dr. Ali Fakhro, Minister of Health and an AUB alumnus, that was attended by other ministers of health of the Gulf countries. Fakhro and I had come to know each other at previous WHO-sponsored meetings. During one of the breaks in this 1977 meeting, I spoke with him about my interest in AUB and the job offer I had from Asper. He encouraged me and pledged his support. That meant a great deal to me, as he was an articulate spokesperson for change among the ministers. As the pieces fell into place, I became increasingly inclined to pursue Asper's offer.

After that 1977 meeting, I wrote Asper to indicate I was considering the position. He extended two invitations. The first was that I join him in a trip he was planning in the U.S. to visit several not-for-profit organizations that had provided AUB support. The second was an invitation to Rose and me to visit AUB in January of 1978. In accepting his invitations, I invited Asper to visit us in Atlanta to meet Rose and to discuss the proposed January visit. Asper and I planned these visits concurrently.

In October 1977, I met Asper when his flight landed at the Washington/Baltimore airport. We rented a car and drove to New York City, where we met his colleagues at the Rockefeller Institute, a foundation that had already been generous in supporting AUB. We also visited the Pew Foundation, AUB offices in NYC, the chairman of AUB's Board of Trustees, and several members of the Board involved with AUB's medical affairs. I was impressed by how articulate and effective Asper was in advocating for AUB's needs. After our meetings, we drove from NYC to Atlanta. I remember the driver's side windshield wiper of our rental car failed during a heavy rainstorm when I was driving into the Baltimore area, slowing us considerably. We exchanged cars and continued our journey.

We welcomed Asper as our houseguest in our Stone Mountain home in late 1977. On the second day, we visited CDC. My agenda for him included meetings with my supervisors, colleagues, and staff. As we drove home at the end of a busy day, Asper said he was satisfied with his vetting. On the last day of his visit, Rose and I invited a group of about 15 local AUB medical alumni to our home to discuss AUB matters. Asper was a great storyteller. He had many interesting anecdotes to share about his experiences at AUB. He spoke of ways AUB had kept above the political turmoil, his work with the news media to ensure their continuing support, and efforts to ensure AUB would be seen as a continuing bastion of academic excellence despite the unsettled conditions. He underscored his belief that the campus had become a sanctuary positioned above the fray by a strict policy prohibiting political meetings and posters on campus. At the end of this visit I reiterated my interests in the position, and Rose supported me. The next step was our AUB visit.

Our trip to Beirut went as planned from January 11 to 18, 1978. We were houseguests of the Aspers. We were awed by the beauty of the AUB campus, the elegant landscape, and the breath-taking views of the Mediterranean Sea. The city was calm. Everyone we met was enthusiastic and supportive of the prospect of our taking on this new AUB role. Indeed, Asper told me during this time that he even had the AUB president's nod to recruit me, as well as the blessings of the Board of Deans. The president felt that my research interests and publications fit with his vision to develop both AUB's opportunities as well as a synergistic network of institutions in the region. He was also enthusiastic about some of the ideas I had shared with Asper.

During this visit, I had many discussions with Asper about crafting a new name for AUB's School of Public Health. We searched for a name consistent with the academic parts, namely, public health, nursing, and laboratory sciences. We considered but dismissed "Allied Health Sciences," as we both saw it as a bit condescending with implications of a subordinate role to the Medical School. I cannot remember which of us first came up with the name, but we both agreed it should be "Faculty of Health Sciences" (FHS). After I left, Asper got the president's approval and the consent of the Board of Deans, including the Medical School Dean. The name seemed settled—at least at that time.

I left with a good feeling about joining the AUB faculty. I looked forward to the challenges of this new job, doing something different in a new career, confident I was up to the task, assured by prior experiences in Lahore, at CDC and with WHO. Most important was the fact that Rose was supportive.

Accepting the AUB offer and first steps in my new role

Factors that convinced me to accept the position were several. I was confident that I could collaborate successfully with the two people whom I thought would be my supervisors, Asper and President Hoelscher. I expected these two to provide able, dedicated, and committed leadership that would enhance my working experience. My enthusiasm was also reinforced when I learned about several other faculty who shared my research interests, most notably Jamal Harfouche and Calvin W. Schwabe[ix]. Despite the financial issues, I was confident in AUB's and the school of public health's academic foundations. AUB's history was in keeping with my own philosophy of social justice. I felt confident I could implement the plan we crafted to attract seniors from AUB's various schools; I believed I could build on the existing collaboration the school had with the Johns Hopkins School of Public Health; I was optimistic that my cholera experiences, evolved as a professional passion for safe water and sanitation, would be helpful; and I was hopeful that my links with CDC and WHO would provide much-needed support from public health luminaries. Rose agreed, and so I accepted the job.

Even before moving to Beirut, I had work to do for AUB. It was necessary to get approval of a revised curriculum for the existing MPH degree. To arrange this from my CDC office, I contacted the New York State Department of Education, located in Albany, NY. Two telephone conversations with a person in charge were encouraging and helpful. The Department explained the accreditation arrangement with AUB, and we exchanged correspondence by mail. What remained was getting faculty approval of the revised MPH curriculum and scheduling a meeting in Albany after settling in Beirut.

Before my next trip to Beirut, I had several other AUB-related meetings in the U.S., and I also attended a conference in Alexandria, Egypt[76]. Each meeting reinforced my decision.

In another stopover meeting in Beirut from June 6 to 7, 1978, I again met with Asper. He had arranged two important meetings for me. The first was to consider appointing someone from the public health faculty to serve as assistant dean. He recommended Jack Ibrahim, an impressive young man serving as an assistant professor in the school's Environmental Health Department. At that time, Ibrahim was a part-time PhD student enrolled in the High Institute of Public Health in Alexandria, Egypt, a leading school of public health in the region. We discussed his doctoral project, and I got his advice as to how best to get faculty support

---

[76] While still at CDC, I arranged to meet Dr. Calvin W. Schwabe while attending a meeting of the American Epidemiological Society in Sacramento, Davis, California on March 30, 1978. We spent hours discussing AUB, mutual friends and colleagues, and shared research interests. The following week, I met again with Asper in Washington, DC, as we had previously arranged. I accompanied him in meetings with the Pew Foundation and several other groups. We spent four days together from April 18 to 21, 1978. In a rented car, we drove to New York and Baltimore to meet with other people and organizations that had supported AUB. We visited AUB's office in NYC, where I met several members of the Board of Directors. During the last weekend in May of 1978, I attended a meeting of the International Epidemiological Society in Alexandria, Egypt. During this meeting, I met with senior staff of the Eastern Mediterranean Regional Office of the World Health Organization with whom I had been consulting on cholera issues. They were supportive of my plans to join AUB.

for the revised MPH curriculum. After our meeting, I suggested we should be on a first-name basis. He said he was a bit uncomfortable with that, but he offered a compromise—he would call me "Dean," since it sounded so much like "Gene." He was being facetious, but I got his point; he envisioned a formal relationship. And so it was for the nearly four years we worked together. He served FHS well and made my job much easier.

The second meeting Asper had arranged for me in this June 1978 visit was to meet with President Hoelscher to discuss administrative issues. Asper accompanied me to the president's office. I was surprised that he left me to wait for the president. The president started rather formally, as if he was a bit uncomfortable in things he needed to discuss. The first had to do with logistical issues: my salary and where my family would live on campus. I was surprised at his offering a salary lower than I had expected. He told me it was not so much an offer—it was just what he had available in view of the university's and the school's financial situation. He mentioned he was aware that I would have my own retirement salary from my CDC service. I was disappointed, but since I was not considering the job for money, I did not make this an issue. The president's second point was the assignment of my family's apartment on campus—an apartment on the fifth floor of one of two university buildings on the lower campus next to the seaside road, a building allocated for faculty residences. Again, I was a bit surprised because I had thought my family would have a small home in the center of the campus. I asked about this; he informed me he had committed that residence to a new Dean of Agriculture he was in the process of recruiting. This Dean's starting date was months later than my planned arrival in early July. As I did not want to start my relationship with President Hoelscher on a sour note, I reluctantly agreed. I noted we had tentative plans to arrive the day after the American Independence Day holiday. I mentioned that AUB would not have to pay my salary for the first three months after I arrived in Beirut because I had accumulated CDC leave that I could take as terminal leave. Thus, I set my first day at AUB for the 5th of July of 1978, and my official AUB starting date as October 1, 1978.

Having discussed these preliminary issues, President Hoelscher mentioned he wanted to talk to me on another important matter; it had to do with the Nursing School. For this discussion, he asked Dr. Samir Thabet, university provost and vice president for academic affairs, to join us. The essence of their presentation was that they wanted me to assume responsibility for the Nursing School in my capacity as Dean of FHS. The president indicated that the situation provided an opportunity for new roles for nursing in the region, though he did not go into detail. As this was totally unexpected, I explained that I had no experience in this arena, so I would have to give this some thought. President Hoelscher indicated that he wanted to settle this matter before I left. A meeting was scheduled the next morning.

Determining my role in the nursing school

As I reflected on this day of unsettling surprises, I had very mixed feelings. I was inclined not to accept the Nursing School responsibility especially given that it came without prior discussion and input of others. Furthermore, I was uncomfortable that Asper had excluded himself from this important meeting. So, before committing myself, I wanted to get his opinion. As I was a houseguest with the Aspers, I talked to Asper about this matter that evening. His position was, "It's up to you, Gene." Since he was neutral, but not opposed, and both the president and Thabet seemed to give me some latitude, I did some soul searching and came up with an idea. At breakfast that morning I shared it with Asper, and he liked it. Later that morning, I presented it to Hoelscher and Thabet.

I proposed augmenting the nursing curriculum training and research with a focus on the control of nosocomial (i.e., hospital-acquired) infections and injuries. I made the point that wherever studies were conducted, the need for such control programs was evident. In fact, studies demonstrating the importance and efficacy of such control programs were done in my own Bacterial Diseases Branch at CDC. The advocacy and leadership for such programs came from my two CDC supervisors and colleagues Drs. John V. Bennett and Philip S. Brachman. They were two of the leading scientists in this field. Their textbook entitled *Hospital Infections* was widely used and accepted in hospitals and schools of public health in the U.S. In fact, I had coauthored a chapter in this book with another colleague, Dr. James M. Hughes, a distinguished CDC scientist, on the topic of controlling foodborne-disease transmissions in hospitals. That was the one aspect of nosocomial surveillance and control consistent with my own interests. CDC had many years of experience developing and testing methods for nosocomial surveillance. Most leading hospitals in the U.S. were actively participating in these surveillance programs, as this had become a requirement for hospital accreditation. In the U.S., it had been recognized as best practice. My plan also addressed another issue that very much concerned me, namely, the challenge and complexity of conducting epidemiological field studies in a country at war. Therefore, I was prepared to accept the assignment with a few conditions.

In my presentation to the president and the university provost that morning, I first reiterated my concern due to my lack of expertise in nursing. I made it clear that I would rather not, but I was willing to accept if they, and the respective faculty and decision makers, would agree to the inclusion of a nosocomial control program in the nursing curriculum. I made this a quid pro quo. My plan called for the assignment of someone among the existing nursing faculty to serve as full-time interim director. I also asked for two new faculty lines—one for an epidemiologist with expertise in such programs, and a second position for a full-time director, a senior-level academic nurse with research and teaching experiences. I was pleasantly surprised that both the president and the provost supported my plan. In fact, the president was complimentary and enthusiastic, seeing a nice fit with his vision of AUB Nursing becoming more responsive to regional needs. They also agreed to provide funding for these two additional faculty lines. Thus, the matter was settled.

I delayed my departure for another day in order to appoint an interim director of the Nursing School from existing faculty. I also felt it would be appropriate for me to talk to the person relieved of her position as director; it seemed to be the right thing to do. I assured her of my support and prevailed on her to continue in her roles teaching and curriculum development in her niche area of expertise. She expressed her satisfaction at the end of our meeting. Later, she proved to be a productive member of the Nursing School.

Because of the urgency of finding a new interim director of nursing that same day, I consulted with Asper and Ibrahim to get their recommendations as to the best-qualified candidate among existing nursing faculty. They both recommended Larry Afifi. At the time, she was an instructor. They felt strongly she had great leadership potential. I met her, and we had a long discussion, during which I, too, became impressed. She asked for time to think about this—at least overnight. I agreed. We met again the next morning. She said I could count on her. I advised the president, and he made arrangements for her appointment as interim director. She proved to be an able administrator and did a great job in facilitating a cohesive and supportive environment among the nursing faculty. Indeed, I was quite happy with the success of the nursing school, though perhaps it wasn't exactly as had been first envisioned[x].

Nosocomial infection control was on my mind during my return flight to Atlanta. I was beginning to see how the turn of events might be a blessing in disguise. Back at CDC, my colleagues were enthusiastic about supporting this new initiative. They encouraged me to consider the possibility of establishing a center of excellence for nosocomial infection control for the region, very much in keeping with the president's vision to extend the Nursing School's footprint into the region. Later, when I investigated what was known about nosocomial infections in Middle Eastern hospitals, I learned, to my surprise, that data about such programs were scant, and surveillance programs for nosocomial diseases hardly existed. While in Atlanta, I also got CDC support for two nosocomial prevalence studies. They would be conducted at the AUB hospital in Beirut and the Sulmaniya Hospital in Bahrain. They were the largest and arguably the most prestigious hospitals in the region. An EIS epidemiologist was identified to conduct the surveys after I got settled in Beirut. We envisioned that these studies would provide important baseline epidemiological data.

Standing behind the new name for the Faculty of Health Sciences

Unexpectedly, the "Faculty of Health Sciences" name was challenged in mid-June of 1978. I received a telegram at home—the 1978 version of an e-mail message—from President Hoelscher, in which he asked me to consider seriously the fervent objections of the Dean and faculty of the Medical School.

340

They had convinced the president that naming our department "Faculty of Health Sciences" inappropriately implied that I would also be Dean of the Medical School, which they argued is also a "health science." They proposed changing the name to "School of Allied Health Sciences." The telegram also indicated that the Medical School was offering me an appointment as Professor of Medicine in the new School of Allied Health Sciences. I was upset and firm in the telegram I sent in response. In the few words customarily used in telegrams, I wrote, "Not willing to change FHS name based on prior concurrence all AUB decision makers. Feel strongly this matter."

The president's support of my position came in a letter dated June 29, 1978. He wrote, "The Board of Trustees has approved my plan for the separation of the present Faculties of Medical Sciences into two new Faculties. One of these will be the Faculty of Medicine, while the other will be known as the Faculty of Health Sciences. I placed your name before the Trustees in nomination for the position of Dean, Faculty of Health Sciences, and am pleased to report to you that the Board has approved my nomination. I therefore now ask you formally to accept this expanded role at AUB." Two additional paragraphs of this June 29, 1978 letter had to do with the provisions of salary, and the conditions of the apartment the university was assigning. Most encouraging were his concluding sentences, "I look forward both personally and professionally to working with you. You may be assured of my support of your efforts." [5] This historically important letter marked the birth of FHS as an independent AUB school on June 29, 1978. With this affirmation I was set and ready to start

Moving to Beirut

My move from Atlanta to Beirut had many twists and turns. I moved my family out of our Stone Mountain (Atlanta) home two days after receiving this letter from President Hoelscher. Rose and I placed most of our household effects in storage, keeping only personal items we intended to carry on our trip. We then arranged to live in temporary quarters pending our departure on July 5, 1978.

To our horror, just after we received this letter and only days before our scheduled flight departure, news media accounts showed horrific pictures of fighting in Beirut. We were shocked—the truce we had counted on had vanished. We were anxiously glued to our television set during that week. With ever-worsening news, on the Sunday before we were scheduled to leave, Rose and I contemplated changing our plans. We anticipated that President Hoelscher would tell us not to come as we discussed other possible plans for our future. Cell phones didn't exist then, and phone calls over "landlines" were very difficult, especially abroad. After several attempts, we finally got a phone connection to the president's residence. President Hoelscher's response to our concerns was, "Don't worry. We are sitting on our patio enjoying a beautiful day. The news media are exaggerating the problem." When we asked what he would do if he were in our shoes, he said, "Come."

With this assurance, Rose and I traveled with our 11-year-old son Paul by air. Flights to Beirut at that time took days, and the penultimate stop was in Cairo. We had no news during the entire trip. Unbeknownst to us, while we were en route from Cairo to Beirut, the worst fighting of the Lebanese Civil War broke out. The truce we thought and hoped would be lasting was completely shattered. The U.S. State Department had issued an advisory for Americans not to travel to Lebanon. When we arrived at the end of an exhausting trip, still not knowing this news, we were greeted by Ibrahim and the Medical School Dean, Raja Khouri. They were somber in their surprise to see us, thinking we would have known of this advisory, expecting that we had cancelled our trip and returned home. Our shock was palpable. They accompanied us to the Marquand House, the residence of the president. En route, I asked Rose what she wanted to do. She said, "I'm so tired I just want to go where there's a comfortable bed, and we'll make the decision tomorrow."

President Hoelscher and his wife Chub greeted us and welcomed us to AUB and into their home. The Marquand House was a historical landmark constructed in 1879. It served as the home of AUB's presidents. We asked about Asper. I was shocked to learn he had resigned. They did not tell us why; they only mentioned Asper and his wife Ann were still on campus, and that a meeting had been scheduled for us in their residence the following morning. In the morning we were taken to their home. Ann greeted us warmly, but they were clearly subdued. They assured us that Asper's plans to leave should not affect our plans. He would not provide details, but it was clear that he had been asked to leave. Later, I learned financial issues arising from the chaos played a role. We were profoundly disappointed.

Beginnings in Beirut

Resumption of the war was an ominous beginning for the newly launched FHS. I was concerned that with Asper's departure, his connections with Johns Hopkins would not be accessible. However, I was secure about support from Johns Hopkins' Dean, D. A. Henderson. I felt assured I would report directly to the president and had his support. I also saw support coming from

CDC. So, I was resigned to live with a new paradigm in the administrative structure of my new job.

We stayed with the Hoelschers about a week. This time made possible discussions with the president about my concerns. He expressed strong feelings, reaffirming his commitment to the new school. These discussions enabled me to see that we had in common a deep sense of social commitment—a shared vision of the challenge and importance of what needed to be done despite the chaos of war. Social commitments come from leaders who believe in social justice—it is the philosophy of public health. In the many discussions I had with the president in this week, I came to realize he had as deep a sense of social justice as I had. These conversations imbued in me great expectations of what my faculty and I could accomplish.

Rose and I hesitantly and apprehensively decided to stay. We moved into the faculty apartment assigned to us on the lower campus along the Corniche, the coastal road thoroughfare beside the Mediterranean Sea. The apartment's fifth-floor location proved to be a greater liability than I had been led to believe. We had to cope with electrical outages and water rationing. The apartment was stark, with little furniture. Essential furniture was provided by the university, but our household goods required many months to arrive from Atlanta. What was allocated was meager and its quality far less than what we had enjoyed in our previous residence. The road outside our bedroom was noisy day and night. Besides the sounds of incessant horns, we could often hear gunfire and rocket explosions from the fighting in East Beirut. Life went on despite the turmoil around us. I so admired Rose's fortitude in the face of those unfamiliar stressful experiences. I am deeply indebted to her for her support, especially during those early months of my tenure. Thanks to her, we made the best of a very bad situation outside of the campus.

Reconciled and committed, I got started. Getting involved was the best medicine. The campus seemed safe. Life went on both on campus and in the adjacent neighborhood called Hamra. My administrative assistant, who had provided secretarial services for several of the previous school directors and interim directors, was a big help. Meanwhile, Rose inquired about possible campus jobs. She decided to volunteer for a position in the library of the School of Agriculture.

Rose and I both worked hard, long hours, and found the work satisfying and the progress gratifying. Some faculty had home televisions, but ours was in our shipment still in storage, so we very much depended on a small radio purchased locally. We especially remember the British Broadcasting Company (BBC), which had news on the hour and a refreshing blend of short news commentaries, short stories, classical music, and some plays. We enjoyed these, but Rose especially missed her piano. These were difficult days, especially for her.

First steps at AUB

In a thick fog of tobacco smoke, I held my first meeting with faculty to discuss various topics, including a faculty retreat and the proposed 2-year MPH program. I was aware of pervasive tobacco use during meetings in my cholera consultations, but I had no idea smoking would be so prevalent among public health faculty, students, and staff. Back then, the effects of second-hand smoke had not yet been documented. This likely explains why so many of the faculty were adamant in their objections to my attempts to curb smoking, seeing it as an affront on their individual rights. I could only get my faculty to agree on restricting smoking during meetings, but not during breaks. Smoking at that time seemed to be gender specific, with a much higher prevalence among men. The nursing faculty was entirely female, and I don't remember any of them ever smoking.

In my visits to the region, I had already met with nearly all of my public health and nursing faculty to discuss individual teaching, research, and service activities. However, up until this time, I had not yet met with two senior faculty members, a biochemist and a botanist, who transferred from the School of Pharmacy when it was closed the previous year. They had no public health credentials and only nominal teaching experiences relevant to public health. My meeting with the biochemist went well, as he responded persuasively to my questions as to what he saw as his new role in FHS. However, when I met with the botanist, a Canadian citizen who had been at AUB for many years, I was surprised and concerned because his role in the School of Pharmacy was to lecture on herbal medications and their role in treating diseases—not a topic suitable for a public health curriculum. Since the School of Pharmacy's closure, he had not found a public health role, he did not teach, and he had no external funding for his research on how insects communicate! I was surprised that the financially stressed School of Public Health was paying not only his full salary, among the highest in the school, but also paying for his research equipment. I made a difficult decision in that one and only meeting—he had to go. I asked him to resign and to leave as soon as possible. He did not object. After only a few days, I joined a party thrown by his friends on the faculty to thank him for his years of service to AUB and wish him well. The following morning as he was about to leave, an explosion occurred near his residence in Hamra. One of my FHS faculty who was with him at the time told me later that the botanist was much relieved that he was leaving, as he saw the incident as an ominous warning.

I enjoyed the academic setting, especially teaching. I taught two MPH courses—a perspective of public health course required for students new to the field, and an elective course on the control of foodborne and waterborne diseases. I also taught medical students in Dr. Haroutune Armenian's *Introduction to Preventive Medicine* course for Medical Students. I lectured on enteric pathogens in Dr. Mattossian's second-year in bacteriology at AUB's medical school. On several occasions I spoke at medical and pediatric grand rounds on cholera and other enteric diseases. I also held adjunct appointments at the University of Bagdad and the University of Basra in Iraq, and at the University of Amman, Jordan. I lectured in Dr. Phil Brachman's Field Epidemiology Training Programs in Kuwait and Saudi Arabia. I mentored two students in prevalence studies of infant mortality in urban and rural populations published with Dr. Huda Zurayk. I enjoyed attending faculty committee meetings and meetings of the Board of Deans. Occasionally Rose traveled with me when I lectured in the region. With her skills in English, she provided me candid and insightful critiques.[77]

At a faculty retreat a few weeks after arriving in Beirut, I presented my plan for the revised MPH program. The faculty provided helpful comments; all approved the curriculum. I

---

[77] During my AUB tenure, I was also able to leverage my CDC connections to bring in outside experts. Since the entire parasitology faculty had left, I arranged for a CDC speaker, Dr. Peter Schantz, a veterinary epidemiologist colleague of Schwabe, to teach a two-week truncated course on the subject. During this time period, I also arranged for another CDC scientist, Dr. Frank Bryan, to visit AUB to discuss the Hazard Analysis and Critical Control Point (HACCP) strategy for safe foods, on which he was a leading expert. CDC had assigned high priority to an international effort to educate and promote the adoption of HACCP at a time when most governmental organizations (including our own USDA) were employing a food-safety strategy essentially built upon long-debunked miasmic principles—dubbed the "sniff and poke" method.

presented the plan at a Board of Deans meeting and got their approval. I learned from some applicants I interviewed that they learned of the program from their deans. I recruited a few adjunct faculty members from the behavioral sciences departments of the School of Arts and Sciences and some who were UNICEF professionals.

About two months later, I returned to the U.S. and spent two days in Albany conferring with staff of the Department of Education. I presented the curriculum of the 2-year MPH degree revised to accommodate AUB college-level seniors. It was a short meeting, during which the curriculum was approved with very few questions asked. On my return to AUB, I reported the approval to faculty and members of the Board of Deans. We then began marketing the program. This MPH curriculum required students to complete core and elective courses during the first academic year. A field practicum was required for the second year—in essence it was a working internship, usually in ministries of health in support of contracts we had in Gulf countries. These internships helped graduates find jobs. This new MPH became the flagship offering of FHS. The only other master's level degree during my tenure was in epidemiology.[78]

Home life

During the first nine months of my tenure, I was preoccupied with home problems arising from the delayed shipment of our

---

[78] In the first year of my tenure we had only one student from the region, a Ministry of Health physician from Yemen funded by USAID. He had already enrolled for the former MPH program for the 1977 – 78 academic year before my arrival. Because he was a physician, he was exempted from the required practicum. He was the exception that proved the rule, the one and only applicant from the region, underscoring why the revised MPH program crafted to appeal to local applicants was necessary.

household goods[79]. We were living with what we brought in our suitcases. The quality of life in our home left much to be desired. The shipping company advised they had to hold our shipment in Brunswick, Georgia because of unsettled conditions in the port of Beirut. The long delay affected Rose's morale, so I decided to appeal to President Hoelscher to permit us to go to Brunswick to sort out household goods in storage. I explained I could combine this visit with my scheduled trip for accreditation of the new MPH curriculum in Albany, New York (referenced above). The president approved. Rose and I flew to Atlanta, where we rented a car and drove to Brunswick. In the warehouse where our household goods were in storage, we spent most of a day gathering the items we most needed. We arranged to have these shipped by air; some we carried back with us. I flew to Albany for the accreditation meeting, while Rose flew to Rochester, NY to spend a few days with her family.

Intermittent fighting in and around the port of Beirut explained why our shipment required nine months from storage in Brunswick, Georgia to the port of Beirut. When it finally came, we were profoundly disappointed because most of the containers were waterlogged. We learned that artillery shells had damaged the roof of the warehouse in Beirut where our

---

[79] Our car, which we had shipped from Atlanta, arrived after about three months, well before we received our household goods. We kept it for only a short while, because day trips were unpredictable and sometimes dangerous. Gasoline was often in short supply. An even greater concern was roadblocks by armed militias. Fortunately, at that time, an American passport was an asset. Driving in the city was tenuous, as traffic lights often did not function, and cars with gunmen extorted the right of way. We were relieved when we sold our car. We spent our recreational time on campus or in restaurants, our church, and a movie theatre in Hamra.

shipment was stored before it was delivered. Rainwater got into cardboard cartons and boxes. It was a heart-breaking experience, especially for Rose, as we had such high hopes that our quality of life would improve after we got our shipment. Water damage was extensive; we had to discard many things we had packed in cardboard containers, including paper records of my research studies in Thailand, India, and Pakistan. This indeed was the low point of our Beirut experience, leaving Rose in tears.

Our family experiences in Beirut were compromised by the chaos of the civil war in other ways, as well. From the time of our arrival in Beirut in July of 1978, and some weeks thereafter, fighting continued on the opposite side of Beirut. Night and day, we could see and hear the battle for control of the eastern part of the city. During the first few weeks after our arrival, as my work was gaining traction, Rose wanted to leave. However, she held on with great pluck and determination, especially after she realized how much progress we were making. I have always admired her and given her credit for supporting me in those very difficult days.

The civil war conflict also caused the Beirut airport to close several times during my tenure, but I fortunately was not traveling on those occasions. Only once, when I was in Atlanta to attend the 1980 Epidemic Intelligence Service (EIS) conference, I had a near miss. I spoke to Rose on the telephone from Atlanta the Sunday morning before the EIS conference began. On that day, news from Beirut was ominous. Rose confirmed the problem—she pleaded for me to return immediately, because we both knew that on such occasions the Beirut airport had closed. I arranged a flight leaving that same day and arrived in the Beirut airport two days before it did in fact close. Such closures were generally time-limited, but they were a continuing source of concern and were enormously inconvenient.

Our daily routines were disrupted from time to time by severe shortages of water and electricity. Water was often rationed, especially in the hot summer months. AUB had several deep wells to supplement the city's water supply, but these were inadequate, especially during the summer. At times, water was available for only one or two morning hours and then during the evenings. Often we showered using cold water. We learned to store water in pails and our bathtub at the first sounds of gunfire.

We had no television in our apartment. All but one of the radio stations we could receive broadcast in Arabic and French, so the British Broadcasting Corporation's English language programming from London became our only source of news, concerts, and entertainment. We lived sparsely, without many of the comforts and conveniences we had enjoyed in our stateside residence. We had no servants except for day services when we hosted guests for meals in our apartment. Rose and I did all the shopping and housework necessary.

Most of the time, we carried our groceries from stores in the Hamra district to our residence, a distance of about a mile; often we had some groceries delivered. During my tenure, I developed an inguinal hernia[80]. I easily reduced the loop of bowel caught in the hernial sac from time to time. Then, one day, on the way home from our shopping, a loop of bowel that I could not dislodge got caught in the hernial sac. I managed to walk to my residence in great pain. I asked Rose to call for help. An AUB surgeon came to our residence to examine me. He diagnosed a

---

[80] Inguinal hernias result when the inner lining of the abdomen is weakened, thereby creating an opening into which a loop of bowel can protrude and get trapped. This causes a bulging of the inguinal area (the area where the leg attaches to the trunk).

strangulated hernia, and I was hospitalized for emergency surgery. Within the hour, AUB surgeons released the strangulated loop of bowel and repaired the hernial sac. The event was traumatic, but since it had to happen, the timing was fortuitous because I was scheduled to travel. Had this happened during a flight across an ocean, the consequences would surely have been much more serious. Incidentally, Asper also developed an inguinal hernia during his tenure, although I'm not sure whether that was a coincidence or a reflection of the chores we all had to do in addition to our jobs.

In January 1981, for the last several months of my tenure, we moved into a second campus residence. It had been David Dodge's childhood home and was located in an especially prized location for the most spectacular views of campus and the Mediterranean Sea. We especially enjoyed the awesome sunsets. The first few months after this move coincided with a period of relative calm, which was especially encouraging. Living conditions were also much more pleasant in this house. In the apartment, we had suffered from constant noise pollution as well as air pollution—the lack of central air conditioning forced us to keep the windows open, so we had no respite. Overall, the house was comfortable[81] and felt more secure even after fighting intensified in April. We used rooms in the lower level of this home as a shelter whenever bombs exploded nearby[82].

---

[81] After one of the not uncommon windstorms, a great deal of sand entered gaps in the windows. All the windows needed insulation, so on one of my trips abroad, I returned with a suitcase full of insulating material. I installed it myself, and after that, no sand entered during sandstorms. I presume other occupants have benefitted from this.

[82] I sent Interim President Dodge a memo recommending conversion of these rooms into an apartment, since it had a separate entrance. I understand this was done after we left.

Despite the inconveniences and risks, we reflect on our life in Beirut with many fond memories. We enjoyed company, especially to play bridge. We found enjoyment in reading and listening to stories, symphonies, and news from the BBC. It helped a great deal that we had physical as well as mental challenges to occupy us[xi]. We were also comforted by Rose having her piano.

Rose's piano

Our Steinway baby grand piano attested to our intention to stay a long time. It was the most formidable challenge in planning our household shipment. Rose's piano meant a great deal to her, as she had majored in piano recital at the Eastman School of Music. Before we married, she taught piano both in a college course and to private students in a studio her father had built especially for this purpose. Concerned about the hazards of shipping the piano, Rose called the Steinway Company for guidance. After explaining her purpose, she was transferred to a member of the Steinway family. At first, he wondered if she was serious about moving the piano to Beirut. After overcoming his disbelief, he was exceedingly helpful. He sent her detailed instructions for the movers about disassembling the piano into separate parts that were wrapped for protection from rain damage and also light enough to be hand-carried up five flights of stairs to our apartment. Thanks to his instructions, despite being kept in storage for months when rainwater damaged so many other items in the same cargo, the piano remained in perfect condition. Watching the movers climb up five flights of stairs carrying on their backs piano parts weighing hundreds of pounds up five flights of stairs was a "have to see to believe" event. After the piano was assembled in our apartment, Rose found a tuner. She spent many hours playing her repertoire of classical music. Chopin was her favorite, and a pleasure for both of us. After several months, Rose performed for a small group of senior AUB colleagues and administrators after a dinner we hosted in our living room apartment. They were impressed—Rose was at her best ever.

A few days later, I got a call from David Dodge, who had attended the event and at the time was Vice President for Administration and Finance. He was puzzled, as he had no record of the university shipping the piano or paying for any of our shipment. I explained that CDC had paid for this, as I was entitled to a final shipment from my home to my new residence when I retired from the Commissioned Corps of the Public Health Service. Dodge raised the issue because he was concerned that the university might be asked to ship the piano back to the States when we left AUB. I assured him that we had no intention of leaving anytime soon and no intention of asking AUB to pay for shipping ever. I explained that we planned to donate the piano to the university together with other large items of our household goods whenever we would have to leave. He was relieved, but wanted to be sure this would not become a problem for AUB. The next day he asked me to put this in writing. I had no problem obliging him, because Rose and I fully intended to stay at AUB for however long my tenure might last, or for however long AUB would want me to serve.

Later, in the days before I left Beirut in November 1981, I called Dodge, who was then interim president. I reiterated our plan to donate to AUB all of our large items of furniture including Rose's baby grand piano. After we left, he arranged to have a plaque for the piano, which had been moved to the Marquand House, the home of AUB's presidents. We were informed months later by one of our Lebanese friends that the plaque was inscribed with my name, "Donated by Eugene J. Gangarosa, Dean, Faculty of

Health Science."[83] I was dismayed by the inscription, as it should have had Rose's name, or perhaps both of our names, since it was in fact her piano. It had meant so much to her, especially when we were all so distressed and anxious because of the chaos. Donation of Rose's piano in fact had a deeper meaning, as it underscored the fact that when Rose and I accepted the AUB challenge, we viewed it as a lasting commitment. Rose and I fully intended that this would be my last job, the final chapter of my professional career.

AUB finances

During my tenure at AUB, my work was set against the backdrop of financial stress that the university experienced due to the war, the chaos of which had quickly taken its toll on AUB. Travel to Beirut became tenuous as news relating to the fighting featured prominently in news media and television broadcasts throughout the world. School enrollment plummeted. The resulting loss of school income was compounded by losses the Medical Center incurred in treating battle casualties. Referrals for medical services from the region came to an end. Serving these patient referrals from the region had been one of the Medical Center's important sources of income. The resulting financial strain was serious, and the consequences weighed heavily on decision-makers. AUB's Board of Trustees had to take drastic steps. In 1977, AUB's School of Pharmacy, which had served the region since 1883, was closed.

Out of concern as to what additional measures might be necessary to deal with strained finances, in particular as to whether AUB should close another school or other academic

---

[83] As I write this, the piano remains in the Marquand House, where we first stayed as guests of the president and his wife in July of 1978.

parts, newly appointed President Hal Hoelscher prevailed on John Munro, Professor of English, to assess "The medium term future of AUB." Professor Munro interviewed many who had vested interests in AUB, including a number of faculty. Two of his consensus findings, reported in a letter to President Hoelscher dated August 22, 1980, were that the civil war had transformed AUB from a regional to a local university, and that cutting costs by eliminating another Faculty "was not the answer" to solving the fiscal crisis [6]. He underscored this point by noting that closing the School of Pharmacy had hardly made a difference in AUB's financial situation. Nevertheless, the president's May 16, 1980 memo to me, referred to below, made it clear that closure of the School of Public Health had been considered as a cost-cutting option. In his letter to the president, Professor Munro also stated, "Everyone believes that AUB's main problem was money and was likely to remain so ... Only if more money is forthcoming is it likely that AUB's situation will improve." The financial strains he articulated were clearly manifestations of the intermittent and unpredictable turmoil.

In the spring of 1980, President Hoelscher expressed his concern about FHS's finances on two occasions, once asking me to clarify the situation "... in the light of the proposed option to close one of AUB's faculties as a budget-saving expedient." Hoelscher's memo clearly indicated the Board of Trustees had considered closing the school [7, 8].

Public information regarding AUB's financial crisis is also in the record of a U.S. Congressional Hearing. Senator Ted Kennedy advocated the university's appeal for urgent assistance in the context of diminishing yearly allocations of support AUB had been receiving from the United States Agency for International Development (USAID). This hearing was held on September 23, 1981. The following selected quotes from Chairman Senator

Mark Hatfield's testimony convey the essence of AUB's plight: "Events of the past few months in Lebanon have placed severe new strains on the university, and, in the absence of new financial commitments to its continued existence, AUB may have to close its doors in the very near future ... The University Hospital has suffered ... in gun battles between warring factions, [E]xpenses have mounted from treating patients suffering from war-related wounds ... I urge the adoption [of the appeal] ..." The last sentence records the affirmative vote of the committee: "The amendment (UP No. 418) was agreed to." What the Committee was considering was an amount half again as much as the USAID allocation committed for the preceding year. The amount and details were not part of the record, but the affirmative action made the point—additional funding followed [9].

Despite the devastating effect of the civil war on the Medical Center (which affected the bottom line of the university), enrollment at AUB was more or less steady until the very end of my tenure, particularly enrollment of local applicants. That remarkable stability was made possible by the university's firm commitment to political and ideological neutrality, which turned AUB into an informal sanctuary. Nearly all of the feuding factions were represented In AUB's faculty, staff, and students. Therefore, stability was in everyone's best interests. Families who had decided to remain in Beirut saw the university as a safe place for their college-aged children. For many families, parental employment in nearby Gulf countries, in addition to endowment funds from AUB, made tuition affordable.

FHS finances

Though the Medical Center suffered heavily from the civil war, FHS was able to achieve a strong financial position. At the end of its first year, FHS recorded income in excess of expenditures.

FHS income increased from all sources, as depicted in the graphics below. In a memo that President Hoelscher sent to the Deans, dated February 19, 1980, he wrote, "I have just received a complete accounting of income generated by RADAC (Research and Development Administrative Center). During the academic year of 1978 – 79, RADAC brought a net income to AUB of $548,613. Of this, $284,233 were generated by the Faculty of Agriculture and Food Sciences, while the balance, $264,380, were generated by the Faculty of Health Sciences." He also noted sharply higher projected incomes for the following years. When he commented on these data at the Board of Deans meeting, his closing comment conveyed a sense of pride that these were the two deans he had recruited. I was pleased but a bit embarrassed, because I felt that it was not me but my faculty who deserved credit. To underscore his pride, President Hoelscher sent copies of this memo to his supervisor, Dr. C. Plimpton, Chairman of the Board of Trustees, and Mr. W. Rice, University Treasurer [10].

I mentioned that closure of our school had been considered in 1977 – 78. In a memo of May 16, 1980, entitled "FHS's Finances," I reported our solid financial footing for my first completed academic year, 1980 – 1981, based on projections from the Comptroller's office [7]. These data are reported in Table 2.

Table 2: FHS Financial Figures

Year	Operating Expenses	Tuition Revenue	Gifts	Sponsored Programs	FHS's Share from RADAC	Total Revenue
80/81	$800K	$921K (corr.)	$65K	$25K	$94K	$1.10M
81/82	$920K	$1.08M	$65K	$128K	$150K	$1.32M

We were all pleased that FHS had emerged financially strong in its first year. FHS had generated income exceeding operating expenses, and I predicted in my memo, "In the not too distant future, [FHS income] will be an important contributor to help grow FHS and to meet AUB's needs." That became a reality in the remaining years of my tenure.

The above financial information was an early affirmation of Asper's strategy that FHS would be financially stronger as an independent school apart from the Medical School. Indeed, he also viewed this separation as a necessary means to protect FHS, as it would have been vulnerable to closure given the financial crises faced by the Medical Center. The above recovery in FHS's financial condition underscored FHS's potential of again becoming a moneymaker for public health and for the university.

Salary increases had been constrained since the mid-1970s, when school income fell short of expenses in several consecutive years. Even the benefits of FHS's overall financial improvements in 1978-79 and 1979-80 had not been reflected in salaries at midyear 1980. Therefore, I wrote a memo to President Hoelscher on June 23, 1980 to request merit-based salary increases of 0% to 25% for all 10 FHS faculty; this would be in excess of the 7% across-the-board increase administratively approved. In another memo I sent him the very next day, June 24, 1980, I made a more compelling case for even greater increases—as high as 70% for the three most productive FHS faculty [11, 12].

I had another card to play with regard to additional income. I wrote to my contact in the Albany, NY accreditation office to ask how AUB's tuition charges compared to peer institutions. They sent me a publication confirming the disparity I had noted between AUB's tuition charges and those of 31 other private medical/public health schools in the United States extant in 1978 – 1979. The average first-year tuition of the 31 U.S. universities was $6,140.45, compared to AUB's tuition of $3,300. I sent this information to the president in a memo dated July 10, 1980. He thanked me, acknowledging the data would be considered in subsequent decisions about tuition increases. This was a difficult matter for decision-makers, but my memo may have played a role in the press release from AUB's Office of Information on October 5, 1981 that students had agreed to a 25% increase in fees to support the university [13].

FHS' Enrollment, Faculty, and Financial data, 1977-1982

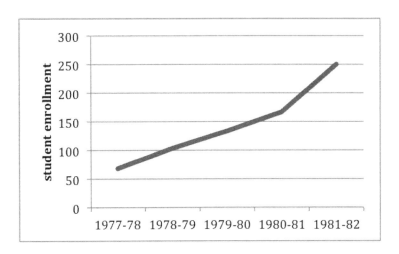

Figure 15: AUB FHS Enrollment, 1977 – 1982

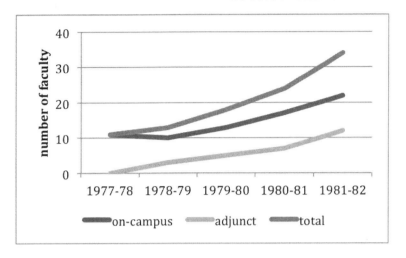

Figure 16: AUB FHS Faculty, 1977 – 1982

FHS' Enrollment, Faculty, and Financial data, 1977-1982

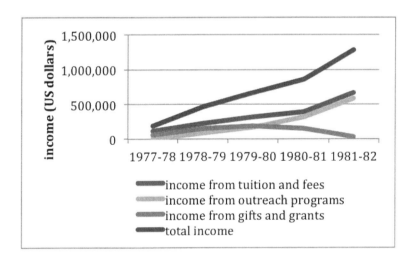

Figure 17: AUB FHS Income, 1977 – 1982

361

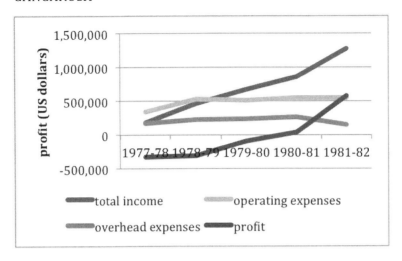

Figure 18: AUB FHS Financial Overview, 1977 – 1982

Even though he had already left AUB by this time, Sam Asper is the real hero of the FHS story. He advocated for the school's independence, which enabled its dean to put funds the school generated towards its own growth, rather than being subject to another dean's priorities for the use of those same funds. This kind of independent status is especially important when a school's survival is the issue—as it was at AUB during the chaos that led to the Lebanese civil war. Asper's lasting mark on AUB was his recognition that the public health school (which became the FHS) should not suffer the recurring financial crises that had already resulted in closure of the School of Pharmacy. In retrospect, I am grateful I was there to carry out his plan.

The school's situation at the outset of my tenure was dominated by years of continual civil conflict, which had both eroded the diversity of the curriculum and completely dissipated its focus on the parasitic diseases of the region. The chaos of war drove away the expert faculty that mentored the master's degree in Parasitology, which had been the school's flagship offering. Most, but not all, of the other master's degrees listed earlier were also casualties of the chaos, with the notable exception of the masters in Epidemiology.

FHS's financial independence leveraged a reinvigoration of the academic directions of the school during this transition. The leadership for this came from the two distinguished PhD Johns Hopkins-trained faculty, Dr. Haroutune K. Armenian and Dr. Huda C. Zurayk. Their research and scientific niches, their epidemiological and biostatistical skills, and their institutional links, including the Johns Hopkins School of Public Health and the World Health Organization, enabled FHS to emerge with much greater breadth and depth in its public health curriculum, as well as with greater distinguishment. At the same time, Dr. Nabil Kronfol provided leadership for academic programs in allied health sciences, particularly nursing, in some of the Gulf countries. Another key personage was Dr. Nadim Haddad[84], who contributed to FHS recovery in several important ways. Haddad played an important role in negotiating contracts between AUB and Gulf States ministry staff. He also arranged practicums for students with Ministry of Health staff and was one of several mentors for these students. Further, he collaborated with junior FHS post-graduate faculty and Bahraini ministry staff in assorted public health research and service projects.

Several other great academics were also critical to FHS's financial recovery. Aftim Acra demonstrated that sunlight could kill bacteria and viruses and then developed that key observation into a breakthrough technology for disinfecting drinking water at the household level. This elegant, simple invention heralded a new era of point-of-use safe water that

---

[84] Haddad was in fact one of the distinguished AUB alumni who had so impressed me when I was vetting AUB after they had offered me a position as Dean, tasking me with reinvigorating the school of public health.

went beyond oral rehydration for *treating* diarrheal diseases, to a new approach for *preventing* them. [85] [14] I previously mentioned the contributions of Zurayk, a biostatistician PhD graduate of Johns Hopkins School of Public Health; Armenian, a physician epidemiologist graduate of Johns Hopkins SPH; and Kronfol, a physician public health administrator, public policy expert, and DrPH graduate of Yale University's School of Economics. All three were outstanding teachers, student mentors, and scientists. I had the good fortune of collaborating with Zurayk on studies of the prevalence of infant deaths. We published two studies comparing infant mortality between rural and urban areas of South Lebanon [15, 16]. Zurayk, Armenian, and Kronfol have had distinguished careers and are highly regarded scientists in their respective fields. Many other scientists were also key contributors to FHS's financial wellbeing[xii]. Thusly, FHS progress was achieved in the region despite the turmoil in Lebanon. I believe President Hoelscher would have been pleased with their accomplishments.

In the years prior to this writing, the academic momentum has expanded and accelerated in excellence, recognition, and potential during Dr. Iman Nuwayhid's tenure as the seventh Dean of FHS. However, I would be remiss if I did not acknowledge the work of all of FHS's previous deans as well as acting deans as described in the reference "The Faculty of Health Sciences at the American University of Beirut: A Brief History: 1954-2004." [3]

---

[85] During my tenure, Professor Accra also served as Chairman of the Department of Environmental Health and coordinator of the Bachelor of Science in Environmental Health offering, a joint academic degree between FHS, the College of Arts and Sciences, and the School of Engineering.

New directions for the Nursing School

Coinciding with my tenure at FHS, the stage was also set for an expansion of and direction change for the Nursing School, whose enrollment had suffered since the intensification of the civil conflict in the early 1970s. Prior to that time, AUB had offered a certificate, three diploma programs, and a bachelor's degree in nursing. By the time I came to AUB, only the BSN program and the Diploma in Nursing remained; although the BSN program had a modicum of public health content in its curriculum, the Diploma in Nursing was strictly clinically focused.

In April of 1980, AUB hosted a conference on nursing education in the Middle East, with representatives from 13 countries [17]. Primary care was urgently needed in the region at that time, particularly in the rural areas, and one of the main themes discussed at the conference was the need to rigorously train nurses in public health so as to be able to meet these community health needs. President Hoelscher made several speeches to the conference participants, from which I identified three elements of his vision for nursing education in the region: 1) to further develop "capabilities in, and ... service to, the needs of primary health care – preventive medicine, family medicine"; 2) to ensure that nursing graduates have the skills and knowledge to provide leadership in all aspects of their profession; 3) to foster among students the skills necessary to understand and utilize technological developments to their full advantage [17]. This was a vision that was in contrast to the prevailing sentiments within the Faculty of Medicine, which favored a more specialized care focus given the university hospital's historical prominence as a tertiary care institution. The hospital's status as a center of excellence in the region was also responsible for a substantive portion of the medical school's income (which in fact translated to the university's income) in the days prior to the civil chaos. At that time, the financial stresses were so great that all academic leaders mobilized whatever resources they had to protect their own turf. It was in this context that the expansion of public health into primary care was resisted, as it was seen as a threat to the very survival of the medical programs.

Despite these challenges, however, AUB did succeed in transforming its nursing education. The person most critical in pushing forward this new vision was Professor Adele Nelson, who served as director of the program in the Division of Nursing within FHS and had in fact organized the conference (no small feat in this climate of limited financial resources). Two words come to my mind to describe her work: quality assurance. I had great confidence in her abilities and expertise, and trusted her to push forward the nursing program with very minimal input from me. Nelson envisioned a rigorous academic curriculum for our nursing students and was successful in securing external funding from the Helene Fuld Foundation for career development of promising BSN graduates. Through this funding (indeed, our only funding at the time for nursing education!), a number were supported in career development programs abroad. Many have since gone on to highly successful careers with well-known organizations.

The following year, however, the continuing civil conflict created a situation that jeopardized our new vision for nursing education. The hospital's need for clinically trained diploma nurses had become urgent, with this shortage in trained nurses partly related to a stigma against nursing that was prevalent among Muslim families in the region at that time. The Board of Trustees proposed transferring the Nursing School to the Faculty of Medicine, partly to facilitate nurse recruitment to the hospital, and also (likely) partly to bolster the financial situation of the Faculty of Medicine, which, like that of most of AUB, was rather dire at that time. A member of the Board of Trustees, Dr. Theodore Van Italie, asked me my opinion regarding this transfer. In a letter to him dated May 7, 1981, I supported the plan to transfer the clinically oriented Diploma Nursing Program to the Medical School. However, I advocated that FHS retain the Bachelor of Science in Nursing Program, in part because it had become popular for applicants aspiring to leadership roles. I also pointed out that Nursing faculty and students enrolled in the BSN program had expressed strong feelings that the program should remain in FHS, based on a belief that this would enable greater development than could be achieved within the Faculty of Medicine. In addition, I noted we had a record 56 applications for the BSN program pending at that time [19]. My view about the BSN degree did not prevail, and nursing faculty morale suffered after this restructuring, which was seen as a demotion of the program. Nonetheless, motivated graduates continued to be successful, with several having superlative careers in internationally known agencies. Academic nursing and health administration was later extended more fully into the Gulf countries under the leadership of Professor Kronfol.

At the time of this writing, nursing education at AUB is strong—the Rafic Hariri School of Nursing is supported by a large endowment from MP Hariri and is considered a center of excellence. I believe that Nelson laid the foundation for this growth and development, beginning with the conference that she organized and continuing through her contributions to the public health curriculum as well as her role in the emergence of the Division of Nursing as an independent school of nursing. I give her great credit for her strong leadership and dedication, without which the School of Nursing may well have faltered during those turbulent times.

Leaving AUB FHS

Leaving FHS was, and still is, a poignant memory. In the fall of 1980, I was considering two other job offers because my three-year contract would expire in January 1981. I was tempted to stay a bit longer because Rose and I were offered the home on campus I had initially requested but which had been assigned to Dr. John Fisher, Dean of Agriculture. He left AUB in December 1980, during a calm period that lasted only a few months. In retrospect, that was the safest period of my tenure. Still, tensions and concerns about the tenuous situation caused me to hesitate, so I ruled out a three-year renewal. I had briefed President Hoelscher that I was considering instead a one-year renewal. I was pleasantly surprised by his letter of January 5, 1981, stating, "... working with you continues to be both a great personal pleasure and a source of continuing professional satisfaction. You took on an activity 'not a Faculty' when you came here and shared with me a dream about its potential significance and importance to AUB and this entire region. You have moved steadily and deliberately to develop that activity ... 'now a Faculty' ... capable of important professional services at a high professional level ... and in the continuing future". I was deeply touched by this. Another factor that affected my decision to renew my contract for an additional year was the fact that I had assured applicants I was planning to stay at least until the end of that academic year. I saw that as a commitment.

In the spring of 1981, fighting resumed close to the campus. We received a letter from my son Ray, poignantly expressing his concern—and the family's concerns—about our situation in Beirut[86]. A new concern gripped me—I could accept risks for my own life, but I would not put Rose and our son Paul in danger. So,

---

[86] A copy of Ray's letter is attached at the end of this chapter.

early in July of that year, the three of us left AUB and returned to our home in suburban Atlanta. For most of that month, I helped Rose and Paul to get settled. I returned to Beirut in late July intending to stay at least until my contract expired at the end of academic year 1981 – 82.

The next few months were exceedingly stressful. I was lonesome; it was the longest time Rose and I had been apart since our marriage. It helped that Rose called, despite difficulties getting phone connections. I often learned of local developments from her, since BBC news had only minimal coverage of the Lebanese civil war. Almost every day, colleagues and students reported intensified fighting in and around Beirut, even in AUB's suburb—Hamra. I kept reassuring Rose I was safe, but she knew otherwise because she realized I had to buy food and other essentials off campus in Hamra. I prepared all meals and ate at home because of hostage-taking and indiscriminant bombings in public places.

I made an appointment with Acting President Dodge to inform him of my decision to resign. I vividly remember that meeting, in which he made no effort to dissuade me[87]. Instead, he expressed deep concern about potential problems in FHS that he, as interim president, would have to address. He worried whether the faculty and resources could handle the record number of students we had recruited, especially since many more applications were still pending. As he was new to this job, he did not know FHS well. However, he understood the dire financial

---

[87] Indeed, Interim President David Dodge wrote a telegram to the Board of Trustees dated June 15, 1981 supporting my request for a one-year renewal of my contract with AUB, on the condition that a distinguished scientist be appointed to the Board of Trustees to advocate FHS issues. I recommended that D. A. Henderson serve in that role.

condition of the university, and realized it was not in a position to rescue a floundering program.

I shared with him my confidence in FHS's strengths. I mentioned that FHS had been in the black for every year since its inception, and revenue growth was still strong. I reassured him that the faculty could manage without me, especially since he had three outstanding choices for acting or interim dean. At the end, he said he wanted me to summarize in writing my assurances, especially regarding FHS's financial strength. Because little time remained, I said I would try my best. He made it clear that was not good enough. As we parted, he said, "See this has your highest priority."

I spent days crafting a memo to President Dodge and finished it on October 14, 1981. From data provided by the registrar's and business offices, I tabulated increasing enrollment, increasing income, increasing numbers of adjunct faculty teaching at little cost, and increasing income from grants and contracts. These findings provided strong evidence that FHS had restored a solid foundation even during the chaos of civil war, so it no longer needed subsidies from the university or my continued involvement. I met President Dodge the next day to present my report [19]. That one meeting with Interim President Dodge was the only time these data about FHS's financial situation had been presented. Decades later, I have rediscovered these unpublished results to help tell this story.

On Monday, November 16, 1981, I was pleasantly surprised to see a front-page story in the campus newspaper, the *AUB Bulletin*, with the headline "Fall Registration: 4,865 vs. 5,028." The article pointed out that FHS had increased its enrollment during that academic year (1980-81), while enrollments in other colleges were lower or little changed [20].

370

My last act as FHS's dean was writing a letter to President Dodge dated October 26, 1981. It documented continuing salary disparities and recommended large raises for key faculty who had extended themselves far beyond the call of duty for teaching, mentoring, and research supported with external grants. I have since felt great satisfaction that those faculty members have had distinguished careers, including two who have served as deans of FHS [21].

In my last evening in Beirut, Interim President Dodge invited me to his house for a memorable going-away party. His home was on the same path next to where we had lived. I was a bit late, as I had much to do to prepare for my flight the next morning. I was astonished that so many had gathered for the informal event—faculty, friends, staff, neighbors, and students who filled the Dodge's home. After an hour or so, President Dodge spoke spontaneously for about 10 minutes. He thanked me for my service to AUB, noted the progress FHS had made during my tenure, and wished me success and a safe trip. In sharp contrast to the anxieties he had expressed in our earlier meeting, his remarks gave me confidence that he recognized FHS's potential and its bright future. That poignant experience, forever entrenched In my memory, assured me things would turn out well for FHS.

AUB FHS after my departure

After I left, Armenian succeeded me as Interim Dean of FHS. The years that followed witnessed the most severe fighting of the Lebanese Civil War, affecting many of the faculty.[xiii] A brochure prepared at the School of Public Health's 50th anniversary, entitled *A Brief History: 1954-2004*, underscored the critical role Armenian played at that time. It has a section, entitled "Surviving War," describing the profound impact of the war on AUB and

FHS. This section cites Armenian's leadership role in maintaining operations, continuing classes with block courses taught by local and external faculty, involving students in research, enlisting them in disease surveillance with funding provided by the United States Agency for International Development (USAID), and collaborating with Save the Children and the Lebanese Red Cross. Its concluding paragraph recognizes his collaboration with another outstanding AUB leader, Dr. Adnan Mroueh, noting they "redoubled their efforts and served dual roles as acting Deans of FHS along with their regular academic appointments." From the work they did, Armenian published a landmark study, *"Epidemiology and the War in Lebanon."* [22] Considered together, these works demonstrate that with such leaders, FHS/AUB was able to adapt through an extended period of instability. They were FHS's heroes, making great academic achievements during the worst chaos of the war. I am pleased the financial recovery that FHS's faculty accomplished during my tenure made their heroism possible. I am encouraged that even now, FHS and AUB continue in academic excellence.[xiv]

I would also like to compliment the dean at the time of this writing, Dr. Iman Nuwayhid, and his network colleagues for their dedication in the face of great hardships, their enlightened plans, and their wonderful work. I wish them continuing success. I am pleased that Emory University's Rollins School of Public Health is part of this network. In particular, I am delighted that Dean Nuwayhid and my colleague Dr. Christine Moe are planning collaborative research to promote safe water and sanitation.

I expect that AUB's founding fathers would have been extremely pleased with the state and focus of the university at the time of this writing. Dean Nuwayhid's ideas fit perfectly with the principles of tolerance that Professor Daniel Bliss articulated in the opening ceremony for the university's dedication, way back in 1871. Bliss's remarks were far ahead of his time. We now see their eloquent echo in the United Nation's Declaration of Human Rights, which provides a beacon of enlightenment for all nations. The Faculty of Health Science's academic work and services to the region also fit perfectly with AUB's motto from the biblical passage in John 10:10, which underscores our concern about quality of life for all peoples.

Another AUB persona—Hajj Omar Faour

I would also like to pay tribute to AUB/FHS administrative staff, and in particular one staff employee, Hajj Omar Faour. I write his story because of his exemplary dedication and commitment to AUB. He left a lasting impression on everyone touched by his service and self-sacrifice.

Omar was a trusted AUB driver and the senior staff member of AUB's carpool. The university's carpool arranged travel required for faculty, staff, and visitors, and provided logistics at the airport to facilitate security arrangements for them. Omar was a caring and friendly person even when circumstances were grim. He consistently found ways to bring staff and visitors safely to campus even in the most difficult and sometimes dangerous circumstances. The importance of his role was underscored on those occasions when fighting was close to the campus, and he had to improvise alternate routes to avoid potentially hazardous situations. For example, he routinely drove nurses through the most dangerous parts of the city and at the most dangerous times. On several occasions when the Beirut Airport had closed because of hostilities, he met Asper at the Damascus airport and returned him to the campus over mountainous roads rendered treacherous by long neglect, wear and tear, artillery shell holes, frequent military roadblocks, and snipers trying to discourage or disrupt travel.

Rose had one particular experience that especially taxed Omar's skills. I had arranged an FHS visit for one of CDC's distinguished scientists, Dr. Frank Bryan, an international expert on food safety. Specifically, he was CDC's point person on promoting the Hazard Analysis and Critical Control Point (HACCP) strategy for safe foods. Unexpectedly, I had to travel to address an urgent matter on the day he was scheduled to arrive in Beirut. I asked Rose to meet him, a task she sometimes did for me. Omar drove her to meet Bryan at the airport and helped him clear security. On the way back to the campus, fighting broke out. Rose recalls that Omar had to stop repeatedly to ask people for their sense of what was happening. He took several detours around troubled areas to avoid hostilities. A trip that usually required no more than an hour lasted three hours. Bryan, with Rose in the back seat, sensed something was awry and became a bit anxious. She confidently assured him that Omar was skilled in such situations. When they arrived, my Assistant Dean, Jack Ibrahim, was anxiously waiting for Omar, Rose, and Bryan at the AUB gate; everyone was much relieved because they realized how hazardous their journey must have been.

On another occasion, Omar helped my brother in a difficult situation when he arrived at the Beirut airport. Dr. Louis P. Gangarosa, Professor of Dental Pharmacology at the University of Georgia in Augusta, Georgia, had invented a technology to deliver high concentrations of drugs, such as antiviral agents, into affected dermal tissues using the electrolytic process called iontophoresis. I invited him to visit (at my personal expense) to teach his methodology to a select group of dental professionals in Beirut. With the logistical information I had provided him, he scheduled his travel from Milan, Italy, where he had been consulting and teaching. Unfortunately, when he arrived, his visa was found somehow flawed. Omar had access to the security area where Lou was being queried. He was informed of the problem and told it could not be resolved at the airport, so my brother would not be permitted to enter the country. I am not sure what Omar did, but he sorted this out, and Lou was allowed to enter. I was grateful when a much-relieved Lou and a smiling Omar came through the check point where I was waiting for them. Omar had convinced a senior customs officer that a group of dentists at AUB were waiting for him so that they could learn and use his method in Lebanon. On similar occasions, without Omar's intervention, people who arrived in Beirut with flawed visas simply had to leave on the next flight to wherever.

Because FHS had a steady stream of scientist consultants who helped in the revival of the school, we depended a great deal on Omar's services. Even before the civil war, Omar's services had been vital for helping Asper until his departure, and then later, to facilitate AUB and FHS work. His encyclopedic knowledge of the city and the goodwill he exerted through his contacts were tremendous assets to the University Hospital, Medical School and FHS. His coworkers, the university's professional faculty, and visiting dignitaries respected his calmness even under great dangers and admired his returning every day to a job that confronted him with such dangers on a regular basis.

Even Omar's everyday task of transporting AUB nurses from the Christian sector of the city to the AUB hospital posed special hazards. The border between east and west Beirut was called the "green line," after the uniform color of the militia that frequently controlled roadblocks there. After I left Beirut, I learned that Omar had been killed one night by a sniper's bullet while attempting to return to campus after driving nurses to their homes in East Beirut. Rose and I have a special place in our hearts for Omar, whom we shall always remember as AUB's shining example of dedication, commitment, loyalty, and determination.

Personal reflections

In summary, during the years 1978 – 1981, I served as Dean of the Faculty of Health Sciences for the specific task of reviving AUB's School of Public Health, whose applicant pool for its many academic offerings had been compromised by the Lebanese civil war. What I had inherited was a faltering academic program that had become financially impaired by the loss of applicants from the region. In the first two decades after WWII, the school had been globally recognized as a center of public health excellence by virtue of its distinguished faculty of internationally recognized research scientists and its rich and diverse menu of academic offerings that had attracted applicants from the Middle East and East Africa. During my tenure, I worked with faculty to change the school's existing Master of Public Health (MPH) degree program into a two-year program to appeal to local seniors recruited from AUB's Colleges. Enrollments in this revised MPH Program and in other FHS academic offerings at the master's and baccalaureate levels increased in each year of my tenure, resulting in budget surpluses that strengthened FHS's academic and financial base.

Despite hardships Rose and I experienced, I benefitted a great deal personally from my time at AUB. I left AUB's FHS with a sense of accomplishment, satisfaction, and confidence. My role in helping FHS reverse its financial fortunes prepared me well for the next chapter of my career—the job I got at Emory University helping its public health graduate program get traction after languishing for seven years. The contrasts between the experiences I recorded in this chapter and those in my role at Emory were stark and striking. At Emory I had responsibility for a graduate program that, despite having existed for seven years, had only 16 part-time students when I started, had never enrolled a full time student, had never enrolled an international student, had never offered more than 12 courses, had never won funding for research, and had never had an income sufficient to cover its expenses. In a sense it had not faltered—it just had never taken off. In contrast, my challenge at AUB was to find a way to reverse the financial fortune of what had been _the_ premier public health institution of the Middle East. However, both these chapters in my career involved institution-building with very limited resources.

References

1.   Asper S, Bergman PS: **Care Amidst Chaos: The story of the Medical Center of the American University of Beirut in the early years (1975-78) of the Lebanese civil strife**: American University of Beirut, Alumni Association of North America; 1994.

2.   Powers LE, Churchill CW: **Bibliography of echinococcosis, with selected abstracts**. Beirut, Lebanon: American University of Beirut; 1959.

3.   Campbell O, Acra A: **The Faculty of Health Sciences at the American University of Beirut: A Brief History, 1954-2004**. Beirut, Lebanon: American University of Beirut; 2004.

4.   Katul M: **Data on AUB Programs, from Registrar's Office**. Pers. Comm. Rec. by EJ Gangarosa. Beirut, Lebanon.

5.   Hoelscher H: **Formal offer letter for the position of the Dean of Faculty of Health Sciences, AUB**. Pers. Comm. Rec. by EJ Gangarosa. Beirut, Lebanon; 1978.

6.   Munro J: **Report on the medium term future of AUB**. Pers. Comm. Rec. by H Hoelscher. Beirut, Lebanon; 1980.

7. Gangarosa EJ: **FHS's Finances**. Pers. Comm. Rec. by H Hoelscher, Memo #1 on FHS financial situation edn. Beirut, Lebanon; 1980.

8. Gangarosa EJ: **Memo #2 on the financial situation of FHS**. Pers. Comm. Rec. by H Hoelscher. Beirut, Lebanon; 1980.

9. **Congressional Hearing on amendment UP No. 418**. 1981.

10. Hoelscher H: **Memo on AUB finances**. Pers. Comm. Rec. by Deans of AUB. Beirut, Lebanon; 1980.

11. Gangarosa EJ: **Request for salary increases for FHS faculty**. Pers. Comm. Rec. by H Hoelscher, Memo #3 on FHS financial situation, merit-based salary increases edn. Beirut, Lebanon; 1980.

12. Gangarosa EJ: **Request for additional salary increases for most productive FHS faculty**. Pers. Comm. Rec. by H Hoelscher. Beirut, Lebanon; 1980.

13. Gangarosa EJ: **Comparison of FHS tuition to other schools of public health**. Pers. Comm. Rec. by H Hoelscher. Beirut, Lebanon; 1980.

14. Acra A, Raffoul Z, Karahagopian Y: **Solar disinfection of drinking water and oral rehydration solutions: guidelines for household application in developing countries**. Beirut, Lebanon: UNICEF; 1984.

15. Shibaru I, Tabbarah I, Zurayk H, Muhana M, Gangarosa E: **Infant mortality in Bekaa-Lebanon, 1979**. *Le Journal medical libanais The Lebanese medical journal* 1980, **31**(3):245-250.

16. Zurayk H, Tawil M, Gangarosa E: **Effect of urban versus rural residence and of maternal education on infant health in South Lebanon**. *J Epidemiology and Community Health* 1982, **36**(3):192-196.

17. **Nursing Education in the Middle East: Community Health Needs and Curriculum Development**. In*: April 14 - 18, 1980 1980; American University of Beirut, Lebanon*; 1980.

18. Gangarosa EJ: **Opinions on the nursing program at FHS**. Pers. Comm. Rec. by T v Italie. Beirut, Lebanon; 1981.

19. Gangarosa EJ: **Memo on FHS financial situation**. Pers. Comm. Rec. by D Dodge. Beirut, Lebanon; 1981.

20. **Fall Registration: 4,865 vs. 5,028**. *AUB Bulletin.* Beirut, Lebanon; 1981.

21. Gangarosa EJ: **Salary disparities and recommendations for FHS faculty salaries**. Pers. Comm. Rec. by D Dodge. Beirut, Lebanon; 1981.

22. Armenian HK: **Epidemiology and the war in Lebanon**. *Takemi Forum on International Health.* Boston, MA: Takemi Program in International Health; 1985.

Appendix: 1981 Letter from Raymond E. Gangarosa

Sunday, April 12, 1981

Dear Mom, Dad, and Paul,

It is with the greatest consternation that I read about the renewed fighting in Beirut. I can imagine how frustrating those events must be for you, especially in view of your recent decision to stay longer. I think now more than ever our family is plagued by a pervasive feeling of isolation because of these events. Dad, I was particularly dismayed by your decision to call off your visit, though I completely agree it was the right and necessary thing to do. But most of all, I am deeply concerned about your safety. I realize you have lived close to the dangers for a long time and are better able to estimate the risks, but I wonder if you can appreciate fully their toll on us who are not exposed except through worry about you. In my travels, I felt far less stress when it was myself at risk and not you. (Dad, I'm sure you had the same feeling last week -- I could head it in your voice). Now every time I read about a terrorist hijacking and the turmoil in the Mideast, I cringe at the possibilities. Remote as they may seem to you in your everyday life, the specter posed by fanaticism and anti-Americanism gnaws at us. Recently after a tough night on call, I was awakened by a nightmare about you. In the past, I can scarcely remember having been jarred from the peacefulness of sleep (seemingly my only respite from the demands of my internship), much less when I was so tired.

I want to encourage you to leave Beirut -- if not for your own sakes, then for ours. I, perhaps more than most, recognize the need for sacrifice in finding a niche, but there are situations that are intolerable, and surely this is one. Dad, how can you effectively recruit faculty when your recruiting campaign is aborted by the fighting? And in the mere policies of promotion and firing, one makes bitter and potentially dangerous enemies in the Mideast. As a foreigner your position is even more vulnerable. And how can we sleep comfortably knowing that an AUB dean was assassinated in his own office on the campus itself? Dad, you are too productive and useful to be working under these unnecessary risks. I've kept fairly quiet about these concerns for a long time, always feeling guilty that if anything happened, I'd never forgive myself for my silence. Regardless of any momentary improvements in the political situation in Beirut, that area will always be unsafe, even on campus. As events and Iran and Pakistan have so dramatically proved, we can't even assume stability from one day to the next, especially in light of the vociferousness of anti-Americanism and pervasive suspicions of Israeli spying -- to say nothing of the enormous power wielded by armed psychopaths in Lebanon.

The difficulties in communication alone are a blow to everyone's morale. (When I talked this week to Dr. Calia about my frustrations about our situation, I had to choke back the tears). This comes a time when there is a lot of turmoil in our family, and the isolation contributes to a lot of stress. With your

concern about trends in Gene's life, surely your isolation is detrimental both to you and to him. And at a time of tremendous growth in my life, I feel deprived of the opportunity to share it with my brothers and parents. Furthermore, in this time of extreme demands on me, it compounds the difficulties to be unable to share my thoughts with you, and, even more, to have to worry about your safety. I think personal factors like these would be sufficient by themselves to terminate a contract. [But, Dad do I understand that you haven't actually signed contract?].
Regardless of the inconvenience of moving again, I believe it is folly not to leave Beirut now, for every possible reason. Tell them it's for personal reasons that you have to leave -- that your family is troubled and worried sick about you. (It's true -- I've been eating more Gelusil than food lately, and Peggy feels the same way. So do Aunt Theresa, Aunt Florence, Aunt Claire -- everyone!)

I know you have a lot of wonderful friends in Beirut, that it's difficult to leave -- to leave work undone and "abandon" friends at a bad time. But you have so many friends in so many places, and so much exciting work to do -- why being such an inconducive and dangerous place? I welcomed (and still do!) your traveling to a new environment, to break out of the oversettled existence you lead in Atlanta -- but now as you are resettling in Beirut again, once again you must break away. You can't let the apparent stability lull you into overlooking the dangers -- of being on the wrong plane, of sudden political upheavals, unpredictable outbreaks of violence -- if only because we in the States have to worry about these on your account.

All of us care a great deal about you, we love you, and hope you will decide to come home very soon.
Love,
Ray

Chapter 14: My Role in the Transition of Emory University's Graduate Program into a School of Public Health

My earliest involvement with Emory

My interest in Emory University began in 1958 when my mentor Garland Herndon left the Walter Reed Army Hospital to work there. He spoke enthusiastically about his future at Emory, and his comments planted the seed in my head that I might someday also have a role at the university.

In 1971, during my tenure at CDC, Tom Sellers sent a letter inviting me to teach in the Department of Community Medicine. I accepted and received a letter of appointment as Clinical Professor of Preventive Medicine and Community Health, signed by Sanford Atwood on September 17, 1971. I began teaching as an adjunct faculty member the following year.

Four years later, in 1975, the Master of Community Health (MCH) program was launched, and John Boring and Sellers asked me to expand my teaching role. I was enthusiastic about teaching Emory students, and lectured every year before my CDC retirement in 1978. These experiences gave me a sense of belonging and prepared me for a future role that I did not anticipate at the time.

As previously mentioned, while serving as Dean of the Faculty of Health Sciences (FHS) from July of 1978 to November of 1981 at the American University of Beirut, I made 3 trips to Atlanta to attend the annual CDC conferences of the Epidemic Intelligence Service (EIS). On each trip, I visited Tom, who was then chairman of the Department of Community Health and Preventive Medicine (DCHPM). I shared with him my progress in transforming AUB's FHS and the satisfaction I had from seeing enrollment rise, the academic program grow, and the new school gain recognition. In my discussions with Sellers, I saw that my challenges at AUB were similar to those he was facing in the MCH Program.

A struggling program

At that time, I recognized that the MCH designation was limiting the growth potential of Emory's program. The MCH was not well recognized in the academic or public health community. According to Dave Sencer, a key player in the organizing consortium, this name was adopted to underscore the commitment to train community health practitioners. However, it seemed to leave MCH graduates on the defensive in their job interviews, needing to explain that they did not have special training or skills in the subspecialty area of maternal and child health, which was the most common interpretation for the acronym "MCH" among public health workers. I also sensed that there might have been a tacit acknowledgement that the degree was something less than the MPH degree awarded by other graduate programs in public health.

Even more serious than the name and content of the degree was the problem that students could escape paying tuition at Emory by taking courses at other Atlanta schools. In fact, students could get full Emory credit for courses taken elsewhere and tuition paid elsewhere, an arrangement that I had never heard of in any academic institution, and one that cost the program a substantial amount of money! It is important to understand how this anomalous situation came about. The MCH program was created by a consortium of institutional partners, with Emory taking the lead. Other partners were Georgia State University, Georgia Tech, and CDC. It was envisioned that Emory's curriculum would grow as the program grew, but that was not happening. The sparseness of the course offerings was the result of a lack of budget for curriculum development. In a Catch 22 situation, continual budget deficits prevented university investment in the program, which made the program unappealing to applicants, which then in turn reduced tuition revenues and exacerbated budget deficits. There was virtually no change in the curriculum between 1975 and 1982. When I came aboard, the curriculum consisted of four core courses and eight electives, a total of only 12 courses! Most of the core courses were taught only during the summer semester. From such a limited academic menu, it was next to impossible for students to complete the required 37 credit hours at Emory. The only solution was to permit students to take public health-related courses at the other consortium institutions. Students I spoke to were, in fact, quite pleased with this arrangement, because tuition at state-supported schools was considerably less than tuition at Emory. Students were thus able to earn Emory degrees without paying Emory tuition except for the four core courses. This arrangement consigned the program to financial stagnation, as without a strong curriculum, it was unable to attract enough applicants to enable growth.

At that time, the MCH program was under the jurisdiction of the School of Medicine, which was absorbing these annual budget deficits. Medical school administrators were impatient. The situation was ominous: I came to understand that administrators were questioning the very survival of the program.

An initiative that failed

While I was at AUB, Garland Herndon was acting dean of Emory's School of Medicine. He encouraged the MCH faculty to remedy the program's problems by starting an Academy of Health at Emory. The plan was prepared and submitted in anticipation of funding. The academy would have four components: (1) problem-solving in public health, (2) multidisciplinary inquiry, (3) research and development, and (4) education of students through a School of Prevention, offering a Master in Prevention degree. The planners met with CDC personnel and developed the proposal that would expand the MCH program, with the ultimate goal of starting a school of public health. In fact, the proposal was prepared so as to compete for funding corresponding to a Request for Proposal from the Department of Health and Human Services. These events raised hope that funding would be forthcoming. It also raised my own hopes for a role in the growth of Emory's program.

Late in 1981, when I left AUB, a visit to Tom Sellers was high on my agenda. I was disappointed to learn that the MCH program's problems were persistent and that the Academy of Health had not been funded. The dean of the medical school was concerned that the academy concept would compete for other funding that had a higher priority at Emory. In the absence of external support, the concept of a graduate program in public health at a private institution was seriously questioned. Mounting yearly deficits undermined the credibility of the program. The reality I saw at that time was a pessimistic future for MCH. I thus wrote off the possibility of a role in transforming the MCH program. I thought the issue was dead.

A new opportunity and a challenge from Emory University

In the year 1982, I had consulting assignments for the World Health Organization. I participated in studies of oral rehydration therapy, and also had a role in an investigation of a longstanding endemic of *Salmonella waycross* in Guam. These temporary assignments required a lot of time away from home and were therefore stressful to my family and me. I yearned for a new reality without short-term consultations.

I began to explore other job options. Several opportunities arose, including an offer from Johns Hopkins, where my classmate D. A. Henderson served as dean of the school of public health. He offered me a position to be the coordinator of his school's MPH program. I turned these offers down because I really wanted to work at Emory, stay involved with CDC, and live in Atlanta—which was Rose's preference as well.

I met again with John Boring, a close friend and colleague going back to when we worked together at CDC in the Epidemiology Branch. I also continued my association with another of Sellers's faculty members, my friend and colleague Jack Shulman, whom I knew from my years at the University of Maryland, and from when we served together in the EIS. I met with both of them to seek their advice regarding the role I believed I could have in helping to solve the MCH problems.

Late in the spring of 1982, I was pleasantly surprised to receive a call from Sellers inviting me to consider a part-time teaching job during the absence of a faculty member on academic leave. It was a small role—assisting in teaching preventive medicine to freshmen medical students. This was an opportunity that, in my thinking, kept alive the possibility of my someday transforming the MCH program. This was still very much a distant hope of mine, though I saw it as a sensitive issue I should not discuss. With this in mind, I accepted the role.

The course was taught in the fall of 1982. As the semester progressed, opportunities arose to discuss the matter of the MCH program. I think my enthusiasm for what might be was infectious. It helped that I had John's support; he more than anyone helped influence Sellers. In her book *A Shared Dream*, Dollie Daniels wrote that Boring exclaimed to Sellers, "We have to find a way to bring Gene Gangarosa on board!" [1] In the early fall of 1982, while the medical school course was in progress, Sellers asked my help in preparing a plan to reinvigorate the MCH program. The possibility I had nurtured was becoming a probability.

Sellers arranged what I called "Sellers's rescue plan," a proposal for the medical school dean, James Glenn, to accept me as director of the MCH program for a trial period to see if I could fix problems compromising its growth. I was impressed by how well Sellers had prepared for this meeting with Dean Glenn. He had made arrangements for letters of support from Bill Foege, Director of CDC at the time, and Jim Alley, Director of the Georgia Department of Human Resources. Their letters were definitely helpful in assuring Dean Glenn of the need for a graduate program in public health at Emory to meet not only Georgia's needs but also national and international needs.

Those letters were particularly important because some naysayers at Emory argued that the major problem of the MCH program was a limited pool of applicants. That impression was based on and seemingly supported by the fact that, at the time, there were very few applicants seeking admission, no full-time students, and no prospects for external support. I saw much more potential.

It was fortuitous that Dean Glenn was a classmate in my premedical program at the University of Rochester. Our meeting with him was cordial. Sellers spoke first, and then I did most of the talking as he listened intently. I sensed that I needed to give more than reassurance of what I thought I could do. So, I offered a plan I hoped he could not refuse: no need for tenure, a salary that could charitably be called modest, and a commitment that if I could not succeed in turning the program around within two years, I would help phase it out and then leave. I think he was persuaded by a combination of my conviction, enthusiasm, and experience at AUB.

The dean accepted our plan. With only a handshake, I made plans to begin my new role as Director of the MCH program on the first workday of 1983.

I later learned that I may not have even had this chance were it not for the work done by Connie Conrad, my predecessor as director. During her tenure, she played a key role in getting the Master of Community Health program accredited by the Council of Education for Public Health (CEPH), which has established rigorous standards. In fact, when the MCH program first began, the CEPH had no mechanisms for accrediting programs of public health—only schools of public health. Indeed, some schools of public health were reluctant to open up accreditation to programs, for fear of new competition! Connie took the initiative to travel to Washington, D.C., to meet with Janet Strauss, the Executive Director of CEPH, so that they, along with another program director, could write the standards of accreditation for programs of public health. Upon her return to Atlanta, Connie ensured that Emory's MCH program met these standards. That first year, Emory was one of three programs to be granted accreditation. That accreditation was a critical point in the acceptance of the program by university decision-makers, buying the necessary time as well as investment to save the MCH program from the fate of Emory's Dental School. Then, in 1982, she volunteered to step aside so that I could implement a recovery plan for the MCH program analogous to what I had done at AUB.

I also learned that, during my vetting for this new position, my curriculum vitae had been forwarded to the Vice President for Health Sciences, who fortuitously happened to be Garland Herndon, my mentor during my Walter Reed Hospital residency training. Another piece of my career puzzle had fallen into place.

Becoming a casualty!

Just as everything seemed to be coming together, I had a personal setback on Christmas Eve of 1982, two weeks before the scheduled start of my new job. My son Ray and I were hanging insulation on a porch to adapt it for winter use. While he was on one ladder and I was near the top of another, I lost my balance, fell, and broke my right ankle. I actually heard the bones breaking at the moment of impact. It was the quickest diagnosis I had ever made!

The injury was a serious fracture of the right foot—a break in several pieces, one of which sheared the joint below my ankle. It required surgical pinning to secure broken bones, a full leg cast, and a long convalescence; it has also caused chronic pain and decreased mobility even up to the time of this writing. I spent the rest of the Christmas holiday in the orthopedic ward of DeKalb General Hospital. However, I was determined that this problem would not stop me.

Despite this handicap, I started my new job as planned. I came to work in my cast, charged with anticipation. My colleagues commented that I got through the civil war in Lebanon unscathed, but before I even started my job at Emory, I had become a casualty! From day one, I found my job challenging; it required working 60-hour weeks. I never missed a day's work.

In familiar territory

The curriculum was my first concern, but at Emory there was an additional twist I hadn't faced at AUB—I had to require students to take their courses at Emory and pay the tuition of a private school. This was priority number one. I was pleased to have the full support of faculty in making this change. Students already enrolled in the program were permitted to complete their course work elsewhere if they wished. That was not a big problem because at that time there were only 16 part-time students and no full-time students! Starting with the first new applicant accepted in the program, all students were required to pay full Emory tuition. This action was an essential step in the evolution of our school.

To institute this new tuition requirement, we had to make the course offerings sufficiently attractive that the Emory curriculum would provide significant added value. Accordingly, I initiated four changes in the program:

1. **Change in degree offered:** For the first time, we offered the Master of Public Health (MPH) degree. In preparation for this change, I made numerous inquiries to get student, alumni, and faculty views on the name of the degree we would offer. We came to the conclusion that the name "Master of Community Health" was inappropriate and was an impediment to our progress. The most compelling reason for change was the fact

that the MPH degree was widely recognized as the basic credential for public health professionals, while the MCH degree was relatively unknown. The MCH curriculum, though sparse and unconvincing, had been generically an MPH offering. In making the change from the MCH to the MPH degree, I was pleased to get the support of students, alumni, faculty, and the accreditation committee for graduate programs in public health. For alumni support, we retroactively awarded the MPH degree to all graduates since the inception of the MCH program. With MPH degrees, our graduates could seek employment with much greater confidence and credibility. This, following the change in tuition policies, was the second milestone event accomplished within weeks of my becoming program director.

2. **Paradigm shift in the use of the MPH degree:** As we had done in Beirut, we changed the concept of the MPH degree from the traditional endpoint degree primarily for physicians, to an entry-point offering for baccalaureate-level students. We opened the door to those with no or little prior public health experience who aspired to pursue careers in public health. In my numerous interviews with prospective applicants both at AUB and at Emory, I found that the newly offered MPH programs were like a magnet for the many who aspired to address social concerns, those who wanted to make a difference in the lives of others. The CDC itself was also a magnet for many reasons, e.g., numerous prospects for working with distinguished scientists, part-time job opportunities for students, and job opportunities after graduation. The program also appealed to those who weren't sure whether to embark on medical or veterinary careers, whether for financial reasons or because of the uncertainty of multi-year commitments to get into the job market. Applicants were attracted to "internships" required for practicums. Often, stipends earned during practicums, however small, served as an inducement. All of these features were further advanced during

my tenure by the network of public health institutions nearby, such as the American Cancer Society, CARE, the Carter Presidential Center, as well as other public health agencies that were headquartered locally, in Washington, and at other sites.

3. **Expansion of curriculum and faculty:** We also expanded the academic menu by offering new courses developed by existing and newly recruited adjunct faculty. We did this without a budget. My Beirut experience gave me confidence to begin recruiting practicing public health professionals with links to the university, including alumni willing to teach and participate in new course offerings. It was far easier at Emory than it had been at AUB because of our proximity to CDC, the source of an almost unlimited pool from which to recruit adjunct faculty. Furthermore, CDC was widely seen as the global center of public health practice and of public health excellence. In Beirut, CDC was half a globe away; in Atlanta, CDC was next door. CDC under Bill Foege's direction played a pivotal role in what I was able to accomplish in the transitions of both of these graduate public health programs.

A number of CDC scientists (including myself, while I was there) had participated in the Department of Community Health and Preventive Medicine (DCHPM) sporadically as lecturers in courses, but I needed a greater level of commitment from them—and thus needed to offer something in return. The lure would be adjunct faculty positions and the prospect of being part of the challenge in creating a school of public health in Atlanta. At that time, the nearest schools of public health were in Birmingham, Alabama (146 miles away); Columbia, South Carolina (211 miles away); and Johnson City, Tennessee (266 miles away); there were none in Georgia at the time.

Then, as now, CDC attracted some of the best-trained scientists in public health; it was almost an academic campus already, with a strong tradition of peer review, open inquiry, weekly grand rounds, and stimulating discussion. For the CDC faculty, the lure of having—and contributing to—a premier school of public health within easy walking distance was irresistible. Master's degree students could provide help for their mentors' projects while getting academic credit. Furthermore, we planned that our school would soon have doctoral programs in epidemiology and biostatistics, wherein CDC could offer dissertation topics to our students and in which CDC personnel could even enroll themselves for career advancement.

A critically important meeting

In the spring of 1983, shortly after assuming the role of director of the MPH program, I received a telephone call from CDC's administrative assistant asking for a meeting that same morning with Bill Foege and Jeff Koplan. At that time, they served as CDC Director and Associate Director. Without hesitation, I agreed.

This proved to be a momentous and historically important visit. They came to my office in what had been the office of the MCH/MPH program, a small house located at 1518 Clifton Road; the same address and the same location later became the Rollins School of Public Health. This place had been a family home purchased by Emory some years previously and subsequently converted to office space.

Foege and Koplan reached out to us to offer CDC assistance at a time when the program was on extremely tenuous grounds. They asked one question, "How can we help to ensure the success of your program?" This was the focus of the meeting. I told them I welcomed and badly needed CDC's support. I said I hoped that I would have the same support at Emory that CDC had provided when I served as the dean of AUB's school of public health, the Faculty of Health Sciences. Again at Emory, as at AUB, my most pressing need was to boost the enrollment. To do this, I had to expand the academic menu by increasing the number of courses and opportunities for students. In particular, I needed to connect our academic program with CDC's surveillance programs, research, and operational activities. I wanted help in making my interpretation of Robert Woodruff's vision into a reality. I believed that by transforming the MPH program we would also be building on his endowment as well as on his gift of land on Clifton Road on which CDC was located. I liked the harmony of this exchange—Emory's gift of land to CDC, followed by CDC's gift of faculty and intellectual resources to Emory's public health program.

We discussed the tenuous status of the program and the steps I had taken to address the most critical problems, which included changing the name of the program, resolving tuition issues, transforming the curriculum, increasing enrollment, and expanding opportunities for students. Most of all, I needed their help to enable me to recruit CDC scientists to serve as adjunct faculty teaching and mentoring students. I expressed my confidence that with their help, Emory would become a leading school of public health. I based my confidence that it could be done on the fact that it had already been done at AUB. During my four-year tenure as Dean of AUB, the assistance CDC provided was a crucial factor in helping to transition AUB's faltering graduate program in public health into a viable school of public health. I explained to Foege and Koplan that my task in both institutions was the same. At the end of the meeting I felt confident they would make things happen. And indeed they acted promptly. Foege gave his permission to permit me to directly identify whomever I wanted to recruit from among those interested in helping us build the program. We decided to make the program flexible enough so the individual faculty members could define their own roles. Thus, this landmark meeting set the stage for future events.

The first two years

In my role as program director, I reported to Tom Sellers, who, as chairman of the Department of Community Health, reported to the dean of the medical school, James Glenn. Glenn had previously been ambivalent to the Department of Community Health and Preventive Medicine because of the need for continuing medical school funding. However, he agreed to support adjunct appointments, and we were off and running. Interest was pervasive among CDC scientists as well as applicants for the program.

The academic program blossomed, and student applicants exceeded our expectations. We even enrolled our first-ever full-time students, three of whom came from Egypt through AMIDEAST, a nongovernmental organization that I had worked with in Beirut. Applicants were attracted by an expanded academic menu that included new courses, new areas of concentrations, and new opportunities for field experiences. The CDC connection was a huge help. In fact, my job was much easier at Emory than at AUB because of Emory's proximity to CDC, Foege's and Koplan's enthusiastic support, and the support of many CDC colleagues. I also recruited adjunct faculty from other Atlanta institutions, following the example set by Connie Conrad and Tom Sellers. Student applicants also came from CDC employees and staff aspiring for an academic credential.

In March 1983, just three months after I came aboard, Dean Glenn sent me a letter complimenting me for the encouraging recruitment to date. The expanding curriculum, the new MPH offering, and the realization of the CDC connection attracted new applicants and new adjunct faculty. To encourage working students and professionals, we offered required courses every semester along with an expanding list of electives, many of which were also offered in evening schedules. We became financially self-sustaining during the very first quarter of the first year of my tenure—a far shorter time than the two years I had thought would be needed.

The momentum of growth during my tenure as director of the program is shown in the graph below. We remained in the black every year. We easily repaid the medical school for all the years of deficits since the program's inception, and then became a revenue generator.

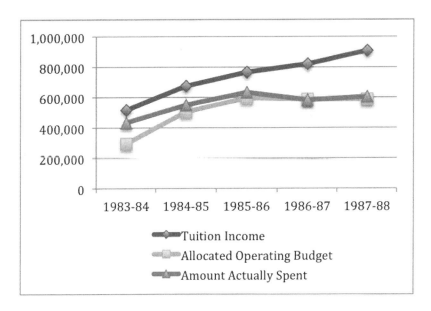

Figure 19: The financial status of Emory's public health program during its transition to a school of public health

By the middle of my first year, the program offered 8 core courses and 56 electives. The number of areas of concentration increased from three (Community Health Administration, Health Planning, and Health Education) to five (the original three, plus International Health, and Environmental and Occupational Health).

Some CDC faculty taught their own courses; others co-taught with other CDC scientists or with Emory faculty. For example, Martha Katz and Bill Watson taught the required public policy course in the fall semesters of 1983 and 1984. President Carter, Bill Foege, Jeff Koplan, and Stan Foster lectured in different courses taught in every year. Students found an increasing number of mentors for their master's theses among new adjunct faculty. We also recruited additional faculty from Georgia Tech and Georgia State, whom we paid with modest honoraria. Academic standards improved. All at virtually no cost to the program!

At the beginning of the fall semester of 1984, well within the two-year time limit I had to turn around the program, we enrolled 51 newly registered students; 26 had previous graduate degrees, including 13 at the doctoral level (10 MDs, two DDSs, and one PhD). All but 11 of the 51 had prior health-related experiences. The average age was 30, with a range of 21 – 42. Twenty-eight (54%) of the 51 were full-time students. Ten (20%) were international students, representing Australia, Bahrain, India, Lebanon, Nigeria, Saudi Arabia, Venezuela, and Yemen. Those from middle-eastern countries were referred by my AUB colleagues and connections, particularly the nongovernmental organization AMIDEAST.

In the 1982 – 83 academic year, only three students graduated. In the 1983 – 84 academic year, 16 students graduated. The momentum increased in every subsequent year of my tenure, and increased further during the tenure of the next dean, Ray Greenberg, and still more during the tenure of the following dean, Jim Curran.

Adding to the program's tuition income, we received a four-year cooperative agreement from CDC to develop our international health track, and another from the National Institute for Occupational Safety and Health (NIOSH) to develop a curriculum in environmental and occupational health. I do not hesitate to assert that these were excellent investments of taxpayer money that have been repaid many times through the synergies of the collaboration between CDC and Emory. Nearly all the full-time faculty arranged for outside funding, many by CDC Cooperative Agreements that paid parts of their Emory salaries. In addition to teaching four courses, I also had salary allocated to work with Dr. Bob Chin in the National Immunization Program. I conducted a study that generated several student practicums regarding the impact of anti-vaccine movements on outbreaks of pertussis (whooping cough)[2].

The net effect of these changes convinced most, but not all, that Emory's graduate program in public health could thrive. We showed that public funding could be obtained, but it was not essential for financial self-sufficiency. Finally, we could make a strong case for a school of public health in a private university. One of the remaining doubters was an unexpected antagonist— the new dean of the medical school.

The start of a rocky road

Dean Glenn left Emory in late 1983, just as we were gaining momentum for the changes described above. We were sad to see him leave. He had become a supporter and a strong advocate of the MPH program. The interim dean, Dr. George Brumley, Professor and Chairman of Pediatrics, was also supportive and encouraging. Emory administrators were pleased that the medical school did not have to provide us additional resources, because we were self-sufficient.

In 1984, Richard Krause was appointed dean of the School of Medicine. He had previously chaired an epidemiology department in the Midwest and had been director of the Institute for Infectious Diseases at the National Institutes of Health (NIH). Sellers and I especially had high hopes that he would support our movement to transform the program into a school of public health. Quite the opposite occurred.

Shortly after Dean Krause came aboard, Sellers and I visited to pay a courtesy call and to share with him our vision of public health at Emory. We had no idea of his negative views on this subject. From the very beginning, he made it clear that our school was not one of the medical school's priorities, that we did not have a mandate to grow, and that he did not want our program to divert attention from his efforts to establish Emory's School of Medicine as one of the top 10 in the country.

Krause and I had profoundly different views of the direction of public health at Emory. His opinions surfaced unexpectedly at a meeting held at CDC in Dr. Jim Mason's office on March 28, 1986. Jim had recently been appointed director of CDC. I attended the meeting with Tom Sellers, Richard Krause, and Charles Hatcher from Emory, and Mason and other staff from CDC. Mason called for the meeting to explore ways of strengthening the bonds between our institutions and to articulate his own commitment as an advocate of Emory's public health program. I envisioned that something would come from the meeting that would further enhance our growth momentum. Mason seemed eager to build on the extraordinary achievements of his two predecessors at CDC, Dave Sencer and Bill Foege, who could be considered founders of the MCH and MPH programs.

Dean Krause articulated a completely different vision than that shared by many of us, including the past program founders and Mason. Krause spoke of a laboratory-based collaboration that would strengthen the basic sciences departments. What he saw did not build on the surveillance theme that had made CDC an internationally recognized center of excellence. His vision would leave traditional epidemiologists completely out of the loop. Instead, he advocated a partnership between CDC's laboratories and the medical school's basic sciences laboratories that would propel molecular epidemiology to a new level of excellence. He envisioned that such collaboration would substantively enhance Emory's ability to compete for funding from the National Institutes of Health. This was important to him because NIH funding had become an especially valuable tool to measure the excellence of medical schools.

I was not prepared for this. Despite (or perhaps because of) his background in academic epidemiology, Krause did not appreciate that "shoe leather epidemiology"—not laboratories— drives investigation of disease outbreaks. Obviously laboratory sciences have played a crucial role in public health. However, even laboratory scientists typically acknowledge that if there is a conflict between epidemiological findings and laboratory results, the former trumps the latter. Mason and I shared a vision that public health excellence would be achieved at Emory through collaboration in applied epidemiology, where the laboratory would be supportive of field activities, and that public health faculty and students would have roles in both spheres.

I chose not to argue the point at this meeting because both Dean Krause and I were recently appointed, and in particular, because it seemed imprudent to disagree with Krause at that time, especially in the presence of Hatcher and Mason. I was also concerned about a confrontational relationship with the Dean arising in such an open forum. A few days after the meeting I spoke to Mason; he expressed surprise at Dean Krause's comments.

An effort at diplomacy

After several days of careful contemplation, I decided to put my views in writing to share with the Emory attendees at that meeting. I sent a letter on April 2, 1986, addressed to Dean Krause with copies to Hatcher and Sellers. This letter gave me the opportunity to express a conflicting point of view as tactfully as I could craft words. I knew that I was taking a chance, that I was putting my job on the line, and that I could have forced Dean Krause's hand in getting rid of me. However, I thought it was important for the future of the program to articulate a more realistic vision of public health at Emory, one that was consistent with the unique resources of both CDC and the university. Sending that letter was perhaps the most important thing that I did during my tenure as director of the MPH program.

However tactfully I had written the letter, it created between Dean Krause and me an antipathy that had consequences in the struggle for school status. It polarized our positions. I believe Dean Krause circulated the letter, and I know he discussed it with his faculty more than once. Practically everyone knew and quoted the Dean's position that "a school of public health would happen only over [his] dead body." I believe Hatcher shared his copy with President Laney and with President Carter. I sent a copy to Foege. I think most of these figures agreed with the vision I articulated. However, I believe my letter contributed to divisions within the medical faculty. I sensed this from the sometimes-cynical comments that some medical school faculty made about "Dr. Fogey" and me. Yet there was a positive side to this story: it led to a debate in the inner circle where Hatcher, Foege, and President Carter had influence.

A favorable report

After this letter, the debate about the future of the graduate program in public health soon took a positive turn. I felt I had support for my efforts from key decision-makers, notably Emory University President Jim Laney, the former CDC Director Bill Foege, and Foege's successor, Jim Mason. Laney knew that Dean Krause was unsettled by my leadership and my vision of public health. Laney also knew that Krause was opposed to Emory having a public health program any larger than it had been, because he felt it would compete for resources with the medical school. To address his concerns, Laney directed Krause to assemble a committee to study the future role of our department in the university. This committee was chaired by Dr. William H. Plauth, Professor of Pediatrics. It included, among others, Dr. John McGowan, who at the time of this writing serves as a professor in the Rollins School of Public Health. The committee deliberated for months, interviewing many medical and public health faculty and CDC staff. I was frankly very worried that the report might be negative and would give Krause the leverage he needed to take a drastic step, possibly even asking me to leave or aborting our renaissance. I was enormously relieved when I saw the report.

The Plauth report was not only a milestone, but also a turning point, as it provided decision-makers with a peer assessment of the program's potential and its promising future. The report highlighted the most promising indications of the program's growth from admissions office data:

"The more than three-fold increase in the number of applicants for the MPH degree (47 to 161), the accepted applicants (44 to 147) and the number of students enrolled (125 to 408) from the academic year 1982-83 to the year 1984-85 speak for a recognition of the value of the instruction and the importance of the degree. During the same interval the quality of the students accepted ... also increased."

Another important point they made addressed a lingering concern: "There is no indication that the job market is anything but favorable and growing." The committee also noted, "The leadership of the MPH program and the support of the program by the Department of Community Health has been energetic, well directed, imaginative, and highly successful." The report is copied in Dollie Daniel's *A Shared Dream*. It was a strong endorsement of our accomplishments and of our vision for the future.

The dean's new strategy

Dean Krause was muted but undeterred. He developed a strategy that, among whatever other objectives he had in mind, seemed to be designed to defuse the need for a school of public health. He reorganized the quantitative medical sciences—the Department of Biostatistics, chaired by Elmer Hall, and the separate Epidemiology Division in Tom Sellers's Department of Community Health. He merged these two groups and appointed Ray Greenberg as department chair. He also ensured the new department substantial funding for faculty recruitment, amounting to millions of dollars. The establishment of a strong Department of Epidemiology in the medical school would surely have undermined the MPH program in its bid for status as a school of public health. To understand the subsequent chain of events, it is necessary to describe my relationship with Greenberg.

My initial acquaintance with Ray Greenberg, and a subsequent conflict of opinions

I first met Ray Greenberg in late 1984 or early 1985 when he visited Emory to be considered for a faculty position in the Department of Community Medicine. Sellers asked me to interview him. I remember being very much impressed with this bright young man who had seemingly accomplished so much in such a short period of time. I genuinely saw a bright future for Greenberg at Emory and shared this assessment with Sellers, who subsequently hired him. Our relationship was strong through the early years of Greenberg's tenure. He was supportive in strategic planning meetings and faculty retreats. He taught our first course in chronic disease epidemiology. The first two years of our relationship went smoothly.

However, a divisive issue surfaced, the question of whether CDC scientists were qualified to mentor our students in their theses and Special Study Projects. Dean Krause objected to my "stream of requests for adjunct faculty appointments" and, since their approval had to go through the medical school, my faculty could not grow to meet our expanding needs unless we had his support. I suspect that Dean Krause persuaded Ray Greenberg to make a major issue of this.

Tom Sellers called for a meeting to discuss this topic. I was asked to attend, along with Greenberg, Elmer Hall, and John Boring. Despite all our previous successes with adjunct faculty from CDC, and the absence of problems in our past experience, Greenberg and Hall argued vehemently that CDC staff did not have the academic qualifications to mentor students, and therefore we should only use them in a few selected instances. They argued that if we continued to enlist them, it would compromise our academic standards. Boring seemed to support them in this concern.

I was strongly opposed, arguing that the adjunct faculty we had recruited were accomplished scientists whose credentials had been scrutinized and approved by a faculty committee of peers. Most were well known nationally, and many others had global recognition. Responses from mentored students and course critiques were favorable. Students coveted CDC opportunities and wanted to be involved in CDC projects. These opportunities were valuable in enabling students to transition to the job market. Further, CDC opportunities were also important in recruiting students. Finally, our relationship with CDC was our unique niche among graduate programs in public health, our *raison d'être* for Emory having a school of public health. I was adamant in this position. I was very pleased that Sellers supported me.

Although I felt vindicated, I sensed that my relationship with Greenberg had been somewhat compromised. Other factors also caused me concern about our changing relationship. Greenberg was initially active as a junior faculty member in the program, having taught a course that was offered in his first two years. His course was well received by students. However, soon after this disagreement, he decided to withdraw from this role. He was also close to Hall, who was an open Krause supporter and cynical about my vision of our becoming a school of public health. Around this time, Greenberg was recruited by Dean Krause to head the new Department of Epidemiology in the Medical School. I understood how difficult his position had become, and that he really had to take this position in support of Dean Krause, who had become his benefactor.

I recall an effort that I made to gain Greenberg's support and to have him recognize the potential of the MPH program. I asked for a meeting in his office in downtown Decatur in the spring of 1988. There we talked about the possibility of the program eventually becoming a school, and the role he might play in it. I showed him five years of financial and student statistics that I thought would impress him. He may have been impressed, but it was still not in his best interests to indicate his support. I left that meeting a bit disappointed, and although he did agree to resume teaching his epidemiology course, I worried that we could not count on him to support our goal of becoming a school.

Endorsement from our accrediting organization

We passed another milestone on August 28, 1987 with the receipt of a two-paragraph letter from the American Board of Preventive Medicine[88]. It was signed by the Secretary-Treasurer, Stanley R. Mohler, and concerned candidate performance on the specialty board examination. It said tersely, "Enclosed are the rankings for the examinations taken in 1984, 1985, 1986. We are pleased to note that the Emory University program ranks at the very top in all three years in regard to candidate performance." Sellers circulated the letter widely. In his covering note, he acknowledged the limitations of this accomplishment, noting that we were aware that we did not have large numbers of students taking this examination. However, he noted that this acclaim demonstrated our commitment to grow while maintaining and enhancing academic quality. This totally

---

[88] A copy of this letter is in the appendix.

unexpected support had a profound impact on Emory decision-makers. President Laney sent his personal congratulations.

I remember encountering Dean Krause one day as I was walking to the medical school in mid-October 1987. He made a cryptic remark about the letter, noting that he doubted that it had statistical validity. He seemed irritated that the letter had been sent directly to the President and Vice President of the university. He felt he should have made the decision whether or not to forward it to his superiors. Nevertheless, most decision-makers were impressed. It certainly helped us achieve our goal.

Our most difficult year, but another milestone—Division status

The year 1988 was by far the most difficult of the years of my Emory tenure. Even though we had long since become financially sound, had increasingly well-qualified applicants, and our income was retained by the medical school in excess of the budgeted allowance for our operation, Dean Krause withheld the funds we needed to grow. His efforts to improve the ranking of Emory's medical school were encountering financial difficulties, and the medical school had a deficit that needed to be addressed. Although seed money for new faculty positions had been promised to the MPH program, the allocation for these positions was not presented to the university's Board of Trustees despite the fact that the MPH program was generating funds far in excess of what we were allocated in our budgets (see Figure 5, above).

Faculty members were already stressed because of the increasing demands of a rapidly expanding student body during five years of rapid growth. We badly needed additional faculty to cope with this growth. Only six additional faculty had been hired during the previous five years, three paid for from the MPH budget, and three from contractual arrangements with CDC. The CDC faculty arrangements were through Interagency Personnel Agreements (IPAs) that paid no overhead and required considerable faculty time for CDC tasks. The bottom line is that faculty workloads were increasing faster than the resources made available to cope with the growth.

This financial crisis was taking its toll on faculty morale. Understandably, they expected more from me, and I could not deliver. There was also increasing pressure to raise academic standards for research and to require faculty to get more of their salaries from other sources. The faculty became testy. They openly doubted that I could prevail in my aspiration to become a school. They questioned the wisdom of my not accepting the reality of Dean Krause's position that he had articulated so often and so forcefully—that we would never become a school of public health. I did not blame them; I knew that if I were in their position, I would probably feel as they did.

The faculty began to question my leadership. This became apparent in a number of ways. It was my custom to take Friday afternoons off to address personal matters and to compensate for the hours I regularly worked on Saturdays and Sundays. Without my knowledge, faculty arranged regular meetings on Friday afternoons to discuss the crisis, knowing that I would not be there to participate. Two faculty members wrote lengthy letters, with copies to the rest of the faculty, questioning my leadership and stating emphatically that they thought the program was "not moving in the right direction." One such memo said that money would be better spent to compensate the overstretched faculty for their heavy teaching loads than to start a school of public health. Some even wondered if my dream of starting a school of public health was delusional! This unrest was particularly difficult for me because it distracted from my sense

409

of accomplishment and satisfaction as the program grew and became self-sufficient—at the same time that administrators were applauding our success.

I wrote a letter to Tom Sellers dated March 9, 1988, by then six years after I was appointed Director, to express my growing concerns about these developments. In it, I wrote, "I need to tell you that faculty morale has been adversely affected; enthusiasm that propelled our momentum in recent years has waned." In a personal note to Sellers on May 29, 1988 (at the low point of my tenure as director), I wrote, "It is my judgment that our own 'revolution' is directed against the policies emanating from my conviction that we will become a school. I find it particularly difficult to reconcile my philosophy to the growing conviction among faculty that we will never become a school." I asked for a meeting "to consider alternatives in a transition to new leadership." With this note, I submitted a letter of resignation. Sellers asked me to withdraw it, assuring me of his support and his conviction that we would prevail.

Sellers's support at this crucial point energized me. I pushed ahead with renewed determination. Dollie Daniels best described my state of mind at that time. She wrote, "Gene Gangarosa took the program by the scruff of the neck and shook it into a school that could not be ignored." It was an imaginative and descriptive metaphor that captures well my energy, determination, and commitment to the school. It also reflected the angst we went through and the ultimate success of our efforts.

An obstruction vanishes—and a school is formed!

The year of 1989 proved to be another turning point in the history of the school. A hint of a change in the dean's office came in early March when I received a call from Bill Todd informing me that the decision had been made that our MPH program was being elevated to division status. He noted this would be a transitional step on the way to becoming a school of public health. In the excitement of this news, I did not ask about Dean Krause. It occurred to me after this call that an important change in the dean's status must have taken place.

On March 16, 1989, I received a most important letter from Charles Hatcher confirming what Bill Todd had told me. It noted that our status had changed from Program to Division. His letter requested that I serve as Interim Director of the Division of Public Health until the university administration could find a permanent director. It noted that John Boring would chair a search committee for the "first leader who can launch this exciting effort to move the division to school status." This letter was copied to President Laney, Jeffrey Houpt, Bill Foege, and Walt Dowdle. The fact that Krause was not copied on this letter confirmed my impression that he was in fact no longer functioning as Dean. This was an enormous relief. Suddenly, my vision of a school had become a reality. Having realized we had reached our goal, I had no problem stepping aside to welcome a new director. I was happy to facilitate this transition since, with the appointment of a new dean to replace Krause, the program would surely be given urgently needed resources.

Because Sellers was also not copied on Hatcher's letter, I called him to share the good news. He too was elated. On that same day, I forwarded the letter to faculty and expressed my appreciation for their patience.

Thus, in 1989, with six years of solid financial performance, a glowing report from our accrediting body, a favorable report from the Plauth Committee, and recognition of the quality of our program by the American Board of Preventive Medicine, the Emory University Board of Trustees elevated the MPH program to division status, provided seed money for faculty recruitment, and gave their blessing to our becoming a school. Provisions were also made for us to occupy a floor of the planned American Cancer Society Building. We moved there in the spring of 1989. This was the moment we had long awaited. When I started, I had thought this would take far more than seven years.

Around mid-August, I received a call from Kathryn Graves, a development officer at the medical school, asking for an appointment. On the phone she was a bit cryptic about the purpose of the meeting, but I figured it could relate to some tangible involvement and possibly support from the university's Development Office. We met at the Houston Mill House restaurant for lunch on August 17, 1989.

At our meeting, Graves asked if I would be interested in having her assist in the development of what would become our new school. I answered hesitantly, noting I would be pleased if this could happen but explaining I had no funding. She informed me that funding would come from the Development Office. What a surprise! She had already discussed this with her supervisor, Phil Mazzara, Vice President of Development for the Woodruff Health Sciences Center. He had suggested that she explore the possibility of a development position in public health. She had also talked to Bill Todd. Graves informed me that William Plauth had written the white paper providing the rationale for this action, and that Bill Todd encouraged her to take this job. Graves's joining our program was great news. It confirmed that the Health Sciences Center was committed to our program. It was an enormous relief. Graves and I met again on Monday, September 11, 1989 to discuss the logistics of her move to the American Cancer Society building. The whole division was pleased to welcome her and offer her space. I vividly recall the faculty meeting to welcome her on September 25th because it palpably changed the mood of the faculty. Ever since, she has played a key role in facilitating the momentum of our program.

Reflections on my interactions with Dean Krause

Dean Krause's single-minded emphasis of medical research introduced considerable friction with clinicians, and his attempts to decrease support for Emory's charity teaching facility, Grady Hospital, undermined his credibility with the university administration and medical faculty [3]. Given the strong support our program had from the university president, it is possible that the disagreement Krause and I had about a school of public health may also have contributed to his decision to leave. This impression was reinforced in an unexpected encounter I had with Krause on April 25, 1997. It took place in the foyer of CDC. He was waiting with an international visitor for a meeting with Dr. James Hughes, Director of the Center for Infectious Diseases. I happened to be walking through the foyer to meet a colleague. When I saw Krause, I walked close to him with my hand outstretched to greet him and shake his hand. He was cool, but proper. He introduced me to his colleague. After exchanging greetings, I asked him if he had seen the new school of public health building. He said, "I know it is there." Then turning to his colleague, he said, "This was the school that I said would only be built over my dead body. And they had to get rid of me to do it." I said I was surprised that he still held this view, because the relationship between the school of public health and the medical school had so persuasively demonstrated the synergy. He said that this was a misconception and that the school of public health was "the worst thing that could have happened to the medical school." As he was leaving the foyer, I said to him, "On that point, we can respectfully continue to disagree."

Krause's views were driven by his concern that a school of public health would be an obstacle to his goal of making Emory's School of Medicine the leader among peer medical schools. No doubt he reasoned that the ascent to the top would bring to Emory a proportionate increase in NIH grants. Getting those grants would bring not only resources, but also recognition and prestige that would attract the best-qualified students and scientists. The recognition he sought for Emory was both national and international, and he envisioned that this would translate into Nobel prizes. I do not fault him for having such laudable goals.

Krause's error in seeing the MPH program as an obstacle to Emory's eminence stemmed from the fact that his vision of excellence was restricted to laboratory accomplishments and breakthroughs. In particular, we disagreed on the issue of the importance of surveillance and field epidemiology. I felt that our proximity to CDC provided us with a perfect niche that was globally unique and linked to attractive opportunities for learning and jobs. In response to this perspective, he told me, "That is the very problem. Gene, we must achieve academic excellence through micro-epidemiology—in the laboratory, not in the field." He reiterated that a school of public health in the mold of traditional field epidemiology was not suitable for Emory's medical school.

Events that transpired after Krause's departure made it abundantly clear that Emory's decision-makers made the right choice. Ultimately, Hatcher and President Laney, undoubtedly influenced by Foege and President Jimmy Carter, decided to pursue a broader vision of public health. The partnership between the School of Medicine and the Rollins School of Public Health has been exemplary. Numerous breakthroughs, both in the laboratory and in the field, have made it apparent that the two philosophies of public health are complementary. From an academic standpoint, both schools have benefited from the partnership with CDC. It is abundantly clear from Hatcher's autobiography that the development of this partnership was "Emory's unique treasure" and its "greatest asset." On page 267 of his autobiography, he writes,

"A School of Public Health was exactly the type of program to kick-start our relationship with the CDC. No other academic discipline lined up as well with the Center's mission. Opening a new school is no small task though. There would have to be committees, faculty searches, fundraising efforts, and of course bureaucratic jostling, but in 1990 we opened Emory's first new School in over seventy years."[89]

The search for the first dean of the new School of Public Health

Although we had finally achieved the reality of becoming a school of public health, the joy of the occasion and the sense of accomplishment were tempered by a new crisis of leadership. I was the logical person to serve in the role of division director, but I had considerable misgivings. After agonizing over this for some time, I reluctantly accepted the role of interim director because no one else would take it. After making this decision, I felt the situation had improved when we learned that Krause had resigned, that our budget for the 1989 – 90 fiscal year would include seed money for new faculty lines, and that there would be a search for the school's first dean. I welcomed these initiatives and renewed my enthusiasm to move forward to finalize our goal.

---

[89] Although we were approved in 1989, our school as such did not exist until 1990.

The search for the dean of the new school of public health initially focused on finding a senior person with an established public health record. Candidates identified in the university president's office included D. A. Henderson, dean of the Johns Hopkins School of Public Health; William (Bill) Foege, executive director of the Carter Center; and Jim Mason, director of CDC. All three declined. D.A. came to visit, to encourage our transition to school status, but he made it clear that he would not accept the position. However, he had played a vital role behind the scenes making the case why we had a unique opportunity to create a school of public health. Foege preferred to retain his role behind the scenes in a function he has played so well, that of an inspirational leader. Mason had his sights on a Washington position; he became Assistant Secretary for Health and Human Services.

The search turned to candidates less well known. The first candidate seriously considered was Dr. Barry Levy. He had distinguished himself as a leader in environmental and occupational health. His interview went well. Members of the search committee were much impressed. Ray Greenberg participated in Levy's interview. I personally think that Levy's visit and the reception he received sparked Greenberg's interest in the position. It was at that time that he stated his desire to be considered for the position; I supported his application, and he was ultimately successful in being appointed to the role.

I was pleased to hand the mantle of leadership to Greenberg, especially as I believed that his ability to generate external funding would be a critical benefit to the program, along with his leadership skills. This was the final landmark I sought, the transformation leading to a school that I likened to a ship that had passed through the storms and had finally arrived safely in port. When I took the helm in 1983, I envisioned myself leading until we had achieved this milestone. Greenberg built on that foundation, just as I had built on the foundation I inherited from Tom Sellers and Connie Conrad. The assets Greenberg brought with him greatly strengthened the infrastructure of the school and cemented relationships with the schools of Medicine and Nursing. These, in turn, enabled him to launch a strong research program, recruit an outstanding and highly qualified faculty, and reinvigorate the momentum that had transformed the MCH into the MPH program. After Greenberg left, the second dean, Jim Curran, exponentially propelled the school's growth, building on rich connections with CDC and its role as a leading global public health capital.

The Emory University Rollins School of Public Health was supported during its gestational period and early inception mainly with tuition funds from its students. Less than four million dollars in developmental funds went into its formation! [1] Once again, I had started a school of public health practically without a budget. It was Bill Foege who committed CDC in this and in the AUB venture, both of which culminated in the transition of marginal programs into flourishing schools of public health. We also owe this accomplishment to the dedicated faculty who did the research, teaching, and service that made the school possible. I especially thank my colleagues at CDC, who gave so much of their time and expertise with little reward except faculty positions, collegial collaborations, and personal gratification. They also benefited from having public health students support their research, especially when federal resources were constrained.

Figure 20: Bill Foege, EJG, and Rose.

On two occasions in my career, CDC's Director Bill Foege asked, "Gene, tell me what you need," referring in 1978 to the American University of Beirut's faltering school of public health, and in 1983 to Emory's anemic graduate program in public health. In both instances my response was the same, "I need resources to expand academic programs." CDC's responses were pivotal in the recovery and transformation of both—AUB's Faculty of Health Sciences and Emory's Rollins School of Public Health have emerged as global leaders among schools of public health.

The team that enabled the transition from program to school

Many faculty played critical roles in supporting the transition from program to school. Over some period of time, various tracks were developed for students to focus on their specific interests. After our historic meeting in spring 1983, Bill Foege endorsed faculty Cooperative Agreements and provided funding for the development of an international health track; these important changes were completed in short order. Then he gave me permission to approach CDC scientists directly. I was especially pleased to recruit Roger Rochat, a globally recognized expert in maternal health. He joined the Emory Faculty as Professor of Public Health in 1985 and continued the plan and curriculum for global health that had been developed by a committee initially chaired by Bill Foege. Rochat was also the first director of the International Health track (forerunner of the Hubert Department of Global Health). Mike Lane joined the Program later as the second director of the International Health track. Phil Brachman contributed in important ways—he came aboard to direct the Hospital Infection Program at Emory Hospital, continued developing global field epidemiology training programs, taught several courses in epidemiology in our school, and later became coordinator of the Hubert Humphrey Fellowship Program. Clark Heath and John Richardson joined the program a year later and, with funding from NIOSH, developed the curriculum for the Environmental Health track. When Clark left, Howie Frumkin joined the faculty as the first Chairman of the newly established Department of Environmental and Occupational Health. Other key persona (most of whom I've mentioned previously) include Tom Sellers, Bill Marine, Connie Conrad, John Boring, Ray Greenberg, and Jim Curran.

The list of CDC scientists who were recruited as adjunct faculty and what they accomplished for our school would fill many pages. With regret, I pay tribute to them as a group because, preoccupied as I was with the school's growth, I was not close enough to be familiar with their many accomplishments in their own niche areas of public health. Furthermore, I did not keep the records that would have enabled me to do justice to them. I acknowledge their important role. I am personally indebted to each of them.

I write with conviction that CDC's support provided during the tenures of Dave Sencer, Bill Foege, and Jim Mason was pivotal in making possible the School of Public Health at Emory. As Director of CDC, Foege facilitated transitions at both AUB and Emory. I was fortunate to have had the opportunity to provide leadership in the transition of the academic programs of those institutions that led to the transformation of AUB's faltering school of public health into the vibrant Faculty of Health Sciences, and exponentially expanding Emory's graduate program in public health from the MCH program into the Rollins School of Public Health, at the time of this writing recognized as a global academic center of excellence.[90] The Rollins School of Public Health emerged because of Robert Woodruff's endowments and his bequest that included the land on which CDC is located. In my view, the Rollins School clearly fulfills Woodruff's vision of close collaboration between Emory and CDC.

At this writing, there are 50 accredited schools of public health in the U.S. In 2011, U.S. News ranked Emory University's Rollins School of Public Health sixth (tied) out of 44 schools rated, giving

---

[90] Indeed, I felt that AUB's revised 2-year MPH for college graduates was the prototype for Emory's own revised MPH program.

it a score of 4.1 out of a possible 5.0. For a school that was only 14 years old and started primarily on tuition funding, against some other established schools that go back more than 95 years, that's not bad! We have already achieved global prominence, but the most exciting part lies ahead. The future is very bright indeed.

My academic activities during this time

My responsibilities during the time I served as Director of the MPH Program were not only administrative—I also taught, mentored students, and engaged in research. In accordance with the high priority I assigned to expanding the program's academic offerings, and thereby its competitiveness, I encouraged faculty to teach as many courses as was feasible. In that spirit, I taught four courses—considered a full academic load for full-time academicians.

One course that is still taught at the time of this writing, albeit in condensed form, is Control of Foodborne Diseases. I initially established this as an elective course because this was my niche area of academic interest. I taught this course from 1983 to 1987, when it was merged with Christine Moe's course on the Control of Waterborne Diseases to become Control of Foodborne and Waterborne Diseases. At this point, it was cross-listed in the Departments of Global Health and Environmental Health. At first, it was offered as a full-semester course. However, in 2010, Rose and I had conflicting plans for our 60th wedding anniversary, and from then until the time of this writing, a condensed version of the course has been offered in the first week of January. From its inception, CDC scientists have featured prominently in teaching this course.

As we had no full time faculty to teach the core required Environmental Health course during the years 1983 – 1985, I coordinated with adjunct faculty from Georgia Tech and CDC/NIOSH to offer it. In 1986, I requested the help of two distinguished CDC scientists—Clark Heath and John Richardson. They provided leadership for the reorganization of this course, which they then proceeded to teach and expand. Ultimately, this effort resulted in the emergence of the Department of Environmental Health. I was a guest lecturer in this course from 1986 through 1990, when Dr. Howie Frumkin became Department Chair.

Perspectives in Public Health was established as a core course for students who had no previous public health or medical experience. Most of the students enrolled in this course had recently graduated from college. I taught this course from 1983 to 1986, when it was no longer needed, as several other courses provided a generic orientation to public health.

I also organized and taught an elective course entitled Communications for the Health Professionals; this was offered especially for students interested in improving writing and/or speaking skills. The course was popular with students who came into our Program sponsored by international agencies such as AMIDEAST, a U.S. not-for-profit organization whose focus is career development of professionals from the Middle East and North Africa[91]. Virginia DeHaan, who has a memorial lectureship to honor her work with the MPH program, promoted, helped organize, and participated in classes with Katherine Baer, who took the lead in this course. We used Baer's book as a required textbook.

---

[91] I worked with this organization during my tenure at AUB.

As mentioned earlier in this chapter, I also had a portion of my salary dedicated to work with Dr. Bob Chin in the National Immunization program. This work, on the impact of anti-vaccine movements on outbreaks of pertussis (whooping cough) provided salient scientific evidence of the harmful effect of these movements. These movements were spawned in part by a physician at the University of Glasgow who published flawed data about the pertussis vaccine—alleging it was responsible for neurological complications. Foege asserted that the physician surely would have been charged with "public-health malpractice" if such a legislation existed, because the resulting anti-vaccine movements resulted in countless illnesses and many deaths due to pertussis. Together with some colleagues, I published a paper in the Lancet that was in essence a report of the consequences of those anti-vaccine movements. One of the scientists in our Emory/CDC team, Dr. A. M. Galazka, provided pertussis surveillance data from countries where high coverage with diphtheria-tetanus-pertussis vaccine (DTP) was maintained, specifically the former East Germany, Poland, and the USA, with countries where immunization was disrupted by anti-vaccine movements, specifically Sweden, Japan, UK, the former Russian Federation, Ireland, Italy, the former West Germany, and Australia. These surveillance data showed that the incidence of pertussis was 10 to 100 times lower in countries where high vaccine coverage was maintained than in countries where immunization programs were compromised by anti-vaccine movements. Our data underscored the efficacy of this vaccine.

Following this work, my student D.A. Salmon mentored other students including Dr. Omar Saad, who at this writing is faculty in the Hubert Department of Global Health at Rollins and a prominent leader in this field. This mentoring sequence is an example of what Stan Foster and I described as "Passing the

Epidemiological Torch from Farr to the Global Legacy of Alexander Langmuir." Farr's development of disease surveillance during the 19th century provided the practice of epidemiology its foundation, linking the 16th century plague mortality records to CDC's multifaceted MMWR. In this historical sequence, we can see a metaphorical relay race, where each mentor passes a baton to students who take that work ever further, and all the participants are linked through their accomplishments to all who preceded them. The conceptual foundations established by Farr and Langmuir stand out as landmarks in this historical relay.

Personal reflections

I feel proud of and pleased with my job as the ship's captain during the difficult years of my tenure. The events I have described focused on management and administrative issues, but there were other facets I found much more exciting, challenging, and gratifying. I refer to the teaching role I had at Emory, which I still maintain at the time of this writing. The teacher's role is what has driven me. It is the opportunity to add something, however small, that transforms the student to become a leader, to nurture as a farmer nurtures a plant, and to witness, as the culmination of a mentoring relationship, a flowering career, and the emergence of a new public health leader. Perhaps it is selfish on my part, but I see that transformation as a means of perpetuating my own immortality, because in each of my students is a small piece of me. This is why I almost feel like I have adopted all of my students. I watch their career development with an almost grandfatherly pride.

References

1.   Daniels D: **A shared dream; the genesis of academic public health at Emory University**. Atlanta, GA: Rollins School of Public Health, Emory University; 2000.

2.   Gangarosa EJ, Galazka AM, Wolfe CR, Phillips LM, Gangarosa RE, Miller E, Chen RT: **Impact of anti-vaccine movements on pertussis control: the untold story**. *Lancet* 1998, **351**(9099):356-361.

3.   Wrobel S: **Raising the Bar: 150 Years of a Medical School in Motion**. In: *Momentum: Forward Thinking from the Woodruff Health Sciences of Emory University.* Atlanta, GA: Emory University; 2005.

Appendix – Relevant letters

August 28, 1987

Eugene Gangarosa, M.D.

Director, H.P.H. Program

735 Gatewood

Emory University

Atlanta, GA 30322

Dear Dr. Gangarosa:

The American Board of Preventive Medicine reque -— *[obscured by Post-It Note]*

Medical Examiners assess performance information— *[obscured by Post-It Note]*

in regard to candidate performance on the preven -— *[obscured by Post-It Note]*

The Board agreed to notify the respective schools of their ranking in this regard. Enclosed are the rankings for the examinations taken in 1984, 1985, 1986. We are pleased to note that the Emory University program ranks at the very top in all three years in regard to candidate performance.

The enclosed tables are released to the respective schools for internal use as an aid in guiding curriculum preparation and training activities.

Sincerely yours,

Stanley R. Hohler, M.D.

Secretary-Treasurer

SRH/jeg

STUDY OF CANDIDATE PERFORMANCE BY MPH SCHOOL

Schools Represented by Five or More Candidates

Name/Location of MPH School	Average Percent Correct	Core Bank Ability, Measure in Logits:		Number of Candidates
		Mean	SD	
LOMA LINDA U	59	.56	.67	10
U CALIFORNIA, LA	61	.66	.66	14
U CINCINNATI	66	.79	.66	13
U ILLINOIS	65	.80	.35	19
U TEXAS	66	.89	.65	60
TULANE U	68	.99	.66	16
U TORONTO	68	1.01	.59	5
WRIGHT STATE U	68	1.02	.55	9
U CALIFORNIA, BERK	69	1.06	.52	31
U MICHIGAN	70	1.09	.52	28
U MOUNT SINAI	70	1.10	.61	6
U HAWAII	71	1.17	.39	9

U MINNESOTA	71	1.18	.57	12
HARVARD	71	1.20	.62	56
COLUMBIA U	72	1.26	.49	10
U PITTSBURGH	73	1.20	.60	6
U NORTH CAROLINA	73	1.30	.67	15
U ARIZONA	73	1.34	.29	5
JOHNS HOPKINS	73	1.36	.56	97
U UTAH	75	1.39	.53	5
YALE	75	1.39	.55	S
U WASHINGTON	77	1.56	.55	12
EMORY U	80	1.76	.77	5
NO MPH SCHOOL	65	.85	.68	132
All 599 Candidates	69	1.07	.64	599

Based on all candidates tested in 1984, 1985 and 1986 (N = 599).

The average percent correct score is based on the scale of the 1986 Core test.

GANGAROSA

MASTER OF PUBLIC HEALTH PROGRAM

EMORY UNIVERSITY SCHOOL OF MEDICINE

DEPARTMENT OF COMMUNITY HEALTH

Atlanta, Georgia 30322

August 31, 1987

Tom Sellers

Community Health

Dear Tom,

I am pleased to share the enclosed information from the American Board of Preventive Medicine showing the outstanding performance of Emory's graduates in the Preventive Medicine Specialty Board Examination. There is a need for restraint in interpreting this information because the number of Emory candidates who took the examination was small and the time period short. Nevertheless the data, however preliminary, are very encouraging. These data support what we have known for some time about our MPH Program, namely that:

1) We are able to attract the very best students.

2) We are offering a rigorous curriculum with high academic standards.
430

3) There is a unique ambience at Emory for training in public health.

Many places grow onions, but there is something unique about Vidalia that enables their onions to excel. The extraordinary resources available to us through our collaboration with CDC and the other institutions that constitute the MPH consortium provide us a uniqueness that is now being recognized internationally. This modest record is the beginning of our harvest that comes from the contribution of land that visionary Trustees of this great University made to the Federal government in the decade of the fifties that made possible CDC's proximity.

We are ready to move ahead in the development of a doctoral track that will also set standards of excellence. I am confident that the combined resources of the MPH Program and the new Department of Epidemiology and Biometry will enable us to offer the finest PhD training in epidemiology offered anywhere. I hope we can get the support of University authorities to make this possible.

Sincerely,

Eugene J. Gangarosa, MD

/om

xc: Dr. James T. Laney

Dr. Charles R. Hatcher

Dr. Richard M. Krause

GANGAROSA

August 31, 1987

Richard M. Krause, MD

Dean, School of Medicine

403 W H S C A Building

CAMPUS MAIL

Dear Dr. Krause,

We have just received some happy news; our most recent group of candidates for board certification by the American Board of Preventive Medicine ranked first among all such groups who graduated from schools and programs in public health. The exact order of finish of the other programs is confidential but our graduates' performance exceeded that of MPH graduates of all the schools of public health including Johns Hopkins, Harvard, University of North Carolina, etc.

The numbers are small of course and only physicians take this examination but we feel that the high quality of our students and their courses of study are confirmed and that they reflect great credit upon the University.

One might argue that the presence of many CDC physicians among our graduates accounts for our high ranking; while such information is not officially available, the only two graduates we know to have taken the Preventive Medicine Board exam have never had a CDC connection.

We are pleased to share this information with you.

Sincerely.

Thomas F. Sellers, MD

McAllister Professor

Community Health

Attachments (2)

cc: Dr. J. A. Bain

Dr. D. E. Brinsfield

Mr. J. T. Bertrand

August 31, 1987

Dr. James T. Laney

President

Emory University

408 Administration Building

CAMPUS MAIL

Dear President Laney:

We have just received some happy news; our most recent group of candidates for board certification by the American Board of Preventive Medicine ranked first among all such groups who graduated from schools and programs in public health. The exact order of finish of the other programs is confidential but our graduates' performance exceeded that of MPH graduates of all the schools of public health including Johns Hopkins, Harvard, University of North Carolina, etc.

The numbers are small of course and only physicians take this examination but we feel that the high quality of our students and their courses of study are confirmed and that they reflect great credit upon the University.

One might argue that the presence of many CDC physicians among our graduates accounts for our high ranking; while such information is not officially available, the only two graduates we

434

know to have taken the Preventive Medicine Board exam have never had a CDC connection.

We are pleased to share this information with you.

Sincerely,

Thomas F. Sellers, MD

McAllister Professor

Community Health

Attachments(2)

PART V: CLOSING THOUGHTS

Chapter 15: From Food Stamps to Philanthropy

My earliest days

I have mentioned in chapters of this book the hardships my family experienced during the Great Depression of the 1930s. During the years of WWI, my father had a good job and the family was well off thanks to his skill as a stonecutter. My father's brother, my uncle who lived in Niagara Falls, arranged with immigration authorities for my father to come to the U.S. with a secure job as a stonecutter. His skills were very much in demand during a road-building boom before and during WWI. The kind of work he did is still evident in roads built originally for horse and buggy traffic. Unfortunately, much of what he earned was squandered in Italian War bonds sold to immigrant families such as ours. Purveyors of these bonds (my eldest brother Sam referred to these unscrupulous individuals as financial "sharks") preyed upon immigrants, taking advantage of their compassion for their motherland to market risky financial instruments at teaser interest rates. These bonds lost their value in the November 1929 Wall-Street crash, leaving many immigrant families ill-prepared for the Depression that followed—the worst in the history of this country. Many of these destitute families decided to return to Italy. In my family, the financial stress played a key role in my father's determination to return to his family quarry in Sicily, where he was assured a job. As I mentioned earlier, this engendered turmoil within our family as my mother wisely and firmly resisted. I also wrote of the many hardships my family experienced—how my next older brother Frank and I accompanied my father in gathering nuggets of coal that had fallen on railroad sidings not far from our home in Rochester, New York, because we could not afford to buy coal essential for winter heat. I described the misery my family experienced when we could not afford monthly charges for electricity, necessitating our making candles for nighttime light. I still recall my elation in getting a dollar bill from my older brother's friend when I was hospitalized for rheumatic fever at the age of 10—as it was the first dollar I had ever owned. On the opposite spectrum of feeling, I also keenly remember my family's distress in losing our home because we could not afford mortgage payments. My mother experienced such adversity in managing a destitute family in the worst of times; the availability of food stamps made a profound difference in our very survival. I mention these events again by way of background to make the point here that my family was among the poorest of families. In such a financially stressed environment, every nickel counted. It was an ambience that encouraged saving, budgeting carefully, finding ways to earn extra money, and stretching every dollar. I was personally deeply affected by these and other Depression-era hardships.

I responded to this situation by finding part-time jobs—the first at age 12 as a farm laborer during weekends (a job I also held during one summer in high school). I continued working part-time throughout high school, spending two summers as a waiter at the Silver Bay Resort on Lake George. With the few dollars I earned, my mother encouraged me to open a bank account. I learned from her that money saved earned money back—that is, via interest rates. I treasured this bank savings account and enjoyed watching it grow as it earned regular bank interest. However, I trace my first investment experience to my hobby as a stamp-collector between ages 14 and 16. I described previously how this hobby helped me in my schooling, but it also played an important role in my financial growth. Through this activity, I learned that certain stamps increased in value. I associated with friends who made money by selling stamps at higher prices than they had paid. One friend in particular taught me how stamps were appraised—how they fluctuated in value, enabling one to negotiate price when purchasing stamps. It was my first lesson in bargaining. In addition, the hobby gave me my first feel for trading—a sense of the marketplace that facilitated purchases and sales. In retrospect, it was the seed for my interest in the stock market, but it also played an important role in my career development, as it sparked my interest in the global issues, historical events, and famous people featured on stamps. It was also the foundation for my wanderlust—my curiosity to explore other places, cultures, people, and academic topics such as geography, history, mathematics, and the sciences. While I earned a bit of money from my stamp collection, it also helped me in many other ways.

New lessons as a young man

I learned more about saving when I entered the army. I exercised an option available to soldiers only when they entered military service, to use part of my monthly pay for a matched government allotment that was sent to my mother. I decided to invest the largest amount permissible, leaving me a meager amount for my living expenses. I learned to budget this to make it last. I also benefitted from a higher rate of interest than what generally prevailed; this was the army's way of encouraging savings. I wrote earlier about my one-time poker-game experience, losing what remained of my month's pay in a matter of an hour or so. It was a memorable learning experience that taught me never to gamble, even during a later trip to Las Vegas. I also wrote about my military savings, which enabled me to earn enough for a down payment on a house I bought for my parents after my discharge. In my assignment in Italy, I took an opportunity to buy a surplus army Jeep for $200. After using it for several years to commute as an undergraduate, I sold it for $500 shortly after I got married.

During my college years, I took advantage of the University of Rochester's extension program to attend late afternoon and evening courses so that I could earn money as a bakery manager. When I purchased my first car after selling the Jeep, I took advantage of an insurance loan rather than pay a higher market rate. In my first year of medical school, I needed a microscope for my anatomy, histology, and embryology courses. I found an ad in a newspaper for an old Zeiss monocular microscope for $100.00, saving hundreds over other options. When I was about to graduate from medical school, I did a library search to find funding from the New Jersey Davella Mills Foundation for a fellowship for a postdoctoral year in the university's graduate program, where I could earn a Master's degree. I had no financial assistance from my family at any point—in fact, I assumed responsibility for assisting my family starting with the purchase of a home for them. However, I did have an inheritance of several hundred dollars from my parents, and Rose's parents and an uncle left her inheritances of several thousand dollars that certainly helped us. Rose's father was especially helpful in providing us an apartment where we lived during the years I attended medical school, and her mother and sisters were exceedingly supportive in so many ways. Nonetheless, Rose and I had primary responsibility for our own finances, and this drove the growth and development of habits that we have kept throughout our lives. In short, I was frugal, I learned several ways to save, and I endeavored to earn extra money—working part-time in my adolescence and full-time as a college student taking afternoon and evening courses. These experiences and decisions helped me to develop a business sense—and I had fun, especially as an adolescent. My experiences trading stamps gave me insight that laid the foundation for my interest in stocks. I became intrigued by financial matters—it was an interest that served as a pathway to the stock market.

Lessons about the stock market

It was during a very hectic internship that I learned about investing in stocks. My first month's salary fell short of our needs because the budget we planned did not take into consideration the added cost of getting settled into a new apartment. By the end of the third week into my internship, we actually ran out of money and had no reserve. We were desperate, but too proud to borrow from friends or family. So, we struggled and stretched in every possible way. By the end of the second month we came to grips with the need for a rigid budget. Our budget included a tithe for our church and charities and another tithe for our personal savings. In our third month, our tithe for personal savings was $35. Some of the military physicians with whom I worked were trading stocks. One of them mentioned Tri-Continental Stock (TY), citing as one of its advantages the fact that as a closed-end investment company, it was selling as a common stock on the New York stock exchange at a price less than its net asset value. So, buying this stock was a way of getting 6 to 7% additional value as compared to most other mutual funds that required an upfront charge. I looked into the quality of the stocks in the TY portfolio and was pleasantly surprised to see stocks for well-recognized brands of everyday necessities in foods, household items, cars, and other products. So I invested our first tithe, $35, in this closed-end investment company. In the months that followed we added more—a process that continued in every month of my internship. It was satisfying to see growth by reinvested dividends. I continued this strategy for years—in fact, I still own some of the shares I purchased over a period of 60 years. At this writing, these shares have a six-figure value, as do several other stocks I hold. It was a pleasant ride as the stock market went up, but daunting when it fell. In down markets, I initially stopped investing until I realized that the lower prices provided opportunity to accumulate more at lower prices. Through the years, compounding regular monthly investments with reinvested dividends convinced me that this was the best way to accumulate wealth. Over the course of years, quality stocks have averaged growth of 10-12%. In no five-year period over the course of these 60 years have we lost money. In summary, we became multi-millionaires by tithing for ourselves, reinvesting dividends, and staying in the market through good times and bad. This is my testimony to the power of compounding, selecting quality stocks, and continuing investing in both strong and weak markets.

If the reader is overwhelmed by the thought of 60 years to reach the same goal, I hasten to add that 1) the years will go by no matter what, and 2) this strategy actually works in less than 60 years. However, no one can predict the future, so I conclude this point by writing, try it—you may be pleasantly surprised, and you may in fact be able to endow your own chair, if not for yourself, for a loved one in 50 years. We completed the funding of our first chair after 45 years.

I had several stockbrokers early in my financial career, but I came to the realization that my investment strategy made it unnecessary to rely on brokers for advice in selecting stocks. I did as well or better than the best of them. Our stock choices were made possible by what I learned from only two investment letters to which I have subscribed. Many of the stocks in our portfolio we have held for decades. They are all highly rated. Nearly all of them pay dividends. Most provide essential services or sell things that are necessary for quality of life. Specifically, the holdings we have include leading companies in practically all categories—pharmaceuticals, including Pfizer, Merck, and other leaders in their field; finances, including the big banks; home improvement, including Home Depot and Loews; service industries such as utilities and rails; and water and sanitation-related services. Most of our investments are in domestic stocks. I have not invested in mutual funds except for the one stock that got me started—TY, a closed-end mutual fund that does not require an upfront charge. I have never bought stocks on margin. I have only once sold stocks short, and after a loss on that one short sale I have never again sold stock short. I have not traded in futures.

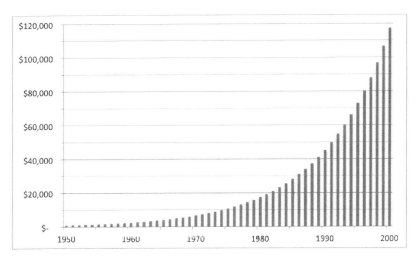

Figure 21: The power of compound interest.
This figure shows a hypothetical scenario in which $1000 is invested and compounded annually at 10%, with no additional investment. At 25 years, the value of the investment is over $10,000. At 50 years, the value approaches $120,000. Young investors would do well to harness the power of compound interest.

Because of my past military service, I joined the United Services Automobile Association (USAA) in 1956. It and TIAA/CREF are the two highest-rated financial companies. I do all of my trading through USAA with stocks I select, buy, and sell at brokerage rates far less than those charged by other financial institutions.

Through USAA I purchased life-insurance policies for my wife and family and an annuity that I was fortunate to buy during an era when high interest rates prevailed. This annuity pays 6% compounded and is another six-figure investment. I have not invested in property or timeshares.

Our philanthropic activities

We find ourselves in a strong financial position, able to give back, due to the habits I mentioned above. We disciplined ourselves in several ways. We paid off the two mortgages for our first and second homes in record time. We never accumulated credit-card debt, and always paid credit card monthly balances so that we never paid interest on our credit-card purchases. We never borrowed from friends or family. Except for our brief mortgages, we have been totally debt free all of our sixty-five years of our marriage at this writing. This has enabled our philanthropic activities.

In 1991, Rose and I established our family foundation, the Gangarosa International Health Foundation, as a 501c organization. I funded it with my earned income from my consulting business from 1991 to 2014, which averaged between $60,000 and $100,000 per year. We have been able to donate, via our foundation, to numerous NGOs each year, and we never solicit from the public.

We share generously with the charities and institutions that made possible our educations. We have established irrevocable endowments with the University of Rochester, where I was educated, and at Nazareth College, where Rose was educated. One of our first endowments was with Emory's Rollins School of Public Health. It was established to support global field experiences (GFEs) for students. I did this because, during my tenure as director of the graduate program in public health (which evolved as the Rollins School of Public Health), I was greatly influenced by my own global experiences (as described in this book) in Italy and in Bangkok[92]. Those two field experiences shaped my career. Touched by the importance of such experiences, I decided to establish an endowment for global field experiences for graduate students in the Rollins School. We also funded the Center for Global Safe Water at Emory University's Rollins School of Public Health with two endowed chairs—one in Rose's name for sanitation, the other in water under my name. We have also established two more endowments at the CDC Foundation. The first endowment was initially to provide seed money for safe water initiatives in developing countries, but has since transitioned to support water-related student practicums, first for Emory students, and now also for students in the College of Charleston's public health program, where our son Paul teaches. The second endowment at the CDC Foundation also supports student practicums in similar topics for these same institutions. A separate endowment that we established with the College of Charleston in 2014 also supports student practicums. Most recently, we established an endowment with the American University of Beirut's Faculty of Health Sciences to support water and sanitation research.

In addition to these endowments, we have supported many not-for-profit organizations that have specific health initiatives to ensure quality of life to the poorest of our global neighbors. Our donations swelled from just a few to 76 in 2014; most of these NGOs we support with contributions of $50, but for those involved in water and sanitation or refugee work, our support

---

[92] In Italy, I worked in logistics during a typhoid outbreak. In Bangkok, I worked on the first urban outbreak in cholera that subsequently spread globally as the 7th pandemic.

has been in four-figure donations. In the early months of 2015, the number of new NGOs requesting support surged to a point where it would have exceeded our foundation's budget to donate to all of them. Rose and I were overextended and overwhelmed by the deluge of increasing solicitations from both old and new NGOs—we were receiving multiple letters, emails, and even phone calls every day. Therefore, in May of that year, we wrote to most of them to request that they delete us from their membership list. However, we continue to support organizations involved in refugee work throughout the year, and we plan to also support NGOs focused on water and sanitation and a select few for blindness control with one-time donations. In February 2015, I had two optic nerve strokes that compromised my vision, preventing me from continuing my consultative practice. This was a factor in asking most of the NGOs we supported to remove us from their mailing and call lists, with the few exceptions noted above.

Even though we are just a small family foundation, we have given over half of our financial wealth to establish our endowments[93]. That is a larger percentage than the payout of the biggest charitable organization. We have set aside the remainder as a reserve in the event that either of us becomes disabled and requires long-term care and to ensure the bequests we have set aside for our children and grandchildren. We have been generous with our children and grandchildren with annual stock contributions to the extent limited by tax constraints.

---

[93] Both chairs at Emory were endowed primarily through our foundation, but also with some money from our personal accounts.

Our motivations for giving back

What motivates us to share our blessings is our commitment to improve the quality of life for those less fortunate. Rose and I have both been deeply moved by our experiences in the developing countries where we have worked and lived. We saw for ourselves the hardships of people who must live in unsanitary conditions. We have been deeply involved in research to find ways to reduce the terrible risks created by unsanitary conditions.

I have delved into my memory to sort out what exactly were the experiences that influenced us in our philanthropy. In fact, Rose has done the same thing and has composed her thoughts in a short essay entitled "Rose's story," at the conclusion of this chapter.

In my own reflections, I believe the one most important event was my experience in Calcutta, India in 1959. After completing my Bangkok study, I planned my return home with a stopover in Calcutta, India because I wanted to share with a colleague the intestinal biopsy method and to biopsy another cholera patient if that was feasible. I was aware at that time of a study published from this institution advocating the use of cortisone for the treatment of cholera. This was during an era when the prevailing dictum was the intestinal epithelial desquamation theory, which likened the pathology of cholera to a burn, for which steroids like cortisone were being used. I had a contact at the School of Tropical Medicine in that city, so I sent him a telegram to brief him of the work I had done in Bangkok and ask if he would invite me to visit him to see the intestinal biopsy instrument and possibly use it there in a cholera patient. He responded quickly with an enthusiastic YES. Accordingly, I routed my return flight with a three-day stopover in Calcutta. The director of the

449

institute made arrangements for my accommodations. I showed him how to use the instrument, and together we biopsied a cholera patient who had recently been stabilized. He permitted me to cut the specimen in half so that we could both compare the appearance from the duodenal epithelium. On the morning of the third day, when I was scheduled to leave, he told me that the intestinal epithelium was entirely intact—exactly what we had found in our Bangkok cholera patients. He was so grateful that he could see for himself that there was no desquamation. It supported him in his opposition to the cortisone strategy. I spent the rest of that day with one of his students, visiting the streets of the city, which were still teeming with refugees from the mass migrations from what was then East Pakistan, now Bangladesh. I was appalled by the plight of these refugees, how extensively they were exposed to the dirtiest water, which was the only thing they had for all of their needs. At the time, these refugees were in the thousands with no home or shelter—many slept and lived on the streets. This was a poignant experience for me, and it is still framed clearly in my memory. In answer to my question as to which experience was most instrumental in my becoming a philanthropist it has to be this one—on the streets of Calcutta.

Another input that was formative in the development of my own philosophy on philanthropy was the planning of the Alma Ata conference on primary health care. This conference, held in September 1978 in Kazakhstan, in what was then the Soviet Union, articulated the ambitious goal of "Health for All by the Year 2000." My consulting work with WHO contributed to the planning of the conference, but I could not attend as I had recently assumed my position as Dean of the Faculty of Health Sciences at the American University of Beirut. Each colleague I spoke to who had attended the meeting was energized by the sense of global commitment to primary health care. Yet all of us soon recognized that the goal, however idealistic, was totally unrealistic. One of my colleagues relayed in an anecdote that in a conference in Thailand, the "Health for All by the Year 2000" goal was translated as "Health for All in 2000 Years." I explain to my students that it may not have been an error in translation—it could have been intentional to make the point that the goal was unrealistic. In fact, it was from the Alma Ata meeting that a new strategy evolved—the Millennium Development Goals, which are focused on specific objectives, e.g., infant mortality, smoking cessation, and obesity. This transition from a simple "wish list" to prioritized, realistic, and measurable objectives is one that I fully support. I strive to align my own endeavors with these goals, so that I can take my own place in our universal responsibility for global health. In doing so, I have some confidence and a sense of accomplishment knowing that our endowments and my work represent our best effort for universal health.

Nonetheless, the most poignant reminders of our contributions are the hand-written messages we get frequently from students who benefit from our GFE endowment. Their expressions of gratitude and their realization that these experiences are career-changing events are the most valued of our investments.

Rose's story

It began in Pakistan in 1962. Each morning, I drove to my workplace, the Lahore American School, where I taught high school English and served as principal. On every journey, I saw women collecting water, children being washed, and people brushing their teeth in a canal where buffalo bathed and latrines drained. They had no other sources for water! I was deeply moved, and these haunting images persisted through the years. How I wished I could make a difference!

Through the years, I encouraged and supported Gene's career in water and sanitation, often editing and critiquing his work. His focus was to prevent the spread of cholera from the deplorable sanitary conditions that were present not only in Pakistan, but also shared by many others of the developing countries of the Middle East and South Asia. In 1978, we moved to war-torn Lebanon, where Gene played a major role in the transformation of the school of public health at the American University of Beirut.

Upon our return to the States in the early 1980s, Gene joined Emory faculty. His interest was in promoting the academic program in public health; this culminated in the development of the Rollins School of Public Health. Gene "retired" from Emory in 1991, and at that time we established our first endowment to support students in their practicums abroad. Students often write letters to us describing their global field experiences as life-changing events. Some were poignant accounts of difficult conditions that further reinforced our commitment.

In 2003, Gene continued his advocacy for safe water by mobilizing a network of professionals in various colleges of Emory, CDC, and local organizations with related interests. A second endowment, a chair in his name, provided the seed money to accelerate this effort and to establish the Center for Global Safe Water.

It has been most gratifying for me to observe the Center's progress. Its impressive growth played a pivotal role in our decision to fund our third endowment—my chair—dedicated to sanitation.

I see we have a long way to go to achieve the goals of safe water and decent toilets for all, but I am confident it will happen. I congratulate those already involved and urge all to hasten efforts to make these goals a reality. When these goals are reached, we can all rejoice in the knowledge that we leave a healthier and safer world for our children. That is my dream!

Reflections on giving and receiving

I have many reasons to be grateful for the largesse of others. I have to credit the Rochester community for paying for my 1936 convalescent hospitalization, mentioned elsewhere in this text. That was in itself a career-changing event: I felt that Whipple was impressed by this story when I told him about my hospitalization and what it meant to me in my interview for medical school. I believe it was instrumental in my acceptance at a time when so many outstanding applicants were being considered. I am also most grateful to those who made possible the relief my family got during the worst days of the Great Depression. I recall vividly how much it meant to my mother that she got food stamps—especially when she, the only breadwinner, was laid off and no one else in the family was working. Those food stamps got us through the worst of times. I can hardly imagine what might have happened without this relief. I am so grateful for the GI Bill that made possible my medical school education. Without it I could not have gotten an education—my whole life would surely have been different. For the pivotal support taxpayers provided for these things, I am most grateful. I am pleased that for each year I have paid taxes in my professional career, I have paid back many times the monetary value of all these things. But the satisfaction that comes from paying taxes is not enough—I can never repay the tax-payers for all the benefits I and my family got from having the chance to live in this country that has meant so much to me, particularly as I reflect on how close we came to losing everything had my mother agreed to return to Italy. So, I am pleased that we can help others with the resources my professional career has made possible. I wish decision-makers in our Congress would see how important this help is for the poor and how much it means to the country to have immigrants who would love to have the opportunity my family and I have had.

In summary, I see "health for all" as a shared responsibility for all of us committed to public health. Thus we see our work—my personal endeavors, our Foundation's contributions, and our endowments—as investments in the shared responsibility necessary to make possible improved quality of life and Health for All. What we have given came from what we received from the largesse of the communities in which we were raised. We hope we will be seen as examples of the payback that comes from such generosity—what the community gains from food stamps and the cost of my education. We hope we will be seen as examples of how such investments through welfare to struggling families and my education have been solid investments not only for our nation, but for the entire global society.

.

Afterword

In this book, I have shared my early life experiences as well as my professional experiences. In this afterword, I would like to relate these experiences to several themes—the "legacy of cholera" and its impact on my own life; the promotion of social justice that is so important to me; and the joys of mentorship and teaching that I have been privileged to experience in many different locations throughout the world.

Summary of salient points in my professional life and how they interrelate

Mine was a career inspired initially by the book *Microbe Hunters,* which I read as a child during a prolonged hospitalization for rheumatic fever. The pathway I serendipitously followed led me to a war-devastated Naples, Italy where, as an army supply technician during WWII, I happened to interact with soldiers from the Walter Reed Army Institute for Research (WRAIR) who were engaged in measures to control a typhus epidemic caused by the war-related destruction of the city's water supply and sanitary facilities. In Naples I had no single mentor, but I identified with these soldiers, and I learned from readings about the disease control measures in progress. I look back on this military experience as a self-taught field practicum in public health. My next immediate professional step was medical school, during which I began to develop my interests in preventive medicine and research, and where I also met several classmates who became lifelong friends and colleagues, most notably D.A. Henderson. After my internship year, I had the opportunity to pursue my research interests at the Walter Reed Army Hospital and the Walter Reed Army Institute of Research (WRAIR), culminating in my cholera experiences in Bangkok, Thailand, Calcutta, India, and Lahore, Pakistan, which coincided with the beginning of the seventh cholera pandemic. These events, and the professional networks I gained during them, contributed to many of my later career opportunities.

Through all these positions and associations, my professional focus has been on safe water and sanitation. My consultations for cholera control provided me opportunities to promote water and sanitary infrastructures. My leverage for this work came from the knowledge, training, and inspiration of distinguished mentors and collaborators in research discoveries—starting with my discovery of the pathogenesis of cholera in Bangkok, Thailand in 1959, at the beginning of the pandemic. I built on this discovery with research in a number of different countries, including Pakistan as discussed in this book. Through this research, I also identified the pervasive intestinal condition known as environmental enteropathy, previously unrecognized. Concurrently these discoveries launched my career as an educator. I have taught medical students, nurses, public health students and practitioners in pediatrics, internal medicine, and public health practice at each of the institutions with which I have been associated[94]. These teaching arrangements have been lengthy—I've spent at least three years in each. Among the many lectures I give concerning water, sanitation, and various public health issues, my single most important topic deals with the transformation of public health in the mid-1850s, made possible

---

[94] These institutions include the Walter Reed Army Institute of Research (WRAIR); the Pakistan Medical Research Center in Lahore, which emerged as the Institute of Public Health; the Centers for Disease Control and Prevention (CDC); the Faculty of Health Sciences (FHS) of the American University of Beirut (AUB); the University of Baghdad; the University of Basrah; the Rollins School of Public Health (RSPH) at Emory University; and the College of Charleston.

by John Snow's investigation of cholera outbreaks in London. In this lecture series, I weave together information from Steven Johnson's historical account and my own experiences in cholera.

My favorite subject to teach in public health—cholera— and the role of a text I use in my teaching

In all the courses I have been teaching, including a course I taught in January of 2016 just a week before this writing, I use Steven Johnson's book *The Ghost Map.* In this book, Johnson leverages extraordinary historical records to document the investigations of a physician-anesthesiologist into devastating cholera outbreaks in mid-1850s London. This investigation, particularly the work that the physician, John Snow, did during the 1854 Golden Square outbreak, is now considered a classic and is taught in many schools of medicine and public health. Further, this is perhaps one of the first examples of what I like to call "cholera's legacy": The results of this investigation eventually prompted the construction of the modern sewer system that enabled London to grow while providing its citizens with safe water. Further, John Snow's investigation resulted in the transformation of public health. For these reasons, and because the book integrates so nicely with my own professional experiences in cholera, it is my favorite text to use while teaching.

I met Steven Johnson on the occasion of his lecture at Emory University in 2010. We had a long discussion on points of mutual interest in the book. On most topics we agreed, but I felt obligated to point out an error in the book—an incorrect speculation on the source of the rice-water stool typical of cholera diarrhea. I explained his speculative account had been the outdated dictum disproved by my Bangkok biopsy study, which showed that epithelial cells of the intestine remained entirely intact during cholera diarrhea. We also discussed how my EIS mentor Alex Langmuir was impressed by William Farr's management of the 1866 cholera outbreak in London, during which Farr engaged the retired parish priest Henry Whitehead to assist in the investigation. This action helped to inspire Langmuir's own strategy of including diverse professionals from varied disciplines in the Epidemic Intelligence Service (EIS). I was pleased to meet with Johnson, and I especially enjoyed his inscription on my copy of his book: "To Gene Gangarosa—a student of cholera for so many years!" His exclamation point tickled me.

The most important topics I teach involve the integration of what I have learned in my cholera work with key points in Johnson's book. Perhaps foremost of these topics is the concept of rates, the basic tool of epidemiology. In one of his landmark investigations into cholera outbreaks in London, John Snow persuasively used rates to demonstrate a link between cholera deaths and water supplied by two different companies. Snow noted that the proportion of households affected by cholera was much higher in those homes supplied by Southwark and Vauxhall, as compared to those supplied by Lambeth. He used this information to link the outbreak to contaminated water supplied by Southwark and Vauxhall.

I also often ask students about what life was like in 1850s London, and why. The answer becomes apparent when I cite Charles Dickens's *Bleak House:* "That is to say, Jo has not yet died." This quote is relevant because it enables students to understand the magnitude of the mortality rate among the working poor, i.e., the fact that the average life expectancy was only 16 years in London at that time. The cause of the high mortality rate becomes clear from Johnson's metaphor in his reference to "the monstrous cancer" extant in London at that time. The monstrous cancer refers to the shit in which people were immersed, and from which cholera emerged, in the Golden Square district of Soho, as well as in other poor districts throughout the city. Although people of the time were correct in incriminating feces as a cause of disease, even going so far as to call for sewers, they wrongly identified the smell of feces as the dangerous agent[95]. Snow was ahead of his time in recognizing, during the Golden Square epidemic as well as a later epidemic, that it was not the smell of feces—but rather some contaminating agent *within* the feces—that was the cause of cholera. He was able to prove his point by comparing cholera deaths in homes with different water suppliers (as described above). The salient point of the *Ghost Map* story is that the modern city was enabled by the realization that infectious agents from human and animal feces cause diseases that kill. Although London's first major sewer system in fact carried contaminated water, a better sewer system was soon designed that eventually eliminated cholera from London and other European urban centers that had adopted it. It is the combination of efficient sewers and safe water treatment plants that keep untreated feces away from water sources, thus preventing the development of a fecal veneer. In result, these infrastructures have eliminated urban cholera and typhoid fever, as well as a host of other water borne diseases, in the more developed countries of the world. The key point I teach is that cholera's "legacy" is the recognition that elected or appointed municipal leaders have the responsibility to provide their citizens with safe water and sanitary facilities. I call this a social contract.

---

[95] Indeed, Edward Chadwick, often lauded for his appeal to Parliament to fund London's first sewer system, leveraged his appeal by persuading Parliament that "all that smells is disease."

However, cholera's "legacy" must not end in the mere construction of sanitary and water infrastructures. These sanitary and water infrastructures must be maintained. Failure to maintain them has resulted in many serious waterborne outbreaks—one example investigated by my own group featured cholera in Portugal in 1975, while an example current at this writing is a lead poisoning outbreak in Flint, Michigan. The latter portends an incredible pending outbreak of dementia and a host of other serious lead-induced diseases, but is unfortunately only the tip of the iceberg of the profound and pervasive deterioration of our water and sanitation infrastructures. The widely embraced concept of social contracts for these infrastructures implies that community leaders must be held responsible for failures to maintain them. I emphasize to my students that the water we drink from our home faucets comes from recycled wastes. The quality of this water is usually good to excellent, but we also share responsibility for whatever maintenance is required to keep it safe. I urge my students, family, and friends to keep this in mind when they vote. Those of us in medicine and public health have to take the lead in advocating for these treasures, and acting proactively to prevent illnesses rather than solely reacting to disasters. When our elected leaders fail, as in Flint, they must be held responsible.

Another important teaching point eloquently demonstrated by *The Ghost Map* concerns the development of the modern health department. During the London cholera outbreaks, the London Board of Health failed to recognize the significance of Snow's work because they were blinded by their adherence to the miasmic principles. They saw only causes that were compatible with the miasmic theory, and could not accept the possibility that a single water source could have caused the outbreak. In contrast, the members of the St. James Vestry Committee were not compromised by such blind adherence to a single principle.

Instead, this diverse committee (including a priest, a surveyor, and a physician, among others) was able, through cross-disciplinary collaboration and open minds, to find and understand the evidence incriminating the Lewis family home as the source of the Broad Street well outbreak. From this experience emerged a realization of the intellectual power of open-minded people from varied disciplines. This in essence was the birth of the modern-day health department—this cross-disciplinary committee was the prototype used for the reorganized British Ministry of Health[96], as well as other health departments throughout the world. Indeed, Alex Langmuir saw the Vestry Committee as the prototype for the membership of the EIS, and Farr's surveillance as the prototype for the surveillance concepts employed by the EIS.

My last teaching point has to do with the discovery of environmental enteropathy, as it too is linked to the same "monstrous cancer" noted in Johnson's book. This condition arises from fecal contamination in settings where inadequate hygiene, unsafe water, and soiled environments coexist. I use a mnemonic to help students remember how pathogens can be transmitted in such an environment: "the five Fs." They are as follows:

1) Feces—are the original source of the pathogens responsible for intestinal infections. Uncontained feces can contaminate water as well as other environments.

2) Food—can become an important source of pathogen exposure particularly where temperature control and refrigeration is lacking.

3) Fingers—can transmit pathogens when they are unwashed.

---

[96]The reorganization of the Ministry of Health was prompted by the "Great Stink" of 1858, which finally convinced officials that the miasmic theory was not valid.

4) Flies—transfer pathogens from feces to food (as can roaches).

5) Fomites—can enable transfer of pathogens from hands to other hands (fomites are inanimate objects such as hand rails, pencils, elevator buttons, and so forth).

In an environment contaminated by a fecal veneer, pathogen transfer by the Five Fs can contribute to recurrent diarrheal illnesses among children, in turn causing environmental enteropathy. Breastfeeding is important in preventing this condition as it enables immunity to develop, but that immunity is often not enough when infants start weaning and become toddlers, at which time they begin to put everything into their mouths. This is a milieu that provides ideal opportunities for pathogens to complete their life cycles, resulting in nutritional problems that aggravate the situation and hasten the downhill spiral leading to early deaths. Specifically, the multiple repeated enteric infections and co-infections that are common in such an environment can cause the human intestine to react by retracting the intestinal villi in an attempt to limit the surface area over which the pathogens (or toxins) can act. In the normal North American subject, recovery of the small bowel pathology from a single bout of intestinal infection is complete in a matter of days, as the damaged intestinal cells are replaced by new ones. However, repeated infections and co-infections (a common situation in many developing countries) can permanently compromise the digestive process. These events lead to early deaths—such as Dickens alluded to in his quote, "That is to say, Jo has not yet died." In *The Ghost Map,* Johnson describes these deaths as due to the "monstrous cancer" prevalent in 1800s London, explaining why the life expectancy at that time was only 16 years among the working poor [1]. The environmental enteropathy resulting from this "monstrous cancer" compromises physical and mental growth, even in the absence of more severe nutritional disease as manifested by marasmus or kwashiorkor [2-5]. Studies have documented that these problems associated with environmental enteropathy may be carried over to impact subsequent generations.

Reflections on my work abroad and the influences of my early family life

I was fortunate learning from my earliest experiences growing up in a large family the importance of sharing, tolerance, accepting differences, and working and playing with others. I enjoy spending time with others, engaging them in mental gymnastics, and I also get great pleasure from helping others. My wife Rose also came from a large family, with similar cultural roots, although her family was more fortunate than mine. They accepted me wholeheartedly into their family, and they were supportive in so many ways. I believe that these early experiences have shaped my personal viewpoints and interactions wherever Rose and I have lived and traveled.

Throughout our travels, Rose and I have spent a great deal of time exploring new places, and have managed to befriend strangers as well as colleagues. One of our favorite things while traveling was to pack a lunch and stop for a picnic—it always attracted a number of curious locals! We often had to ask strangers for assistance, sometimes in another language or using sign language, hand gestures, maps, and tourist handouts to try to understand each other. Throughout our lives, though especially while living abroad, we have enjoyed entertaining neighbors, students, staff and faculty in our home, often even hosting visitors. In turn, we were often invited to the homes of faculty, where we enjoyed conversations with family members and their children. We fondly remember meals with these families—often extending into the late evening hours.

In our dwellings abroad, we managed with water and sanitation facilities more tenuous than what we had in our stateside homes. These experiences gave us still more empathy for those dealing with water and sanitation infrastructures even more primitive in our own, and inspired our philanthropy as well as our daily dealings with our neighbors and employees. For instance, in Pakistan, we permitted nomads who set up their tents in a vacant lot across the street to get water from a faucet at the side of our house. Although this practice was discouraged by our provider, we appealed and eventually succeeded in changing policy. The principles of social justice have guided me to similar advocacy throughout my life and career.

Everywhere I've taught—abroad as well as in the U.S., I have had a close working relationship with my students. I also enjoy employing former students to serve as teaching assistants in subsequent courses, and feel great gratification when I see their own careers develop. In Calcutta and Lahore, I taught faculty colleagues how to use the intestinal biopsy instrument that I had used in my biopsy studies. Upon my departure, I donated the instrument. Later, some of these faculty conducted independent studies. I was greatly pleased when they published their work.

I have also had opportunities to promote and support education below the graduate level. While we were living in Pakistan, I was a board member and chairperson of the Board of Directors of the Lahore American School, where Rose served as principal and taught English to high school students. I served on a committee to raise funds to support Pakistani students at our school. In Lahore and in other places we lived, I also was able to help facilitate connections to enable educational opportunities abroad for the children of our faculty friends.

We have treasured memories of each of the places we visited—where we lived, the many faculty with whom I taught, students I taught and mentored, friends we made, and places we visited. Throughout our travels, we acquired many beautiful items that still adorn our home at the time of this writing, and took many photographs that we love to share with family and friends. Rose and I feel privileged to have had such a variety of outstanding experiences.

Concluding thoughts

I feel fortunate to have had such a long and exciting career, and to have benefitted from the support of family, friends, and outstanding mentors. My early family life taught me about the value of hard work and the impact of poverty on a family. I have personally benefitted greatly from social welfare programs (a debt I've now been able to repay many times over in taxes) as well as from the kindness of family. These experiences, as well as others, have instilled in me a great passion for social justice that has underpinned my career. I also have my family to thank—specifically, my mother and my brother Sam—for encouraging a commitment to education, a dedication that I continue to the time of this writing.

My family story comes full circle with this book, dedicated to my four siblings—"now angels"—whose untimely passing provided one of the seeds of my career interests. Their premature deaths, caused by intestinal and respiratory disease, were likely also related to environmental enteropathy—now recognized as a common problem in settings similar to my family's home in Sicily, where livestock proximity and limited water supplies requiring rationing contributed to a pervasive "fecal veneer." My family's move from Comiso, Sicily, to Niagara Falls, New York, proved to be an escape from the fecal veneer that claimed the lives of my four siblings. Had my family not moved, it is likely that myself and my other siblings unborn at the time would have also succumbed to the effects of environmental enteropathy. So I am especially indebted to the decision my parents made to emigrate. Now, as I conclude what I have written here, I finally have a sense of satisfaction reconciling the circumstances of my siblings' deaths in this historical postmortem analysis.

References

1. Johnson S: **The ghost map: the story of London's most terrifying epidemic — and how it changed science, cities, and the modern world**. New York, NY: Riverhead Books; 2006.

2. Keusch GT, Rosenberg IH, Denno DM, Duggan C, Guerrant RL, Lavery JV, Tarr PI, Ward HD, Black RE, Nataro JP *et al*: **Implications of acquired environmental enteric dysfunction for growth and stunting in infants and children living in low- and middle-income countries**. *Food and Nutrition Bulletin* 2013, **34**(3):357-364.

3. Keusch GT, Denno DM, Black RE, Duggan C, Guerrant RL, Lavery JV, Nataro JP, Rosenberg IH, Ryan ET, Tarr PI *et al*: **Environmental enteric dysfunction: pathogenesis, diagnosis, and clinical consequences**. *Clinical Infectious Disease* 2014, **59 Suppl 4**:S207-212.

4. Prendergast A, Kelly P: **Enteropathies in the developing world: neglected effects on global health**. *American J Tropical Medicine and Hygiene* 2012, **86**(5):756-763.

5. McKay S, Gaudier E, Campbell DI, Prentice AM, Albers R: **Environmental enteropathy: new targets for nutritional interventions**. *International Health* 2010, **2**(3):172-180.

END NOTES

[i] My son Ray, an avid history buff who remembered aspects of this "cruise" better than I did, helped me reconstruct why it turned out the way it did.

The Landing Ship Tank was conceived because when the British retreated hastily from France in May 1940, they had to leave their valuable tanks and trucks on the beach for lack of ships to transport them across the English Channel. Although some of the earlier versions were adapted from existing designs and reasonably well suited for long voyages across open seas (like transatlantic voyages), the LST became adapted to a specialized function crucial to winning the war:

- LSTs were hurriedly designed to be cheaply and sloppily built in huge numbers. In rushing the ships into production, little attention was paid to making them more controllable or stable in heavy seas. Still less attention was paid to any niceties.

- To cram closely parked tanks into their holds, the ships were shaped like boxes, with flat sides completely without streamlining.

- The bow was also flat and even less streamlined, because its huge door swung down and opened up in the front so that tanks could drive side-by-side straight from the hold onto the beach. This was the essential feature that made them so well adapted to amphibious landings—LSTs could travel up to the water's edge where heavy equipment could drive right into combat, without the need for deep-water ports, piers, cranes, etc.

- Most important of all, most LST had an extremely shallow draft (i.e., the distance from the waterline to the bottom of the keel), so that they could unload tanks directly onto a beach with minimal exposure to corrosive salt water. Some kinds of LSTs had drafts as shallow as 4 feet. With so little ballast below the waterline, LSTs wallowed like drunken sailors in heavy seas!

- The shallow drafts of some LST models made them so unstable that many were retrofitted to pump water into ballast tanks when going into deep, choppy, and/or stormy seas. That approach is often used in thoughtfully constructed ships, but for a poorly researched design like the LST, it amounted to partially sinking the vessel so it could manage more treacherous waters! Many were designed with extremely shallow drafts in the bow for beach landings and slightly deeper drafts in the stern for more stability. Needless to say, these sloppily implemented ad hoc modifications did not help the vessels' seaworthiness very much.

- In one dramatic example I read, when American troops landed by LSTs near Agrigento in the invasion of southern Italy, they were so seasick they could not fight! Fortunately, they had air cover, so they were able to hold the beach, despite the delay in the invasion until they recovered.

There were many varieties of LSTs with different characteristics, and I don't know which kind we took. However, Ray searched the internet and came up with a comparison between various LSTs and the premier luxury liner just before (and troop ship during) World War II, the Queen Elizabeth, which would be fairly similar to an average cruise ship at this writing. This comparison highlights why LSTs were so unseaworthy:

	Typical LSTs	Queen Elizabeth	Comments
Draft	14' (Mark I) 3' bow, 7' stern 5' bow, 11' stern	38'	The LST's shallow draft allows it to beach instead of unloading at a deep harbor pier, but causes it to wallow in the open ocean.
Length	350 – 400'	1,030'	The LST's shorter length makes for a much choppier ride in high seas.
Beam (width)	50 – 65'	118'	The LST is unusually wide for its length and draft, allowing powerful waves to push it around.
Horse-power	6,000	160,000	The LST is grossly underpowered, especially considering it is also far less streamlined.
Top speed	18 knots (Mark I) 9 – 13 knots (others)	30 knots	The LST's lack of power and streamlining make it slow, especially against powerful incoming waves.
Displace ment (tons)	2,000 – 6,000	84,000	The LST's light displacement makes it like a bobbing cork compared to the Queen Elizabeth!
Cargo capacity	20 tanks or 35 trucks or 200 troops	10,000 troops	The LST took on a lot of cargo weight for its size, power, displacement, and seaworthiness.

ii Dr. Alex Langmuir's role featured prominently in the early years of the development of the Dhaka Laboratory primarily through Epidemic Intelligence Service (EIS) Officers he selected, starting with Dr. Henry Mosley, whose cholera studies contributed so much to our understanding of the epidemiology of the disease. I was involved only peripherally in the selection of two of the EIS officers, Dr. Roger Rochat and Dr. Barth Reller, who conducted the first investigation of oral fluid therapy in a field study separated from a hospital. They published their work with their collaborators David Nalin and Cash McCall in a landmark study that launched ORS as the treatment of choice for diarrheal diseases of any etiology. [Cash RA, Nalin DR, Rochat R, Reller LB, Haque ZA, Rahman AS: **A clinical trial of oral therapy in a rural cholera-treatment center**. *American J Tropical Medicine and Hygiene* 1970, **19**(4):653-656.]

iii Early in the 1960s, Drs. Joe Smadel and Bud Benenson arranged for visits of scientists involved in the Bangkok studies to brief and teach scientists how to use the biopsy instrument to study intestinal infections. I was among those assigned to that duty, and we visited and taught at several academic institutions. After receiving our training, some of our students did studies with the biopsy capsule that greatly expanded knowledge of other intestinal infectious diseases.

iv When we had moved to Pakistan from our home in Wheaton Woods, Maryland, our largest single piece of furniture was Rose's baby grand piano. Having it was an essential part of the quality of Rose's life, so we agonized and made difficult decisions—excluding many things we had wanted to take to stay within our weight allowance. We had even greater anxiety about
470

the piano when faced with our abrupt return to the States. Our situation was complicated by the additional weight of other household items we had acquired in Pakistan—hand-woven rugs and handcrafted woodwork. We consulted with Fred McCrumb, who advised us to leave the piano in our Lahore home, pledging he would make arrangements for it when Dr. Woodward arrived as my replacement. We never knew what happened to it, but some months after we returned to the States, Fred wrote us a poignant letter that included a check for what we had told him was the value of the piano. We used the money to buy another similar piano for Rose in our home in Stone Mountain.

[v] When we lived in Pakistan, cars did not have seat belts. Car-related injuries were common and often serious. On our return journey to the States, we bought a new Mercedes 190 at the factory in Germany, which offered a shoulder-only seat belt option. At $2300, that Mercedes was the most expensive car we had ever purchased, but seat belts added only $100 to the price. We waited an additional decade to buy our next new car, at which time we could buy one that had hip and shoulder seat belts as standard equipment.

[vi] The full text of Dr. Rashid's email is below.

"[The Center] has assumed a great learning center status in Punjab province. After you left in 1964, the Pakistan Research Center and International program of the University of Maryland, School of Medicine, Baltimore collaborated in genetic research on mosquitoes till 1979. Dr. Baker was one of the researchers working on *Anopheles Culicitacies* with Pakistani scientist collaborators. The research center continued its work till the late 1980s.

6 Birdwood Road has a great history as a seat of learning and research. It housed the first public health facility, called the Institute of Hygiene and Preventive Medicine, established in 1949, and later it became the College of Community Medicine, now called the Institute of Public Health. It has an active MPH program, also it awards the degrees for Master's in Hospital Management, M.Phil in Community Medicine, in addition to training in sanitation, food inspection, and other paramedical fields. It also has an active department of entomology that is continuing its research into dengue fever and other parasitic infections. It has carried its work from your center and is under the Punjab Department of Health, getting some technical support from WHO and other international organizations. It has other teaching and service programs in maternal and child health, a department of environmental health, a center for rabies and snakebite, other vaccination programs, and family planning programs.

The most important institute that is also housed there is the Postgraduate Medical Institute, which has been in existence since 1975. It is part of the University of Health Sciences, along with various teaching hospitals. It imparts MD and other degrees in clinical subspecialties. It is the foremost institute in medicine in Punjab and is meeting the needs for primary care and specialists in Lahore, Pakistan. This institute found its home in 1995, after Allama Iqbal Medical College moved to its current location.

Also, currently, a government agency, the Punjab Population Welfare Department, is located exactly in your building at 6 Birdwood Road. A neighbor is the postgraduation institute for Nursing.

The Center you left has continued to build on your efforts and research. It has continued mosquito research and has added many important medical and postgraduate institutes that are still serving the Punjab region and Pakistan as a whole.

The address is still called 6 Birdwood Road, although alternatively it is named as 6 Abdur Rehman Chugtai Road, after one of the foremost painters and architects after Pakistan came into being in 1947."

vii Even though DDVP had only been in use for about 15 years by the time of our research, pioneering environmentalists had already raised warning flags about serious adverse environmental impacts of DDT, the insecticide DDVP had been intended to replace. In 1961, Rachel Carson published her landmark book *Silent Spring*, which warned of the pervasive environmental hazards of insecticides like DDT (which she claimed should be called "biocides"). Her recent work on the cutting edge of environmental science had not reached our attention at the time, but she and others had been incubating the ideas for some time before that. As a naturalist, Carson had developed concerns about pesticides in the mid-1940s, and as early as January 1958, newspapers published accounts of bird kills attributed to aerial DDT spraying. During FDA hearings in the late 1950s regarding pesticide policies, Carson observed the chemical industry's hardline stance and commented on perverse incentives that even extended to government programs. Needless to say, chemical companies interested in marketing new pesticides were not receptive to her objections.

Long after our research project, serious questions were raised about health hazards and ecological damage from DDVP. In fact, it is no longer approved for use in human living spaces, as we had used it, and the Environmental Protection Agency has considered banning it many times since 1981. One of the health effects of most concern was the very symptom I had— neurological toxicity—which, with increasing exposure dosage, can progress from fasciculations to seizures to coma to death. When I experienced those symptoms, organophosphate chemical poisoning was not even considered in the differential of neurological symptoms, but now with widespread insecticide use, especially by farm workers, such toxicity has moved to the top of the list, far above amyotrophic lateral sclerosis (ALS; Lou Gehrig's Disease). Even some of my own colleagues were so preoccupied with controlling disease vectors like mosquitoes that they discounted the adverse side effects of the measures used.

In retrospect, it boggles my mind that we were performing clinical trials to determine the efficacy of a potent insecticide before significant safety studies had been done by the manufacturer! Clearly we put the cart before the horse in evaluating efficacy before establishing safety, but that misstep was the product of the social, economic, and scientific culture of the time, including an undeveloped regulatory environment as well as unresponsive corporations. As it turns out, the research we did evaluating DDVP for malaria control was nullified by its significant toxicity. That insecticide, at least, proved to be a dead end for mosquito control.

viii Hans Zinsser (*Rats, Lice, and History*) makes the point that it is not the generals who wage battles, but rather infectious diseases, that have determined the course of history. Among the most common diseases that featured prominently in Zinsser's book was bacillary dysentery. Zinsser cites several anecdotes—during the Civil War, General Lee's army at Gettysburg was compromised by dysentery, and he himself had the disease in the days of that battle. During WWII, the disease was rampant among recruits, in concentration camps, and in prisoner of war camps. More recently, the Andersonville, Georgia Museum documents the awful plight of union soldiers who suffered and died in large numbers from dysentery in the Confederate Prisoner of War camp located in that town and now the site of the National Prisoner of War Museum. Hand-washing and personal hygiene are key control measures. Where sanitation compromises water and food, the disease becomes endemic or hyperendemic with periodic outbreaks.

[ix] Two of the School of Public Health's faculty, Drs. Jamal Harfouche and Calvin W. Schwabe, had an especially important influence on my AUB recruitment. Both were global leaders in their fields. I met and got to know both of them. Their research interests and mine intersected in different ways.

Asper introduced me to Harfouche in my 1977 visit. Our meeting was cordial and upbeat, as we had mutual friends at the WHO and we knew of each other's research. What we had in common was infant mortality, though we approached this subject from different directions. She was a pediatrician focused on infant growth and development, while my work dealt with the pathophysiology of infectious diseases of the intestines and the consequences of these infections on infant mortality. I was well aware that her research had set global standards for monitoring infant growth. These shared interests forged a bond between us.

Schwabe was a veterinary epidemiologist whose scientific contributions were focused on the zoonotic diseases, i.e., animal diseases transmitted to people. From 1956 to 1964, Schwabe had joint appointments in the school and in the Medical School.

He founded and chaired a Department of Tropical Medicine, and in 1962 he founded the Department of Epidemiology and Biostatistics linking the three health schools—Medical, Nursing, and Public Health. In 1964, he took a leave from AUB to serve as director of WHO's parasitic diseases control programs. I knew of his research because at the time my work at CDC included the surveillance of foodborne diseases—some of which are zoonotic—and in particular salmonellosis, for which I was CDC's point person. I also shared office space at CDC with Schwabe's colleague Dr. James H. Steele, with whom he conducted research and taught. Both Schwabe and Steele are still seen as veterinary giants who together created the niche specialty of veterinary epidemiology. I worked with Dr. Myron (Mike) Schultz, another distinguished CDC scientist who had a close association with Schwabe. Schultz paid tribute to Schwabe in his biography published in Emerging Infectious Diseases in 2011. [Schultz MG, Schantz P: **Calvin W. Schwabe**. *Emerging Infectious Diseases* 2011, **17**(12):2365-2367.] What Schwabe contributed to the world is lauded in Schultz's biography and in Schwabe's obituary, written by Philip H. Kass and Richard H. McCapes. [Kass PH, McCapes RH, Pritchard WR: **Calvin W. Schwabe, Professor Emeritus of Veterinary Epidemiology, Davis, 1927 - 2006**. In. Davis, CA; 2006.] Both sources credited Schwabe as the "progenitor of the modern era of veterinary epidemiology." The quote that makes my point is this—"There is scarcely anyone in this field throughout the world today who cannot trace their legacy, either directly or indirectly, to Calvin Schwabe." Harfouche's and Schwabe's impressive scientific contributions were part of AUB's grandeur.

In addition to Harfouche and Schwabe, many other distinguished AUB scientists contributed to the school's prominence in the years before the clouds of the civil war gathered in the early

1970s. A number of them and the important roles they played were cited in the publication of AUB's 50th anniversary event. [Campbell O, Acra A: **The Faculty of Health Sciences at the American University of Beirut: A Brief History, 1954-2004**. Beirut, Lebanon: American University of Beirut; 2004.]

x Though great progress was made in extending academic nursing education, there was less focus on nosocomial infections. Initial surveys of nosocomial prevalence in two of the leading regional hospitals revealed high rates, but follow-up and surveillance plans could not be implemented for various reasons.

xi My daughter Peggy (Margaret Ann Gangarosa) lived with us in our apartment while she attended her first two years of medical school at AUB. She had been interested in medicine during her undergraduate work at Emory University and did well in the Medical College Admissions Tests (MCAT). When she learned of my interest in AUB, she became intrigued by the possibility of attending medical school there. Encouraged by two of her Emory professors who were AUB alumni, she applied and was accepted. Although she had studied Arabic, she recognized she was limited in her ability to communicate with patients as she contemplated her clinical years. So, after completing her basic medical courses, she applied to Emory University's Medical School to complete her medical education. She was accepted with advanced standing and completed her two clinical years at Emory. After her graduation, she completed a pathology residency at Emory and then joined a group of pathologists in Brooksville, Florida. She organized her own pathology group practice serving hospitals in that area. After 30 years of distinguished service to patients and communities, she developed an aggressive kidney cancer that caused her death in the fall of 2012. Even as I write this, her loss weighs heavily on us.

[xii] People and institutions who contributed substantially to FHS's financial recovery included: William (Bill) Foege, CDC director; Phil Brachman, director of CDC's Epidemiology Branch; his successor Dr. Carl Tyler; Dr. Peter Schantz, a parasitologist who taught a truncated semester course for medical and MPH students; Dr. Ann Kimball, an Epidemic Intelligence Service Officer who was the lead investigator of a cholera outbreak in infants in Bahrain; Kimball's supervisor, Dr. Robert Gunn [Gunn RA, Kimball AM, Mathew PP, Dutta SR, Rifaat AH: **Cholera in Bahrain: epidemiological characteristics of an outbreak**. *Bulletin of the World Health Organization* 1981, **59**(1):61-66.]; Dr. Frank Bryan, who conducted a truncated course on food safety for medical and public health students; Dr. José Rigau, an Epidemic Intelligence Officer who conducted prevalence studies of nosocomial infections at AUB hospital and Sulmaniya Hospital in Bahrain and then presented his findings in grand rounds at AUB's Medical Center; Dr. Carl Tyler, who, along with Phil Brachman, enabled a career pathway for prospective FHS faculty in CDC's EIS training program, from which three AUB physicians were recruited (Drs. Hani Atrash, Rima Khabbaz, and Muin Khoury); the Beirut office of UNICEF, which provided adjunct faculty to teach courses and mentor students; the WHO offices in Alexandria, Egypt and Geneva, Switzerland, which provided technical advice and support; and D. A. Henderson, Dean of the Johns Hopkins School of Public Health, who provided on-site consultation and funding support for students in AUB's College of Engineering.

In 1981, a philanthropist (Rafic Hariri) pledged a large tract of land in the Bacca Valley for a primary care center to train AUB MD and FHS public health graduates. This was intended to be a demonstration program for what could be accomplished in primary healthcare. Dr. Hani Atrash was the intended director, but the plan did not materialize because of the chaos caused by the civil war. Instead, he interviewed for and was accepted into the Epidemic Intelligence Service (EIS) of CDC. He later served the Ministry of Health in Bahrain. In 1985, he and his family moved to Atlanta, where he attended Emory's Rollins School of Public Health for his MPH degree and later served with CDC in Maternal Health. He has had a distinguished international career benefiting people of many countries.

xiii Interim President David Dodge was taken hostage on July 19, 1982 and released exactly a year later. He was incarcerated both in Lebanon and in Iran. His service with AUB was distinguished as administrator and President.

Dr. Malcolm H. Kerr was appointed President of AUB on March 20, 1982. He was a highly respected scholar and teacher, fluent in Arabic, and widely recognized for his distinguished studies of the Middle East. Rose and I interacted with him at social events during Board of Trustees visits. He was assassinated by two gunmen on January 18, 1984.

Frank Regier was taken hostage in February 1984 and freed from his captivity on April 14, 1984. He and his wife Mary were close friends of ours and neighbors residing in the same faculty apartment building. He was among 96 westerners—most of whom were Americans—taken hostage during the Lebanese civil War.

Mr. Peter Kilburn, Librarian for the Faculty of Engineering and Architecture, was taken hostage in December 1984. He was detained in Libya and murdered in reprisal for a U.S. attack on a Libyan target. Rose knew him during the years she volunteered her services as librarian.

Dr. Haroutune Armenian succeeded me as the second dean of FHS in 1981 and served until 1987. I have noted his exemplary leadership in maintaining FHS's academic presence during the chaos that followed in 1982-83.

Dr. Huda Zurayk followed Armenian as Interim Dean, 1986-87, and Dean, 1998-2004. During her tenure, FHS's research, enrollment, and external funding flourished. She was the first woman dean in any AUB faculty, and one of the few women deans to head schools of public health anywhere. I was one of the Emory faculty who hosted her when she visited Emory University in 2003. She gave Emory's annual Genie DeHaan Lecture describing her research in Lebanon, which involved collaboration with Emory faculty. She encouraged an expanded academic link between FHS and the Emory Rollins School of Public Health. The water and sanitation endowment that Rose and I established with FHS in December 2013 is a step in making this happen.

xiv In 1991, ten years after I left Beirut, Asper invited me to serve with him on the Educational Commission for Foreign Medical Graduates for which he was executive director. I served on this committee for seven years. I appreciated that opportunity to work with him, which had previously been denied by his abrupt departure in 1978. This renewed friendship enabled me to reflect on things I have written in this chapter. One of the treasures he left me his hand written note on the title page of his book "Care Amidst Chaos," published in 1994. It reads, "To Gene and Rose Gangarosa, very dear friends, who gave much to AUB, with my sincere thanks and best wishes." I see him as one of the great mentors in my professional life. He died on November 9, 1999.

Dean Iman Nuwayhid invited me to critique his report for the reaccreditation of FHS by the Council on Education for Public Health in the summer of 2011. This documented substantive and continuing progress in achieving academic excellence. I replied that his application convinced me that FHS ranked high among world-class schools of public health. The accreditation committee implicitly agreed with my conclusion by awarding FHS a full seven-year accreditation, which is only given to the most outstanding schools of public health. AUB was the only one outside of the United States accredited for seven years. Emory's Rollins School of Public Health in Atlanta, Georgia was another. In April 2012, Dean Nuwayhid's book, *Public Health in the Arab World,* gave a masterful blueprint for public health in the region. [Jabbour S, Giacaman R, Khawaja M, Nuwayhid I (eds.): **Public Health in the Arab World**. New York, NY: Cambridge University Press; 2012.] From his work, I see it again appropriate to recognize FHS as a jewel in AUB's crown.

For the School of Public Health's 50th anniversary, Oona Campbell and Professor Aftim Acra wrote a brochure about FHS entitled *A Brief History: 1954-2004.* It was published together with a second publication for the 50th anniversary: *The Faculty of Health Sciences at the American University of Beirut: The Present and the Future.* These records provide the best historical account of academic public health at AUB.

A TRIBUTE TO MY FATHER, EUGENE J. GANGAROSA, SR.

Raymond E. Gangarosa, MD, MPH, MSEE

Gene Gangarosa has been an unheralded historical figure in public health. Outside his fields of expertise, large circle of professional friends, and university contacts, his accomplishments are not widely known. His mild-mannered personality is a refreshing throwback to a more thoughtful, respectful age. Many of his personal friends have no idea how much impact he has had on the course of human events.

Gene's modesty belies his impressive professional legacy: he has contributed to every categorical aspect of the development of public health during his 70-year career except one: mathematical methodology. Any of his contributions to basic research, disease surveillance, outbreak investigation, practical interventions, academic administration, teaching, history of public health, and philanthropy would easily fill an entire, highly productive career. Gene Gangarosa is the elder statesman in a field that has saved more lives than almost any other human endeavor. Innovations to which he professionally contributed in both the treatment (oral hydration) and prevention (safe water technologies) of enteric diseases have already saved many millions of lives, and will continue to do so throughout the indefinite future. He has seen more of a span of scientific achievement than virtually anyone who has ever lived. Starting as the junior member of the research team that first investigated cholera with modern medical tools, he made the first conceptual breakthrough that opened the floodgates, and now can see in retrospect how his career has reverberated through public health practice.

I want to give a personal account of what Gene's example and influence have meant in my life, as both his son and professional colleague. My career has followed an unconventional path, and despite his mentorship of many people who have accomplished great things in public health, my father has been very supportive in letting me find my own underachieving way.

It's quite obvious to anyone who knows both of us that my father's many amazing skills skipped a generation in me, so I have worked hard to develop complementary perspectives. At every step, I have thought long and hard about following my father's career path, each time preparing myself ahead of time to find my own niche. Before applying to medical school, I concentrated in engineering graduate school on learning how biological systems work; after my internship, I did research in magnetic resonance imaging and developed an expert system that performed a new kind of tradeoff analysis, which I planned to use for public health policy when I entered the MPH program at Emory; I did my MPH thesis in enteric disease epidemiology, but investigating a different application and using methods quite different from my father's specialty; and before I entered a PhD program in epidemiology, I was among the first to develop a comprehensive plan for suing the tobacco (and alcohol) companies for societal healthcare costs.

I envisioned a career in the mathematical interface between public health, economics, and public policy, focusing on corporate accountability for product-attributable social costs. My advisor was excited about my dissertation as it coalesced around novel topics of infrastructure viability, adaptive problem-solving, unanticipated consequences, biological analogies, and conscious social evolution. However, I developed a gnawing apprehension that the two major initiatives I was exploring—corporate accountability and social evolution—were not in sync. It took many years for me to realize the source of this cognitive dissonance: adaptation and evolution present fundamentally conflicting tradeoffs, as explained in the Appendix. Rather than continuing research that might be flawed and publishing results that I felt were premature and possibly counterproductive, I dropped out of the doctoral program before finishing my dissertation. I was determined to continue my research, but couldn't publish it until it was ready, and I couldn't get funding to work on it until I had some tangible output. In the publish-or-perish career I was seeking, I had just committed professional suicide.

Neither of my parents ever criticized me for that decision, even though I had left the academic program my father had helped to start, and I couldn't really articulate my concerns. If any of his colleagues said anything to him about me, or if he felt embarrassed about my quitting, he never said a word to me. He had been very proud before then that I had a promising career in academic public health ahead of me, but didn't express the slightest hint of discouragement as it completely collapsed. It seemed amazing to fail so visibly and not have anyone say, "Get with the plan," "I told you so," or "What are you going to do with yourself now?"

Nor did my father miss a beat in offering me a precious opportunity, which ultimately was responsible for keeping my research effort alive for the last 20 years. He had been doing consulting work for some time, and I had previously helped on one occasion when he surveyed the public health impact of anti-vaccine movements. At that moment when I found myself completely rudderless, he asked me to be a partner in his public health consulting firm.

We made a great team! Although consultations were sporadic, that part-time job paid well enough to support my time-consuming hobby of interdisciplinary research. Almost all our consultations involved litigation enlisting my father as an expert witness in infectious diseases; although I would rather have worked together on public health research or interventions, I see now in retrospect that I served in a role similar to an EIS officer. Gene Gangarosa was one of the best mentors I ever had, and it was a great honor getting to know the great man who was my father as a professional colleague. When he had worked alone on cases, the information overload had been a bit overwhelming for him, but we managed very well sharing the load between us. He was happy to give me as much work as I wanted, so I would organize each case assessment with a timeline and initial impression, write the first draft of our reports, and work with him throughout the entire course, whether for trial preparation or a final report. I had writing, organizational, analytical, and computer skills that freed him for teaching and research projects he preferred, and I helped him with those activities also.

I was also gratified to help my father start work on his autobiography. Neil Shulman had long been impressed with my father's accomplishments in public health, and urged him to write a book about his experiences. Our three-hour meeting in the American Cancer Society cafeteria on June 23, 2011 was an absolute delight, in which Neil's humanity, compassion, and enthusiasm spurred us to forge ahead. As I subsequently learned the details of my own father's life and career, I felt I was getting back to my own roots. Our consulting work took on new meaning, as I could appreciate the deep humanity, intellectual depth, historical context, and experiential background behind his enormous expertise.

My sister Peggy's diagnosis with clear cell renal carcinoma in March 2012 and tragic death seven months later devastated our whole family, and put the brakes on both our consulting business and the autobiography. Peggy had designated me as executor of her estate, and her dying wish was that I serve as trustee caring for her three beloved pets. I spent a year in Florida at her house managing the estate and trust, but so far away from the resources I needed, I couldn't accomplish anything on our consulting business, the book, or my research. So I moved back to a house in Atlanta, located just 9/10 of a mile away from my parents' home, that was perfect for my expanded menagerie and ideal for my work.

On my return, I was overwhelmed with a backlog of pending tasks, health problems with my newly acquired dog Beau, and a flood of new insights about civilizational evolution. We were very fortunate to enlist Rachel Burke's help replacing me as editor, and also fortuitously, our consulting business dried up (probably because of my father's advancing age) just at the time we both needed to move on to other things. I participated for a while in drafting most chapters in the autobiographical narrative, but Rachel did most of the work, eventually taking over those aspects entirely. As she fluently juggled her doctoral dissertation in epidemiology, management of public health projects abroad and domestically, and her writing and editing tasks on the book, her administrative skills reminded me a lot of my father's. During the year she worked with us, we were delighted that she was admitted to the EIS program, where she will start next month and no doubt have an illustrious career.

With Rachel's capable help in the background, I turned my attention to incorporating insights into the book about the evolution of human civilization. Given the expansive scope and impact of Gene Gangarosa's career, I realized there would never be another publication more suited to introducing the concept of civilizational evolution than his autobiography. My father's Emory faculty library account allowed me to intensify and expand my research of the scientific literature, so I quickly uncovered and amplified many rich connections with ideas I had been developing in past years using less comprehensive resources available on the Internet. During this time, my own thinking and writing seemed to be directly experiencing the very percolation processes I was studying. In that way, a subject I would have found abstract and difficult came to life and became very intuitive.

At first, I wasn't sure what concepts were ready for publication, as I started to ghostwrite more limited perspectives where they related to various narratives scattered throughout the book. My father encouraged me vigorously to include my ideas, but was dismayed about my intention to remain anonymous. He kept insisting that I write an authored section in the book, then publish a series of related articles, and establish my credentials as a historian of public health. We reached a breaking point when both my parents were unhappy with the reviewer's draft we circulated—my mother because there was nothing about Gene Gangarosa's contribution in the long opening historical section, and my father because he didn't feel comfortable taking credit for my work and felt unqualified to field questions from colleagues about sections I had written in the book.

I couldn't pass up my father's generous offer of his own autobiography for introducing ideas that fit so well with the themes of his career, so I reluctantly agreed to write an appendix. A number of problems arose in rapid succession: the rest of the book was nearing completion just as I was starting this phase; Rachel's schedule imposed a tight deadline; I hadn't organized my ideas to present in that way; I wanted to avoid follow-up publications on this topic for various reasons; my early drafts were extremely confusing; there was no getting around that the ideas are very dense; the literature search was time-consuming and never-ending; every time I encountered a new vein of research, I would lose track of where I had left off. Gene and Rachel generously gave me a bit more time, but the real breakthrough came from enlisting Diane Dougherty's help.

I met Diane a couple years ago through a mutual friend, Lisa Parsons, who has expressed enthusiastic moral support for my projects over more than 15 years. Diane is a former nun and now renegade priest, who, because of the Catholic Church's medieval sex discrimination policies, was ordained and excommunicated in the same motion! When Diane and I met at a presentation I gave on corporate accountability, she asked the most insightful question (about creative destruction) that anyone has ever posed to me.

When we started working together on the appendix, things looked bleak. I had fruitful ongoing conversations with a few friends, but I couldn't hold all the ideas in my mind at one time, and the deadline (before Rachel gave me another month) was a couple weeks away. Diane studied my notes and got up to steam right away, serving as a sounding board, asking great questions, and soon anticipating what I was thinking and suggesting important ideas of her own. She brought a wealth of her own experiences and had a great command of the spiritual literature on evolution. My pets loved her. I asked my vet to come to my house to euthanize Beau when he became completely disabled, and Diane said a beautiful prayer as he slipped away peacefully under a gorgeous blue sky with his family and furry friends around. And as each deadline approached, Diane camped out in my basement apartment or (to keep from oversleeping) on my den sofa, both of us working around the clock until we were exhausted, sometimes out of phase so one would prepare what the other would continue after waking. I appreciate all the hard work and long hours that Diane put in to help translate the very unpromising initial draft she read into the preceding appendix, which we both hope is a reasonably creditable bookend for my father's autobiography.

And I am even more grateful to my father, for pushing me to write the appendix to his autobiography, insisting that I do the impossible, prodding me to get an unimaginably expansive concept out within an unmanageably tight deadline, forcing me to stretch my perspective in areas that are almost completely unfamiliar to me, trusting my judgment in fields he doesn't understand after verifying that our ideas mesh perfectly in fields where he does. Looking back on our 30-year history of working together, this autobiography is a wonderful culmination in itself. But the greatest gift he gave me in the process was to let me put my own signature on it and to offer the book as a way to advance what's left of my less-than-impressive career.

How can I express how lucky I am to have such an amazing father? I remember an incident during what I hope was a very brief blind spot during my teens, the time when I imagined I knew much more than he did. I was hopping mad at him because he didn't indulge my spendthrift ambitions to build a state-of-the-art radio controlled airplane. Instead, he asked me to draw up a budget, start slowly with something simple, and keep developing my skills and understanding. He assured me if that hobby meshed with my interests in aerospace engineering, he would support me fully, but he needed to see some commitment first. I was too impatient to produce a masterpiece on my first foray, so I didn't take that offer. That interaction probably goes a long way toward explaining why I'm not very good as a practical engineer. As I said, that pragmatic mindset skipped over me. When I worked in MRI research, my colleagues could not help noticing, usually with amusement and/or disdain, what a theoretical egghead I am. Who knows? If I had inherited my father's pragmatism, maybe I would have pioneered drone technology 40 years earlier than it actually emerged! But in retrospect, it's obvious that my father invested the money I would have spent on electronic hardware much more wisely. And maybe it's better that I concentrated on civilizational evolution than on drone technology.

I am so proud of my father for his generativity in sharing the story of his life and career with the world. I have felt deeply honored to help him tell that story. Knowing personally his generous personality and brilliant mind, I want everyone to experience the inspiration he sparks in everyone around him. That spark of inspiration is a message I want to tell here as a postscript to the appendix. Part of the evolutionary process that is better conveyed in this tribute is the spirit of generosity and generativity that can flow from generation to generation. I have seen that personally and intuitively throughout my life, and two generations of Gangarosas want to pass that flow on as far into the future as it can go.

Raymond E. Gangarosa

As my parents both turn 90, still incredibly sharp but slowing down physically, it's wonderful to see them reflect with satisfaction on their lives and accomplishments. My father is looking forward to sharing his autobiography with former colleagues and signing copies at gatherings. My mother, Rachel, Diane, and I are all pleased that we could help him do so, knowing the impact his presence and story will have on others.

APPENDIX:

The emerging role of public health in civilizational evolution: healing the schism between science and religion

Raymond E. Gangarosa, MD, MPH, MSEE[1]

with Diane Dougherty, MAE, MSE, EDS

[1] I wish to thank Diane Dougherty for her dedicated and enthusiastic help, keeping me organized and focused as I struggled to encapsulate three decades of research during the preparation of this appendix. I could not have captured this full span of ideas without her thoughtful assistance. Not having been spiritually oriented until doing this research, I also thank a number of friends (including Diane) for valuable discussions and correspondence that helped me put these ideas into a broader perspective (although any mistakes or omissions are mine). Most of all, I want to thank my father, Gene Gangarosa, for generously providing the best imaginable medium for getting these messages across—his own autobiography—and the permission to express my views in so personal a forum. Space does not permit me to amplify examples from his own career of the principles I've described, but his own life and career have been the ultimate inspiration for every aspect of this research, so I hope a discussion of these concepts will bring his legacy into a wider focus.

In this world we humans do not occupy the center of the universe, neither are we superior to all other living beings. Rather the interconnectedness of life in our universe means that we are part of the web of life. Integral systems tell us that our universe is thoroughly interconnected, so that even our own being is not our own. Reality by its very nature is interconnected.

– Ilia Delio, The Emergent Christ (p. 27)

Table of Contents

Overview of humanity's current crisis

Only within the moment of time represented by the present century has one species—man—acquired significant power to alter the nature of his world.

– Rachel Carson

Simply stated, life is a never-ending uphill confrontation with forces that create disorder. Disease is a manifestation of disorder at the physiological level, which can propagate up to the global level as pandemics, especially when disease processes interact with cultural dysfunction, which is a typical manifestation of disorder at the societal level. Improved designs make life almost effortless within the right environment, whereas a mismatch between design and environment makes it a terrible struggle.

Life has two broad timescales of its own: adaptation (the processes of living for organisms currently alive) and evolution (the transmission of designs for living from current to future generations). As we will see, this principle applies both to biology and civilization, despite differences in the underlying rules, players, and dynamics. The commonality of this principle could be enormously helpful as one of many guides that humanity can use for civilizational evolution, hopefully to establish wiser and more compassionate ways of living, in ways that have never been available to biological evolution.

Adaptation can easily get stuck in a "race to the bottom" engendered by shortsighted, greedy, ignorant, careless, and/or irresponsible behavior. Such behavior undermines higher-level structures (like the biosphere) that provide bounties far greater

A-1

than would be attainable within the parochial adaptive framework—they "bite the invisible hand that feeds them." Ultimately, such adaptive ruts arise because greed is rewarded more than cooperation, so under the action of incentives alone, cooperators will go extinct.

To counteract such tendencies, evolution is a kind of "advice for living" that one generation passes on to all future generations through the way in which its experiences, harsh and otherwise, are reflected in its design. A bit more precisely, evolution can improve designs through "synergistic complexification," escaping from such adaptive ruts by developing levels of organization with wider perspectives, economies of scale, improved flexibility, greater capabilities, and expanded compassion (e.g., democracies, market institutions, universities, philanthropies, communities). In biological evolution, such complexification emerged at glacially slow rates, in fits and starts with many collapses, via an unsystematic tinkering process [1, 2] that gradually harnessed cooperation, specialization, diversity, interactions, and cycles to build synergistic higher-level structures.

Evolution entails generativity, sacrifice, and faith, because it requires learning from mistakes and investing for posterity, with no way to envision the outcomes. Although there is no assurance if, that, or how these new societal structures might benefit future generations, the hope is that they will provide some unfathomable kinds of dividends and interact with other social institutions to generate virtuous cycles.

In biological evolution, that concept of genetic transmission as "advice" is very sloppy, but it doesn't have to be for human civilization. We can think of civilizational evolution as the transmission of wisdom across many generations over the course of millennia. Civilization is the trajectory (path) that unfolds over long timescales through dynamic interactions among culture (i.e., shared ideas), society (i.e., shared actions), and the external environment. The concept of civilizational evolution raises two critically important questions that, at least for now, characteristically require thoughtful consideration and consensus development more than urgent, immediate action:

1. An adaptive question: How can humanity take responsibility for the consequences of our actions as a species?

Question 1 refers to an imminent awareness that people alive today ("humankind") must address by transforming culture and society.

2. An evolutionary question: How can humanity take responsibility for our path as a civilization?

Question 2 refers to a subsequent ongoing awareness that humankind must spark and people alive throughout all time ("humanity") must continually address to establish sustained waves of transformative changes in culture and society in response to changing conditions and emerging insights.

At present, humanity is not doing a very good job of either living adaptively or designing evolutionarily, and practically the only usable advice we are providing to future generations comes from examples of what not to do and how not to do it! The current human condition can be likened to a monkey fist trap (which, in fact, we have set for ourselves through ignorance and greed that has reshaped our environment, much to the detriment of all life on earth). According to legend, hunters lured monkeys with delicious cracked coconuts placed inside wire cages. The bars were wide enough for monkeys to insert their arms, but too narrow to withdraw the prized coconut held by a clenched fist. Struggling endlessly in its frustrated greed, the distracted monkey became easy prey for the hunter to club it to death and serve it for dinner. The human condition is yet further complicated because we have gained so much knowledge and power that we are a danger to ourselves, other species, the earth's life support system, and the future of life on earth. Therefore, the risks of having so little insight could hardly be more serious.

Nonetheless, thinking about evolution as a process opening up to human civilization presents tantalizing opportunities. Species do not just occupy adaptive niches, but actually construct them; humanity does so to a greater extent than any species that has ever existed because of our unique development of cumulative culture. We understand a lot about biological evolution, metabolic processes, and physiological designs as a starting point, but we also have enormous engineering experience with our own technologies and even more valuable theoretical understanding from mathematics and science. The history of technological progress even informs us of the enormous advantage we might gain by going from unsystematic—and almost unconscious—tinkerers to deep thinkers and systematic engineers. And the understanding of how serious the stakes are could provide the extraordinary motivation needed to overcome the daunting obstacles.

Unfortunately, the rationality that has bequeathed humanity our vaunted sciences and technologies has not been tempered by commensurate wisdom to contain such advances in knowledge and power. Our dangerous creations have turned us into children playing with flamethrowers. Frustration engendered by that misuse has spawned a cynical, self-centered, materialistic, and anthropocentric viewpoint. Under these conditions, the prospect of enlisting cooperation at the level of human civilization seems like a worst-case scenario of herding cats!

Epidemiology is the study of the distribution and determinants of health and disease in populations; the word is derived from Greek words meaning "upon people". By posing these questions, I propose extending the definition of epidemiology beyond the study of what is visited "upon the people" to include "what the people visit upon themselves." To get the point where we can create wise, effortless ways of living and provide helpful advice to future generations, we need to reconsider all past human experiences in this broader context. The whole historical span of past mistakes—feudalism, crusades, inquisitions, oligopolies, weapons of mass destruction, dictatorships, pogroms, genocides, global wars, arms conflicts, massive pollution, perverse incentives—is just as useful, if not more so, for guidance than what little success we've had thus far trying to cooperate and coalesce as a civilization.

The problem is that living the required design changes would involve accepting responsibility and exerting discipline in ways we have not yet conceptualized. Seemingly routine life functions require a stunning degree of self-sacrifice and cohesion to attain the extremely capable, coordinated designs of our own bodies. So far, technological progress has only provided us the monkey fist equivalent of coconuts and wire cages—i.e., the illusion of reinforcing feedback ("benefits") that we chase, but also the unintended consequence of a huge amount of corrective feedback ("error signals") that something is wrong. Science and technology cannot help resolve the dilemmas, because the flaws reside in our own character.

However, as we will see, there is much more to the story. Biological evolution has confronted the diverse challenges of making bickering protoplasm cooperate, and has achieved a stunningly harmonious resolution. Awareness of nature's miraculous design innovation is one of the greatest revelations of our time, an inspiration for our own creativity, and a promising pathway for civilizational evolution.

Perhaps you can already see why this discussion is relevant to Dr. Eugene Gangarosa's "life in service to public health." The field of public health is precisely the precedent humanity needs to bridge what currently manifests as a gap between struggling to adapt and failing to evolve. Even when humanity acts like the greedy primate *Homo economicus*, outbreaks of deadly disease are such a threat to reinforcing feedback that societies are willing to suspend business-as-usual and finally listen to the corrective feedback, even to the extent of developing fundamental knowledge, systematic methods, preventive measures, and treatment methods.

In evolutionary processes, it's not uncommon that a huge advance ratchets the system into a state that demands greater performance. Now, the vast human population and our greedy lifestyles are taxing the earth's carrying capacity. My father's generation of epidemiologists, by virtue of helping to save so many lives, has yet further increased population pressures, thus indirectly escalating demands for humanity to start living wisely.

A-6

I hope his example and some of the principles described here will spark discussions about how we might do just that. This appendix draws so much inspiration and so many examples from his autobiography that I hope it will be a worthy bookend to his life's narrative. I present it as a tribute to his generosity of spirit in telling his story, in hopes of highlighting another less obvious dimension to his already unprecedented legacy.

The mission of public health

To expand the scope of epidemiology to address contemporary crises, I propose that the mission of public health, which already plays a large and crucial role in human affairs, be extended considerably to address the needs of civilizational evolution. Here is how I would identify the current and expanded roles for public health.

Current mission

In its currently recognized role, public health is the science and technology authorized and designed to protect and improve the health of people and communities at all levels, from the individual to the entire human population, through various strategies, most notably research, prevention, outbreak investigation and control, governmental administration and intervention, education, community assessment and outreach, healthcare delivery, and reduction of social disparities. To prevent the emergence of new pathogens and community dysfunction, public health must make special efforts to protect vulnerable populations from harsh living conditions, exposure to pathogens and toxins, inadequate and/or inaccessible healthcare, societal neglect, and political disenfranchisement.

The methodology of public health is informed by historical awareness; interdisciplinary sciences (especially medicine, biology, social sciences, epidemiology, and biostatistics); disease and exposure surveillance; community service through outreach and communications; a strong tradition of mutual support, especially through education and mentoring; critical self-appraisal, e.g., through academic research and peer-reviewed publication; a natural propensity for compassion; and strong philosophical and theological roots.

The issue of compassion in public health deserves special attention in light of this mission. From the most basic considerations of public health, poor living conditions, toxic and infectious exposures, and social dysfunction can foster evolution of virulence in microbial pathogens, especially when genetic material passes between species in weakened hosts or unsanitary environments, e.g., potentially transmitting antibiotic resistance or creating "super-bugs." Thus, if only as protection from explosive epidemic outbreaks, everyone has a stake in the health and wellbeing of everyone else on the planet.

Efforts by the rich and powerful to isolate themselves from these hazards reflect a lack of awareness of these fundamental realities of life—a kind of "sleepwalking" through civilizational evolution that fails to make the necessary investments and sacrifices for the wellbeing of current and future generations. As a result, we can observe an extremely large and widening gap between rich and poor—this should be seen as a danger signal. It provides the rich too much more of a cushion against the hazards of living in society, and when the rich also exert disproportionate political influence, societal leaders become insensitive to those hazards.

A-8

Without correction, these hazards may then become full-blown, sometimes irreversible, and even potentially perpetual crises.

But beyond those practical reasons, public health is an opening for the human community to express life-giving and restorative compassion on every scale, from the interpersonal (one-on-one) to the humanitarian (society-to-society) to the civilizational / planetary (society-to-planet). This generosity is usually anonymous, since most preventive interventions give little evidence of who was saved, and even those who have reason to be grateful generally cannot determine whom to thank. Therein lies the basis for a profound spirituality inherent in this unique segment of the healing profession. As a result, public health tends to attract intensely idealistic people with progressive inclinations.

Unfortunately, as I write this, we exist in a rancorous, polarized, public and political climate whereby conservatives begrudge these basic investments in humankind and in humanity's future. The long and tragic history of totalitarian regimes built on the premise of radical wealth redistribution, and equally totalitarian regimes opposed to that premise, has poisoned rational discussions about this subject, so even a mutually acceptable vocabulary is conspicuously unattainable. Ironically, fiscal conservatives frequently argue, "The budget deficit is too large, and so we have to cut expenditures"—even as the gap between rich and poor increases to an unprecedented degree, and such budget-cutting measures have already created huge public health disasters that will incur staggering social costs.

In actuality, conservatives have recognized that an unsustainable impasse has developed, but on the basis of their own vested self-

A-9

interests, resist the conclusion that human actions are largely responsible for it. However, as I will show, progressives also do not understand this situation properly, and should resist the inclination to ascribe cynical motives and assign blame. A huge part of the problem is that human activity, as currently conducted in virtually all its aspects, is toxic to life on earth. The mere act of aggregating to such numbers and consuming to such an extent has caused us to pollute our environment so much as to cause a mass extinction event, poisoning numerous other species even as we are barely becoming aware of the problem. No actions taken at the individual or community level and no technology can save us from ourselves if we continue to deal with these issues as in an adaptive fashion.

Proposed expansion of the mission

The key to resolving this impasse is reorienting our focus to scales of time and social structure at the level of civilizational evolution. That framework is the basis for expanding the mission of public health to address a constellation of issues outside its traditional boundaries.

Because of the urgent need to respond to disease outbreaks, within that setting, public health is the only institution that has been given a fairly universal mandate to respond to corrective feedback. In that role, the public health community has proved itself to be reasonable in its advocacy for societal interests, despite the fact that commercial interests clamor to market harmful products without the encumbrance of any oversight.

At whatever rate the public can be convinced to extend its mandate, public health should also address the broader unintended consequences of human activity. Much of the focus

A-10

should be on social dysfunction and dynamic imbalances that can be traced to design deficiencies in social institutions, even in cases where interventional remediation seems possible only in the distant future. To address those situations, public health needs to develop and expand its theoretical framework to model the dynamics of current designs and identify alternatives that might function better.

Public health should establish partnerships with organizations that address issues beyond human health but currently lack the same mandate to respond to corrective feedback. Fortunately, the issues that are the most important, e.g., planetary health, are the ones with the longest timescales. However, the imbalances have accumulated for so long that a catastrophic tipping point might not be that far off, so we should avoid further delays under the conservative assumption that we may be at the cusp of disaster. Still, the public will have to be convinced that the need warrants whatever adjustments are appropriate to the social contract—even if humanity has to experience catastrophe—since it's even more important that we reach a solid consensus that can be relied upon indefinitely than that we solve any specific problem(s). As human activity encroaches on one habitat after another, it's vital that we recognize that the future course of life on earth could be exquisitely sensitive to some kinds of human actions, so we should abandon or severely curtail time discounting (the shortsightedness manifested by basing decisions on fairly immediate rewards while ignoring possible future adverse consequences).

The immense challenge of this approach lies in the profound patience, investment, and sacrifice it will require. We must be prepared to create social structures that will lead only to benefit

A-11

for future generations, and to do so with no expectation that we will reap any rewards ourselves. In that regard, this approach entails foregoing certain kinds of reinforcing feedback that we currently get from our actions and instead becoming intensely aware of and responsive to corrective feedback. The upside is that this approach could extend our compassion and spirituality even beyond the current limits of public health, in the process making us more attuned to the meaning of human existence.

In the rest of this section, I will give specific examples from the history of public health that illustrate the need to extend its mandate in these ways.

The current impasse

We live in interwoven layers of bondedness. The world is not a "machine," but an integrated whole, which means the network of phenomena that compose the stuff of life is fundamentally interconnected and interdependent.

– Ilia Delio, The Emergent Christ (p. 27)

How utilitarianism replaced spirituality

In sketching three vignettes from the early history of medicine, I will explain that science broke off from religion because science was so much more effective in dealing with life's problems: utilitarianism replaced spirituality.

- *An early application of empirical science to wound care.* Ambroise Paré (1510 – 1590) was a poor barber-surgeon who had diligently studied the surgery textbooks of his day and joined the French army early in his career to get experience. At the siege of Turin in 1537, there were so many casualties that he ran out of the boiling oil that was the standard treatment for gunshot wounds. So, he improvised, applying a soothing balm of egg yolks, rose oil, and turpentine. Arising the next morning after a fitful sleep, he was astounded to find the patients he had treated with his improvised regimen to be resting comfortably, without fever or wound swelling, in sharp contrast to all the patients whose wounds had been treated conventionally with boiling oil! As a precursor to survival analysis, he followed patients in both treatment groups over their convalescence and verified the gentler treatment gave better results in every way throughout the entire course. As a matter of compassion, he resolved immediately never to subject a wounded patient to the excruciating "treatment" of boiling oil, and over the course of his long and distinguished career, developed many revolutionary surgical techniques based on the principle of minimizing tissue damage. He verified his results over and over in 20 military campaigns, and wrote 20 profoundly influential surgical texts—all in the vernacular, since he didn't know Latin—so other barber-surgeons of his day could learn his methods. His status as an esteemed teacher allowed barber-surgeons to become university professors, and he replaced unquestioned acceptance of ancient Greek physicians with careful empirical observation. His position in the royal court isolated him from political intrigues and vendettas, and he exhibited great courage at the end of his life by unsuccessfully advising the surrender of Paris during the siege of 1590 because the poor were starving in large numbers.

Thus, three centuries before John Snow investigated the cholera outbreaks of London, medicine had started developing cultural traditions that would serve public health as well, e.g., empirical observation instead of unquestioned acceptance on authority; wide dissemination of results; compassion and gentleness; collegiality and mentorship; mutually supportive professional societies. To discuss professional cultures in these terms is a very recent phenomenon, scarcely mentioned before the mid-20th century, but the ideas and approaches became well established in universities, hospitals, and clinics without formal conceptualization of the processes involved. The social structures and traditions developed by and for the medical profession established a scaffold that supported the growth of related cultural elements in public health three centuries later.

- *The first controlled scientific experiment.* Francesco Redi (1626 – 1697), called the "founder of experimental biology" and the "father of modern parasitology," made a career of challenging myths of his time using newly emerging scientific methods. He is best known for refuting the theory of spontaneous generation with the first controlled experiment ever published. He attracted flies with various kinds of meat in jars; however, the experimental samples were covered with gauze, inhibiting the flies' access, while the control jars were open. Redi observed that maggots only formed in the control (uncovered) jars, whose meat the flies had been able to access in order to lay their eggs. He followed up this experiment by showing that dead flies could not spontaneously generate maggots even in the absence of the gauze covering. Louis Pasteur's more sophisticated experiments in 1859 established a milestone in microbiology by definitively disproving the theory of spontaneous generation.

- *The basic epidemiological method: risk calculation.* Pierre Charles Alexandre Louis (1787 – 1872) introduced the basic numerical method used in epidemiological analysis: a calculation of risks. A risk is an expression of the frequency with which an event occurs in a defined population. In 1828, Louis published an analysis of one group of patients who had undergone bloodletting for fevers and another group that had not. Louis added other refinements to the method that are recognized as very important: (1) he matched the two groups by age, diet, severity of illness, and other treatments that had been given, such that the comparisons would reflect the impact of bloodletting instead of extraneous variables (although he didn't recognize the importance of randomized assignment), (2) he accumulated data for a large study population to "average out" individual differences (reasoning that diversity among people is so great that medicine can only study commonalities, and offering a rule of thumb that the study population should contain 500 individuals or more), and (3) he followed clinical courses over time, in an explicit use of survival analysis. As he expected, his analysis showed bloodletting was counterproductive as a treatment for pneumonia.

These and countless other incidents contributed to the rise of the scientific method, with each one promoting yet further rejection of the faith-based perspective that had preceded it, in proportion to the previously unprecedented capabilities it conferred. The patience and compassion of St. Francis himself seemed irrelevant in comparison to a paradigm that could solve increasingly difficult problems and invent previously unimaginable technologies on behalf of human interests. But as we will see, that kind of utilitarian calculation led down a slippery slope to the panoply of dangers that now confront humanity.

Uniquely to the human experience, the evolutionary emergence of this kind of adaptation is manifested as problem-solving behavior, which has become a paradigm in itself, most fully expressed through the scientific method and technological progress. It's not that the problem-solving paradigm is wrong or dangerous in and of itself, but along the way, humanity has lost the sense of balance that is needed to keep its blind spots in check. We have let it become a substitute for wisdom, and in the process, have become very unwise indeed. This appendix is a plea to get back to our roots.

Design flaws in evolving systems

Love is the only force which can make things one without destroying them ... Some day, after mastering the winds, the waves, the tides and gravity, we shall harness for God the energies of love, and then, for the second time in the history of the world, man will have discovered fire.

– Pierre Tielhard de Chardin. As quoted in Seed Sown: Theme and Reflections on the Sunday Lectionary Reading (1996) by Jay Cormier, p. 33

In this work, I describe a new class of dynamic instabilities and design flaws that can undermine a society's operation, through feedback of unintended consequences to its environmental niche and cultural/social milieu. When it indiscriminately uses the problem-solving paradigm over long civilizational timescales without overriding accountabilities and responsiveness to corrective feedback, those side effects can accumulate like

A-16

deleterious mutations, as in the case of environmental lead contamination. Such conditions can cause the culture/society complex to become a kluge.

The term "kluge" is engineering slang for an extremely clumsy, inelegant, and dysfunctional design, with the implication that everyone would be better off if it were scrapped to allow the evolution of a completely new and different system, redesigned from scratch. This definition implicitly describes a sequence of events starting with an adaptive rut (the deficient design), progressing through an evolutionary transition (the unpleasant process of abandoning and redesigning the klugey product) and resolving in an evolutionary transformation (the drastic redesign). Physiological systems show evidence of such dead ends that occurred during biological evolution, for example, by mass programmed cell die-offs of specific anatomical structures during embryogenesis that serve no purpose for a given species (e.g., the budding tail of human embryos).

For example, this perspective exposes the interacting flaws of social Darwinism (in all its forms, blatant or insidious), neoclassical economics, and polarizing politics that rationalize unregulated pursuit of self-interest as a panacea for addressing common interests. In fact, allowing selfish individuals to pursue reinforcing feedback without accountability for adverse social consequences creates incentives for a race to the bottom, which is related to the evolution of virulence. Accountability is lacking because harm can accumulate insidiously when social structures are not designated to respond to corrective feedback at higher societal levels.

This is the flaw inherent in the human condition: the very processes that make us successful also make us an invasive and dangerous species. This is also a less blatant flaw inherent in public health: unlike most of the rest of society, at least we are responsive to corrective feedback, but only as applied to specific problems, and not to redesign of aspects of the culture/society complex that are unworkable kluges. In our defense, we have not been given the mandate to initiate that redesign process, but on the other hand, we have not fully recognized the extent of the systemic imbalances.

Our failures to protect the public health are in settings that defy identification of specific problems and lack a mandate to implement specific interventions. However, by thereby overlooking systemic imbalances, we also have failed to recognize specific blind spots in humanity's perspective that gave rise to them. For example,

1. The carnage of worldwide wars and genocides stemming from the toxic idea of social Darwinism, which was wielded by extremists on both ends of the ideological spectrum to kill hundreds of millions of people during the 20th century.

2. Perverse economic incentives, arising from a glaring blind spot in neoclassical economics—the assumption that society is nothing more than a collection of selfish individuals—which ignores global instabilities that flow from lack of accountability at aggregate levels.

3. Pervasively unstable dynamics, resulting from the fact that the forces holding our current adaptations together have gotten completely out of sync over time, especially as our technological abilities have caused them to diverge at an accelerating rate. Thomas Robert Malthus anticipated this

A-18

conundrum in 1798 when he predicted a miserable course for human civilization because population tends to grow exponentially while agricultural output tends to scale up only linearly, resulting in a mismatch where demand would eventually outpace the food supply. Although developing nations frequently fall into this Malthusian trap of famine, disease, and social strife, technology has always pushed back this bogeyman—until now, when we also have to consider the side effects of how we forestall population pressures. These instabilities are the prod that forces us to live wisely, so transformative evolution is our only option for escaping this adaptive version of the Malthusian trap.

It's imperative that we correct these systemic design flaws because they are relentlessly squeezing the life out of human civilization. Yet the impetus for that correction lies in the indefinite future, so the constituencies who would benefit from actions we take now will not be born for decades, centuries, or maybe millennia. Stuck in this adaptive rut, it's much easier for politicians to respond to voter pressures to increase jobs (even by supporting commercial enterprises that exacerbate the systemic dysfunction), to pander to vested interests that deny the fundamental flaws, to fan the flames that have caused deep cultural and social scars (e.g., raising campaign contributions by pitting their own constituency against others with opposing agendas), and to build prisons to incarcerate people who fall through the cracks as a result of these misguided policies (e.g., undermining the effectiveness of schools in disadvantaged communities and fostering a punitive, intolerant attitude to make up for their own lack of insight).

And yet the situation keeps getting worse! Even recognizing these systemic design flaws may encourage using that knowledge adaptively in ways that continue to dig us deeper in our current rut. We have gotten so accustomed to treating technology as the "solution to our problems" that we are quite ready to accept the concept of "geoengineering" (changing the earth's atmosphere to overcome the effects of global climate change, despite all the unknown consequences such large-scale intervention might have) so we can keep feeding our appetites for energy without changing our own attitudes.

Oddly enough, our amazing abilities for rational thought and fluent problem-solving are at the heart of this systemic flaw of the human condition. It's not that rationality and problem-solving are inherently bad or wrong. Instead, they have fostered a perspective that is too narrow for the broader issues at hand and have blinded us to a higher spirituality that might help us learn to cooperate on levels and in ways we have never considered before.

- The flaw in rationality. As the crucial tool of utilitarian adaptation, rationality is also a vehicle for rationalization. Pragmatism is the ultimate barrier to vision and transformation. For example, an economic system that makes it cheap to burn liquid dinosaurs is creating a planet that future generations will find unlivable.

- The flaw in problem-solving. In response predominately to reinforcing feedback, almost to the exclusion of attention to corrective feedback, a bewildering patchwork of adaptive problem-solving has generated myriad unintended consequences that interact turbulently in our societal echo chamber. The same process that cross-pollinates technological innovation also creates harm, which can go

A-20

unnoticed until it accumulates as huge burdens, societal dysfunctions, serious design flaws, and dangerous instabilities.

Over the past few centuries, humanity's culture/society complex has unconsciously adopted a klugey, dysfunctional seven-step design attempting to address unintended consequences of problem-solving with insight development, notably scientific knowledge and technological innovation. However, the "improved" design further decreased responsiveness to corrective feedback even as it greatly increased system capabilities, with no compensatory safety measures, thereby compromising stability of the entire biosphere and initiating a mass extinction event. Mathematically, the design has allowed endless suppression of manageable low-dimensional chaotic instability to contaminate overall system operation with intractable high-dimensional chaos, caused by turbulent, irreversible mixing in a "societal echo chamber." The design has further accelerated buildup of deleterious mutations while blinding the population to its limitations, thereby increasing frustrations and making the system more and more ungovernable, even as it perpetuates the seductive illusion that science and technology will somehow, someday solve all its problems. A more fundamental issue is that we have been "sleepwalking" through history, advancing extremely slowly and completely unsystematically, so previous advances have been made with no real understanding of how we accomplished them, and correspondingly little insight for guiding upcoming transitions, including the one we now face. Thus we need first and foremost to develop responsibility and discipline, as a way of pushing back against the disorder and harm that we ourselves are creating.

A-21

Redesigning this flaw would require the emergence of new kinds of cooperation. A catastrophic collapse could convince future leaders of the folly of our current obliviousness and inaction, but we also may have the option to anticipate and avert disaster, if we choose to accept the realities that confront us. A perspective of the human condition that is based on scientific principles can finally reconcile the longstanding conceptual rift between science and religion—providing justifications to set aside selfish attitudes and behaviors, hopefully helping to usher in a new paradigm of constructive cooperation.

A percolation threshold marks the transition from adaptive behavior to evolutionary design transformation

Adaptive and evolutionary behaviors reflect percolation processes, which are marked by a sharp transition, called a percolation threshold. Loosely speaking, percolation theory relates to the statistical behavior of interconnected, interacting lattices (like communities) functioning as dynamic systems that are embedded within interdependent network (like large-scale societies and/or ecosystems). That behavior changes as a function of the density (perhaps also as a surrogate for types and intensities) of interactions. Adaptive systems are characterized by low interaction densities, below a percolation threshold, where the effects of network interdependencies are negligible, so within-lattice interactions can be considered in terms of the much simpler characteristics of isolated individuals. For example, centuries ago, in earlier stages of technological development, humans interacted sparsely with the global ecosystem, so the effects of human activity did not have to account for interactions with natural environments.

By contrast, in evolving systems, e.g., those influenced by rapid technological change and population growth, interaction densities increase rapidly, and when they exceed the percolation threshold, network interdependencies abruptly become predominant effects. Under those circumstances, the rules of system operation change dramatically, forcing a phase change, or evolutionary transformation, that allows the system to account for interdependency effects within the larger network environment. Typically, such evolutionary transformations manifest as profound design changes that allow the system to function within the fundamentally different parameters of dense network interactions.

For example, as hyperexponentially accelerating technological development and rapid population growth encroach on natural ecosystems, a percolation threshold is reached where human activity resembles a virulent invasion of the biosphere. Under those circumstances, the percolation processes (cultural rules and societal structures) that worked for the low-interaction density, adaptive realm become dangerously obsolete, so a fundamentally new design is required to account for profoundly altered operating conditions.

Introduction to the problem-solving paradigm

The problem-solving paradigm is an adaptive process that works in the stepwise fashion described below. Although the seven core steps (numbered 1-7) are entirely in the adaptive realm (i.e., operating within the current generation), the settings that arise both before (0: niche) and after (8: dissonance) are even more important to the vital transitions between adaptive problem-solving (in the here and now) and transformative evolution (i.e., developing wisdom and transmitting it to future generations). Accordingly, we will discuss those initial and final stages in some detail here, and then return to them in the final section on spirituality (the rediscovery and renewal of what is sacred in human civilization).

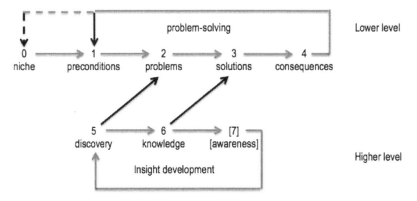

Figure 1.

The problem-solving paradigm takes two linked passes through the same process: a lower-level problem-solving phase and a higher-level insight-development phase.

The problem-solving paradigm eventually reaches an impasse where its internal contradictions are compounded by its escalating capabilities, forcing a phase change, i.e., a complete redesign of its cultural and societal underpinnings. We can think of such phase changes like transformations in a physical system (e.g., transitions from steam to water to ice on cooling), speciation during biological evolution (e.g., the transitions from lower primates to hominids to humans), discovery of a revolutionary scientific principle (e.g., electromagnetism, relativity, quantum physics, chaos theory), or development of a fundamentally new and life-changing innovation (e.g., broadcast media, computers, the Internet, smart phones—or, in the context of this book, oral rehydration therapy and household safe water technologies for developing countries). By contrast, adaptation is a process of refinement of existing designs, e.g., proliferation of variants of computer hardware, software, and applications to meet different consumer needs. Humanity is at a stage of development where our shared worldview has progressed as far as it can by addressing only adaptive issues, and must now reflect and act on the future we have seemed intent on destroying by considering how that worldview must evolve. The world is a whole, fragile, interconnected life form, and our own worldview must acknowledge and respect it as such.

These examples give a sense that adaptations are transient, and cannot withstand the test of time indefinitely: the trajectories of evolution, science, and technology are inevitably punctuated repeatedly with displacement of old paradigms with new ones. However, as we will see, the phase transition that humanity now confronts as the problem-solving paradigm outlives its usefulness presents challenges that are (almost) entirely unique in evolutionary, scientific, and technological history.

Stages in the problem-solving paradigm

Here I will describe the entire sequence in the problem-solving paradigm. As indicated above, the first and last stages involve contextual perspectives instead of steps, and so are much more important with regard to transformative evolutionary change. Therefore, I will elaborate on those stages in much more detail than the others.

Table 1. The Stages of Problem-Solving.

	stage	label	brief description	
—	0	niche	the environmental setting of life's challenges, realities, and potential	
step	1	preconditions	the societal "echo chamber" that processes all feedback	problem-solving phase
step	2	problems	the set of challenges we decide to address	
step	3	solutions	the interventions we implement	
step	4	consequences	the results of our actions	
step	5	discovery	the crucial observations that trigger an avalanche of associated innovation	insight-development phase
step	6	knowledge	the understanding that coalesces as shared information	
step	7	awareness	recognition of our limitations	
—	8	dissonance	an emerging perspective that the paradigm is fundamentally flawed and must be replaced	

Where we start this evolutionary iteration

0.   niche: the setting of life's challenges, realities, and potential.

Before any steps are taken, a preliminary stage of the problem-solving paradigm is cast in the setting of humanity's place in the world, i.e., our niche. Evolutionary theorists have only recently come to recognize that species do not just occupy ecological niches; they actively define and shape them. *Homo sapiens* has taken this process of niche construction to a new level, in large part because the problem-solving paradigm, which is an exclusively human tool, has given us the capability of remolding our entire planet to serve our own interests.

Given the way humanity has been destabilizing the earth's vital life support systems, we need to appreciate the wholeness of nature and resolve to respect its resilience. Unlike any other organism that has ever lived on earth, humanity is making an engineering project out of niche construction, despite the fact that we are complete novices tinkering with natural systems that took billions of years to form and stabilize. The unintended consequences, blind spots, and design defects inherent in the problem-solving paradigm (which are described below) make it inconsistent and incompatible with viable evolutionary processes. As a species and as a civilization, the whole of humankind is acting like the Sorcerer's Apprentice, watching in horror as our clumsy attempts at control unravel disastrously. Given our short lifespans (and profound unsophistication), these events seem to be unfolding in slow motion, but in actuality, they are cascading into an avalanche of mass extinctions that is precipitous on the timescale of biological evolution, triggered by our careless and ignorant inattention to the building codes of

A -27

life. Countless other species have gone extinct blundering into evolutionary dead ends in the same way, blindly relying on adaptive mechanisms that only accumulate deleterious mutations until a lethal threshold is reached that makes them nonviable.

One advantage we have over other species traversing this same trajectory is our ability to comprehend and analyze life's dynamics. Ironically, the problem-solving paradigm itself is the source of that ability, leading to the compelling but surprising prediction that it will ultimately prove to be an exaptation— which is defined as an adaptation that arose to address a need that was entirely different from its ultimate purpose[2]. There are two reasons why the problem-solving paradigm has gone through this two-step process: (1) it has been perfectly adapted as a utilitarian tool to increase humanity's power and influence, and (2) feedback from our actions affects our environment in ways that are typically hidden from view for long periods. Thus a combination of increasing power, denser interactions, delays induced by habit and complacency, and accumulating harm had to reach a percolation threshold at which the intrinsic flaws of utilitarianism become obvious.

The dynamics of the natural systems affected are glacially slow and utterly guileless, but human influence on them is spectacularly powerful, rapid, and deliberately invasive by comparison. The accelerating pace of technological advancement

---

[2] The classic example of an exaptation is feathers, which initially evolved (before any species could fly) in the role of thermal insulation. As natural selection favored species capable of flying, that preexisting exaptation was pressed into new service, as a component in the flight apparatus.

A-28

cannot predict the long-term effects of any new technology, much less the combinatorial explosion of interactions it might have with all the others mixed into our chaotically evolving civilization. The net result of this high dimensional chaos is unpredictable emergence, multiplication, amplification, propagation, and further interaction of harmful effects.

It's not clear how such escalating harm will turn out. Will it lead to collapse, or even extinction? Deep insight and fundamental readjustment? A sudden flip into a new state that reintegrates all the chaotic elements in a new way? Or some other outcome we cannot possibly envision? Biological evolution has followed all these paths countless times at one time or other (including, surely, many variants of the last scenario), and we cannot be sure which is our fate, but developing awareness of the underlying processes will allow us some capacity to steer the right path through all the potentialities. All these issues now necessitate an alternative paradigm of taking responsibility for our influence on the bounties that bless our existence.

Aside from sudden meteor impacts, no events occurring during the 3.5 billion-year span of life on earth have altered its trajectory as rapidly as aggregate human activity. Not being conscious in the way that we are, the earth has no defenses against our determined encroachment. However, its life support systems have evolved into extremely powerful feedback loops storing vast amounts of energy, which are capable of generating huge catastrophes in response to severe, persistent degradation of carrying capacity and stepwise, unrelenting, destabilizing pressures. Given this standoff between our selfish exploitation and the earth's inevitable pushback, our continued stubbornness may precipitate a Malthusian catastrophe of unthinkable scale,

A -29

either causing a huge population collapse or forcing us to change our ways. These harsh alternatives would seem to be a certainty if humanity lets the dynamic forces get more and more unbalanced by continuing to sleepwalk through this process. The biosphere's interaction with our civilization's careless indifference is teetering on a hair-trigger instability, where further continuation of business as usual will inevitably tip us catastrophically into a severely unfavorable state. Worse than that, the perverse incentives that engender such negligent carelessness resemble conditions that promote evolution of virulence, whereby a parasite has every incentive to plunder its host when it can readily "jump ship before the ship goes down." So far, humanity's evasion of accountability for commandeering the earth's life support system—simply to advance provincial and shortsighted human interests—has maladapted us as the most voracious parasite life on this planet has ever encountered. As we will see, the so-called "Great Acceleration" in human activity since 1950 [3] has been the most rapid and drastic niche construction by any single species in the earth's history [4, 5], already transgressing four of nine "planetary boundaries." Two of these measures of planetary health, climate change (relating to atmospheric CO_2 and energy imbalance that cause global temperature increase) and biosphere integrity (relating to extinction rate and biome diversity), are near dangerous tipping points [6]. Furthermore, the rate of anthropogenic carbon release is 10 times higher than at the earth's previous temperature maximum, 66 million years ago, suggesting that our impact on the biosphere has no past analog. [7]

However, further consideration of this perspective summarily dismisses any notion of "sustainable solutions" as completely misleading and ultimately counterproductive. The ultimate lesson of biological evolution is that species that get comfortable in static niches go extinct. Human civilization has enforced that rule unconsciously on nature, but with a vengeance, causing mass extinctions of species unable to keep with the pace of our accelerating power and advancing encroachment. Environmentalists would be so happy to arrest the pace of ecological destruction that they often devise plans that fail to consider this rule (e.g., simply assigning value to the earth's resources within the existing adaptive market structures). By now we should understand that the only equilibrium in life is death. To proceed from here, humanity must abandon pipe dreams of easy adaptation and utopian panaceas and embark consciously on a path of continual transformative renewal.

This detailed picture of the niche that humanity has constructed for itself illustrates where we are beginning this phase of civilization, now finally waking up from a long slumber. By taking this point in the feedback process to be both start and end, we can also see from a theoretical standpoint where humanity's knowledge and power have led us. As a matter of fact, the details of the flawed problem-solving process are essentially irrelevant to the deeper evolutionary questions we face. Even before we characterize the steps themselves, we can recognize they have become obsolete and dangerous, at least insofar as we use them now, as our sole interface with the world.

The two core subsets of the problem-solving paradigm

The problem-solving paradigm should not be considered either "good" (helping us learn about the laws of nature and address humanity's needs) or "bad" (because it has unleashed our most virulent nature and made humanity a danger to all life on earth).

Instead, the problem-solving paradigm has been an intermediate process in civilizational evolution that has allowed humanity to keep expanding the context of its shared worldview. Although it is dangerously obsolete in its current form, some aspects of it can serve as an exaptation on the path toward humanity's quest to manifest wise self-governance.

The stepwise process within the problem-solving paradigm entails two core subsets at two different levels, one phase addressing adaptive concerns, and the other at the next-higher level looking ahead to the upcoming evolutionary transition. The lower, purely adaptive-level phase has four steps and is concerned with everyday problem-solving. The higher-level phase consists of three steps and is involved in insight development.

The lower-level subset: the problem-solving phase

The premise of the problem-solving paradigm is that a complex world can be abstracted functionally to a two-step process: problem definition followed by intervention that flows toward a resolution, or solution. As we have seen, this is a seductive illusion, because the dynamics of life superimpose all kinds of complexity around such efforts to control its trajectory. This observation should in no way be interpreted as a rejection of problem-solving, since it is a necessary part of life—typically the pragmatic component of existence. The hallmark of pragmatism is that we must take action and move on with life despite any reservations that our choices are less than perfect.

Since 1997, a computational analog of the simplified four-step subset of the problem-solving paradigm has gained considerable attention as an extremely versatile search and optimization algorithm, termed "differential evolution" [8]. Researchers have found a wide class of differential evolution algorithms [9] that can apply to a huge number of problems [10] of many different classes [11] without any knowledge of the mathematics of the system under control, using feedback from the system as a kind of analog computer. These algorithms can be implemented computationally in a wide variety of ways (called "metaheuristics") [12], many of which are naturally inspired (for example, biologically oriented approaches, like evolutionary algorithms, e.g., genetic or evolutionary programming; socially oriented approaches, like particle swarm optimization or ant colony optimization; physically oriented approaches, like simulated annealing; and culturally oriented approaches, like tabu search). Simulations of multilevel metabolic control networks can exhibit characteristics of economic systems, like classic supply-demand curves [13]. They can also function through a wide range of approaches [14], some simulating very familiar human-like behaviors, such as greed, exploitation, oppositional activities [15, 16], with different approaches getting very different results, sometimes in ways identified here (e.g., shortsightedness of memoryless greedy algorithms, which can be overcome to some degree by swarm strategies that mimic democracies with great diversity).

Such strategies, to one degree or other, resemble the operating paradigms of bacteria, which, although brilliantly successful in life, are not renowned for their ability to create life-sustaining high-level structures analogous to the invisible hand. As I will show, mainstream neoclassical economics is predicated on the same operating paradigm as bacteria, and shares the same design limitation: it can only break down structures, not build them up. As humanity must increasingly attend to common

A -33

interests and its future trajectory, that design has passed the threshold of being just limited in capability and vision, to a point where its overconfident, incompetent muddling is downright toxic. I don't want to discourage such research, but I have called out in this appendix many of the pitfalls of an even more general and nuanced version of that class of algorithms, which, despite the name "differential evolution," are all quite clearly adaptive and not fundamentally transformative in nature, at least not in the sense that I am considering here.

The problem-solving phase is a familiar set of steps from everyday experience:

1. preconditions: the societal echo chamber that processes all feedback.

In contrast to the niche stage above (which relates to the external environment and does not involve any action on our part), this first step of problem-solving per se concerns itself with the cultural milieu. This is the step that might be summarized in the "background" section of a scientific journal article—although if we really admitted the truth to ourselves, we would realize we can never fully capture the entire context of humanity's aggregate culture. As much as we try to ignore the confusing cacophony of interactions by attempting to isolate problems in the next step, all of life's feedback pours into this societal echo chamber, leaving many people and institutions feeling alienated and rudderless. As we approach a crescendo of internal contradictions, this stage accumulates a vast store of unexamined antecedent conditions that cannot possibly be considered in the subsequent problem-solving efforts.

Like the preceding stage that relates to the environmental niche, this corresponding stage in the cultural realm is a major source of noise in the problem-solving paradigm, for better and worse. That noise is part confusion but also part inspiration. The theme of noise as inspiration is recurrent in biology and society. As a result, we need to be tolerant of variability, accepting of diversity, and compassionate despite our differences—they are what gives life its vitality.

For this reason, we need to resist the inclination to suppress every problem, cure every ill, stomp out every social disorder. The noise and discomfort of life provide motivation to get involved and shake things up. The rationale for helping people then shifts from making them comfortable to mobilizing their potential. The excruciatingly slow shift from feudalism and slavery to democracy and free markets had the critical effect of vastly increasing the number of participants in the process of cultural and social change, i.e., from a king to an entire population of voters. Free markets still harbor echoes of slavery (e.g., through commerce in addictive products), large pockets of slavery still persist (e.g., in human trafficking), and democracy can get hijacked by oligarchs manipulating public opinion, but even those design flaws help us from an evolutionary standpoint, if only as the grains of sand that irritate us to grow pearls.

2. problems: the set of challenges we decide to address.

The second step of the problem-solving paradigm involves identifying what aspect of our world we want to control. In terms of a design process, problem definition relates to specification of system parameters and/or desired outcomes. In systems with realistic complexity (typically involving multiple variables and subtle dynamics spanning a range of hierarchical levels to be managed over a range of timescales), problem definition typically involves (1) restricting attention to the set of levels and variables of interest, (2) assigning priorities and identifying constraints for the desired outcome, (3) recognizing (or postulating) relevant feedback interactions, and (4) implicitly or explicitly developing a framework for assigning tradeoffs in anticipation of the unfolding outcome. We often choose to respond to reinforcing feedback (outcomes we desire) with some variables and negative feedback (outcomes we want to avoid) with others. Tradeoffs can get more complex when we identify variables to control within an acceptable range (like temperature) or processes that interact.

3. solutions: the interventions we implement.

In the third step, the stimulus of a manageable problem often leads to the response of a doable intervention, which resolves as a solution. This is the enticement of the problem-solving method—if we ignore all the complications surrounding the paradigm, one quick observation leads to one simple action; project that paradigm onto a divide-and-conquer strategy and the answers to all life's questions will follow straightforwardly in one (vector) fell swoop[3]! Good luck with that, I say!! The secondary problem of eliminating all those vexing interaction effects is left as an exercise for the reader!

---

[3] This description fits perfectly the way engineers design technologies, by choosing linear components, avoiding complex interactions, and constructing feedback circuits to conform to neat, infinite-dimensional matrix equations. The nonlinearities, interactions, and interdependencies of natural networks assure us that life can never work that way! Therein lies the fallacy that science and technology are panaceas for solving humanity's problems.

A-36

4. consequences: the results of our actions.

One of the most profound revelations of our age is the nature and behavior of complex dynamic systems, which offers tremendous insight into the consequences of our actions. In a prescient 1936 article, Robert K. Merton [17] discussed in broad terms what was then known about "the unanticipated consequences of purposive social actions."[1] Starting from a stimulus-response framework, John Platt's 1973 article discussed "social traps" [18], including two dysfunctional variants of the "invisible hand" that Adam Smith described as the guiding force of economic systems [19]: "the invisible fist" (a race to the bottom) and "the invisible chain" (a cycle of co-dependency). George Richardson surveyed both control ("servomotor") and communications ("cybernetic") models of social behavior, starting with a fascinating historical analysis, including an account (pp. 64-66) of how the designers of the United States Constitution used insights about time constants for self-regulating steam engines to establish three branches of government with short-, medium-, and long-term accountabilities appropriate to their respective purposes [20]. The development of chaos theory has provided insights into dynamic systems that eluded mathematicians and scientists for centuries. [21, 22]

In the sweep of civilizational evolution, the impact of human activity is making earlier theoretical insights evident from empirical observations. Humanity has developed so much power that the unintended consequences of our actions have pervasive, interacting impacts that spill over onto multiple levels and reverberate on a wide range of timescales. It's increasingly clear that the invisible hand we create is the invisible hand we get.

A -37

In this setting where human actions are affecting the entire planet and its future, we might wonder what is the broader significance of those impacts at much lower levels, e.g., on individuals. This question is especially important because that's where many of the motivations arise for the causative actions. We are ephemeral beings, with short lifetimes in relation to civilizational evolution: when I complained about trivial issues as a child, my father once used to say, "10,000 years from now, nobody will know the difference!" (That message never resonated, so he quickly stopped saying that!)

However, it's important to realize our behavior extends ripples far beyond our sight and comprehension. The defining characteristic of chaotic systems is sensitivity to initial conditions, which gives both assurance and caution that the consequences of even trivial actions can amplify tremendously through the "butterfly effect" over long timescales. Civilizational evolution provides a vehicle whereby those influences can pass on through social interactions in ways far subtler than how genetic traits are transmitted in biological evolution.

We might consider these effects in terms of amplification and propagation of humanity's potential, which is not acknowledged enough as a rationale for public health and public policy. This is a profound justification for compassion, mercy, liberty, love, and generosity. We are building something beyond our lives that will persist for all time. This realization should give pause to those who wage war, kill and injure others, destroy lives, induce addictions, compromise livelihoods, and limit human potential. By the same token, this is also a refutation against lesser transgression, like shortsightedness, mean-spiritedness, greed, intolerance, discrimination, and pettiness. Even those seemingly smaller insults can amplify, propagate, multiply, and interact, first to affect subsequent generations, perhaps just slightly, but eventually to affect all of humanity on a much larger scale. An understanding of modern mathematics makes us wonder how both everyday activity and major policy decisions are influencing the trajectory of civilizational evolution, taking God's matters into our own hands.

The upper-level subset: the insight-development phase

Insight development is a three-step process occurring at a higher level than problem-solving itself, but tightly linked as a systematic information source and guide. The three steps in this core set are discovery (of isolated key observations), knowledge (coalescence of ideas into bodies of shared information), and awareness (of our limitations). As described above in connection with the early development of scientific thought and methods, the insight-development phase has emerged as a dominant adjunct to the problem-solving phase. This aspect of the problem-solving paradigm has taken advantage of the human species' unique capacity for cumulative culture by systematizing the process and its widespread communication. In its most noble manifestations, there is an implicit recognition of the enduring legacy that we may all participate in constructing. Through amplification processes, the responsibilities we individually and collectively face in niche construction may extend for all time through civilizational evolution to build something that God can use for a higher purpose. From the technologies we ourselves have started to develop only recently, we now can appreciate the role that intelligent components can play in the function of a complex dynamic system. We can thereby get a mathematical sense of how God has enlisted humanity as co-creators of our

A -39

world. This concept invokes the idea of generativity at the level of humanity as a whole, which compels us to abandon the self-centered veniality of anthropocentric conceptual frameworks that have dominated and misguided us for far too long. By shaping culture and building social structures, we can stop sleepwalking and consciously steer the path of human civilization in a constructive direction.

5. discovery: the crucial observations that trigger an avalanche of associated innovation.

This first step in the insight-development phase is aligned above the first step in the problem-solving phase. The diversity in the societal echo chamber generates inspiration, from which creative, empowered individuals, groups, and/or corporations can seed the culture with revolutionary ideas—e.g., the periodic table of elements, biological evolution by natural selection, special and general theories of relativity, quantum physics, chaos theory, the DNA double helix, the genetic code.

6. knowledge: the understanding that coalesces as shared information.

As more and more people reflect on creative theories, they interact, at first sparsely, and then more and more densely as a percolation process. Once that process crosses a threshold, in an abstract sense, we might consider the associated body of ideas as undergoing a self-organization process, mediated by those interested people, organizations, and institutions. Societal structures, like universities, foundations, corporate research, and governmental agencies, play key roles in launching and sustaining these efforts.

A-40

The knowledge obtained in this step is critical for expanding the population's perspective. A major distinction between the discovery and knowledge steps is the activity of communication channels that disseminate ideas widely. Even though the knowledge is predominately used to support the status quo at first, it eventually turns the tide toward transformative change. As the transition approaches, the system resists change, and a wide range of intense clashes ensue, like the ones we see at this writing between conservatives (defending the status quo) and progressives (advocating reform).

7. awareness: recognition of our limitations.

Awareness is related to wisdom, but shared on a population scale. Wisdom is rare enough among people, but given the uncritical emphasis on individual autonomy that is endemic as the chief obstacle to coalescing as a culture and society, it's almost impossible now to imagine an entire population exhibiting the trait. A biology analogy is clear: some elements of our society—notably corporations, governments, and public health—have arisen from autonomous unicellular origins and begun to function like a multicellular organism, but neither all our behaviors nor all the population has adjusted to that reality. The metabolic byproducts of our klugey implementation of multicellular life—pollution, discrimination, injustice, war, violence, alienation, addiction, crime; the list goes on and on— have been highly toxic. It's uncomfortable to discuss these topics publicly, because they seem to defy resolution. But all life is committed either to evolve toward improved designs (however arduous a process that may be) or else eke out a marginal existence on the edge of extinction. As we have picked up potential and kinetic energy on that trajectory, the only two options we have are to derail the train and thereby fail as a species, or to get control and pull into the next station, in anticipation of setting up routes to other destinations in the future. Like it or not, at this stage in civilizational evolution, we're in the railway business. Sometime in the distant future, we'll get enough fluency with wise self-governance in this regime to add the societal equivalent of an interstate highway, an airline industry, and the Internet.

On a wide scale and to a large extent, awareness is currently absent, but pockets are emerging as people here and there pick up bits and pieces of insight amid the noise of our echo chamber. Therein lies another irony: the echo chamber that is such an obstacle to coherence is also a fertile source of invention, as different cultures and spiritual traditions share insights that are required to overcome inertia and learn how to recover from the imbalances. This is a time when we must be especially grateful for our differences, because the diversity of ideas is a substrate for awareness and wisdom. In the end, those differences will allow different cultures, communities, and nations to express their individualities in new ways, like different tissues and organs in the division of labor within the new cultural body or ecosystem we are poised to start growing. Celebration of our current cultural diversity also provides the seed for healthy evolutionary experimentation along the path to populating that ecosystem, and when the time is right, humanity will experience a blossoming of evolutionary potential analogous to the Cambrian explosion 800 million years ago, which established the design blueprint for all animals since then.

Even more to the point, the diversity we have now will provide the range of perspectives to facilitate making future evolutionary transformations, the specifics of which we cannot envision, except to know they will involve entirely different challenges. Recall that the definition of civilizational evolution raised an adaptive question about living responsibly but also an evolutionary question about steering a sensible course henceforth. In our weighty time, it is not enough that we are faced with the challenge of waking up to one of the most significant transitions in human history; we must also set up conditions to facilitate future evolutionary transformations so they are not as traumatic and difficult. In terms of biological evolution, we must not only correct the defect in our metabolism, but also use our experience through this transition to develop vision that will guide us in future transformations.

Historical experiences with technological innovation provide insight here: resistance to the "technologies" of wise self-governance has made us a population largely of Luddites, some trying to throw their wooden shoes in the gears to stop the machinery, not realizing on the other side of the transitions ahead are the means to overcome societal problems, improve living standards, cure diseases, accelerate the design process, and provide previously unimaginable opportunities By extension, we can imagine a day—even though we may not enjoy it ourselves—where our current wrenching, stumbling experience at this terrifying cusp in civilizational evolution reaches an inflection point and becomes a fluent process, a great adventure, and a lot of fun. We might even envision that future generations see rapid progress along these lines, something like the way computer technologies have evolved within a lifetime from cumbersome mainframes with punch card inputs to cell phones that can communicate instantaneously across the globe in many ways and allow any person to carry once-unimaginable storage and processing capabilities everywhere. The prospect of making such abilities available to future generations—only this time, in the realm of shared wisdom, and not just mere technology—should make us glow with excitement and motivation at having the privilege of living in this pivotal time!

In this phase of human development, we have become so intently absorbed in the cultural and social edifice that serves us in the immediate present that we have given little thought to passing ideas and practices from generation to generation. More than any past time in human history—and, if we really learn the lessons of the experience we are undergoing, at any future time as well—we have no good way to convey wise practices across many generations without corruption in the societal echo chamber. This is a well-known limitation in biological evolution: deleterious mutations accumulate if no mechanisms have emerged to purge them. Many design innovations (the genetic code, sexual reproduction) have arisen in biological evolution to correct this limitation, but it's not clear how they might translate into cultural and societal practices in civilizational evolution. That is another challenge of our time.

The final stage of the problem-solving paradigm: dissonance

Uncertainty about the future produces "the truly cosmic gravity of the this sickness that disquieted us." We lose the conviction needed to act when we worry that evolution may have no future.

– Patrick H. Byrne "The integral visions of Tielhard and Lonergan: science, the universe, humanity, and God," (p. 107) from chapter 6 in From Tielhard to Omega: co-creating an unfinished universe, Ilia Delio (ed.) (2014).

8. dissonance: an emerging perspective that the paradigm is fundamentally flawed and must be replaced.

The last stage in the problem-solving paradigm is where everything falls apart in the adaptive realm, so we are forced to transition into a transformed way of life. Obviously, this is the difficult place where we are now. The old klugey design has long since failed, and despite our misplaced attachments to it, we must abandon it to complete the redesign process.

Human civilization is like a clunky locomotive with a decrepit boiler, which slowly percolated at low temperature in the background after being jury-rigged at the outset of the Industrial Revolution. Since then, it has been rapidly picking up steam as we have attempted to use a cumbersome locomotive engine to power us past the jet age toward interplanetary travel, even though it is completely unsuited to propelling us into flight! Now its haphazard, dangerously overstressed design—with no safety features—is threatening to explode under the pressure, while we force it to keep accelerating to a deafening crescendo! We haven't even bothered to ask what would happen if we ever managed to become airborne with such a poorly designed system!!

The task in this stage is to solidify and channel the commitment to transformation, pull together various parts of the puzzle that have been emerging all along, and create a new design that offers stunning possibilities for humanity's future. We are lucky to live in an era with the highest living standards, the greatest freedom, the most understanding, and the most powerful tools. God has equipped us well to co-create this unfinished universe, but we mustn't delay this process, lest our encroachments on life cause

A -45

our environment to collapse around us, thereby leaving us with much less to help accomplish the task.

The evolutionary process gives us another set of tools to complete this process, which make tarrying here a particularly unpleasant and toxic experience. The feeling of dissonance we have in this stage comes from at least three sources. Ideally, the most important source of discomfort should come from an ever-deepening intuition that there are better ways to live that can only be attained through transformative change. The next healthiest source would be what manifests as "sickness behavior" in systemic illness [23]—the internal signal that the body broadcasts throughout itself to shut down all unnecessary activities to let the immune and repair systems take over and repel whatever stressors have been attacking. It's sobering to think of genocidal wars and endemic violence in this way, but it would be preferable that they stem from that second source of dissonance than from the third and last one: the buildup of crippling mutations. As we have lingered in our adaptive rut, developing greater and greater power without the ability to recognize pain or track down its source, we have been inflicting serious injury on ourselves; however, far worse from an evolutionary standpoint, that damage may have cut off future options for our growth and development. To whatever extent we find positive motivations insufficient for undergoing transformative change, ending that self-inflicted constriction of humanity's future is compelling enough reason for abandoning our seemingly comfortable adaptations and taking the leap into the unknown.

The other side of the evolutionary transition

> *There is something afoot in the universe, something that looks like gestation and birth. In other words, a plan, a purpose for it all.*
>
> *– Pierre Tielhard de Chardin; (Jane Goodall, Reason for Hope: A Spiritual Journey. New York: Warner Books, 1999: xi-xii.)*

By the very nature of transformative change, it's almost impossible to imagine what's on the other side as we approach a transition. By definition, the evolutionary transformation involves a complete and profound state change, so before we experience that leap into the unknown, it will seem like a black hole of uncertainty.

However, that uncertainty does not mean we should fear the change. Ordinary life experiences and historical examples give some idea what to expect. The stepwise transition from childhood into adulthood suggests a reasonable model of the maturation of wisdom, and when we project those experiences to the population level, we imagine the subject of that maturation would be humanity's shared worldview. We easily identify examples of such maturation from earlier advances made when civilizational evolution was sleepwalking through the process: transitions from feudalism to democracy, from serfdom to free markets, from illiteracy to universal education. While resisting the inclination to engage our adaptive compulsions (e.g., developing a business plan for attacking evolutionary transitions!), we might envision the process as developing a technology for wise self-governance.

A helpful way to put these ideas into perspective might be to consider the revelations that unfold for each era. The

A -47

commonalities and repetition of the themes of life occurring on many levels and over many timescales give us ways to see the path ahead, i.e., to develop evolutionary vision as we also alter our adaptive metabolism to be less toxic to ourselves and to our world. Revelations emerge in stages because interactions are sparse initially as a new technology is introduced; then interactions multiply through a combinatorial explosion; until finally a percolation threshold is reached when what was once unimaginable becomes obvious to all. A few decades ago, computer networks were an abstraction, but now the Internet is a profoundly empowering new connection with the world, and the source of intuitive understanding that once was also just abstract (e.g., communication bandwidth as connection speed).

In this setting of percolation thresholds, nobody could have really known about the hazards of our own actions beforehand. We had no experience with the power we would prove to develop. On that basis, we can be more forgiving with each other for our transgressions, to look beyond toward higher purposes that reflect how the design of our civilization is unfolding over long timescales.

Far more than any other species that has ever lived on earth, we humans have the capacity to anticipate events and alter our own actions accordingly. We can fit ourselves into the preexisting reality of nature, but our inclinations to do so in familiar cultural terms have misled us into constructing a synthetic reality, viz., a distorted worldview that is both maladaptive to current existence and obstructive to evolutionary change. Our long sojourn through the scientific era has also given us an appreciation of life as design, pattern, and function that have evolved over time, even as it has further separated us from the realities of life and nature. Now humanity is in a position—actually, forced by the unintended consequences of our own actions—to reflect on why our past methods have broken down, how our old worldviews blind us to reality, and how we might transform ourselves to fit within life's plan.

The underlying flaw with the problem-solving paradigm is its antagonistic complexity. Recall that evolution improves design by "synergistic complexification," i.e., building up a hierarchy of levels that provides bounty to life that lower levels could not attain for themselves. The problem-solving paradigm is based on a quick-and-dirty shortcut, the seductive illusion that defining a problem and implementing a solution can eliminate life's obstacles one at a time, with no further ramifications, implications, or complications.

The irony of that logic is that the problem-solving paradigm itself is the flaw that undermines the synergistic aspects of complexification. This paradigm short-circuits life's ingenious structures that create bounty, providing those looking for immediate gratification, easy answers, or a quick buck with opportunities to "bite the invisible hand that feeds everybody." It gives free rein for shortsighted adaptive interests to undermine potential, create resentment, and steal the future. In that way, its own antagonistic complexity predisposes it to collapse, and thereby to take down the entire elaborate hierarchy that evolutionary processes had previously built up over vast timespans to support life on earth.

However, there is a purpose even in this dismal situation. Again, the stepwise percolation of life's evolution does not allow us to see far ahead, so we have to learn from mistakes. Until now, our sleepwalking course has been slow and haphazard, so as we have bumped clumsily into one insight or pitfall along the way, we really haven't developed any understanding of what we did right or what we did wrong. Not having eyes to see our evolutionary path is a pretty big obstacle to developing good designs and transmitting them to future generations.

If nothing else, the problem-solving paradigm has developed our skill in combining systematic observation with analytical thought. What a gift that is, coming at just the right time! We can turn that insight into reflection on the paradigm itself to identify the sources of its instability. As will see, it has too many steps, creating too many moving parts to go wrong. When adaptation runs the show, it transforms the magnificent edifice of the evolutionary process into a future-sucking machine that fattens and emboldens virulent parasites.

Evolution piles insight upon insight, if we're willing to step back from the harshness of its lessons to learn from them. As we will also see, parasites can turn into allies, and from there, into great friends, and from there, into indispensible parts of our own lives.

These are the healing themes our generation is poised to recognize. Life is providing us the opportunity to bridge schisms so old that nobody can remember firsthand when wholeness existed. This awareness could serve as an inducement to sacrifice unnecessary and counterproductive short-term gain to invest in humanity's potential and future. It could impel us to cooperate compassionately to nurture a sense of community that has long been fractured.

The history of public health in problem-solving paradigms

Is it possible that these insoluble crises are signs of a passage or transition in our national development and in the evolution of humanity? Is it possible we are going through a fundamental evolutionary change and transcendence, and crisis is the birthplace and learning process for a new consciousness and harmony?

– Margaret Swedish Living beyond the "End of the world": a spirituality of hope (p. 173)

The problem-solving paradigm is a societal design based on purposiveness, cumulative culture, response to feedback, and (thus far, unconscious) niche construction. Its success is based on the fact that it can operate on its own terms embedded within any ecosystem, simply by using the environment's response as an analog computer providing feedback. Its serious drawback is in directing its actions on the basis of its own internal motivations—and even generating its own culture to justify its attitudes and behavior. That self-oriented, self-referencing perspective encourages development of a synthetic reality, which historically has percolated unconsciously to cause great damage to the biosphere and life in it. These are exactly the dynamics that foster evolution of virulence. Also, as humanity has aggregated into larger and larger cities and gained more and more power over the last few centuries, history has shifted from a story of epidemics inflicted on populations due to ignorance of scientific principles to a story of the harm we inflict on ourselves.

Public health is the subsystem within that whole parasitic system that has been commissioned to ameliorate the worst side

A -51

effects of its operation, at least insofar as they affect humanity. However, its mandate has only been a passive one—it can react to the unintended consequences of human activity, but not prevent excesses that cause harm either to human populations or to the world as a whole.

Thus the history of public health since its inception reflects a series of phase transitions, as excess after excess percolated until the density of interactions exceeded a threshold beyond which the side effects were intolerable. At that point, the public health community responded to the corrective feedback, developing a new analytical framework for dealing with that specific problem.

As it turns out, at least for enteric disease epidemiology embedded in public health as a whole, the entire history of human civilization over that period can be framed in terms of one entire cycle of the problem-solving paradigm inside another. I'm not sure why that holds so neatly.

The birth of epidemiology

Epidemiology is the study of the distribution and determinants of disease frequency. It is the scientific underpinning for public health practice. The word comes from the Greek epi (upon), demos (people), and logos (doctrine), and so, in etymological terms, is the study of what happens within a population. The Greek word epidemia also came to mean the presence of an epidemic disease, especially the plague.

Table 2. The historical development of enteric disease epidemiology expressed in terms of the stepwise problem-solving paradigm.

steps	stages	events	causes
0	life's challenges	niche: migration into large cities	job opportunities from the Industrial Revolution
1	preconceptions (echo chamber)	mismatch: concentrated population with no sanitation	no experience with large cities
2	problems	dislocations: 1. stench of accumulated shit 2. cholera epidemics	no understanding of the need for or technology of sewage systems
3	solutions	dysfunctions drain cesspools into the Thames River	miasma theory interpreted stench as disease
4	consequences	unintended consequences deadly cholera outbreaks	Londoners sharing intestinal pathogens via water
5	insight-development	discovery of crucial principles Snow: cholera transmitted via water Whitehead: epidemiological follow-up Farr: surveillance, health departments Bazalgette: visionary sewer system design	recognition that large cities are unsustainable without sanitary infrastructures
6		understanding (knowledge) Pasteur: microbiology Koch: bacteriology	extending insights to other infectious pathogens
7		awareness of limitations epidemiological modeling: Kermack/McKendrick: theoretical model Anderson/May: computer simulations	development of epidemic theory
8	dissonance	epidemic of tobacco-related diseases	inapplicability of the infectious disease paradigm for other public health problems

We can think of John Snow's founding of epidemiology as an implicit application of the problem-solving paradigm, specifically to dreaded epidemics of cholera. Subsequent researchers extended epidemiology as a scientific body of knowledge, first to other infectious diseases and then in sequence to a variety of categories of noninfectious public health issues.

The precipitating Malthusian mismatch that caused widespread cholera outbreaks during the 19th century was the growth of

A -53

large cities before adequate knowledge of sanitary practices had emerged. Technology had advanced far enough to supply large populations, but the miasma theory of disease causation (that infectious outbreaks were transmitted by foul odors) suggested counterproductive interventions, most notably draining accumulating cesspools into rivers used as drinking water sources. Thus, instead of being exposed to localized and isolated pockets of enteric pathogens (so the population could develop diversity in its immunity), all Londoners were sharing their intestinal flora through drinking water (thereby fostering evolution of microbial virulence). Table 2 frames this sequence of events in terms of the problem-solving phase, steps 1-4 of the overall problem-solving paradigm.

John Snow's genius was in sparking the discovery step of the insight-development cycle that has become the engine for all of public health. As the father of anesthesiology, Snow was convinced by his experiences administering gaseous ether and chloroform that the miasma theory was implausible, and he conducted brilliant outbreak investigations during three cholera epidemics between 1848 and 1854 that established that contaminated water was the transmission vehicle. His colleague Reverend Henry Whitehead was instrumental in epidemiological follow-up of controls with whom he maintained contact after many of his parishioners fled the danger zone. The collaboration between Snow and Whitehead identified the index case, and from there, the initial site of the contamination (the Broad Street pump), and from there, the causative environmental breach (a severely damaged encasement). Snow had not expected to live long enough to see his insights come to fruition, but upon his death, William Farr took up the torch to establish a corresponding set of public health practices. Meanwhile, it wasn't Snow's insights that prompted construction of London's visionary sewage system but instead The Great Stink—the combination of a hot summer and bacterial overgrowth that led to a terrible smell throughout the city—and lingering fears about miasmas. However, the dramatic success of this sewage system in containing a subsequent cholera outbreak just before its construction was completed vindicated Snow's legacy.

That success with cholera prevention prompted Louis Pasteur and Robert Koch to develop germ theory, establishing a body of knowledge about microbial pathogens that cause infectious disease. Using rigorous scientific methods, they established laboratory techniques for identifying causative pathogens, which they also adapted clinically for diagnostic purposes. That knowledge accumulated as the methods were applied to other diseases and linked to the corresponding pathogenic organisms.

William O. Kermack and Anderson G. McKendrick made the first leaps beyond those empirical methods in 1927 with their development of compartmental SEIRS (susceptible → exposed → infected → recovered → susceptible) models of infectious outbreaks. Without computers, their models were analytically intractable, so their theory lay dormant for almost 50 years. Roy Anderson and Robert May revived their methods in 1976, using numerical simulation of compartmental flow models to study infectious disease outbreaks, later including HIV/AIDS.

New conceptual and analytical methods were required when entirely different public health problems emerged. As we will see, the historical development of public health indirectly help unleash that sequence of problems, as its response to corrective feedback removed constraints on human activity. Its handling of

A -55

those problems retroactively is a prime example of the "sleepwalking" course of human history.

A case study: environmental enteropathy

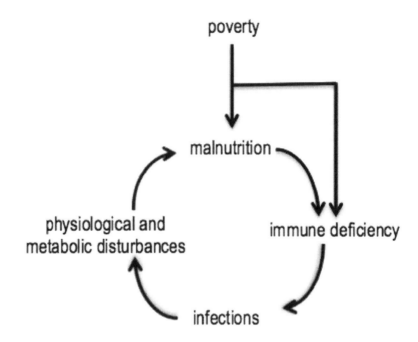

Figure 2.

The vicious cycle of malnutrition and recurrent infections in environmental enteropathy (adapted from [24]).

Although I am focusing primarily on the problem-solving paradigm, it's useful to examine a feedback loop that doesn't meet that definition in itself, but which would often be a target system for control. Environmental enteropathy illustrates some important aspects of dynamic imbalances, vicious cycles, and multilevel dysfunction. The physiological dysfunction in this condition does not exhibit the features of the problem-solving paradigm because the system lacks the characteristics of design,

A-56

purposiveness, intentionality, teleonomy, and (in a theological setting) teleology.[4] As we will see, even when biological and civilizational evolution "sleepwalk" through those processes, those characteristics are still present. The underlying distinction is that there is no purposive behavior intrinsically driving system dynamics, but that the severe concomitant health problems warrant urgent attention and intervention (i.e., purposive action).

In environmental enteropathy, poverty, which is typically the result of a dysfunctional society, can initiate a vicious cycle of malnutrition and infection that feeds on itself in a downward spiral. Though the infectious agent(s) may benefit from a weakened host, this dynamic imbalance is not a race to the bottom, as it is not driven by competitors seeking to gain advantage by undermining each other. Most notably, this dynamic system does not have the stepwise structure of the problem-solving paradigm since it lacks purposive behavior.

In a sense, this case study of environmental enteropathy might seem more relevant to my father's autobiography than to this

---

[4] I am using the terms "purposive" and "purposiveness" in the sense that one or more sentient beings, typically humans, work to advance specific goals. Intentionality is purposiveness that is further based on a sense of mission, direction, aspiration, commitment, etc. Teleonomy is the quality of apparent purposefulness and of goal-directedness of structures and functions in living organisms brought about by natural laws. Teleology is the explanation of phenomena by projected or proposed purpose(s) they are thought to serve rather than by postulated causes. Scientific thought has long discarded the notion of teleology in favor of teleonomy, but in this document I argue that all these terms are comparably useful, each at its own appropriate level of application.

appendix, at least to this point, especially since he was the first to describe the condition. Obviously, a disorder like this that causes severe stunting, developmental deficits, lingering health effects and compromised productivity throughout life, significant economic impact at the societal level, and the potential to incubate and unleash virulent emerging infections would be a high priority for targeting as a significant problem.

However, what's important here is that the problem-solving paradigm doesn't necessarily target this kind of problem well because of its tendency for self-referential focus. Problem definition is an internal process, which gives plenty of leeway for indifference within a self-insulating, self-justifying culture that denies the dynamic realities of the world outside it. That is indeed a prime feature of human culture and society today, which creates a synthetic reality of excess and triviality, complains about budget deficits, creates problems that impose huge social costs, and begrudges the modest expenditures that might prevent such social problems. Other tropical diseases, like malaria, also get short shrift because they do not afflict the more affluent countries of the world, even though global warming may extend their geographical ranges back into what are now temperate zones. And even looming health hazards that are poised to unleash global pandemics that could affect everyone, like microbial antibiotic resistance that threatens to send clinical medicine back to the pre-antibiotic era, are not enough to mobilize research because pharmaceuticals that treat chronic conditions are far more profitable.

The problem-solving paradigm has fostered rationalization for promulgating enormous social and environmental damage under the banner of utilitarianism, although that rationale has also brought out much darker cultural and societal undertones. Cost-cutting was the rationale used for the bureaucratic decision to change the water supply of Flint, Michigan to a lead-contaminated source, but the governing structures that did so had usurped control of an impoverished community's fate as an "emergency fiscal measure" even as it lowered taxes on the rich. The shortsightedness of that decision is staggering, because of the social costs of lead contamination—the lifelong disabilities incurred by childhood lead exposures; the social dysfunction and criminal activity attributable to lead-associated attention deficit disorders, impaired aggression and impulse control, and dementia—and, on the other hand, the tremendous cost-effectiveness of lead abatement measures. Starting in the late 1920s, the first manufacturer of leaded gasoline pioneered a multi-industry, multi-generational corporate strategy to deny health hazards and social costs of harmful commercial products. That strategy, first articulated by Robert Kehoe in what would be called the Kehoe paradigm, was first used to unleash aerosolized tetraethyl lead into the environment as an anti-knock gasoline additive; the strategy was then quickly adopted to lull the public to sleep about the dangers of cigarettes, asbestos, pesticides, and many other commercial products that now impose huge negative externalities (costs not absorbed by the commercial market), as well as the environmental hazards of chlorofluorocarbons and nuclear power.

The problem of environmental enteropathy gets to the heart of social justice, which is a core principle of public health. Because the public health community has to deal with such major health problems on a population and global scale, it cannot ignore the social conditions that seed, propagate, and amplify such problems and further impinge on the function of societies at all

A -59

levels. Nor can it deny problems that will inevitably return in even greater force because of delays, neglect, misinformation, and lack of preparation. The mean-spirited, narrow-minded mindset that cuts essential services to poor communities and sends them in a downward spiral can only backfire viciously as a dog-eat-dog culture that will undermine the emergence of cooperation when it is needed later. The invisible hand we establish is the invisible hand that nature and society will force on us as well. It's ridiculous for humanity to emulate functional strategies employed by life's bottom-dwellers, who could not build higher-level social structures even if they could manage to think of them, but that's exactly the mindset of mainstream economics. An expansive, compassionate, forgiving perspective sets the stage for a life based on grace, as distinguished from a narrow, legalistic, punitive, and self-protective mindset that parses through the laws and nature word by word. Religious zealots aligned with the social conservatism promulgated by neoclassical economists have plenty of opposing evidence from their own sources that should recommend a different track. And even aside from the utilitarian aspects of responding to corrective feedback, social justice is a matter of compassion to all of humanity, which can liberate human potential to enrich humanity's future in unforeseen ways.

Already we have seen that the problem-solving paradigm does not serve the process of evolution well when shortsighted interests dominate the trajectory of civilization to strip-mine human potential, the prospects of future generations, and even our planet's life-support system. Now we see, even in an adaptive setting (i.e., as restricted to present human interests) the paradigm is poorly suited to serving common interests.

There is a prime candidate for replacing the problem-solving paradigm, which has been the focus of the major religious traditions since early in human civilization: a perspective centered on establishing balance in society and the world. This philosophy played an important role in public health since its inception, when medicine was poorly equipped to understand infectious outbreaks, so clergy filled the vacuum in emerging health departments. It would seem a perfect antidote to the harm we do ourselves because of greed, carelessness, and ignorance. In light of the vast timescales and monumental implications of civilizational evolution, we would do well to admit we are ephemeral beings and take our own interests out of the picture as much as possible, even to whatever extent they seem aligned with a reasonable trajectory in our own times. As we will see, many lines of convergent thought are focusing in that direction at this pivotal time in human history.

The remaining history of public health development

The preceding account of enteric enteropathy presented a microcosm of the development of public health since John Snow's day. Susser and others [25-27] identified four waves of public health development, and Richard Horton and others [28-30] have advocated extension of the public health model to planetary health. However, based on the stages of the problem-solving paradigm, I have identified four more developmental waves that are not commonly considered in the realm of public health because they don't present as discrete problems that can be attacked under that paradigm, even though they have caused tremendous morbidity, mortality, and social costs: (1) wars, (2) perverse economic incentives, (3) societal dysfunction, and (4) systemic imbalances. As shown in the next table, public health

A-61

development has exhausted the potential of the problem-solving paradigm and is now stuck in an unsustainable adaptive rut, consistent with an interpretation that this system is poised at the cusp of transformation. I will discuss below why these developments have spilled into the successive stages of the problem-solving paradigm: its role-oriented structure (a) fosters pursuit of shortsighted selfish interests, (b) results in dynamic interactions that spin off new health hazards, and (c) casts the public health community, cleaning up the resulting mess by responding to corrective feedback, in the role of an enabler. These are conditions that promote evolution of virulence, consistent with the interpretation that humanity has become the most voracious species that has ever existed on earth. Ultimately, this analysis advances the premise that problem-solving cannot address systemic imbalances, so some other regime is required to escape the current adaptive rut and take the leap toward transformative change.

In stage 0 (niche), public health decisions were made only on the basis of the most obvious evidence, the senses: as cities without sanitation facilities grew, the huge accumulating cesspools stank, and so therefore they were the cause of disease!

In stage 1 (preconditions), the interventions from the previous stage, draining cesspools into drinking water, precipitated deadly cholera outbreaks, requiring breakthrough discoveries and disciplined laboratory investigation of infectious diseases. Construction of well-designed sanitary infrastructures made large cities sustainable.

In stage 2 (problems), large cities provided economies of scale that allowed mass production (a manmade invisible hand). The most-profitable industries, picking the low-hanging fruit, marketed addictive products, like cigarettes, to a customer base enslaved by chemical dependency and advertising. All other industries were forced, in a race to the bottom, to compete with harmful industries that were unaccountable for social costs they imposed, and therefore implicitly subsidized. The worst actors in the economy were the ones who reaped the largest rewards, while industries that generated real benefits were not compensated for their added value, so the bounty that could have been realized from multilevel organization slowly shriveled away after delays of several decades, as chronic diseases, lost productivity, and healthcare costs accumulated (biting the invisible hand that feeds us). Public health responded to the chronic disease epidemic with risk-factor epidemiology, crafted to investigate statistical associations between exposures and illness, while adjusting for confounding, under the assumption of individual-level multifactorial disease causation [31, 32].

In stage 3 (solutions), in the wake of World War II, especially during the hiatus before the peak of tobacco-related disease and costs, commerce spread globally, along with sedentary Western lifestyles and diseases, whose rapid jumps across international boundaries were enabled by jet travel. Computers had become powerful tools after intensive military development during the Second World War, the Cold War, the space race, integrated circuit evolution, and somewhat later, spatial mapping technologies. Biostatisticians and epidemiologists responded to the waves of pandemic infectious diseases by analyzing transmission in terms of compartmental flows, using SEIRS [33] and Markov chain [34-36] models.

In stage 4 (consequences), pervasive dynamic imbalances generated by human activity (including those from stages 5 [discovery] and 6 [knowledge] that were used to support the lower-level problem-solving activities) spilled over across multiple levels, spanning from the physiological (addiction, chronic disease, infection) to the individual (alienation, discrimination, violence) to the community (neighborhood blight, homelessness, infrastructure decay, gentrification and de facto exile, geographic funding inequities) to the national (compassion fatigue, culture clashes, political polarization, shock jock mass media) to the multinational (international environmental accords, rise of corporations, trade agreements). In that setting, multilevel "contextual" analysis, previously developed in educational settings for standardized test score evaluation, was adapted for epidemiological investigations. That new tool circumvented the ecological fallacy of one-level analysis at the population level and the related flaws of victim blame and infrastructure neglect of individual-level risk factor analysis. On the other hand, the almost entirely empirical nature of such analysis, combined with the turbulent cultural/political dynamics and lack of awareness of the underlying problem-solving structure, did not bode well for effective causal inference.

In step 5 (discovery), to some degree concurrently with the preceding events but at the population level of insight development, the century-old animosities stemming from the bitter aftermath of World War I, social Darwinism (reaching its peak in fascist totalitarianism, especially Nazism), state-sponsored terrorism (epitomized by Stalinist pogroms and the Holocaust), development of broadcast propaganda, and the devastation of all-out war (especially carpet-bombing of population centers, culminating in the atomic bombings of

Hiroshima and Nagasaki) led to efforts to ratchet down tensions, e.g., through the United Nations, the Marshall and MacArthur Plans for reconstructing war-torn Europe and Japan, and NATO. These efforts were informed by historical, not analytical, observations, and were not recognized as public health initiatives, in part because Stalin's heavy-handed takeover of Eastern Europe encouraged the resurgence of militarism and inspired a massive nuclear arms race in the Cold War. In an era where the public was drilled to "duck and cover" if an atomic bomb falls nearby, public health was not seen as a major theme!

In step 6 (knowledge), free enterprise, bolstered by wartime trade, rationalized by neoclassical economics, and seen as a bulwark against the excesses and flaws of communism, interacted with military technological innovations, postwar government expenditures on veteran benefits, and advertising to promote a culture of compulsive consumption to ward off economic boom-bust cycles. Corporations became extremely profitable and gained unprecedented power, effectively inserting themselves as a fourth branch of government, which, by virtue of far greater funding, eventually came to exert even more external influence on the executive, legislative, and judicial branches than these branches were designed to exert on each other without such de facto corruption. In this stage, perverse economic incentives combined with dysfunctional government to accentuate the imbalance between seeking reinforcing feedback (typically profits) and responding to corrective feedback (doing the right thing). Emboldened by these trends, extremist neoclassical economists advocated radical ideologies that quickly proved extremely destructive. [37, 38]

In step 7 (awareness, which has not yet emerged on a wide scale), polarizing politics began to make human institutions increasingly ungovernable, as the manifestations of corruption and government dysfunction prompted social conservatives to undermine the operation of government, in large part to solidify corporate influence over democratic institutions. The historical trajectory of culture clashes (e.g., the hippie movement and its antiwar, free love, and women's rights messages) drove religious conservatives into alliance with social conservatives. The availability of huge cash reserves offset the inherently chaotic and unappealing conservative message centered on wedge issues (with opposition to abortion being one of remarkably few that bear any convincing resemblance to a high moral ground) and corporate elitism, sponsoring a well-funded media industry prostituted to anti-government conspiracy propaganda, based on the ironic implicit assumption that businesses can govern better. The shotgun marriage between robber barons and Bible-thumpers, blessed by neoclassical economists (or is it a ménage à trois?), has led to a full retreat from generous, forgiving Christian ideals back to the Old Testament, with heavy discriminatory overtones, and has blinded believers to the revelations of our own age. Conservatives have argued (correctly) that the left has not worked out solutions to the problems its policies has raised, but here, too, difficulties of causal inference have surfaced, with hardly anyone offering convincing explanations. At this late stage in the process, the high-dimensional chaos of all past efforts to solve problems makes further solutions impossible without transformative change. We have passed a percolation threshold where the culture/society complex has become a kluge, and the system, perched at the cusp of evolutionary transition, can only manifest the effects of accumulated deleterious cultural mutations, sickness behavior (malaise that allows repair functions to work), and anticipation of those with a glimmer of awareness.

In stage 8 (dissonance), humanity's dysfunction threatens planetary health and accelerates our own evolution of virulence. The widening gap between rich and poor is evidence of hoarding behavior, which threatens to create a dog-eat-dog culture even as global systems collapse around us. It seems very unlikely that these are the End Times, given that those who proclaim loudest to be believers are utterly clueless about what is obviously happening, allying themselves with the forces that are driving God's creation off this cliff, distracting everyone with their own intolerances, and stupidly insisting that God would put everything right if we just removed all constraints on profit-making activity. The Word of God is supposed to instill wisdom for trying times like these, but the ever-widening schism between science and religion, coupled with longstanding theological denial that God would allow biological evolution to run creation, has driven the faithful to view the King James Bible as a substitute for reality, where neither the prophets nor the translators could have foreseen the processes that are emerging or the conceptual frameworks that might resolve the ubiquitous contradictions. So far, humanity is lucky, because we have been exploiting the earth to buffer our living standards, but in the process, we have initiated a mass extinction event, and although it is not as large as others evident in the fossil record, it has a shockingly sharp leading edge and is the only one precipitated by a single species. Our reliance on the adaptive tactics and scientific/technological prowess that have made us so comfortable is not reassuring either. No adaptation can hold together over indefinite timespans, and as the cohesive forces weaken, resistance to transformation intensifies the pent-up

A -67

tensions. We will eventually get this message one way or another, but if we wait until catastrophe strikes, we will have far less reserves, resilience, and goodwill with which to work through the transition.

The fact of the matter is that humanity is an evolutionary adolescent, exerting our newfound power in irresponsible ways verging on juvenile delinquency, but with great potential if we can recognize our purpose, manifest responsibility and discipline, and develop wisdom—on the level of the entire human population. It's not unreasonable to suggest this will happen if our actions lead to worldwide calamity and force us to reflect on the causes, but we also have the option of developing awareness, anticipating the hazards, and rising to the challenge.

The public health community has taken on that role for past crises, and some are already advocating that it step up again to this new opportunity. A key aspect will be to understand why the current structure of human culture and society are failing. To push this conversation along, I will continue to examine the roles played by key actors so far, then examine how biological evolution dealt with similar crises, and finally meditate on some theological implications.

Table 3. The problem-solving paradigm explains the sequential development of public health. Here I have identified 5 developmental waves that Susser and Susser omitted (shaded).

	stage	precipitating event	insight ("wave of development")	analytical paradigm	example	comments
0	niche	reliance on senses	miasma theory	"It stinks, therefore it's diseased." (WRONG!!!)	sewage	proven wrong
1	preconditions	population increases, inadequate sanitation → enteric diseases	infectious disease epidemiology	outbreak investigation, microbiology	cholera	
2	problems	economies of scale, perverse incentives, exploitation of addictions	risk factor epidemiology	multifactorial causation, adjustment for confounding	cigarettes	
3	solutions	globalization, "diseases of civilization"	epidemiological modeling	computer simulation	obesity, AIDS	
4	consequences	neglected imbalances → percolation across levels	contextual models (eco-epidemiology)	multilevel analysis	social dysfunction	little insight into causes
5	discovery	social Darwinism: exploitation, terrorism, propaganda	evolutionary processes	historical analysis	war	not appreciated as a public health issue
6	knowledge	neoclassical economics: imbalance of reinforcing feedback, problem-solving paradigm	purposive systems	kludges, feedback analysis	corporations as a 4th branch of government	inappropriately categorized as a political issue
7	awareness	polarizing politics: increasingly ungovernable	"sickness behavior" at an evolutionary threshold	percolation thresholds, trinitarian dynamics	Flint, MI water contamination	unrecognized
8	dissonance	evolutionary adolescence	planetary health	evolution of virulence	global warming, mass extinction	evolutionary rationale not well recognized

Appendix

Representative roles in the emergence of public health

An exercise in role playing for societal design specification

As I've discussed, the underlying design flaw of the problem-solving method is its overemphasis of roles and underemphasis of dynamic balances. Arrow's impossibility theorem [39, 40] proves that voters in a democratic society cannot translate their ranked preferences into consistent public policy priorities—there are too many people with too many different wish lists to map them onto a single agenda that is consistent with all of them.[5] Be that as it may, the roles and preferences of political, economic, and cultural constituencies have profoundly shaped history thus far, so we must understand them to recognize where we have been, in the interests of charting better paths for civilization. Looking forward, such insights into the past could help us reframe the inferred motivations of the various constituencies in terms of needs that any new system should meet, expressed as design specifications.

Traditional game theory models, such as the prisoner's dilemma (see below), are too simplistic even to explain current social interactions, much less to identify historical forces, account for sequences of past events, or suggest ways to resolve impasses. On the other hand, the problem-solving paradigm might offer promise for historical deconstruction and constructive

---

[5] Kenneth Arrow earned a Nobel Prize as a young man for that useful insight and its elegant proof, and even more to his great credit, has been spending the remainder of his illustrious career discovering constructive ways to convince the public of common interests, e.g., by demonstrating the enormous economic value of resources provided by the natural environment.

A-70

reinterpretation, rooted as it arguably is from first principles in all of the following:

1. human civilization's primary systematic approach to adaptation;

2. a. sequences of prerequisites that set up historical cascades,

or (considered more rigorously from the opposite perspective),

   b. the historical introduction of novel ideas that lead, in turn, to interacting dynamic processes, percolation thresholds, and ensuing event cascades;

and (as shown below)

3. its adaptive origin, the stimulus-response reaction

and

4. an equivalent evolutionary sequence that may have served the same purpose of design transmission in biological evolution through natural selection.

In this informal thought experiment, I will re-apply the problem-solving paradigm to a historical analysis of the evolution of public health, but now, in the spirit of game theory, considering sequential moves by five players who have influenced the dynamics of civilizational evolution over that time period:

- public health (responders to corrective feedback)
- corporations (responders to reinforcing feedback)
- governments (mediators of societal response)

- vulnerable populations (human potential likely to be sacrificed as a system fails)
- wealthy populations (players inclined to insulate themselves from system failure)

While this exercise may paint these constituencies with too broad a brush and (perhaps inevitably) generate a messy picture of historical sequences, it clearly tabulates a rich matrix of testable hypotheses and offers historians an opportunity to repeat the analysis with empirical data. Over the long timescales of civilizational evolution—where polling data reflects little more than transient noise, like asking unicellular organisms about philosophical aspects of life—this qualitative tool could help recognize deep-seated motivations and undercurrents. And on a personal level, I found this exercise exceedingly helpful in resolving longstanding impasses—clashes between corporate accountability and broader concerns of civilizational evolution—some of which I will discuss further.[2]

In the broadest of terms, here is how the five players I've identified would characteristically respond to challenges, structured in terms of steps in the problem-solving paradigm:

Table 4. How the problem-solving paradigm influences the actions of five players involved in the development of public health.

public health

stage		
0	niche	Review of historical experiences
1	preconditions	Analysis of underlying processes
2	problems	Surveillance, data analysis, and computer simulation
3	solutions	Public health interventions and infrastructure development
4	consequences	Community education and program review
5	discovery	Basic research
6	knowledge	Epidemiological science and the precautionary principle
7	awareness	Cultural sensitivity and interdisciplinary studies
8	dissonance	Overarching theological outlook beyond the limitations of science (e.g., compassion)

corporations

stage		
0	niche	New firms that squeeze out profits (perfect competition)
1	preconditions	Loss of sunk costs in winner-take-all situations (dollar auction game)
2	problems	Complexity as an obstacle to control (inventory control game)
3	solutions	Exploitation of vulnerable populations, safety nets and governments (free-riding and rent-seeking)
4	consequences	Adaptive rut that causes a race to the bottom (undermines what the invisible hand should provide)
5	discovery	Reliance on technological progress to escape the adaptive rut (research and development)
6	knowledge	Denial, minimization, and obfuscation of product risks (promotion of time discounting through ads and public relations)
7	awareness	Exertion of influence on government (lobbying, campaign contributions, legislative proxies, model laws)
8	dissonance	Polarizing politics, e.g., on talk radio, television, and Internet (increasingly shortsighted, nihilistic, cynical, defensive, and obstructive)

governments

stage		
0	niche	Accountable to electorate, in principle for common interests
1	preconditions	Subject to fickle voters and corporate power
2	problems	Vexing dilemmas arising from too much power and not enough wisdom
3	solutions	Shortsighted efforts and obstructive delays on behalf of unenlightened interests
4	consequences	Clashing, ineffectual, self-defeating, backfiring policies
5	discovery	Recognition of unintended consequences
6	knowledge	Recognition of increasingly rancorous political environment
7	awareness	Acknowledgement of systemic failure
8	dissonance	Intensifying ungovernability

vulnerable populations

	stage	
0	niche	History of discrimination, e.g., slavery
1	preconditions	Desire to fulfill potential
2	problems	Difficulty recruiting help and resources
3	solutions	Hand-to-mouth existence
4	consequences	Poverty trap passed across generations
5	discovery	Education and mutual support as potential escapes
6	knowledge	Insights into frugality and resourcefulness
7	awareness	Pride in heritage and/or capacity to overcome obstacles
8	dissonance	Potential to have the greatest insight into the human condition

wealthy populations

	stage	
0	niche	History of privilege
1	preconditions	Desire to protect position
2	problems	Resistance to limitations of their own freedom
3	solutions	Investments that maintain personal and family wealth
4	consequences	Dynasties, which may lose initiative from generation to generation
5	discovery	Opportunity to invest in humanity's future
6	knowledge	Access to education, information, and resources
7	awareness	Double-edged sword
8	dissonance	May have blinders to the realities of life

The following table presents my impression of how each agent's response to challenges might have unfolded during the historical sequence previously presented for the waves of public health development. In this table, grayed-out cells represent ongoing processes. This exercise corroborates some of the same causal interpretations as before. There's no way to tell whether that concordance simply reflects that both interpretations came from my own impressions, but certainly more systematic and objective methods suitable for hypothesis-testing could be developed.

Table 5. Characteristic responses of the remaining 4 players. Grayed processes are ongoing.

	historical sequence of events	humanity's developmental stage + example	corporations	governments	vulnerable populations	wealthy populations
0	rural migration →	niche e.g.: "stink"	concentration in cities	nominal concern for the plight of the poor	cholera terror	flight from epidemic areas
1	population increases, inadequate sanitation →	preconditions e.g.: cholera	economies of scale	sewers, safe water, health departments, surveillance	passive protection	burgeoning success of commercial entrepreneurs
2	perverse economic incentives →	problems e.g.: cigarettes	exploitation of addictions	bribed by corporate contributions into shirking duties	poor living conditions, addiction as self-medication	investment in global enterprises
3	globalization → "diseases of civilization" →	[misguided] solutions e.g.: obesity	expansion, outsourcing	trade agreements	redistribution of opportunities	increasing gap between rich and poor
4	neglected imbalances → percolation across levels	[unintended] consequences e.g.: social dysfunction	shortsighted policies characteristic of an adaptive rut	escalating dilemmas	homelessness, unemployment, etc.	increasing defensiveness
5	social Darwinism → exploitation, terrorism, propaganda	[opportunity for] discovery e.g.: war	expansion of weapons industry	misuse of military power; neglect of domestic priorities	increasing marginalization in the face of competing agendas	increasing indifference to the plight of the poor
6	neoclassical economics → unbalanced reinforcing feedback	[opportunity for] knowledge e.g.: corporate influence on government	superficial perspective that exerts disproportionate influence	pandering to diverse forms of corruption	diversion of national priorities and distortion of employment opportunities	alteration of investment opportunities away from the common good
7	polarizing politics → increasingly ungovernable	[opportunity for] awareness e.g.: lead contamination	public relations to deflect awareness of issues contrary to corporate interests	focus on distracting wedge issues even in the face of profound policy errors	disempowerment by misguided policies	self-isolation from misguided policies
8	evolutionary adolescence	dissonance e.g., global warming; extinction event	misalignment with the meaning of human existence	extreme time discounting; no awareness of civilizational evolution	little voice in humanity's future	distorted perceptions of reality

Four existential threats to civilizational evolution, framed in terms of problem-solving

Is it any wonder we witness the impacts of impasse among us—anger, confusion, violence—since real impasse or dark night highlights destructive tendencies? Frustrated desire fights back.

– Constance Fitzgerald, quoted by Margaret Swedish in Living beyond the "End of the world": a spirituality of hope (p. 173)

Each time a man stands up for an ideal, or acts to improve the lot of others, or strikes out against injustice, he sends forth a tiny ripple of hope, and crossing each other from a million different centers of energy and daring those ripples build a current which can sweep down the mightiest walls of oppression and resistance.

– Robert F. Kennedy, Ripples of Hope, South Africa June 6, 1966

The evolutionary transition humanity faces amounts to a leap in cooperation from a unicellular to a multicellular design. The invisible hand that acts through that transition must revise the rules of society to favor coalescence over autonomy. Corporations and the public health community have already made that transition within their own local spheres of influence, so this is not such a foreign concept. However, capitalism is still structured like a design for unicellular life—businesses are on their own, and most fail after a very short period.

Laying out responses to the problem-solving paradigm in the preceding table, especially if derived from some firm basis in fact, could, in principle, establish specifications for the invisible hand that a society is creating as it builds higher-level structures. In biological evolution, the emergence of multicellularity passed a point where cells first could no longer thrive, and then no

A-76

longer live, by themselves. After that point, the higher-level structures that sustained them could no longer renege on the (fairly explicit) covenant to meet their needs. Any complete interruption in that agreement would mean extinction for that particular species and collapse of its participation in the evolutionary trajectory to advance the design of multicellularity.

Thus, even though the problem-solving paradigm is a poor way for a civilization to guide its actions, it is a powerful framework for specifying the design parameters as it evolves. A design path that takes these response characteristics into account might, in some sense, circumvent the limitations of Arrow's impossibility theorem. In 1651, Thomas Hobbes described the social contract in terms of how a population surrenders the right to harm other citizens in exchange for the privilege of living in a civil society. Why can't an evolving civilization establish a similar social contract that surrenders a flawed design to attain stable operation and evolutionary potential? A key aspect of the redesigned system, analogous to civil society, would be to address the needs of its citizens in exchange for fundamental enhancement of internal cooperation. We currently think in terms of a quid pro quo, like a business contract, "I'll cooperate better if you meet my needs," but that's the way unicellular organisms operate; the emergence of multicellularity in biological evolution required a far greater commitment to the wellbeing of the whole system.

I don't pretend to know how society should look; in fact, I think its appearance will always keep changing in response to changing pressures, even though it should remain a vehicle for expressing timeless values. In fact, a good warning sign that

A -77

we're not on the right track is that we're not living the ideals that most people would wish we could.

However, it's not quite so hard figuring out where we *shouldn't* be. I have identified four aspects of modern existence that are inconsistent with where civilization needs to evolve, structured, as before, in terms of the problem-solving paradigm.

1. Preconditions: escalation of hatred following isolated terrorist attacks.

World War I started as a chain reaction from the assassination of the Archduke Franz Ferdinand and his wife Sophie in Sarajevo on June 28, 1914 by a Serbian terrorist aggrieved at discrimination by the Austro-Hungarian Empire. Over the next three-quarters of a century, those two simultaneous murders had been amplified into two World Wars and a nuclear standoff, manifesting as state-sponsored killing of hundreds of millions of people. That single episode triggered societal forces, analogous to biological mechanisms of programmed cell death (apoptosis) and autoimmunity, via reinforcing feedback through the turbulent dynamic system that extended from the level of our primitive limbic systems to the global cultural/societal echo chamber. The mediating forces were insensitive, asymmetrical exploitation that fomented lingering resentment; outrageous terroristic attacks calculated to elicit disproportionate response to precipitate large-scale confrontation; propagandistic saber rattling to recruit public support and soldiers to throw into the fray; the horrors of industrial warfare that created an epidemic of shell shock, nationalistic resentment, and lust for revenge; and application of advancing technology to devise and mass-produce weapons of ever-greater destructive power.

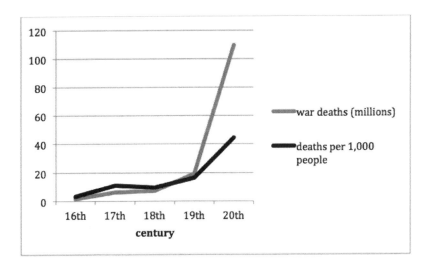

Figure 3. War-related deaths, 1500 - 1999. Plotted from [44], table 14.6.

This kind of amplification is profoundly destabilizing to human civilization. Human memory can echo these vendettas across generations for millennia; resentment still exists in the Middle East about the Crusades. It's not that we should be necessarily passive in the face of outrageous acts; instead, without escalating the cycle of violence, we should try to protect those who are brutally victimized by egregious exploitation and genocidal onslaughts. However, an even more appropriate response might be to ask what we did that precipitated such an attack in the first place. Awareness of percolation processes might make us attuned to situations where our actions appear to be, or perhaps actually are, exploitative but we receive no feedback to inform us of our transgression.

The bottom line, and the real danger signal, is that after having endured such horrible carnage during the 20th century, we are reacting to terrorist attacks in precisely the same way! God was trying to tell us something during a period when we subjected civilization to intense trauma and almost pulled the nuclear trigger of self-annihilation, but we still don't get it.

Part of the problem is that we rely too much on formalized models of human behavior that have fixed payoffs, most notably the prisoner's dilemma. The prisoner's dilemma is a two-agent game played repeatedly during an extended session lasting many turns, each time with a fixed payoff matrix. At the end, both agents receive the sum total of their winnings over the entire session. The game has a payoff matrix on every turn that looks something like this, as a function of whether the players cooperate or defect, where I have reformulated the narrative to consider motivations like emerging compassion or escalating hatred—which we might also consider in terms of evolution of altruism or of virulence in adaptive or evolutionary settings.

Table 6. A passive model of human motivation: the prisoner's dilemma

		Player A	
		COOPERATE	DEFECT
Player B	COOPERATE	MUTUAL COOPERATION BOTH: MODEST REWARD Living in harmony earns its rewards and encourages trust for cooperation in future turns ...	DEFECTOR : HIGH REWARD COOPERATOR: MODEST LOSS ... but I eat better during this turn if I take your lunch in addition to mine ...
	DEFECT	DEFECTOR: HIGH REWARD COOPERATOR: MODEST LOSS ... but I eat better during this turn if I take your lunch in addition to mine ...	MUTUAL DEFECTION BOTH: LARGE LOSS ... but fighting for each other's lunches imposes far greater costs and invokes tit-for-tat responses in future turns that reduce cumulative earnings.

It's really not possible to simulate the emotions of escalating hatred in a sterile game like this, especially one that is played by computer circuits or college freshmen. But imagine a real-life

A-80

situation where two antagonists have their problem-solving apparatuses in close proximity, and the strong one is pushing its problems onto the weak one and sucking up its solutions, further weakening its neighbor and causing significant resentment.

Now imagine the dialog proceeds from there as follows:

STRONG ANTAGONIST: "I'll eat my lunch and yours, too!"

STRONG (burping, but not a full meal's worth): "Your lunch wasn't good enough, so I'm gonna eat you also!"

WEAK ANTAGONIST: "No, you won't!! You've stopped the flow in my life force long enough—now I'll retaliate in a way you'll never forget!"

STRONG (completely oblivious that the weak antagonist was a person in the first place, and not willing to accept him as one now after that outrageously violent act!): "How could you consider doing that to me when all I was doing was having lunch! I am going to annihilate you for that!!"

At that point they are both at each other's throats, diverting industries, resources, manpower, and innovation from the business of living to that of draining life from their neighbor. Each act of violence elicits more vengeance and renewed compulsion to divert even more energy to killing the adversary. That diversion of energy away from the problem-solving apparatus and into warfare reduced the life forces flowing through to a trickle—intensely motivating the other to strangle it off completely. There is no more listening on either side, except internally to messages intended to whip up even more hatred and recruit more naïve volunteers to carry out the dirty business of warfare. All too many return with shattered bodies and tortured minds, escalating the desire for revenge. Grandchildren see the horrible scars and hear the horrible tales, and pass on the posttraumatic stress disorder like genes. Of course, what is transmitted culturally and socially across generations are memes, either as specific ideas (e.g., self-defeating attitudes), general worldviews (e.g., through disempowering childrearing practices and educational experiences), and/or social inertia persisting from higher-level stressors (e.g., lingering effects of disease or famine on future generations). Years later, when some faraway event sounds even remotely like any of the stories that had been told, the grandchildren's grandchildren's grandchildren are clamoring for their government to extract retribution for their ancestors' wounds. Constant reminders of those ancient transgressions set up a robust, highly profitable arms industry, which has vested interests in fanning the flames to keep up its own revenue stream. It recruits ancillary industries, like mass media, to keep the resentments fresh and raw, and stoke them up from time to time when it needs additional revenue. Those industries cannot shift easily to making other products, and will not tolerate shutting down, so they create tremendous pressure for the government to keep funneling public funds into weaponry.

Obviously, this dialog is a cartoon, but it's a better characterization of reality than the prisoner's dilemma!

Equally obviously, this behavior is very detrimental to a system trying to coalesce around a paradigm of cooperation. It's not clear how to interrupt the cycle, but just realizing it has to end is a start.

The recent history of terrorist attacks, kidnappings, invasions, and genocides by Al Qaeda, ISIL, and Boko Haram may shed further light on this situation. The issues involved are too complex to discuss here: for example, different rates of technological development, different cultural and moral reactions to the side effects of contemporary society, deep-seated historical resentments, longstanding refugee crises, localized Malthusian collapses, pockets of radicalization, factional strife and/or civil war—the list keeps going on and on. However, as the example of the 20th century shows, the bottom line is that the military threat of localized terrorist attacks is far less than the consequences of escalating war. Compared to previous eras in world history when huge superpowers slugged it out in all-out industrialized warfare, terrorist attacks do not present existential threats to humankind—contrary to the claims of those whose militaristic knee-jerk reactions actually would immolate the world in systemic conflicts.

This is true even if terrorist organizations acquire weapons of mass destruction, because defensive reaction should target the specific sources of threats and not drag uninvolved subpopulations into the conflict. Terrorists have an intrinsically unpopular message—convincing struggling populations to expend scarce resources on protracted, perhaps even all-out, guerilla war of attrition against a powerful enemy—unless we provide them the tool of escalating anger.

We have seen how influxes of military equipment into developing countries gives radical militias both the means and the incentives to assert selfish interests, often kidnapping their own population and hijacking its future. Lacking political persuasiveness, terrorists use outrageous pinpoint attacks to

A-83

elicit retaliatory reactions for psychological leverage to radicalize the populations they have enslaved at home. Thus, branding entire countries or even a whole religion with the transgressions of radical pockets plays right into the hands of the terrorists. Given how state-sponsored violence amplified and spread during the 20th century, it's utterly insane that we can't recognize how this is happening again!

Thus it's extremely distressing that focal attacks by isolated, deranged terrorists prod our sleepwalking civilization first to trigger an indignant systemic defense of its values and then to rationalize disproportionate military retaliation on whole regional populations, most of whom initially wanted nothing to do with radicalism and a protracted guerrilla war of attrition. When we finally accept that the Western way of life is deeply flawed (although not in ways that terrorists have articulated or can understand), we might recognize that _all_ the tensions in the human condition are canaries in the mine—warning us that the (mal)adaptive echo chamber of technologically advanced countries is draining the life out of human culture, society, and civilization; the biosphere; and the future of life on earth. Fundamentalists are hijacking Western Christianity as well as Middle Eastern Islam, and the bottom line is that this cultural clash just amounts to more of the same extremely dangerous and destructive sleepwalking behavior. We are most destructive, as children playing with flamethrowers, when we deliberately turn that weaponry against each other.

We must keep in mind that the dynamics of hatred have strong irreversible components. It's vital to realize that the longer we let our reptilian limbic systems set our agendas (e.g., with labels like "radical Islam" and comparable terms on the other side of the conflict), the more we risk passing a point of no return. World War I was avoidable, but once Hitler was in power, his venom made World War II inevitable. Enmity has not progressed to that point yet, but Western politicians and terrorists throughout the world have been at each other's throats for so long that we are no longer naïve populations just starting this process. As a result, we must do additional work to ratchet down the prevailing tensions.

Obviously, I am not offering an apology for terrorism. Instead of letting terrorist atrocities trigger widening war, this perspective should promote widening the international cooperation needed for criminal prosecution of violent perpetrators. In sharp contrast to intensive military retaliation, international accords that learn from historical experiences would allow authorities to pursue perpetrators to the ends of the earth. Whenever practical, this framework should mobilize the international community to mount missions to protect and save victims of terrorist aggression. Thus this framework is consistent with peaceful coexistence, mutual acceptance, good will, respect for differences, and coordinated protection against internal and external attack.

2. Problems: corporate invasion of government

Here is another aspect of societal dysfunction, showing how our lack of awareness has caused us to create a dysfunctional society—corporations have invaded the democratic process by essentially inserting themselves as a fourth branch of government:

Appendix

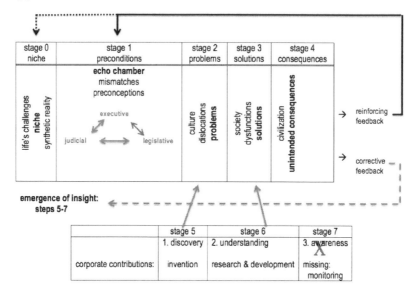

Figure 4.

The structure of American society, with government configured as intended by the U.S. Constitution.

The original design of American government was a remarkably stable structure, but corporations have come to dominate it by virtue of having more money than any of the original branches:

Figure 5.

Invasion of every branch of government by corporations, which thereby effectively become a fourth branch.

A-86

The whole social structure is intractably complex:

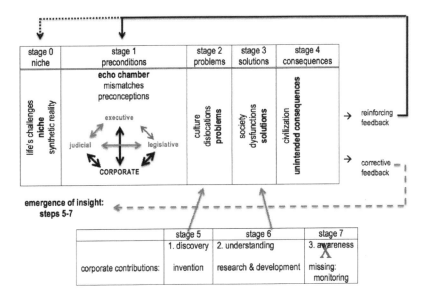

Figure 6.

The structure of American society with corporations having effectively inserted themselves into government as a fourth branch. It's significant that this invasion occurred in stage 1 (preconditions), the "societal echo chamber," where causal influences are especially difficult to discern.

3. Solutions: The seductive illusion of gambling

Strictly speaking, there can be no gambling "industry," because that "commercial enterprise" simply shifts money around—from the poorest, who are so desperate they would make the worst possible investments, to the richest, who are so corrupt they would ensnare the poor in their mutual cycle of greed—without ever producing anything of value. As a result, gambling enterprises could not make a profit if held accountable for the enormous social costs they impose in wasted time, misplaced priorities, lost human potential, blighted lives and communities,

A -87

broken families, suicides, embezzlement and other white collar crimes, security breaches (e.g., by military personnel who sell secrets to pay for gambling losses), dysfunction transmitted in every dimension and level, and a pervasive and persistent corrupting influence. Even when the gambler temporarily "wins," how can that be considered "earnings"? Even if skill were somehow involved, every winner in a negative sum game is offset by a sucker who loses—and a cut to the creep who ran the game. What's worse is that the social disease of gambling has metastasized to government as lotteries, holding out hopes of winning hundreds of millions of dollars to someone who trusts their "good luck" with precisely as much sense as someone betting on the "bad luck" of a perfectly good parachute not opening. Far from being some lucky individual's ticket out of poverty into sudden wealth, that sick surrogate of "hope" should be seen for what it really is—a public health problem.

Everybody realizes that predatory lending creates poverty traps in the adaptive realm, but most people think of gambling as a fairly innocuous voluntary activity, which Thomas Jefferson extolled as a "voluntary tax" (he wanted to raffle off some of his own estate in a lottery to get out of debt.) What makes gambling so poisonous in the evolutionary realm is that it subverts motivations, substituting seductive illusions of "good luck" as a "get-rich-quick" engine, when, in fact, Samuelson and Norhaus's classic economic textbook [43] clearly indicts gambling as a counterproductive activity. In a much broader context, as I've indicated, the mindset of gambling is an existential threat to civilizational evolution, even more than payday lenders and pawn shops are a blight on the cultural and social fabric of communities. In other words, predatory lending is a drain in the here and now, but gambling establishes a constellation of mindset pathologies that obstruct the development of insight, responsibility, and discipline that are necessary for establishing cohesion, communication, and cooperation that can catalyze transformative evolution.

The reality the gambling enterprise doesn't want its clientele to see is the statistical certainty called "gambler's ruin": if an agent plays endless fair wagers against an infinite bank, the bank will outlast the agent, who will thereby go bankrupt, almost surely. The situation is yet further biased in commercial gambling by an additional take that amounts to a rigged game in favor of the house.

By contrast, if the agent invests the same money frugally at compound interest, the ultimate payoff will be substantial, likely amounting to millions of dollars. The downside is that the agent has to wait, but as shown by the large fraction of lottery winners who soon squander their winnings and go bankrupt, the delay allows adjustment to the change in fortune.

Gambling is another commercial enterprise that derives a significant fraction of its revenues from consumers enslaved by addiction, in this case by pathological and problem gamblers. Even acknowledging that making a profit is difficult under the current impasse, we can still express exasperation that this economic sector essentially is perpetuating the institution of slavery in a sanitized form. The whips, plantations, foremen, and lynchings are gone, but new laws, social structures, and technologies hold people in bondage just as surely, with the obscene side effect that gambling magnates can hypocritically claim that they are providing an "entertainment service." To run such a business means abandoning any interest in customers'

A -89

interests, other than keeping them comfortable, fed, and drunk so they are temporarily oblivious to the fact that they are losing money to the house. The institution of gambling is a microcosm of sleepwalking on both sides of the transaction—the marching chant for a zombie mentality of greed, shortsightedness, exploitation, indifference, innumeracy, and ignorance.

Nothing entraps the vulnerable like gambling. It is not a voluntary tax; it is a deliberate exploitation of vulnerability. In some ways, it is worse than bureaucrats poisoning community drinking water, since it enlists the victims in the duplicity, and thereby "launders" the transaction. Gambling is a social design with an invisible hand that, far from delivering bounty, makes the gambler bite every other hand that feeds him/her.

Nothing would serve the cause of the poor better than to boycott all gambling. That is the Boston Tea Party they should mount against oppression, to articulate their Declaration of Independence. Anyone else who fails to help in the boycott, say, because they want to sustain an "entertainment industry" they have enjoyed, should feel deep shame for continuing to support this modern-day slavery. As we begin to develop an evolutionary perspective, we must realize that our actions and support, however seemingly mundane and acceptable in our adaptive present, will shackle the potential of future generations for an entire segment of the population.

Gambling has come in waves in America; we are currently in the sixth one. Each time the cycle ends with public exposure and widespread recognition of the corrupting and destructive influence of an intrinsically counterproductive and uncaring way of life. As humanity approaches a transition where a new perspective of balance must prevail over selfishness, the segments of society that have hosted this parasite must administer their own antibiotic to eradicate it once and for all.

4. Consequences: pervasive, deep-seated dynamic imbalances

The eight-ton elephant in the room is that the global economy, as currently structured, is not just unsustainable, it is hyperexponentially destabilizing itself. Thomas Malthus's predictions of endless gloom seem to have been trumped by endless technological advances, triumphantly permitting the economist's holy grail: endless economic growth. Everything is growing at once: scientific discovery, technological innovation, investment, revenues—what could be better?

However, we must remember that humanity's experience in the scientific era is a mere blink in evolutionary time. It's bad enough that the unintended consequences of economic activity impose such staggering social costs that when we factor them in, the gross domestic product has actually been declining since the 1960s. However, what's most disturbing is that we have found ways to sweep dysfunction out of sight—to seemingly distant ecosystems, to unneeded species that won't be missed when they're soon gone, to populations without the power to complain, to pollution that might not be noticed—without realizing that a combinatorial explosion of steep exponential and hyperexponential growth curves, amplifying each other through multiplicative interactions, is the evolutionary equivalent of a violent explosion. Although the exploding consequence of human activity is unfolding slowly by comparison to our perceptual timescales, it contains vast amounts of matter and energy, and is storing more coiled energy than humanity has ever encountered.

There are no brakes to this train, so we are committed to either the biggest derailment ever or development of a fundamentally new way of transportation. This instability is the most important issue we face approaching the upcoming evolutionary transition.

What this tells me is that we as an entire civilization and species have to earn the right to thrive. Of particular concern is the power a robust economy has, which projects well into the future for human society, ecosystems at all levels, and toward the biosphere as a whole. We want to control our own fate, but we also create the invisible hand that the entire earth experiences, so we must take responsibility for its consequences. If any other species were behaving towards us as we do to all of life now existent and the future of life on earth, we would consider it the most virulent emerging pathogen that has ever existed, and would do everything in our power to eradicate it. We need to extend the Golden Rule to all of life, get our balances in order, and reject the notion of redesigning anything outside our own sphere of direct involvement, so the earth doesn't mount an immune response against us.

Biological origins of the problem-solving paradigm

The logic of domination, violence, reward and punishment that prevails in the everyday world is challenged and replaced by a new logic, the logic of grace, compassion and freedom.

– Peter Hodgson, quoted in Diamuid O'Murchu's Christianity's dangerous memory: a rediscovery of the revolutionary Jesus (p.5)

A-92

1. Adaptive origins: the stimulus-response reaction

As an adaptive process, the problem-solving paradigm derives from the biological stimulus-response reaction, which humans also exhibit individually at lower levels of consciousness or upon reverting to basic instincts. That instinctual response is built around behavioral reinforcement, where positive reinforcement is associated with stimulus-seeking responses (analogous to what I have termed reinforcing feedback) and negative reinforcement is associated with stimulus-avoiding responses (analogous to corrective feedback in my terminology).

Stated more directly and less clinically to emphasize its significance, this basic instinctual reaction is what creates the motivations both to seek pleasurable stimuli and avoid noxious ones. Thus, the unexamined antecedent of the problem-solving paradigm is that it steers our behavior based on our appetites. We have already identified that as a significant design flaw, but tracing the biological origins of this instinct and its precursors shed considerable light both on the human predicament and possible ways out of it, as shown below.

On top of that basic instinct, we have also superimposed all the trappings of civilization that stem from cumulative culture, including a second run through the stimulus-response reaction at the population level (the insight-development phase). This additional go-around adds two more steps that are uniquely associated with the greater depths of human thought and emotion—awareness and dissonance. The other steps are systematized and formalized at the population level through culture and social structures, reflecting our capacities to analyze situations and communicate our impressions:

A -93

1. perceptions → preconditions

2. stimulus → problems

3. response → solutions

4. reinforcement schedule → consequences

5. learning and imitation → discovery

6. group culture → knowledge

That is as far as nonhuman organisms take adaptive responses, even at within their own social communities, but as indicated above, the two final stages in human problem-solving are not evident in other animals:

7. awareness

8. dissonance

So far, the analogy between the stimulus-response reaction and the problem-solving paradigm only applies at the level of individual organisms. In other words, a direct comparison only goes as far as addressing how the human cultural framework and social structures socialize a person from childhood throughout life. In fact, the stimulus-response reaction was not designed to direct population-level response.

As we've seen, a serious flaw in the problem-solving paradigm is the assumption that no interactions occur. The stimulus-response reaction is limited enough in its scope that such interactions are unlikely. By running the stimulus-response reaction on steroids, the problem-solving paradigm has pumped up levels of harmful interactions that were not designed to be addressed by animal appetites.

A-94

So the bottom line is that human civilization has harnessed an animal instinct that is centered on seeking reinforcement or retreating from pain to shape our world, systematize our interpretation and reaction to it, communicate and coordinate our findings among ourselves, design an entire way of life, create powerful weapons and other technologies, and stumble through history as we have applied it to our own narrow-minded, shortsighted benefit along the way! All these things have separated us from the natural world and wrapped us in a synthetic reality that profoundly distorts our view of life. The trappings of science and technology that we have added to this instinct have provided us the tools for strip-mining our own society, our environment, our planet and all life on it, the prospects of future generations, and the future of life on earth. That is the fundamental design flaw that makes our culture/society complex function like a kluge and steers our civilization in overtly dangerous directions. Though we now have weapons of mass destruction, we are still letting animal instincts steer our responses, which were designed for use only with the power of teeth and claws!

What's far more significant is that human civilization also provides the impetus for considering these responses at the population level, and now even up to the level of our entire species. From that standpoint, niche does not enter into the stimulus-response reaction for organisms, while the problem-solving paradigm has become humanity's main interface with the world and the primary vehicle for niche construction. Now that the consequences of our paradigmatic extension of that instinctual reaction are apparent, we are forced into analyzing the design flaws stemming from our use of it.

A -95

2. The path from natural selection to cooperative biological networks

> *Beyond the culture of owing, depending and giving back, there is a gift economy. This is a cycle of giving and taking where all creatures share the fruits of the natural world.*
>
> *– Darcia Narvaez, Neurobiology and the development of human morality: Evolution, culture and wisdom*

As it turns out, biological evolution has been driven by a sequence of steps similar to the problem-solving paradigm, but with a few twists that have profoundly confused their interpretation since Charles Darwin first articulated the idea. Before we look at the actual stepwise sequence for biological evolution, it will be instructive to examine the cultural response—both stubborn resistance and misguided acceptance—that got in the way of putting the pieces together into a meaningful picture.

Confusion about the nature of evolution

The most obvious thing about biological evolution is one of the prominent early steps in the sequence, natural selection—survival of the fittest—which, to refined human sensibilities, seems harsh, brutish, and murderous; discriminatory, racist, and genocidal; disorderly, unthinking, and unmanageable. From the very start, it was difficult for those with religious backgrounds to accept that a personal God would run the universe on such principles. How could believers be persuaded to pray to a God like that? The knee-jerk reaction was to dismiss the scientific evidence, or deny that such evidence existed, and retreat into the Bible as the only valid source of all knowledge. Denial of evolution and other similar scientific descriptions then became a litmus test for true believers.

That idea of natural selection had an opposite but equally polarizing effect on scientists. They answered the question about praying to God the opposite way: evolution was evidence that a personal God did not exist. Scientists interpreted Darwinian evolution to be the nail in the coffin of religion, essentially a mathematical proof of an atheistic universe.

The application of survival of the fittest as a principle in human society had a far more corrosive and insidious effect. Bigots of every stripe had to look no further than the subtitle of Darwin's book, *On the origin of species by means of natural selection, or the preservation of favoured races in the struggle for life*, to find support for a panoply of elitist, extremist, eugenicist, imperialist, fascist, totalitarian, and even genocidal views. The tremendous acclaim and controversy the book received egged on both scholars and kooks to think they were really onto something. The combination of Darwin's premise of survival of the fittest and Malthus's premise of population pressures leading to episodic catastrophe was given the name "social Darwinism" (over the objections of Darwin himself), and interpreted as giving license for those in power to purge humanity of what they deemed to be "genetic weakness." The wide variety of methods used to enforce those policies, from involuntary sterilization to gas chambers, cut a wide swath through human history, giving plenty of ammunition to critics to argue on religious grounds that the very idea of evolution was sheer, unadulterated evil.

The idea of survival of the fittest was also applied in the economic sphere with less brutal but equally uncompassionate enthusiasm. Earlier, Adam Smith's *The theory of moral sentiments* (1759) presented a communitarian perspective of society, while *The wealth of nations* painted a view of economics that leaned strongly toward laissez-faire policies. The bloodthirsty excesses of the French Revolution, the angry rhetoric of Karl Marx, and social Darwinism generated a strong pendulum swing away from communitarianism, which was further reinforced when Marxism was implemented with such brutality as communism in the Soviet Union. Some neoclassical economists have basically interpreted these ideas something like a mathematical proof that compassion is incompatible with a properly functioning economic system.

In a very profound sense, the stumbling course that humanity followed with the concept of biological evolution was itself part of the evolution of human culture—the sleepwalking phase of exploring dead ends and drawing a complete and total blank. Part of the controversy can be resolved by recognizing that biological and civilizational evolution are different manifestations of a general class of evolutionary processes. Recently, evolutionary theorists have shed considerable light on the process of biological evolution and compared it to civilizational evolution (more commonly called "cultural evolution"). The stumbling block, even since Darwin's time, is the question of how bickering protoplasm can put aside entrenched self-interests to exhibit the profound internal cooperation that is the most obvious manifestation of our own bodies, which ultimately provided an evolutionary platform for the development of thought, culture, society, and civilization. The key focus for this inquiry has been the evolution of altruism, which is a far more difficult concept than the evolution of virulence because it works in the opposite direction of known biological principles. The prisoner's dilemma shows that, in a "flat" society (loosely speaking, one with no "invisible hand" at higher levels) defectors attain greater rewards and thus drive out cooperators.

The emergence of invisible hands within biological designs

Biological evolution from prokaryotes to eukaryotes exemplifies the gradual transition from "flat," internally unsupportive, single-level designs to rich, internally cooperative redesigns characterized by a complex, multilevel scaffolding of mutually supportive "invisible hands." Eukaryotes span a wide range of organisms from fungi to plants to animals, including humans. They can be unicellular (like yeasts), but most have evolved into obligate multicellular species, whose cells cannot survive independently. As we can appreciate by observing the wide variety of multicellular organisms around us, the intrinsic structure of eukaryotes promotes a wide range of functional capabilities—in the case of humans, serving as a platform for the evolution of thought and complex societies. By contrast, bacteria are intrinsically unicellular, at most only capable of assembling into loose colonies.

The design capabilities of bacteria and eukaryotes are determined by internal structures. Bacteria have a single cell membrane that separates their internal components from the outside world, while eukaryotes are defined as having internal membranes as well, surrounding the nucleus (with genetic material) and various organelles (performing specialized metabolic activities). By separating its critical internal cellular reactions, the design of eukaryotes has achieved "constructive complexification" that reduces internal "echo chamber" effects

A -99

and allows its subsystems to support each other much better. These mutually supportive networks act like invisible hands to each other, and natural selection pressures have installed defensive safeguards against their internal exploitation and degradation.

Bacteria are spectacularly successful species, comprising by far the largest numbers and biomass of organisms on earth. However, because their essential design feature precludes widespread and extensive cooperation, it intrinsically limits their capabilities to one basic function: catabolism, or breakdown of organic material. When an organism dies, especially one with rich structure like a eukaryote, bacteria proliferate to decompose it—and if an organism is unhealthy, they may not wait to begin their dirty work.

Mathematical games that neoclassical economists use to model societal operation, like the prisoner's dilemma, share this intrinsic design limitation with bacteria. The fundamental irony and irreducible contradiction of neoclassical economics is that it postulates that such designs, predicated on the assumption that society operates as an aggregate of selfish individuals, can achieve the ultimate goal they set for economic systems: to grow constructive social structures that address common interests.

As we see now, that flat social design structure explains perfectly why humanity actually has instead been doing the exact opposite: acting like a parasite, breaking down the natural networks in which we are embedded and even cannibalizing our own societal infrastructures! As the density of dynamic interactions has long since crossed a percolation threshold, the paradigm of neoclassical economics cannot handle the drastically altered operating parameters. As that klugey economic framework tries to muddle on through the pervasive incompetence of its fundamental design limitations, its own misguided overconfidence in its capabilities has become yet another of its intensely toxic influences!

Biological evolution dealt with these dilemmas in the emergence of eukaryotic cellular design, which led to viability of multicellular organisms, which created a body plan capable of supporting neurological development, which established a platform for emergence of awareness, which encouraged sentient beings to aggregate into mutually supportive communities, which provided the impetus for problem-solving and insight development, which made *Homo sapiens* the most successful species that has ever lived on earth. This long series of anabolic-like processes, which built up complex structures, has required setting up layers of invisible hands and protecting them from breakdown. It's remarkable how seemingly esoteric internal structural changes at the microscopic level were able to propagate under natural selection pressures to produce profound enhancements in design flexibility, functional capabilities, and evolutionary responsiveness. Bacteria could not proceed down this path toward development of robust and capable higher-level structure—and neoclassical economics, the prisoner's dilemma, and our current adaptive economy cannot follow it now—because there were/are no incentives, hooks, or ratchets to sustain and preserve them against regression, collapse, and degradation, especially from the action of internal and external scavengers. These are profound lessons for both evolutionary science and long-term public policy.

A -101

Appendix

The responsibility that comes with understanding

But now our own success has also made us the most voracious quasi-bacterial scavenger that has ever chomped its way through the earth's environment and into its very life support system. And furthermore, the multifaceted dysfunction we've caused is inducing humanity to cannibalize our own society, instead of making the harder choices that can take us down the evolutionary pathway blazed by our own eukaryotic body plan toward greater sophistication and awareness. In principle, our technology gives us the capability for constructive complexification, but we have not matured enough to restrain ourselves from grabbing for the easy way out, so we are causing life to collapse around us. No technology will save us from our own virulent inclinations until we are prepared to exert restraints on our own behavior—the nature of which is just now beginning to come into focus.

Our evolutionary immaturity puts us in the situation of the early whaling industry, which hunted the largest animals on earth almost to extinction, greedily grabbing for huge, magnificent sources of biological order and sophistication only to boil them down for lamp oil. Now we are doing the same with fossil fuels, burning "liquid dinosaurs" as gasoline and natural gas—long after recognizing the ways their combustion products affect the earth's climate; identifying plentiful renewable energy alternatives with limited adverse side effects; and thus having no reason to deplete valuable, irreplaceable hydrocarbon deposits that future generations will need and could use sensibly (e.g., to synthesize materials comparable to plastics, but more benignly than we do now). In so many other ways, our economy is constructed around dismantling what nature has built up,

A-102

instead of synthesizing something new from smaller building blocks. Like bacteria, we have become specialists in decomposing organic material, opting for the easy route of catabolizing nature's wonders instead of the infinitely more promising and more spiritually rewarding path of anabolic synthesis of our own creative inventions.

We can now appreciate from historical and dynamic perspectives how we got to this point. When powerful technologies were first developed, they were not perfected and mass-produced to the point where they had much influence on the interdependent networks in which we are embedded and on which we, along with all life, depend. As technologies proliferated and interacted to inspire fundamentally new inventions, as an unanticipated side effect, percolation processes also caused human actions to influence natural networks. As with technology, these effects on the environment were negligible at first, but incentives to exploit natural resources encouraged economic development of interfacing networks, which expanded in size and influence until a percolation threshold was crossed. After that point, the rules that worked when interactions were sparse no longer applied in the new setting where interactions are now extremely dense and proliferating hyperexponentially.

When these dysfunctional effects first came to researchers' attention, it became clear that cooperation is key to making societies function. However, the experiments they developed only pertained to cooperation in flat social structures in the adaptive domain, and thus only applied to the limited kinds of cooperation that bacteria can exert when they either clash in warring factions or peacefully coexist in colonies. The lack of sophistication of those models of cooperation makes them utterly blind to proliferating interactions in multilevel structures, percolation thresholds that undermine invisible hands, changing operating conditions that cause design failure, systemic collapse that demands evolutionary transformation, and fundamental redesign to establish a new operating regime capable of functioning in the presence of dense interactions. These are not just analytical advances—they require new kinds of commitment to life in a more complex and capable whole.

Thus, to go beyond that quasi-bacterial mindset, we need more sophisticated models of cooperative processes, which can extend our understanding beyond the adaptive realm and into the evolutionary reality of creating stable, generous invisible hands. We can build an economy and society that is based on creating beautiful and sophisticated things instead of tearing down nature's beautiful and sophisticated works, but first we must invest not just in adaptive infrastructures and institutions, but also in the (r)evolutionary quasi-eukaryotic mindset that is required to evolve and protect the invisible hands that can sustain that momentum indefinitely. We need to create cultural and societal ratchets that can keep that evolutionary progress from going backwards, getting degraded, and collapsing on itself like a failed civilization.

But before humanity is entitled to use this knowledge to create social structures to correct our civilization's design deficiencies, we must meet our responsibilities as a citizen of the biosphere. Thus, rather than use these ideas adaptively to solve our current problems, we must first ask ourselves deeper evolutionary questions about humanity's spiritual mission as co-creators of our own biological niche, which interacts intensely with the rest of life. The same percolation processes that are sabotaging our own prospects also present serious threats to all life on our planet, as a result of our own actions. Obviously, the viability and functionality of the earth's life support system are far more important than human interests. So we must reflect on the cooperative processes that build up and protect complex structures, initially not to benefit ourselves, but instead so we can serve a greater purpose—and from there, to reshape our thinking, restructure our society, and reform our actions— ultimately to embark on a new and far more promising evolutionary path.

The cooperative processes that create invisible hands

So how could an internal climate of pervasive altruism remain stable enough to sustain eukaryotic evolution over billions of years from its unicellular origins to the emergence of human physiology, cognition, and civilization, without some colony of defectors taking over the show somewhere along the way and causing the whole structure to collapse and be forever lost? As slow and vulnerable to extinction events as biological evolution is, the process must have incorporated some kind of ratchet to keep its progress from going backwards [46].

Three general lines of thought have converged to explain both biological and cultural evolution as the creation of internally altruistic societies: niche construction [47], group selection [48-50], and the processes of cooperation and communication [51]. The explanation below is my synthesis of similar interpretations, translated into terms that were developed in this appendix:

- Niche construction at some higher level (physiological for the emergence of biological structures; ecological for the emergence of human culture) creates an invisible hand that provides bounty not readily available at the lower level.

- Group selection emerges as a way to attend to and tap into that higher-level source of bounty. We can see how economies and societies have organized around group selection principles, through formation of corporations and public health departments. That process has repeated itself many times in human history since the emergence of agricultural communities.

- Cooperation and communication are the natural channels for carrying out that organization. Such cooperative-communicative processes were especially important early in biological evolution, for example, during the development of basic conventions (like DNA inheritance and the genetic code, which established a firewall between adaptation and evolution), fundamental interactions (like the foundations of metabolism and sexual reproduction), and cycles (like the atmospheric oxygen-carbon dioxide cycle, which I'll discuss at length below). At this early stage in humanity's conscious evolution, we need to replace competitive paradigms that are driving us into a rut with similar cooperative and communicative practices.

These principles provide a resonant, intuitive explanation of cultural transmission and civilizational evolution, without having to resort to genetic metaphors (kin selection, selfish genes, memes, etc.). Furthermore, we can observe those steps occurring in real time, or at least over historical timescales. This explanation fits with both religious and scientific interpretations of evolution, reconciling the former with biological evolution as a baseline process in nature and the latter with civilizational evolution as having sacred implications (the future of humanity and all life on earth).

A coherent picture of stepwise biological evolution

– I sometimes quote Santayana who said that we don't know who discovered water but we know it wasn't fish. The person in Stage Three is like the fish sustained by the water. To enter Stage Four means to spring out of the fish tank and to begin to reflect upon the water.

– James Fowler, referring to his stages of faith development [52-54]

Here are the steps of biological evolution (on the left) corresponding with those of civilizational evolution (on the right):

background:

1. mutation ↔ niche

lower level:

2. natural selection ↔ preconditions

3. cooperation ↔ problems

4. specialization ↔ solutions

5. diversification ↔ consequences

higher level:

6. interactions ↔ discovery

7. cycles ↔ knowledge

In a sense, nature has mapped out its own problem-solving paradigm, at the lower level giving free rein to selfish behavior, but also allowing cooperation, by virtue of the higher level and the path of cooperation → specialization → diversification to tap into its bounty. However, there's a significant difference at the higher level for biological evolution—a firewall between the lower and higher level, whereby ephemeral creatures that live adaptively at the lower level do not control the interactions and cycles at the higher level. As a result, nature contains both the brutish realm of natural selection at the lower level, cooperative processes at the lower level that permit emergence of complex biological structures, and the invisible hand at the higher level that can be interpreted as God's providence. Scientists didn't pay much attention to the spiritual aspects of God's bounty, and fundamentalists were too stubborn in their denial to recognize the existence and function of the firewall.

Or at least that firewall was in place until humanity came along, with the power to alter the invisible hand. Indeed, our knowledge of natural selection at the lower level tempted some leaders to translate that harsh operating principle to the invisible hand as well, thereby biting the invisible hand that feeds us. Now realizing what we did then with social Darwinism, and how we're doing even worse now to our environment with the scientific method, we are in a position to identify a design flaw that is common to both biological evolution (at least with us in the picture) and civilizational evolution (at least so far): both run on a variant of the problem-solving paradigm.

Nonetheless, we have the opportunity to use our understanding to rise above those limitations and find a better way of structuring our interaction with the natural environment. Both science and religion are in agreement, pointing the way toward a transformative way of life that resonates with ancient wisdom.

A-108

The unhealthy relationship between human activity and nature

This feedback diagram shows how humanity's problem-solving paradigm (on the left) mismatches with the biosphere's evolutionary process (on the right):

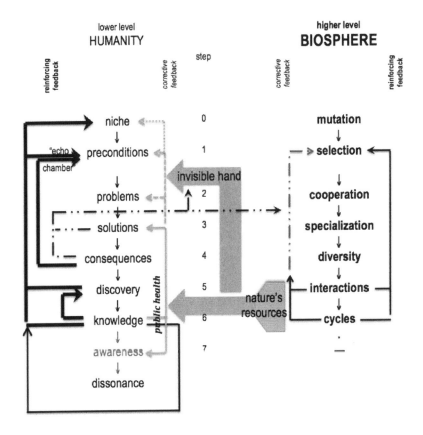

Figure 7.

Interaction of humanity's stepwise adaptive processes with nature's evolutionary processes.

Key features of the feedback diagram:

- Adaptation promotes a race to the bottom because competition favors ruthlessness and exploitation.

A -109

© Raymond E. Gangarosa, 2016

- Evolution escapes from those vicious cycles through complexification, i.e., by building multilevel systems featuring linked virtuous cycles.

- Those systems (which have emerged through humanity's sleepwalking process of niche construction, on which nature has further superimposed corrective feedback) comprise "the invisible hand" that Adam Smith described for free market economies.

- As we strip-mine both nature and our own society, we skew our activity heavily toward reinforcing feedback (left side of the human problem-solving system) and undermine the corrective feedback of the natural system (left side of the natural system). Only the public health sector is attentive to corrective feedback (right side of the human problem-solving system).

- Evolution employs a stepwise sequence very much like the problem-solving paradigm. Significantly, however, the last step is missing, the whole process is much slower, it can't see the whole picture, it can't learn from mistakes or anticipate obstacles, etc.

- Humanity's intelligence and creativity position us as the intelligent component embedded in natural feedback loops; our own experiences with the technologies of artificial intelligence give us a sense of quantum leaps in capabilities that might thereby ensue.

- We benefit more from the multilevel structure of natural systems than human economies can generate. When they are functioning properly, higher levels of organization have access to larger resource pools, economies of scale, wider interconnections, more coherency, and greater energy than lower levels. However, we can poison the well by disrupting the natural cycles that sustain us: "The invisible hand we create is the invisible hand we get." Constructing and maintaining such higher-level structures takes a lot of work, and they are tempting targets for resource robbers of various kinds, so those complex structures are often frail and subject to collapse.

Figure 8 shows a multilevel expansion of the previous diagrams, illustrating how we are destabilizing higher-level structures— "biting the invisible hand that feeds us"—by neglecting the listed infrastructures.

This hierarchy, buffeted by all its internal turbulence, is predisposed to instability, particularly when it is nested many levels high with large gaps in between. To increase the system's bounty and improve its robustness, we could build in more and more intermediate levels to shore it up, but we also need a configuration for the basic building block that is intrinsically much more stable.

As we will see, a more compact and simply interconnected structure is better suited to this task—the triad. In that configuration, each level suppresses selfishness and simplifies its own structure so the whole system can attain synergistic complexity.

Appendix

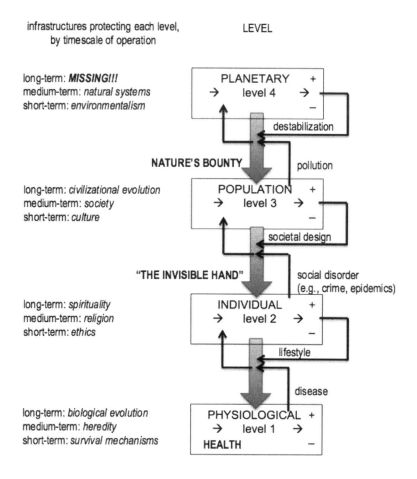

Figure 8.

Depiction of the hierarchical (multilevel) interface between human civilization and natural networks.

Summary: where adaptation and evolution are stuck right now

Below we see the common themes of biological adaptation, cultural/societal adaptation, and biological adaptation. They all share two common design defects:

• too many moving parts to go wrong

A-112

- too much opportunity for selfish interests to commandeer the system and steal the future

Thus for building synergistic complexity, these three paradigms introduce too much complexity of their own, which comes with an invitation to selfish interests to exploit higher-level structures with antagonistic complexity. As a result, these paradigms cannot build reliable higher-level structures that will serve as a bounteous invisible hand without making them fragile and subject to collapse. Evolution builds on past designs, requires enlisting greater and greater cooperation, and extends into the indefinite future, so it depends on higher-level structures to serve as generous, robust invisible hands. If such structures collapse after lower levels have become dependent on them, the system dies and goes extinct.

Table 7. Comparison of humanity's adaptive problem-solving paradigm (at right) with nature's adaptive stimulus-response reaction (at left) and the processes of biological evolution (middle).

stage	biological adaptation: stimulus-response reaction	biological evolution	cultural/societal adaptation: problem-solving paradigm
0	–	mutation	niche
lower level			
1	perception	natural selection	preconditions
2	stimulus	cooperation	problems
3	response	specialization	solutions
4	reinforcement schedule	diversification	consequences
higher level			
5	learning, imitation	interactions	discovery
6	group culture	cycles	knowledge
7	–		awareness
8	–	–	dissonance

A -113

How civilizational evolution might overcome this impasse: a modest proposal that seems consistent with both science and religion

It is not a story we are writing, but a story we are coming to understand.

– Margaret Swedish, Living beyond the "End of the world": a spirituality of hope (p. 147)

I've hinted at aspects of the transformative paradigm:

- Identify design defects that keep us mired in an adaptive rut—most notably, the selfishness and ignorance that have caused humanity to sleepwalk through history—and explore alternatives from every possible source.

- Help nature create an invisible hand that meets various needs identified by the problem-solving paradigm.

- Establish a firewall that protects that invisible hand and allows it to function smoothly, for all of life into the indefinite future.

The basic concept is that a triune (triadic) structure is the simplest configuration that can provide stability to purposive systems. A simple analogy is a three-legged stool. However, the concept is much deeper in connection with the Trinity from Christian doctrine. That structure provides a framework in which one vertex can establish a balanced high-level platform to support lower-level subsystems (i.e., an invisible hand), while the other two can specialize in addressing opposite poles of a dominant dichotomous variable (e.g., in this case, reinforcing and corrective feedback).

A-114

The concept of the Trinity is the accepted doctrine from the early writers of Christian tradition, derived from the Jewish interpretation of God as Abba, Father; the experience of Jesus as the Word made flesh; and encounters with a transformative Holy Spirit that spread a new Gospel of good news. The Trinity was not mentioned in the Bible, but was felt to be the only way to interpret the mystery of three different ways that God seemed to intervene in biblical narratives. The concept was first mentioned in regard to Christianity by Theophilus of Antioch around 170, and after considerable controversy, was formalized in Catholic canon in 325. The idea has long been a riddle, but the notion of trinitarian dynamics now applies to the mysteries of evolution, both biological and cultural, at a pivotal time in human history.

As it turns out, the elements of the Trinity correspond extremely well to the conceptual framework presented here as an alternative to the problem-solving paradigm, to meet the needs of agents who must solve problems while creating a firewall separating greedy control efforts from the highest concerns of life and the timeless progression of civilization. In other words, trinitarian structures could establish boundaries between adaptation (the concerns of people living here and now) and evolution (the concerns of humanity over all time), thereby preventing those in control from draining the potential from life and its future.

At the same time, it provides a framework for coalescing around a community, around which people might cooperate to build the structures that establish the "invisible hand" that meets the fundamental needs of its constituents, possibly even expressed in relation to life flows rather than material terms. These are also characteristics that may resonate with Christian doctrine.

A-115

Appendix

The elements of the Trinity are:

Table 8. The three vertices of trinitarian structures.

God		
Father Creator	Son Redeemer	Holy Spirit Sanctifier
1	2	3
oneness	sacrifice	nurturance

Consistent with Christian teachings, this highest level in the universe is the ultimate source of bounty. Respecting God as a higher authority is a basis for protecting the earth, coalescing around a common structure, and finding a constructive evolutionary pathway. This framework can meet our needs, so we must not be greedy. More to the point, by taking ourselves out of the evolutionary driver's seat, we preserve what is valuable to us, our future, and all of life.

Table 9. Evolutionary scientists have recently homed in on elements that relate to the trinitarian structure.

1 niche construction	2 group selection	3 cooperation and communication
• Alter the environment in constructive ways that will provide benefits to the system.	• Respond to evolutionary pressures at the population level, not just at the individual level.	• Share ideas and tools that will be used henceforth in the evolutionary process.

Table 10. My theory also developed these same themes. For example, if the problem-solving collapses into a triadic structure and the insight-development stages assume the following roles.

1 discovery discard extraneous stages	2 knowledge reinforcing feedback	3 awareness corrective feedback
• Participate in creation of the invisible hand … • …. but respect nature's design.	• Don't undermine the community's infrastructures. • Make pursuit of reinforcing feedback contribute to the community's wellbeing.	• Recognize and respect mutual interdependencies. • Be attentive to corrective feedback.

From a scientific standpoint, this simpler framework also provides a better internal setting for causal inference. The links between the three elements can be bilateral, not stepwise, so information can be shared directly from one repository to another, without the ambiguous reverberation through a massive feedback loop that funnels all feedback through an impenetrable societal echo chamber. The ambiguity of determining causal effects gives license to those with ulterior motives to fabricate conspiracy theories, sponsor propaganda, and foment confusion. By contrast, the architecture of the triadic structure is predicated on a social contract tailored to address shared needs.

In a manner of speaking, this conceptual framework bridges the gap between priorities and constraints that relate to tradeoffs for purposive agents and the integrity of multilevel systems, which are well situated to provide reserves as long as they are not raided by selfish agents. This consideration links to generativity issues in civilizational evolution, especially in relation to a society's responsibility to itself to create an internal environment that fosters goodwill. If a cycle of escalating anger emerges through a dog eat dog culture, all higher-level structures that had been previously built could be in danger of collapsing. Conversely, a society that nourishes human potential, validates contributions, expresses generosity and compassion, and prevents deprivation could go a long way toward creating an internal environment conducive to an indefinite series of future transformations. In that regard, this insight into the longstanding mystery of the Trinity provides a backdrop for the development of cooperation—a scientific riddle since Darwin's day.

In this way, science and religion can finally return to a common path, after diverging for over four centuries. We can see how God is enlisting humanity to be co-creators of the unfinished universe, but requiring us to take the initiative to work things out on our own. God has shown great love and patience as we have floundered around, but has provided an infinite number of clues, even in our own mistakes.

Even when we follow this triadic plan that God has laid out for us, we have no assurance it will always work. It requires constant attention and protection, especially from our own greed and ignorance. Although it is a more stable and resilient design architecture, it still challenges our free will to do the right thing.

And in that regard, too, our perspective of the universe returns to its roots. Instead of a blind watchmaker who wound up a cosmic escapement spring and left the universe to unfold on its own, we see the normative rationale for a moral culture and society. Economic anthropologist Elinor Ostrom [55-58] began making this shift in her studies of societies that successfully protect common pool resources (like fisheries) by using collective action, trust, and cooperation in management practices. She cataloged guidelines those societies used to defend the invisible hands that nourished them. As humanity approaches a transition where we must exert responsibility and discipline, this is the kind of economic theory that will allow us to function on the opposite side of the transformation. Looking back at history from that perspective, future generations will look back at neoclassical economics as a theory for unicellular organisms, completely unsuited for building higher-level structures—although if biology is any guide, likely to remain successful in breaking them down when they die and must decompose.

Societal implications of this transition

There is not only a dark night of the soul but a dark night of the world. What if, by chance, our time in evolution is a dark-night time—a time of transition that must be understood if it is to be part of learning a new vision and harmony of the human species and the planet?

– Constance Fitzgerald, OCD, quoted by Margaret Swedish in Living beyond the "End of the world": a spirituality of hope (p. 158)

The problem-solving paradigm has the seed of trinitarian dynamics within it—the insight-development phase of discovery, knowledge, and awareness. These seeds have been coalescing for centuries, and are well developed. They currently feed the lower-level problem-solving phase in much the same way as the invisible hand, so their current mission would not have to be revised much. The main changes that would bring the current system in alignment with a trinitarian dynamic are these:

- The discovery stage would have to emphasize getting the system in balance, viz., inventions should focus on averting instabilities and attaining overall control.

- The knowledge stage would have to ensure that pursuit of reinforcing feedback respects system infrastructures and avoids imposing major social costs. Once the system stabilizes in this configuration, corporations (or whatever institutions provide society its sustenance) would be held to full and complete accountability for the costs they impose on others.

A-119

- The awareness stage would have to give a sweeping mandate to subsystems entrusted with responding to corrective feedback, viz., the mission of public health should be expanded to planetary health and civilizational evolution.

Meanwhile, extraneous stages from the problem-solving paradigm would have to be eliminated:

- The niche stage, and its associated aggressive niche construction, would be replaced by a gentler peace with the biosphere. Upon finally confessing fully to the harm we have been doing to life on our fragile planet and its future prospects, we would do well to commit our part to a contract or covenant structured like a generalization of the Golden Rule to all life for all time.

- We should commit to abandoning the social echo chamber and its childish preconceptions. It's very hard for us to imagine how civilization would look without the cacophonous, reverberating din that surrounds us in everyday life, e.g., the Donald Trumps of the world. Abandonment of the echo chamber is the difference between knowledge and wisdom, e.g., comparable to the maturation from crazy adolescence to serene adulthood.

All these changes, especially humanity's relationship with our environmental niche, will require seeing reality for how it actually is. New cultural awareness and social structures will likely be required to reverse incentives directed at individual gain and establishing a social contract that encourages cooperation.

Just when this triadic structure replaces the nine-stage problem-solving paradigm, what is now a lower level of the conduct of life (the purview of religion) will no longer be separated from the higher level of thought to support it (the realm of science). In that setting, the schism between science and religion will likely become an anachronism that arose along the blind path of history.

How might we get there from here?

I used to think the top environmental problems were biodiversity loss, ecosystem collapse, and climate change.

I thought that with 30 years of good science, we could address those problems.

But I was wrong.

The top environmental problems are selfishness, greed, and apathy ...

... and to deal with those, we need a spiritual and cultural transformation,

— and we scientists don't know how to do that.

– James Gustave Speth, former administrator of the UN Development Programme and former dean of the Yale School of Forestry and Environmental Studies

Here is one possible dynamic transition from our current adaptive rut into a suitable evolutionary transformation:

- The similarity between problems in life and discovery at the population level with regard to assessing the nature of life suggests merging steps 2 (problems) and 5 (discovery), respectively, across both levels, into role 1 of the triad, oneness. Instead of seeing problems as separate challenges to attack through a divide-and-conquer strategy, we could view life's challenges within a single overarching framework that requires establishing functional balance and dynamic

A -121

stability. Note, however, that a benefit of this holistic framework is that we can abandon the artificial construct of "sustainability" that limits our thinking when we address problems separately. By definition, life is out of equilibrium, and our models of it should reflect the way transformation uses manageable imbalances as momentum to proceed from one state to another. By seeing the whole, we can replace the outmoded concept of homeostasis with the more realistic one of homeodynamics. [59, 60]

- The similarity between solutions in life and knowledge at the population level with regard to seeking reinforcing feedback suggests merging steps 3 (solutions) and 6 (knowledge), respectively, across both levels, into role 2 of the triad, sacrifice. The message for the subsystem that seeks benefits is not to go hog-wild, that is, to temper animal appetites with the needs of the invisible hand that will support everyone and provide a platform for future transformative advances.

- The similarity between consequences in life and awareness of limitations at the population level with regard to responsiveness to corrective feedback suggests merging steps 4 (consequences) and 7 (awareness), respectively, across both levels, into role 3 of the triad, nurturance. This is the subsystem that would protect the higher-level invisible hand from harm.

The three insights that emerged become the triadic elements. Insight itself is the driving force behind this self-organizing process.

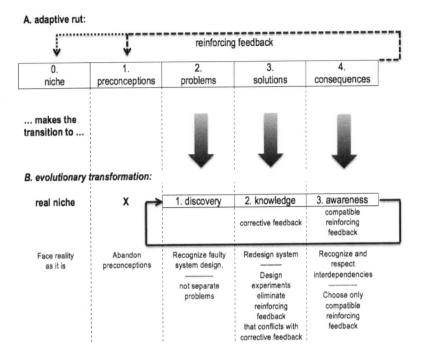

Figure 9.

One possibility whereby the problem-solving paradigm could undergo transformation to a triadic structure.

It almost seems as though humanity was set up to go through this transition, as though God had a preexisting plan for us to develop these insights.

- No other species has the cumulative culture required to develop a deep understanding of natural laws.

- Humans are the only species that combines highly structured societies (eusociality) with a high degree of intelligence.

- Humans are the only species capable of theory, analysis, and invention, all of which are required to progress beyond the limitations of biological evolution.

- From our own recent experiences with the technology of artificial intelligence, we can now recognize what intelligent components can bring to a functional design—e.g., the difference between smart phones and dumb phones. Through that engineering experience, we can appreciate ahead of time what we might offer as co-creators of God's kingdom—and what aspects of our own rebellious nature must be surrendered for us to function in that capacity.

- We have accelerated the evolutionary process by many orders of magnitude, now to a feverish pace. Whereas the timescale of biological evolution is measured in millions or billions of years, the timescale of civilizational evolution is in centuries, decades, or even years.

- As we will see shortly in the work of Darcia Narvaez, our brains are wired with three centers that correspond to the respective ethical demands of the three axes of the triad:
  - the ethics of security corresponding to oneness
    (primitive structures from reptilian neurological development)
  - the ethics of engagement corresponding to sacrifice
    (structures from mammalian neurological development)
  - the ethics of imagination corresponding to nurturance
    (cerebral cortex development, a uniquely human structure)

- Historical experiences over the past century have given humanity awareness that misinterpretation of the true nature of evolution can be very costly in terms of life and suffering.

- This is an era when a large fraction of the population has leisure time and sufficient living standards to reflect on where we are and where we could be.

- Democracy has spread rapidly over the last few decades, empowering large populations, potentially to contribute their creativity to evolutionary experimentation. Diversity of experience and characteristics is important in evolutionary settings, both for searching a rugged optimization landscape from many starting points and for reaching numerous viable end points that would correspond to different nations in the global community or different organs in an organism's body.

- Events have happened at such a rapid pace that we can readily witness evolution in the scientific and technological realms within the spans of recent memory.

- We can easily see how science and technology have transformed our lives in beneficial ways. Thus we are in a rare point in history when this rapid flow of events need not seem threatening, as it has in the past.

- The crises we have created leave us little choice but to address these issues. Humanity has waited as long as we safely could to awaken to these realities.

Two examples where triadic systems emerged

I have identified two examples where a system oriented toward stepwise progression reorganized itself into a triadic configuration. These scenarios could hardly have been more diverse—the first involving the interaction between photosynthetic and unicellular aerobic organisms during the first major crisis of biological evolution, and the second providing the latest insights into the moral functioning of the

A -125

human mind. Yet despite representing opposite ends of the consciousness spectrum, both speak profoundly to the very issues humanity faces just at this point in civilizational evolution.

1. Emergence of life cycles in the biosphere

It's instructive to consider comparable phases in biological and civilizational evolution. Corporations are playing an aggressive role now that mirrors the impact that photosynthesis had on the earth's early atmosphere. It's hard for us to imagine plants as aggressors or opportunists, but before a synergistic life cycle emerged between photosynthetic and air-breathing organisms, they were the worst of bad citizens in the emerging biosphere. These observations have profound implications for the potential future role of corporations.

Joel Bakan has compared the behavior of corporations to the DSM-IV diagnostic criteria that define psychopaths [61]:

1. callous unconcern for the feelings of others
2. incapacity to maintain enduring relationships
3. recklessness with others' health and safety
4. deceitfulness
5. inability to feel guilt
6. failure to follow social norms

Having been an activist advocating for the same issues, I am very sympathetic to that perspective. But this is a dynamic world, where positions and effects can change.

There were other times of great imbalance early in biological evolution. Before the emergence of aerobic respiration, during the period 2.5 to 3.5 billion years ago, photosynthetic organisms played the role that corporations are in now, by poisoning the atmosphere with oxygen. Oxygen was extremely toxic to all other life forms, which all were anaerobic at the time, so its accumulation in the atmosphere posed an existential threat to the future of life on earth.

However, the oxygen crisis proved to be a great boon for biological evolution. Of course, photosynthesis captured energy from the most widely available source, sunlight. At the level of other individual species, that Great Oxygenation Event created an impetus for aerobic metabolism, which attained far greater efficiency taking advantage of the high free energy of oxygen, and the incorporation of mitochondria as the aerobic metabolic centers in eukaryotes, which led to extensive specialization and diversification. Even more significant, on a global level, the biomass of aerobes grew quickly to match that of photosynthetic organisms, so each class's main gaseous waste product was the other's metabolic input, thereby setting up the first of the metabolic cycles of earth's life support system.

So, in fact, the unbalanced activity of business has been to harness a new energy source—science and technology—in pursuit of reinforcing feedback! Despite causing great instability, corporations have been doing civilizational evolution a great favor in the extremely long run. Although the corporate component of this triadic paradigm lacks wisdom, awareness, and compassion, there's no need to criticize corporations for their quasi-psychopathic traits. There are many reasons why

A -127

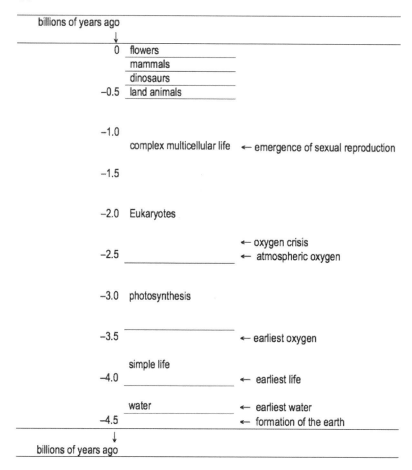

Figure 10.
The evolution of life on earth.

they have become so dumb and uncaring over the last few centuries (even aside from the ones business majors learn in economics courses):

- That's just the way plants evolve! Awareness is a lagging trait that requires emergence of some identifiable problem. The first "plant-like" evolutionary step involves blithely pursuing self-interests, under the implicit assumption that repercussions are not even a possibility! Although some

A-128

people and institutions have called attention to such repercussions, on the whole, corporations are still in denial.

- Pioneers can't afford to attend to cultural and social niceties.

- The rationale for their seemingly reprehensible behavior (like exploitation of vulnerable populations, free-riding, rent-seeking, denial of risks, time discounting) is that their profitability is squeezed at every turn (e.g., by perfect competition, sunk costs in winner-take-all games, and the inventory control game). They are behaving particularly badly now to build a cushion in the face of intractable financial pressures that make the current adaptive realm nonviable. In essence, without acting in a way others interpret as cynical and misanthropic, they would go extinct.

- Life has to fix reinforcing feedback into its virtuous cycles before it can address corrective feedback.

- Tapping into science, technology, and business will inject enormous innovation and productivity into civilizational evolution, as technological progress has shown.

The crisis that corporations have caused helps trigger awareness under increasingly difficult circumstances—analogous to the apoptotic crises in imaginal centers of a caterpillar chrysalis—which is good preparation for emerging in a transformed state where all the rules are changed.

- The system loses wisdom as it gains power. That's the "children playing with flamethrowers" effect.

- A system of such complexity creates obstacles to establishing causal inference because the one-way arrows, throughout every part of the loop, mix everything together. This problem

A -129

- intensifies as the system gains more and more power, because observability and controllability deteriorate.

- The system was running open loop for so long it saturated all available buffers. Once the system reached a percolation threshold, where humanity's newfound prowess exceeded its wisdom, it was increasingly obvious something was wrong.

- Their increasingly virulent behavior was just a signal that the system needs to balance the unanticipated consequence of their activities.

- So Donald Trump's leaving the business arena to show how he would govern is just a wake-up call how far out of touch social conservatives in the corporate world can be. The fact that he has received more votes in primary elections than any other Republican in history testifies how irrationality, intolerance, xenophobia, and faux populism have hijacked "the party of Lincoln."

- The dissonance we feel (or should feel) is our manifestation of "sickness behavior," a malaise informing us of a "systemic cultural infection" that our "societal immune system" must recognize and reject, as an early healing step in the evolutionary transformation toward a fundamentally more harmonious way of living.

So what if corporations only care about making sufficient profits consistently, maintaining cash flows, sustaining payrolls, satisfying investors, gaining market share, and innovating new products? That's also what plants do! Corporations have just tapped into a new source of human potential, and we haven't had enough time to figure out what was happening and restore balance! All we have to do now is evolve a complementary paradigm/technology to establish a virtuous cycle.

A-130

Table 11. The early atmospheric Oxygenation Crisis vs. the current Great Acceleration.

	plants	animals	corporations	public health
exchanges	"toxic" waste: O_2 requires: CO_2	requires: O_2 waste: CO_2	"toxin": selfishness requires: cooperation	promotes: cooperation heals: selfishness
response	slow, to nutrients	full, to environment	reinforcing feedback only	nuanced responsiveness to corrective feedback
awareness	none	evolved toward cognition	limited to adaptive problem-solving	path to transformative evolution
	CONDITIONS EARLY IN BIOLOGICAL EVOLUTION		EARLY IN CIVILIZATIONAL EVOLUTION (NOW)	
metabolism	**negative externalities:** Photosynthetic cell polluted the atmosphere with toxic oxygen.	**positive externalities:** Aerobic cells closed a resource-recycling loop. Aerobic metabolism was a huge improvement over anaerobic metabolism in efficiency and capacity.	**negative externalities:** Most industries impose environmental costs greater than their profits.	**positive externalities.** Public health has responded to each wave of externalities, gaining experience and robustness using the same methods for different purposes.
cycle development	**negative externalities:** A billion years elapsed before oxygen started accumulating in the atmosphere, but after surface minerals were oxidized, and oxygenation crisis developed quickly.	**percolation threshold:** It also took a long time for the interaction between photosynthetic and aerobic metabolisms to create a stable cycle — a suggestion to be patient, because planetary evolution spans many generations.	**negative externalities:** Longstanding denial of product-attributable social harm and costs suggests there may be long lags before corporations accept the responsibilities required to balance reinforcing and corrective feedback.	**percolation threshold:** Epidemiological methods are not well suited to causal inference in multilevel systems this complex.
"citizenship"	**entrepreneurship:** Photosynthetic cells took the initiative of harnessing on behalf of all life the best energy source, before all the details were resolved. **initial harmlessness:** Photosynthesis was not harmful at first because free metals reacted with oxygen to prevent its accumulation. **transient threat to life:** Before the advent of aerobic metabolism, oxygen was one of the most toxic organic poisons.	**phase transition:** The $CO_2 - O_2$ cycle was the first and most basic component of earth's life support system. It set the stage for all life by providing both photosynthetic and aerobic organisms the highest available energy for metabolism. In addition, they both cleared each other's wastes, so each could operate metabolically at peak efficiency.	**entrepreneurship:** Corporations took the initiative of fixing the benefits of science and technology into business activity — a dramatic innovation of cumulative culture. **initial harmlessness:** When science and technology interacted rarely, it seemed they could do no wrong. **current threat to life:** Corporate actions are leading to climate change, mass extinction, social unrest, growing gap between rich and poor. Some actions have been compared to the clinical definition of psychopaths!	**impending phase transition:** These insights suggest ways to design high-level structures to meet lower-level needs and work out a cooperative social contract.

Public health has already started the process by using many of the same methods of science, technology, and management. As a result, it has many of the metabolic advantages as corporations and can therefore act robustly to restore the feedback that become so unbalanced.

By being responsive to corrective feedback, this expanded mission for public health is not only a complementary metabolic process, but also a complementary perceptual process. So public health is taking the role not only of aerobic organisms, but also the path leading to animals! Table 11 gives a tabular comparison.

2. From developmental psychology to triune ethics

Darcia Narvaez's triune ethics theory is a perfect example of both a) an elegant triadic multilevel explanation of human thought and culture and b) implicit derivation of that theoretical framework from a theory of sequential processes. Her three-process concept was inspired by the six-step theory of moral development articulated by her mentor, Lawrence Kohlberg. His stages of moral development bear some resemblance to the problem-solving paradigm, based as they are on the assumption of sequential prerequisites. Narvaez describes Kohlberg's theory as "top-down" (based on observational studies) and her own theory as "bottom-up," being motivated by insights from neurobiology, viz., three brain centers that direct three categories of thought.

However, my earlier discussion of triadic dynamics shows that the ultimate top-down perspective, the Trinity, also connects with the ultimate bottom-up theory, neurobiology, as though God designed our minds in His image! The fact that we have free will to think instrumentally in problem-solving mode or socially

A-132

under trinitarian dynamics also speaks to the moral alternatives with which God has presented us.

The three brain centers in Narvaez's theory relate to (1) the ethics of security, (2) the ethics of engagement, and (3) the ethics of imagination. They correspond perfectly with the three trinitarian vertices: (1) oneness, (2) sacrifice, and (3) nurturance. Her theory accounts for both moral behavior and moral lapses. Table 12, excerpted from her own summary [62], shows how her theory corresponds to some aspects of mine.

Table 12. Sketch of Darcia Narvaez's triune ethics theory.

ethical orientation	security	engagement	imagination
behavioral basis	instinct	intuition	deliberation and narrative
characteristics	routine & tradition following precedent dominance & status	emotion ongoing memory reality & truth emotional self in present more right brain	logical & imaginative problem solving foresight, planning, learning self in past and future more left brain
basic human needs	personal autonomy (goal driven) instrumental efficacy	trust people belonging social efficacy	understanding purpose self-enhancement
moral dispositions	in-group loyalties hierarchy, purity concrete reciprocity tradition, rules, rituals, symbols	love and fellow feeling justice, reciprocity shame, responsiveness	cognitive empathy abstract reciprocity reasoning, creative response
morality	self-protective (afferent) self-assertive (efferent), self-concerned interpersonal relationships	inclusive of immediate other in-group membership tied to emotional feelings	inclusive of non-immediate other human heartedness when linked with engagement ethic

Table 13. Various perspectives of triadic structures and systems.

level			
Trinity (as pattern)	Creator	Redeemer	Sanctifier
principle	oneness	sacrifice	nurturance
axis	whole	reinforcing feedback	corrective feedback
dictum	Don't redesign the environment	Invest in system potential	Recognize and respect interdependence
process in biosphere	atmosphere	photosynthesis	aerobic metabolism
planetary recycling	atmosphere	oxygen	carbon dioxide
biological evolution	ecosystem	plants	animals
civilizational evolution	environment	culture (ideas)	society (actions)
organism	environment	physiological systems	immune system
ethic (Narvaez)	security	engagement	imagination
neurological structure	reptilian axis	mammalian axis	cerebral cortex
biological interaction	environment	host	microbe

Note: This table should not be construed to suggest these relationships always operate synergistically (see following table). For example, in the last line, while human life requires the support of beneficial microbes, obviously harmful microbes can upset the balance to cause disease and epidemics.

Synthesis of these two examples

Triadic systems are ubiquitous at every level in nature, providing stable intermediate platforms that, with proper maintenance, can serve as "invisible hands" to levels below. In Table 13, we also look ahead to other examples we will examine.

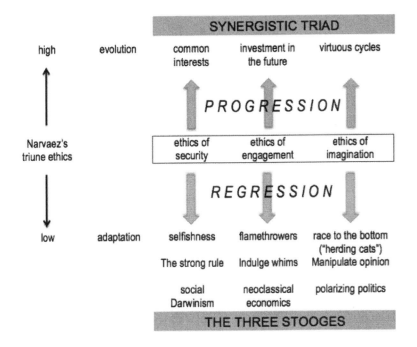

Figure 11.

Emergence of triadic systems is not a guarantee of success; they also can fail.

Spiritual implications

<u>The notion of spirituality in the context of civilizational evolution</u>

An evolutionary perspective revises and renews what we hold sacred. It is a conceptual breakthrough for enabling each generation to comprehend the revelations that unfold in its era. It is a framework for expanding humanity's contextual perspective with each evolutionary transition and transformative change. It allows us new ways to appreciate the wisdom of the past and to expand our awareness of the meaning of human existence, based on the monumental implications our choices can have for the future of all life on earth. In contrast to the sterile, distracting debate that was sparked by the revolting brutality of natural selection in biological evolution, questions about civilizational evolution encourage us to explore how God is enlisting us as co-creators of the universe to install a wise and compassionate alternative. These are just a few practical aspects of an evolutionary spirituality arising from issues raised in this appendix.

<u>How far along is humanity in evolutionary development?</u>

So then where does the current human culture/society complex fall in comparison to known evolutionary touchstones? Since we have evolved in a unique way—via cognition, social organization, and technological development—we have progressed at different rates according to different measures:

- With regard to cooperation at the individual level, we are at the stage of slime molds Dictyostelium and Volvox, which live as single cells when environmental conditions are favorable but join together as a primitive multicellular structure under stress. Similarly, cooperation in human culture and society is sporadic because overriding coherence is so poor that most selection occurs at the individual level. So far, individual-level initiative has driven the technological progress that has propelled the economy at all levels, but now we are drowning in the adverse consequences of our own actions. The higher-level consequences of that accumulation—of harm that we ourselves do—defies individual-level actions.

- Architecturally, the design of human social structures has progressed to the stage of sponges: with little coherent internal order and insufficient cohesiveness to provide strong incentives for internal cooperation. As if that wasn't already a vicious cycle of poor structure mutually reinforcing poor cooperation, the experience of drowning in our own wastes is causing conditions to deteriorate.

- Functionally, humankind is acting like a jellyfish: preoccupied with digestion but with a very poor distribution system; barely able to perceive what's around us or move in a sensible direction; at the mercy of the winds and waves— but with very good stingers! As modern leadership attests, a jellyfish might be thrilled at the prospect of incremental improvement to its digestive system (or its stingers), unable to envision anything more of life because it lacks eyes, minds, communities, nations, and civilizations to appreciate the far greater functionality of people swimming very close by. Projected to humanity's current predicament, that jellyfish mentality anticipates a bright future of never-ending exponential jellyfish growth (and not a thought of blowback from the rest of creation) if it can just cut all future-oriented expenditures to eliminate its budget deficit. A jellyfish bitching and moaning about its budget deficit is a poor excuse for Life As We Know It, and not likely to help its offspring and descendants cut a very dashing niche for themselves in the long run.

- With regard to cooperation at the societal level, humanity is on one of only 20 independent evolutionary paths (clades) from diverse evolutionary origins (insects, marine crustaceans, and subterranean rodents) that manifests eusociality—generally defined by cooperative care of the young, overlapping generations, and division of labor (most often in biological designs relying on reproductively barren castes)—and the only one of those eusocial species characterized by high intelligence and large body size. Such species exhibit high degrees of cooperation, so their colonies function like superorganisms. In many cases, such cooperation has conferred enormous adaptive advantages: for example, the 20,000 species of social insects comprise about 2% of all insect species, yet make up about 75% of insect biomass. Humanity's own version of eusociality, driven by culture and innovation rather than instinct, allowed us to begin dominating the earth many millennia ago, and now to contemplate the consequences of that domination. We now have the potential to be the first eusocial species to give back to all of life the benefits of living in cohesive communities.

- Environmentally, we are like the archaic photosynthetic organisms who polluted the early earth's entire atmosphere with what was then a deadly poison—oxygen—but thereby set up the ecological cycles that govern Gaia's operation. This comparison portends contrasting tales of both serious caution and great potential. When oxygen first built up in the early earth's atmosphere, its toxicity derived from the much

A-138

greater chemical reactivity, i.e., oxidation potential, which is quickly lethal to anaerobes. A new kind of metabolism evolved to take advantage of that greater reactivity: aerobic respiration. Not only was this metabolic foundation far more efficient than anaerobic respiration, but it was also complementary to photosynthesis, so each major form of life could breathe the other's gaseous waste products. This remarkable synergy—which one might argue could not have been anticipated by the early photosynthetic organisms choking the rest of life on the increasing concentrations of oxygen they were generating—was the basis for all subsequent ecological cycles that now make life flourish on earth.

- Evolutionarily, we are like early RNA-based life: mixing metabolism with inheritance (or, equivalently, adaptation with evolution, or, in the human sphere, problem-solving with transformation) without a genetic code for transmitting shared wisdom from generation to generation. In our case, every idea has to run the gamut of the societal echo chamber, thereby running the risk of transforming even humankind's best insights into its worst applications. The genetic code obviously allowed spectacular increases in hereditary information flow across generations, but it also created a firewall between adaptation and evolution, and a corresponding arrow of time that prevented adaptive self-interests from contaminating the vital design improvements developed through harsh experience. By virtue of not having developed a cultural genetic code for transmitting shared wisdom uncontaminated by perverse incentives, the blueprints humanity has transmitted through civilizational evolution have been kluges.

A -139

- Historically, humanity has been sleepwalking through most bifurcations in our trajectory, making choices for the wrong reasons even when those choices were sensible. For example, even after John Snow published conclusive evidence that cholera was transmitted by contaminated drinking water, only a massive olfactory assault, called the Great Stink, could finally prompt London to protect its citizens from deadly outbreaks by investing in a well-designed sewer system. As humanity faces our first encounter with our own power to foul our own nest at a global scale, it's possible that only one or more large-scale catastrophes could kick us out of our current rut.

- Ideologically, we are fragmented: we continue to squabble whether to drive only to the left or only to the right, when the best either alternative could do is drive around in circles! Democratic government was set up to allow negotiating a complex path involving turns in both directions as needed, and as recently as the 1960s, there was a keen appreciation in the U.S. for developing healthy public-private partnerships. However, the very innovations that have given us extraordinary technological capabilities have also compromised our governability, and the ensuing frustrations at being unable to exhibit wise self-governance have yet further blinded and entrenched clueless ideologues.

- Scientifically, we lack a cohesive vision: theoretical and basic sciences are healthy, but applied sciences are overwhelmingly more responsive to reinforcing feedback than to corrective feedback, in ways that preferentially reward harmful commercial enterprises. Furthermore, many scientists exploring constructive societal responses suffer intense harassment from ideologues and entrenched commercial interests threatened by proposed accountability for social costs.

- Spiritually, we are adrift: three centuries of scientific advancement have created an impression that rationality is a panacea, when, in fact, our own hyper-developed problem-solving capacities are causing systemic imbalances, huge blind spots, rising addiction to piecemeal adaptive problem-solving, and massive impediments to transformative evolution. Cooperation is an urgent priority, and science has no clue how to promote it, even as selfish interests create enormous barriers to evolutionary transformation. We finally need to recognize that life is not about us. Belief in a higher power and the religious traditions that have mobilized faith into large-scale action have been waiting throughout the course of civilization to be harnessed for this purpose.

- Emotionally, humanity has no more maturity than an adolescent, and our behavior has bordered on delinquency. Here are current features of human development that resemble adolescence:

  - young
  - growing in power
  - uncoordinated
  - self-conscious
  - argumentative
  - unpredictable
  - vulnerable
  - easily manipulated
  - prone to outbursts
  - invasive

A -141

- o intently focused
- o undisciplined and shortsighted
- o peer-dependent
- o unaware of consequences of actions
- o increasingly cognizant with increasing experience
- o questioning
- o wrestling with moral dilemmas
- o not sure how to resolve all this confusion

- I discussed corporations as psychopaths, but given where humanity is on an evolutionary timescale, we should instead be considered a juvenile delinquent! Here are current features of human development that resemble delinquency:
  - o egocentrism
  - o narcissism
  - o risk-taking behavior
  - o sexual immaturity
  - o crime
  - o violence
  - o lack of self control
  - o weak future orientation
  - o developmental lags
  - o unusually pronounced peer influence
  - o emotional volatility
  - o excessive orientation to the present

- However, thought and communication are always the wild cards in human civilization. We are unique among the elite stratum of eusocial species in being highly intelligent, and, despite our vulnerability for self-delusion that can create glaring blind spots, we have significant capacities for introspection and self-criticism. Having had many historical opportunities to learn related lessons through trial and error, it's possible we could develop awareness of the realities we have created, recognize the lack of accountabilities and associated systemic dynamic instabilities, anticipate the impending disasters if no action is taken, and draw from extensive public health experiences to initiate preventive measures. For example, it's obvious how our predicament, drowning in the waste products of an advanced technological civilization, relates to that of John Snow's London, when large 19th-century cities outgrew sanitary technologies and contaminated their water supplies. So instead of waiting for obvious cues—it stinks!—we have the alternative to respond to the many different kinds of relevant insights we have developed since then.

The sweep of biological and civilizational evolution

The feeling of compassion is the beginning of humanity.

– Mencius

The real tragedy of human existence is not that we are nasty by nature, but that a cruel structural asymmetry grants to rare events of meanness such power to shape our history.

– Stephen Jay Gould, Eight Little Piggies: Reflections in Natural History

A -143

It's useful to get a sense of how things are unfolding, and to compare the pace of biological and civilizational evolution. As we contemplate the unprecedented course of events, one can't help wondering where this Great Acceleration could be leading. The timeline below hints that recent insights in civilizational evolution may be leading humanity to some kind of crescendo unattainable by biological evolution. In any case, an abrupt transition is inevitable, precipitated by the unprecedented planetary crisis we have created. It behooves us to accept the phase transformation willingly and enthusiastically.

Table 14a. The gradual pace of biological evolution, in relation to the much faster pace of civilizational evolution.

recent events (date)	event	distant events (millions of years ago)
	age of the earth	4,543
	biological evolution	
	first organisms (like prokaryotes)	3,800 (3,900 - 2,500)
	earliest oxygen	3,500
	earliest multicellular organisms (cyanobacteria)	3,000 - 3,500
	atmospheric oxygen	2,500
	emergence of eukaryotic organisms	1650 (1,600 - 2,700)
	oxygen crisis	2,300
	emergence of sexual reproduction	1,000 - 1,200
	emergence of multicellular animals	600
	emergence of mammals	65
	emergence of primates	50-55
	emergence of hominids	8
	emergence of humans	1

Table 14b. The accelerating pace of civilizational evolution.

recent events (date)	event	distant events (millions of years ago)
	civilizational evolution	
	first tool use	1.76
	control of fire	1.6
3500 BC	first civilizations (Middle East)	
800 - 100 BC	Old Testament	
54-110	New Testament	
1440	printing press (Johannes Gutenberg)	
1776	James Watt's steam engine	
Nov 24, 1859	publication of Charles Darwin's *Origin of Species* [63]	
1927	publication of William O. Kermack and Anderson G. McKendrick's "Contribution to the mathematical theory of epidemics" [64]	
1953	James Watson and Francis Crick's DNA double helix: "Molecular structure of nucleic acids: A structure for deoxyribose nucleic acid" [65-67]	
1969	publication of Stuart Kauffman's "Metabolic stability and epigenesis in randomly constructed genetic nets" [68]	
1976	publication of Richard Dawkin's *The selfish gene* (popularized Darwinian explanation for cultural evolution) [69]	
1978	publication of Roy M. Anderson and Robert M. May's "Regulation and stability of host-parasite population interactions" [70, 71]	
1983	publication of Paul Ewald (evolution of virulence): "Host-parasite relations, vectors, and the evolution of disease severity" [72]	
1994	publication of David Sloan Wilson and Eliott Sober's "Reintroducing group selection to the human behavioral sciences" [73]	
1996	publication of Kevin N. Laland, F. John Odling-Smee, and Marcus W. Feldman's "The evolutionary consequences of niche construction: A theoretical investigation using two-locus theory" [74]	
2001	publication of Liane Gabora's "Cognitive mechanisms underlying the origin and evolution of culture" [75]	
2005	publication of Darcia Narvaez's "The neo-Kohlbergian tradition and beyond: Schemas, expertise, and character" [76]	

Appendix

Proposal for a partial synthesis

I don't know how evolutionary transformation will unfold, because I am stuck like everyone else on this side of the transition. However, having thought about these issues for a long time, I can see certain aspects of the mindset we will need and the nature of the process:

- First and foremost, we have to recognize that life is not about us. Anthropocentrism has been toxic to human society, the environment, our civilization, and the future of life on earth. We must shift focus from human interests (however enlightened and widely shared) to the responsibilities we are called upon to manifest.

- We must stop thinking in economic terms and finally recognize that life cannot be reduced to a univariate measure related to currency. It's not enough to stave off disaster to save our own skins or to preserve the earth's resources because they will be valuable to humanity's future; we must make ourselves of value to the rest of life, as the only citizen of the biosphere potentially capable of intelligent, coordinated action.

- During the transition to a more enlightened, nuanced perspective, we might temporarily consider how humanity stacks up as a responsible citizen in each dimension where we have influence, and from there, insist that we earn our right to use the earth's resources (gently) and thereby reward ourselves with comfortable living standards.

- A good way to conceptualize that responsibility is to imagine extending the Golden Rule to life as a whole. Acknowledging that we have behaved virulently in a way that threatens our own wellbeing is the first step toward contrition for the mass

A-146

extinction event that we are rapidly precipitating. With that foot in the door, we might connect our own vulnerability with that which we are exploiting from other species, and then resolve to treat the rest of life the way we would like to be treated.

- That being said, we don't have to be needlessly harsh on ourselves for past transgressions. If we commit ourselves toward a mutualistic relationship with the rest of life on earth, our stability also serves a higher purpose. We cannot act as the intelligent agent within the biosphere if our own collapse prevents us from acting cohesively.

- Next, our emphasis should be on "constructive complexification," viz., creating densely cross-supported, intrinsically stable multilevel systems of nested invisible hands, with each one supporting the levels below it. Meanwhile, every level must be strictly accountable for costs it imposes on all higher levels, to prevent disrupting the invisible hands that feed it. This kind of mutual support and accountability should go partway towards enlisting the cooperation that transformative evolution requires.

- Since triadic structures confer greater stability than the current (and familiar) problem-solving paradigm, it may be helpful to speculate how they might work (For a description of the three vertices, see table 10).

  - Vertex 1 (corresponding to oneness or coherence) must create a language or culture from which the rest of the system can develop awareness and expand its perspective. In an abstract way, we might consider this language/culture like the composition and performance of a musical score.

A -147

- o Vertex 2 (corresponding to sacrifice or cooperation) must build constructive social structures from the available options, like assembling a jigsaw puzzle.

- o Vertex 3 (corresponding to nurturance or coordination) must look far ahead to the future of generations to come, much like a chess player sees many moves ahead under many different contingencies.

The key features that make a triadic system better suited to transformative evolution and more stable as a platform for promoting cooperation than the problem-solving paradigm are (1) the structure is simpler, viz., it has fewer variables and eliminates extraneous steps (niche and preconditions) that cause the most confusion ("societal echo chamber"), (2) all interconnections are two-way, so every step can communicate fluently and directly with every other, so causal influences are much more easily established, (3) it takes only one pass at reality, leaving the triads at higher levels to address the (higher level) insight-development phase, (4) the system avoids getting stuck in an adaptive rut by constantly reconfiguring itself in response to the demands of its evolutionary trajectory, (5) beyond the scope of its impending transition, the system looks as far ahead as it can to determine how to configure itself to set up a never-ending series of constructive transformative changes, (6) the system must balance the demands for retaining its intrinsic mission while also promoting constructive evolutionary experimentation.

These stabilizing characteristics have interesting implications in terms of the analogies I described. As the complex musical score (language/culture), jigsaw puzzle (construction of social structures), and chess game interact over time, they change each other's rules!! Thus a new melody or harmony might reconfigure the pattern of the jigsaw puzzle (as if in a computer memory instead of a traditional cardboard version) and/or alter the way the pieces move, and, in turn, those reconfigured games open up new possibilities for musical expression. Thus the system builds on its own richness to become ever richer in its evolutionary potential, while always seeking directions that are constructive and learning from setbacks when its judgments were flawed.

- This perspective formalizes Stuart Kauffman's idea of the "adjacent possible," the hypothetical span of all conceivable states that might emerge from a given point in evolutionary development [77, 78]. By way of comparison, game theory with fixed payoff rules does little more than calculate earnings for drones with different adaptive strategies; the problem-solving paradigm provides a little more inspiration in explaining how events with different consequences can cascade like dominoes when we play adaptive roles; however, this triadic framework of interacting inventiveness suggests how we might expand the frontiers of possibility for humanity and life as a whole. We see how well this possibility-generating engine has worked over long timespans in biological evolution without the benefit of cognition and how well it works now to proliferate technological innovations without the benefit of wisdom. Those touch points provide an opening for faith that new kinds of cooperation can allow human populations to emulate the evolutionary apparatus that expanded life's possibilities to generate the rich panoply of biological designs. However, there's a big caveat: this invention belongs to life as a whole, so we must use it to develop wise self-

A -149

governance, and not to advance our own interests. Benefits will accrue to us, but only if we agree not to hijack the process and thereby collapse it back to the accountants' realm of game theory or the economists' realm of problem-solving. Eventually the process will achieve the fluency of scientific discovery and technological progress, but our task at this stage of human civilization is to demonstrate that we can wield it with insight, responsibility, and discipline.

- The rest of the way toward developing cooperation necessary for civilizational evolution is a matter of ensuring that higher-level social structures provide enough support for lower levels to avoid permanent collapse, which would resemble extinction in biological evolution. The historical deconstruction exercise presented above suggests one way to consider motivations of each player in the past unfolding of civilization. Somehow we might extract from related empirical evidence (e.g., from subpopulations of each player that acted like good citizens) some kind of design specifications for within- and between-level interactions that will protect the system from irreversible collapse.

- At the same time, we cannot insist on protecting ourselves from all collapses. Our best insurance against such risks is to govern ourselves with wisdom, responsibility, and discipline.

- In the context of the problem-solving paradigm, I described a social contract whereby the higher-level system would meet lower-level needs in exchange for fundamentally improved cooperation, but even then cautioned that this must not be conceptualized like a business deal or governmental safety net in the sense of our failing adaptive constructs. This new evolutionary way of thinking will require a far greater leap of faith that recognizes a different set of priorities. We can see this easily by considering the difference between various modes of governance—e.g., democratic socialism (where government provides safety nets to ensure a basic material living standard) or laissez-faire capitalism (where entrepreneurs are free to pursue their material interests)—and the rules that bind cells in the human body (where all cells die if they cannot collectively maintain the system's health). Yet the remarkable thing is that the body, operating on principles that strongly suppress expression of individual interests that impinges on the whole, manages to deliver far better nourishment, more stability, and greater security by virtue of the vastly improved capabilities that accrue from cooperative co-evolution. And yet, as indicated above, even that level of commitment would represent an excessively anthropocentric perspective, since we would need to prioritize planetary health over long timescales far greater than currently seems natural.

- In that regard, the social contract might seem like an inversion of Maslow's hierarchy of needs, reflecting faith in a system's competence to meet low-level needs so that new kinds of cooperation can allow new kinds of higher-level capabilities to evolve. It's not clear how this faith might get started (especially in the current climate of distrust in government), but we can see what has happened after that threshold was passed with technological progress. Although markets have hijacked science and technology to do a lot of harm, it's pretty clear that they also improve living standards, to the extent that few people would want to go back to "the good old days." If you imagine then that technology would be applied to wise self-governance instead of just fancier gizmos, and then consider how much more leverage higher-level systems have to create an invisible

A -151

hand with abundance, stability, and security, you can begin to appreciate the appeal of a social contract that makes this exchange. It's not perfect, since cancer cells still try to bilk the system, and immunocytes scour the body to kill them off before they can drag every cell to ruin. So to suppress yet further that residual of destructive selfishness, you have to envision that much greater dedication to the operation of the whole.

Don't hold me to this perspective (and especially this embryonic description) of the role of the social contract in civilizational evolution. There's no way anyone can predict how this design would play out, but I throw this out as a modest proposal, or more specifically, an evolutionary experiment to evaluate. These are just unsystematic impressions plugged into nebulous aspects of this complex of ideas: assessment of problem-solving needs, projection of those needs into an unfolding problem-solving matrix, structuring a social contract for an evolutionary path, the irreversible physics of cooperation in an evolutionary setting, agreements to participate in construction of higher-level structures, consideration of what the resultant invisible hand should do, specification of the design of evolutionary transformations, etc. It seems quite likely that we don't even have the language yet to envision how this process would look.

Seeing God in an evolutionary perspective[6]

As a scientist who first approached these issues with a pragmatic activist agenda, it surprises me to reach the conclusions that are now so starkly compelling. Science and technology have given

---

[6] This concluding section was inspired by reading [79].

humanity not only new eyes, but also the blinders that have been with us longer than any human memory. The schism between science and religion has manifested as separation from life, wisdom, and meaning.

Pope Francis' recent encyclical *Laudato si' On care for our common home* [80], provides a framework for healing that schism. His thoughtful, compassionate vision of humanity is an inspiring vision for constructive transformational change and the public dialog required to achieve it. Since the core of the ideas presented in this appendix were developed before the release of that encyclical—and most were completed before studying it—it's impossible to convey how gratified I feel that the Pope and I share the same views[7].

Civilizational evolution is a process that extends far beyond our lifetimes, so the best we can do is look to the future toward the capacities we wish to create for future generations. And in the process we introduce our own personal stamp on the irreversible flow of civilizational evolution. Thus from the standpoints of functionality and intentionality the whole process has a mystical anticipatory character. We can see analogies in biological evolution, as cells coalesced into multicellular patterns with ever-greater coherence and capability, an insight that informs our participation but takes none of the mystery out of where all this is heading.

---

[7] Since my thoughts and words cannot match his vision and eloquence, I strongly recommend that the reader consult this document, which can be downloaded at no cost from the Internet.

Appendix

An orientation toward the future is guided by a sense of a compassionate, empathetic God embodied in multilevel self-organizing processes that imbue humanity with purpose. The fact that we want this for ourselves is part of the reason we must act generously toward life as a whole over all time, but we are also acting on behalf of higher purposes, as if to coalesce into cells in a body with new capabilities that never existed before. This conceptual framework accommodates both the reality of biological evolution and the incomparably expansive possibilities of a loving God engaged in the world using us as vehicles of co-creation.

References

1. Jacob F: **Evolution and tinkering**. *Science* 1977, **196**(4295):1161-1166.

2. Mandrioli M: **Epigenetic tinkering and evolution: is there any continuity in the role of cytosine methylation from invertebrates to vertebrates?** *Cell Mol Life Sci* 2004, **61**(19-20):2425-2427.

3. Steffen W, Broadgate W, Deutsch L, Gaffney O, Ludwig C: **The trajectory of the Anthropocene: the Great Acceleration**. *The Anthropocene Review* 2015, **2**(1):81-98.

4. Kolbert E: **The sixth extinction: an unnatural history**; 2014.

5. Lovelock J: **The vanishing face of gaia: a final warning**. New York: Basic Books; 2009.

6. Steffen W, Richardson K, Rockstrom J, Cornell SE, Fetzer I, Bennett EM, Biggs R, Carpenter SR, de Vries W, de Wit CA *et al*: **Planetary boundaries: Guiding human development on a changing planet**. *Science* 2015, **347**(6223):11.

7. Zeebe RE, Ridgwell A, Zachos JC: **Anthropogenic carbon release rate unprecedented during the past 66 million years**. *Nat Geosci* 2016, **9**(4):325-329.

8. Storn R, Price K: **Differential evolution - A simple and efficient heuristic for global optimization over continuous spaces**. *J Glob Optim* 1997, **11**(4):341-359.

9. Chakraborty UK (ed.): **Advances in Differential Evolution**. Berlin: Springer-Verlag Berlin; 2008.

10. Das S, Mullick SS, Suganthan PN: **Recent advances in differential evolution - An updated survey**. *Swarm Evol Comput* 2016, **27**:1-30.

11. Storn R: **Differential Evolution Research – Trends and Open Questions**. In: *Advances in Differential Evolution. Volume 143*, edn. Berlin: Springer-Verlag Berlin; 2008: 1-32.

12. Talbi EG: **A taxonomy of hybrid metaheuristics**. *J Heuristics* 2002, **8**(5):541-564.

13. He F, Fromion V, Westerhoff HV: **(Im) Perfect robustness and adaptation of metabolic networks subject to metabolic and gene-expression regulation: marrying control engineering with metabolic control analysis**. *BMC Syst Biol* 2013, **7**:21.

14. Boussaid I, Lepagnot J, Siarry P: **A survey on optimization metaheuristics**. *Inf Sci* 2013, **237**:82-117.

15. Rahnamayan S, Tizhoosh HR, Salama MMA: **Opposition-based differential evolution**. *IEEE Trans Evol Comput* 2008, **12**(1):64-79.

16. Rahnamayan S, Tizhoosh HR, Salama MMA: **Opposition-Based Differential Evolution**. In: *Advances in Differential Evolution. Volume 143*, edn. Edited by Chakraborty UK. Berlin: Springer-Verlag Berlin; 2008: 155-171.

17. Merton RK: **The unanticipated consequences of purposive social action**. *Am Sociol Rev* 1936, **1**(6):894-904.

18. Platt J: **Social traps**. *Am Psychol* 1973, **28**(8):641-651.

19.   Smith A, Skinner AS: **The wealth of nations. Books I-III.** Harmondsworth, Middlesex; New York, N.Y.: Penguin Books; 1982.

20.   Richardson GP: **Feedback thought in social science and systems theory.** Philadelphia, PA: University of Pennsylvania; 1991.

21.   Kiel LD, Elliott EW: **Chaos theory in the social sciences: foundations and applications.** 1997.

22.   Cambel AB: **Applied chaos theory : a paradigm for complexity.** Boston: Academic Press; 1993.

23.   Blank T, Detje CN, Spieß A, Hagemeyer N, Brendecke SM, Wolfart J, Staszewski O, Zöller T, Papageorgiou I, Schneider J *et al*: **Brain Endothelial- and Epithelial-Specific Interferon Receptor Chain 1 Drives Virus-Induced Sickness Behavior and Cognitive Impairment.** *Immunity* 2016, **44**(4):901--912.

24.   Bhaskaram P: **The vicious cycle of malnutrition-infection with special reference to diarrhea, measles and tuberculosis.** *Indian Pediatrics* 1992, **29**:805-814.

25.   Susser M, Susser E: **Choosing a future for epidemiology .1. Eras and paradigms.** *American Journal of Public Health* 1996, **86**(5):668-673.

26.   Susser M, Susser E: **Choosing a future for epidemiology .2. From black box to Chinese boxes and eco-epidemiology.** *American Journal of Public Health* 1996, **86**(5):674-677.

27.   Susser M, Stein Z: **Eras in epidemiology: the evolution of ideas.** Oxford; New York: Oxford University Press; 2009.

28. Horton R: **Offline: Why the unity of life matters for our planetary health**. *Lancet* 2015, **386**(9991):323-323.

29. Horton R, Beaglehole R, Bonita R, Raeburn J, McKee M, Wall S: **From public to planetary health: a manifesto**. *Lancet* 2014, **383**(9920):847-847.

30. Whitmee S, Haines A, Beyrer C, Boltz F, Capon AG, Dias BFdS, Ezeh A, Frumkin H, Gong P, Head P *et al*: **Safeguarding human health in the Anthropocene epoch: report of The Rockefeller Foundation-Lancet Commission on planetary health**. *Lancet* 2015, **386**(10007):1973-2028.

31. Kleinbaum DG, Sullivan KM, Barker ND: **A pocket guide to epidemiology**. 2007.

32. Rothman KJ: **Modern epidemiology**. Boston [etc.]: Little, Brown; 1986.

33. Mollison D (ed.): **Epidemic models : their structure and relation to data**. Cambridge [England]: New York, NY : Cambridge University Press; 1995.

34. Privault N: **Understanding Markov chains : examples and applications**; 2013.

35. Norris JR: **Markov chains**. Cambridge, UK; New York: Cambridge University Press; 1998.

36. Ibe OC: **Markov processes for stochastic modeling**. 2013.

37. Klein N: **The shock doctrine: the rise of disaster capitalism**. New York, NY: Metropolitan Books/Henry Holt; 2007.

38. Klein N: **This changes everything: capitalism vs. the climate**; 2014.

39. Arrow KJ: **A difficulty in the concept of social welfare**. *Journal of Political Economy* 1950, **58**(4):328-346.

40. Arrow KJ: **Social choice and individual values**. New York: Wiley; 1963.

41. Gangarosa RE: **The economics of common interests: A call for a movement to hold harmful industries accountable for the social costs they impose**. In. Global Humanitarian Summit: Emory University; 2012: 20.

42. Gangarosa RE, Vandall FJ, Willis BW: **Suits by public hospitals to recover expenditures for the treatment of disease, injury, and disability caused by tobacco and alcohol**. *Fordham Urban Law Journal* 1994, **22**(1):81-139.

43. The Economics of Ecosystems and Biodiversity for Business Coalition, World Business Council for Sustainable Development: **Natural capital at risk: the top 100 externalities of business**. In.: Trucost; 2013: 82.

44. Christian D: **Maps of time: an introduction to big history**: University of California Press; 2011.

45. Samuelson PA, Nordhaus WD: **Economics**, 16th edn. Boston, Mass: Irwin/McGraw-Hill; 1998.

46. Hoffmann PM: **Life's ratchet how molecular machines extract order from chaos**. 2012.

47. Vandermeer J, Odling-Smee FJ, Laland KN, Feldman MW: **Niche construction - The neglected process in evolution**. *Science* 2004, **303**(5657):472-474.

48. van den Bergh J, Gowdy JM: **A group selection perspective on economic behavior, institutions and**

organizations. *Journal of Economic Behavior & Organization* 2009, **72**(1):1-20.

49. Laland KN, Odling-Smee FJ, Feldman MW: **Group selection: A niche construction perspective**. *J Conscious Stud* 2000, **7**(1-2):221-225.

50. Salomonsson M: **Group selection: The quest for social preferences**. *Journal of Theoretical Biology* 2010, **264**(3):737-746.

51. Gabora L: **An evolutionary framework for cultural change: Selectionism versus communal exchange**. *Physics of Life Reviews* 2013, **10**(2):117-145.

52. Fowler JW: **Faith development at 30: naming the challenges of faith in a new millennium**. *Religious Education* 2004, **99**(4):405--421.

53. Fowler JW: **Stages of Faith: The Psychology of Human Development and the Quest for Meaning**. *Horizons* 1982, **9**(1):123--126.

54. Fowler JW: **Stages of faith: the psychology of human development and the quest for meaning**. San Francisco: Harper & Row; 1981.

55. Ostrom E: **Crossing the great divide: Coproduction, synergy, and development**. *World Development* 1996, **24**(6):1073-1087.

56. Ostrom E: **A General Framework for Analyzing Sustainability of Social-Ecological Systems**. *Science* 2009, **325**(5939):419-422.

57. Ostrom E: **Polycentric systems for coping with collective action and global environmental change**. *Global Environmental Change* 2010, **20**(4):550-557.

58. Ostrom E: **Social traps and the problem of trust: Theories of institutional design**. *Polit Psychol* 2008, **29**(1):136-139.

59. Yates FE: **Order and complexity in dynamical systems: homeodynamics as a generalized mechanics for biology**. *Mathematical and Computer Modelling* 1994, **19**(6–8):49-74.

60. Lloyd D, Aon MA, Cortassa S: **Why homeodynamics, not homeostasis?** *The Scientific World* 2001, **1**:133-145.

61. Bakan J: **The corporation: the pathological pursuit of profit and power**. New York, NY: Free Press; 2004.

62. Narvaez D: **Triune Ethics Theory and Moral Personality**; 2009.

63. Darwin C: **On the origin of species by means of natural selection, or the preservation of favored races in the struggle for life**.

64. Kermack WO, McKendrick AG: **Contribution to the mathematical theory of epidemics**. *Proceedings of the Royal Society of London Series A* 1927, **115**(772):700-721.

65. Watson JD, Crick FHC: **Molecular structure of nucleic acids: A structure for deoxyribose nucleic acid**. *Nature* 1953, **171**(4356):737-738.

66. Watson JD, Crick FHC: **Genetical implications of the structure of deoxyribonucleic acid**. *Nature* 1953, **171**(4361):964-967.

67. Crick FHC, Watson JD: **The complementary structure of deoxyribonucleic acid**. *Proceedings of the Royal Society of London Series A* 1954, **223**(1152):80-+.

68.   Kauffman SA: **Metabolic stability and epigenesis in randomly constructed genetic nets**. *Journal of Theoretical Biology* 1969, **22**(3):437-&.

69.   Dawkins R: **The selfish gene**. Oxford; New York: Oxford University Press; 1989.

70.   Anderson RM, May RM: **Regulation and stability of host-parasite population interactions .1. Regulatory processes**. *J Anim Ecol* 1978, **47**(1):219-247.

71.   May RM, Anderson RM: **Regulation and stability of host-parasite population interactions .2. Destabilizing processes**. *J Anim Ecol* 1978, **47**(1):249-267.

72.   Ewald PW: **Host-Parasite Relations, Vectors, and the Evolution of Disease Severity**. *Annu Rev Ecol Syst* 1983, **14**:465-485.

73.   Wilson DS, Sober E: **Reintroducing group selection to the human behavioral sciences**. *Behavioral and Brain Sciences* 1994, **17**(4):585-608.

74.   Laland KN, OdlingSmee FJ, Feldman MW: **The evolutionary consequences of niche construction: A theoretical investigation using two-locus theory**. *J Evol Biol* 1996, **9**(3):293-316.

75.   Gabora L: **Cognitive mechanisms underlying the origin and evolution of culture**. Brussels, Belgium: Free University of Brussels; 2001.

76.   Narvaez D: **The neo-Kohlbergian tradition and beyond: Schemas, expertise, and character**. In: *Moral Motivation through the Life Span. Volume 51*, edn. Edited by Carlo G, Edwards CP; 2005: 119-163.

77. Kauffman SA: **Prolegomenon to a general biology**. In: *Unity of Knowledge: The Convergence of Natural and Human Science. Volume 935*, edn. Edited by Damasio AR, Harrington A, Kagan J, McEwen BS, Moss H, Shaikh R. New York: New York Acad Sciences; 2001: 18-36.

78. Johnson S: **Where good ideas come from: the natural history of innovation**. New York: Riverhead Books; 2010.

79. Haught JF: **God after Darwin: a theology of evolution**. Boulder, Colo.: Westview Press; 2000.

80. Pope Francis: **Encyclical letter Laudato si': on care of our common home**. In. Vatican City: The Vatican; 2015: 184.

End Notes

[1]Robert Merton's farsighted and far-reaching paper shows how choices affect actions in complex ways, anticipating more sophisticated computer demonstrations of chaotic processes. It's beyond the scope of this appendix to discuss this rich, qualitative essay of deep mathematical insights, except to note that Merton anticipated multilevel analysis (p. 895); the interplay of people, society, culture, and civilization (p. 895); the role of the existing state of knowledge (p. 898); Henri Poincaré's pioneering 1912 studies of chaotic phenomena (p. 899); complexity (p. 900); difficulties in controlling feedback processes (p. 900), as in the inventory control game (see table 4, corporations, step 2: problems); issues of time discounting (p. 900); consequences of having expectations (p. 900); the importance of time budgets and division of labor (p. 900); the importance of gathering information but also eventually acting (pp. 900-1); comparison of error with ignorance (p. 901); habit as an impediment to learning (p. 901); the analogous inertia of social structures (p. 901); cultural blindness (p. 901); wishful thinking (p. 901); short-sighted behavior (p. 901); a hierarchy of needs (p. 902) (many years before Maslow articulated this concept!); the unintended impacts of self-interests on society through Adam Smith's "invisible hand" (p. 902); the truths and the errors in assumptions of economic rationality (p. 902); common interests in a social environment (p. 902); tradeoffs (p. 902); birth control and the demographic transition (pp. 902-3); a classic study of the Protestant ethic and capitalism (p. 903); transformative events (p. 903); complex dynamic interactions in interdependent networks (p. 903); normative philosophies (p. 903); cognitive

A-164

dissonance (p. 903); self-fulfilling prophesies, including collective bargaining that thwarted Marxism (p. 904); the impossibility of anticipating contrafactual scenarios (p. 904); and a hint about "the implications of this analysis for social prediction, control, and planning" (p. 904).

2 Constructing the responses for corporations was an eye-opener for me, to say the least. I once held an obstinate view that harmful industries must be fully accountable for all social costs [41, 42], but in preparing this appendix, I found a report concluding that almost no industry would be profitable if held accountable for environmental costs alone. [43] While absolute accountability for social costs should be an ultimate goal over the long course of civilizational evolution, it's clear that is too strict a criterion for now. In many other ways (most notably dynamic mismatches), transformative civilizational evolution requires much more than just corporate accountability, probably involving a number of intermediate steps along the way.

Also, as I filled out the responses to challenges for corporations, I realized that they, too, are trapped in an adaptive system that cannot meet their needs, any more than it can anyone else's. As previously stated, their profitability is squeezed by the same kludgey societal design that is causing everything else to fail, so their apparently cynical and predatory behavior is a self-protective adaption to avoid extinction.

This realization provides an opening for sympathy, even for a former firebrand activist like me, which I call "empathy for slime." A society could not function without economic activity, but our current system was sleepwalking as it evolved capitalism and corporations, and even then under entirely different conditions from now. It makes no sense to penalize the caretakers of that economic institution, now manifesting as extremely powerful corporations, at a time when we all need to reach a mutual agreement how to evolve from here.

I offer this personal experience as a concrete example that might have wider applicability. For three decades, I have wrestled to reconcile the stern advocacy position I had staked out with the overriding concerns of civilizational evolution described throughout this appendix, suspending both initiatives because of seemingly intractable clashes. Tabulating this historical deconstruction of public health history, combined with this glimmer of sympathy, helped open my mind to a comparison with the Great Oxygenation Event in biological evolution, described toward the end of the appendix. This exercise showed me how this form of historical analysis could expand my own worldview beyond current impasses, nudging me toward the healing perspective I have described here. Perhaps the leap that occurred in my own mind past the impasses I faced might suggest ways that humanity could make similar transitions on a much larger scale.

Legend for cover images

Front cover

Painting, upper right

Angel and Girl at the Pearly Gates of Heaven
Lorenzo Scott (American, born 1934, still active in 2016)
Undated, probably early 1980s
Oil on wood panel
33" high x 26" wide
Found frame decorated with Bondo and dark gold paint,
    38" high x 31" wide
Collection of the Lorenzo Scott Project, Stone Mountain, GA,
    http://lorenzo-scott-project.org/

Drawing, lower left

Death's Dispensary
George John Pinwell (British, 1842 – 1875)
Originally published in the August 18, 1866 edition of *Fun
    Magazine* (London, 1861 – 1901)
Pencil on paper
Public domain (University of Florida Digital Collections,
    http://ufdc.ufl.edu/UF00078627/00010/206x?searc%C2%
    ADh=fun)

Background

Bills of Mortality for London, England for the week of September
12-19, 1665, at the peak of the Great Plague epidemic, when
7,185 deaths were attributed to bubonic plague in the city.

London's *Bills of Mortality* were the birth of disease surveillance, probably originated in November 1532, expanded in 1570 to include baptisms, designed to tabulate weekly burials from 1592 to 1595, restarted continuously in 1603, expanded in 1629 to tabulate causes of death, expanded in the early eighteenth century to include age at death, and discontinued on September 28, 1858. William Farr significantly improved on them in his *Weekly Returns of Births and Deaths* in London in the middle of the nineteenth century, as did Alex Langmuir in his *Morbidity and Mortality Weekly Reports* in the middle of the twentieth century. Other countries have adopted CDC's iteration as the prototype for disease surveillance and the centerpiece for CDC's Epidemic Intelligence Service and counterparts in multiple other countries.

Back cover

Photograph, left upper corner

Gene Gangarosa with cholera patient. Chulalongkorn Hospital, Bangkok, Thailand, 1959.

Inset image, right upper corner

Intestinal biopsy from upper ileum of purging cholera patient, showing intact intestinal epithelium (border) and transmigrating inflammatory cells (black). This study disproved the prevailing dictum—originating in 19th century autopsy studies now understood to reflect postmortem cellular disintegration—that ascribed the purgation to sloughing of the intestinal epithelium, analogous to a severe burn.

Hematoxylin and eosin stain, x 770. Figure 5 in Gangarosa EJ, Beisel WR, Benyajati C, Sprinz H, Piyaratn P: **The nature of the gastrointestinal lesion in Asiatic cholera and its relation to pathogenesis: a biopsy study**. *Am J Trop Med Hyg* 1960, **9**: 125-135.

Background

Intestinal biopsy of a former cholera patient, one year after acute illness, showing blunted, fused, shortened villi resulting in dramatically decreased digestive surface area resembling pathological changes of the acute clinical malabsorption syndrome called tropical sprue. This study was the first to recognize such pathological changes as a chronic condition (now called environmental enteropathy) and to suggest the causative influence of frequently recurring acute infections.

Modified from figure 7 of Sprinz H, Sribhibhadh R, Gangarosa EJ, Benyajati C, Kundel D, Halstead S: **Biopsy of small bowel of Thai people. With special reference to recovery from Asiatic cholera and to an intestinal malabsorption syndrome**. *Am J Clin Pathol* 1962, **38**: 43-51.

About the cover

It's rare to see a book cover with two biopsy slides and statistics from the Great Plague juxtaposed with a pediatric patient, the Grim Reaper, and angels. It seemed risky putting so many untested ideas on the outside of the book when we knew the inside had finally come together so well and conveyed such important messages. However, this artwork speaks to Bill Foege's admonition that we epidemiologists must see the faces of the people we help when we are crunching their data.

In a literal sense, the visual appearances of these two obscure biopsy specimens, acquired by the author's scientific team six months apart around 1960 and now celebrated on the back cover, have catalyzed an influential field of public health that has saved tens of millions of lives. The image in the upper right corner surprised scientists by demonstrating that the intestinal epithelium in cholera patients with life-threatening diarrhea was completely intact, while the background image showed that those who recover from such repeated illnesses often have a greatly reduced digestive surface area characteristic of malabsorption syndromes. The first result ultimately led to a simple, inexpensive, practical way to rescue such patients from rapidly fatal dehydration, while the second result proved that treatment is not enough. To turn the tide on enteric diseases, treatment and prevention must go hand in hand. In a sense, these unheralded pathological specimens from the past are now abstract symbols how our compassion for acutely ill patients must be accompanied by a commitment to accept them as lifelong partners in humanity's journey into the future.

The front, back, and (blank) spine covers of this book also symbolize stories of the past, present, and (undetermined) future, respectively, that are told inside it. The two parts of the book—the autobiography and the appendix—address different levels of those evolutionary processes. The autobiographical narrative describes that vast temporal sweep in terms of the author's life and his field of public health, while the appendix projects the conclusions from that experience across the course of human history. The front cover relates to the author's appreciation for history; the back cover to his scientific discoveries; and the blank spine to the enormous human creativity that unfolded from his mentorship and generativity. In public health, the front cover relates to the historical and societal roles of epidemiology; the back to the knowledge it has generated; and the spine to the open mindedness needed to launch into the future. In human civilization, the front represents the responsiveness of public health to the corrective prod of human vulnerability; the back to its efforts to integrate and inform everything else that gets unceremoniously dumped into the bustle and confusion of everyday pursuits; and the spine to our as-yet-unfully recognized common interests, shared fate of future generations, and responsibilities to the rest of life on our fragile planet.

We are so fortunate not only to have such beautiful images available to symbolize these momentous forces, but also to have license to modify them in this artistic collage. We especially want to thank Lorenzo Scott for his beautiful angel painting, and Dr. Jim Farmer, his curator, for the rights to display and respectfully modify this gorgeous work of art. I want to thank two people at Book Baby who implemented this cover design: an anonymous graphic artist, who deftly interfaced the visual elements, and John Burton, who gently nudged me to recognize our looming deadline and relinquish artistic control. It was an odd feeling assembling this mosaic in some degree by remote control, with aspects that I could not adjust directly turning out very different from how I had conceived them. The appearance of this cover is as much of a surprise to me as to anyone!

As we, father and son, were writing those two parts of the book, we thought of them as bookends. Now as we collaborate on the last step of finishing the artistic composition of the book cover, it seems they are more like related books in a library row, and the cover forms the bookends that (again, literally) bind them together.

So as my father, mother, and I wrap up five years and one month of our lives devoted to this labor of love, we note with sadness that my sister, Dr. Margaret (Peggy) Gangarosa, who was a pathologist, is no longer with us to appreciate how her profession also fit into the telling of this story about our family. When she was diagnosed with renal clear cell carcinoma in March 2012, our work on the book slowed to a crawl, and our focus shifted entirely to her as she died in October of that year. We did nothing on the book when I moved 400 miles away to her house in Florida to manage her estate for a year, so to get back on track on this and other projects, I had to return to Atlanta. Still caring for the last of her three pets that still survives, I have thought of Peggy every day since throughout this creative process.

Peggy is also on our minds as we reflect how two hematoxylin and eosin stained biopsy specimens—the kind she would have read every day in her practice—have changed the world. As we resurrect those images and honor the patients who graciously swallowed the biopsy capsules when they were in great distress with an infamously life-threatening disease, we think of Peggy's professional skills rescuing the patients whose clinical specimens she interpreted. Seeing how those biopsy images have transformed human history, it's not hard to imagine Peggy, along with other pathologists and clinical scientists like her, as guardian angels, both in life and in death.

And finally, we honor those who suffered and died so that science, public health, humanity, and life as a whole could learn to evolve constructively. The cover memorializes the people behind the artwork who died, as well as those who donated their fates to humanity's growth—the 7,185 residents of London who perished from bubonic plague during one week in the fall of 1665; the nineteenth-century cholera victims so poignantly captured in George Pinwell's drawing *Death's Dispensary*; the author's two brothers and two sisters who died of childhood infections before he could get to know them; the Thai cholera patients whose intestines revealed nature's inner workings so civilization could finally learn from life's harsh experiences.

In juxtaposing the George Pinwell drawing and Lorenzo Scott painting, I thought of all these people in the broad sweep of what we had discussed in the book. Taking liberties with these two great works of art seemed like writing another book. The girl to the right of the pump looks like the angel kneeling at the altar, and the gaze of the Grim Reaper is directed at her in life in eerie similarity to the way the angels are looking at her in death. And thus I imagined the four aunts and uncles I never knew being selected by fate for a different role in humanity's growth than my father's.

Yet through it all, we're all in this together.

– Ray Gangarosa, July 2016